BEYOND EMPIRE AND NATION

This monograph is a publication of the research programme
'Indonesia across Orders. The reorganization of Indonesian society.'

Indonesia across Orders
The Reorganisation of Indonesian Society

The programme was realized by the Netherlands Institute for War Documentation (NIOD) and was supported by the Dutch Ministry of Health, Welfare and Sport.

Published in this series by Boom, Amsterdam:
- Hans Meijer, with the assistance of Margaret Leidelmeijer, *Indische rekening; Indië, Nederland en de backpay-kwestie 1945-2005* (2005)
- Peter Keppy, *Sporen van vernieling; Oorlogsschade, roof en rechtsherstel in Indonesië 1940-1957* (2006)
- Els Bogaerts en Remco Raben (eds), *Van Indië tot Indonesië* (2007)
- Marije Plomp, *De gentleman bandiet; Verhalen uit het leven en de literatuur, Nederlands-Indië/ Indonesië 1930-1960* (2008)
- Remco Raben, *De lange dekolonisatie van Indonesië* (forthcoming)

Published in this series by KITLV Press, Leiden:
- J. Thomas Lindblad, *Bridges to new business; The economic decolonization of Indonesia* (2008)
- Freek Colombijn, with the assistance of Martine Barwegen, *Under construction; The politics of urban space and housing during the decolonization of Indonesia, 1930-1960* (2010)
- Peter Keppy, *The politics of redress; war damage compensation and restitution in Indonesia and the Philippines, 1940-1957* (2010)
- J. Thomas Lindblad and Peter Post (eds), *Indonesian economic decolonization in regional and international perspective* (2009)

In the same series will be published:
- Robert Bridson Cribb, *The origins of massacre in modern Indonesia; Legal orders, states of mind and reservoirs of violence, 1900-1965*
- Ratna Saptari en Erwiza Erman (ed.), *Menggapai keadilan; Politik dan pengalaman buruh dalam proses dekolonisasi, 1930-1965*
- Bambang Purwanto et al. (eds), *Citra kota lama, citra kota baru*

Published in Indonesia:
- Freek Colombijn, Martine Barwegen, Purnawan Basundoro and Johny Alfian Khusyairi (eds), *Kota lama, kota baru; Sejarah kota-kota di Indonesia / Old city, new city; The history of the Indonesian city before and after independence* (2005). Yogyakarta: Ombak.
- 'Indonesianisasi dan nasionalisasi ekonomi', *Lembaran Sejarah; Jurnal Sejarah dan Ilmu-Ilmu Sosial Humaniora* 8/2 (2005)
- Taufik Abdullah and Sukri Abdurrachman (eds), *Indonesia across Orders; Arus bawah sejarah bangsa, 1930-1960* (2011). Jakarta: LIPI Press.
- Sarkawi B. Husain, *Negara di tengah kota; Politik representasi dan simbolisme perkotaan (Surabaya 1930-1960)* (2011). Jakarta: LIPI Press.

Several other workshop proceedings are in preparation

Indonesia across Orders

# BEYOND EMPIRE AND NATION

The decolonization of
African and Asian societies,
1930s-1960s

EDITED BY
ELS BOGAERTS AND REMCO RABEN

KITLV Press
Leiden
2012

*Published by*:
KITLV Press
Koninklijk Instituut voor Taal-, Land- en Volkenkunde
(Royal Netherlands Institute of Southeast Asian and Caribbean Studies)
P.O. Box 9515
2300 RA Leiden
The Netherlands
website: www.kitlv.nl
e-mail: kitlvpress@kitlv.nl

This book is volume 244 in the Verhandelingen Series of the Koninklijk Instituut
voor Taal-, Land- en Volkenkunde

KITLV is an institute of the Royal Netherlands Academy of Arts and Sciences
(KNAW)

KONINKLIJKE NEDERLANDSE
AKADEMIE VAN WETENSCHAPPEN

*Cover illustration*: '"Een jonge heethoofd"; Merdeka. Jonge Indonesiër op het
Koningsplein te Batavia'. Collection NIOD beeldnummer 49174

*Cover*: Creja ontwerpen, Leiderdorp

ISBN 978 90 6718 289 8

Printed editions manufactured in the Netherlands

# Contents

ELS BOGAERTS AND REMCO RABEN

# Prologue

Decolonization has become one of the major themes in twentieth-century historiography. Within the span of three decades, most of the countries that had been colonized by European powers became independent. Discussions tend to concentrate on the causes of decolonization, particularly on the motives and policies of the European powers. As a result, writings on the history of decolonization have for a long time been primarily about unmaking and about departure. Recently, however, the perspective has shifted, with more weight being attached to global dynamics on the one hand, and greater agency being ascribed to local actors on the other.

This volume aims to enhance the debate by moving the analysis away from the political interpretations of decolonization that have been used by both the departing powers and the new national leaders, interpretations that have subsequently dominated our retrospective view of the period. In the next pages, twelve authors give their views on the meaning of decolonization in African and Asian societies. They all view decolonization over a long span of time in order to assess the convergences and divergences between major social changes and political decolonization. Most articles concentrate on social and institutional changes in the middle decades of the twentieth century, ranging in topic from land titles, urban symbolism, racial and class segregation, the banking system, plural economies, neighbourhood associations, and competing nationalities. The authors uncover the experiences of peoples and institutions that were part of the history of decolonization but whose experiences do not easily fit into the temporal dichotomy of a 'before' and 'after'. Avoiding a strictly political interpretation of decolonization causes the process of disentanglement from formal colonial relations to become part of a much wider trend of re-thinking and re-ordering societies. This concern has been central to the large research programme 'Indonesia across Orders; the Reorganization of Indonesian Society, 1930s-1960s', initiated and coordinated by the Netherlands Institute for War Documentation in Amsterdam, which led to the articles in this volume.

The chapters in this volume approach the mid-twentieth-century transition as a story of experimentation and adjustment that started long before and continued far beyond formal independence. By stressing the long-lasting concerns in late-colonial and newly-independent countries, they try to restore a concept of history as a development by fits and starts, and offer an approach to overcome the 'epistemological rupture' that the departure of the colonial powers brought about (Le Sueur 2003:2). We have attempted to cover neither most countries nor all aspects of the decolonization and reorientation of these societies. Instead, the authors have focused on a few main themes to illustrate the multiple dynamics of societies under the strain of decolonization and modernization.

The volume begins with an exploration of decolonization away from conventional parameters. Bogaerts and Raben suggest an alternative approach, beyond political narratives and western temporalities, and across the fissures in history that are so often taken for granted. They argue in favour of an approach of decolonization as part of a much wider history of reorientation and plead for a focus on, in the words of Ousmane Sembène, 'the people that are never mentioned', to reveal the diverging experiences of the various groups and communities that do not comfortably fit the nationalized discourses of independence and thus offer alternative perspectives on changes and continuities in the societies during decolonization.

Raymond Betts sets off with a discussion of the meanings attached to the term 'decolonization'. He shows how our thinking about decolonization has followed the evolving concerns in the world. It demonstrates how much, as Betts (2004:1) wrote elsewhere, decolonization was 'historically loose-ended'. The term 'decolonization' was minted to serve the concerns of the colonial powers and to describe the retreat of the West from formal dominance, offering an apt image of imperial departure and global repositioning. Soon, however, the idea of decolonization was tied up with questions of the lasting effects of colonial dominance, thereby shifting the focus from the former and soon-to-be former imperial powers to the postcolonial societies in the south. Many studies tried to explain how colonialism had crippled the local economies and how Western powers continued to exert their economic hegemony. In the cultural field too, the colonial past left an almost indelible imprint on the cultural and intellectual life, giving rise to protests ranging from Ngũgĩ's *Decolonizing the mind* to Dipesh Chakrabarty's call (2000) to provincialize Europe.

The echoes of colonial mindsets point at the open-endedness of decolonization in economic and cultural terms. But from a political perspective as well, as Frederick Cooper argues, decolonization should be seen more as a process than as a discrete moment. More importantly, he emphasizes that the outcome of the process was far from predictable, but full of uncertainties and possibilities. In West Africa, political independence was the unforeseen result of heightened political mobilization, which was directed, first, at achieving fuller citizenship. It is this mobilization that characterized the transition from colonialism to postcolonial rule – and continued to be an issue in African politics since. But as Cooper warns us, decolonization should not be reduced to 'a singular phenomenon with certain determinant effects'.

The issue of citizenship also has links with the plural character of colonial and postcolonial societies and economies. According to the famous account by J.S. Furnivall, in most colonies in Southeast Asia, colonial subjects had different rights and played different roles in the economy; in most places indigenous peoples had little opportunity and few incentives to develop businesses. Anne Booth in her article shows how both in the late-colonial and postcolonial periods, governments tried to stimulate indigenous participation in non-agricultural sectors, with varied results. This occurred more intensely after independence and with the articulation of ethnic nationhood, when antiforeign policies drove many trading minorities out of business and out of the country, but the impulses had been present in colonial times.

The concern for a stable and autonomous economy urged postcolonial regimes to reform the financial system as well. In a comparison of the monetary policies in the Philippines and Indonesia, Willem Wolters addresses the question of how the governments of these countries coped with the economic and financial legacies of the colonial past. Here the effects of the decolonization process were felt strongly. In Indonesia, the new central bank grew out of the pre-existing colonial framework, but it had little power and expertise and had to submit to the political demands of a government and leader in search of the support of the population. In the Philippines, by contrast, the United States was instrumental in setting up a strong and independent central bank.

Another legacy of colonialism was the absence of national unity. Karl Hack's chapter offers a broad perspective on the postcolonial struggles for the nation and on their links to the periods of colonial rule and the transition to independence. These struggles were not against colonial powers but between contenders of different visions for the nation. The essence of colonial societies was the fragmentation of identities; Hack prefers to speak of *nations-states* rather than *nation-states*. He argues that the fragmented character has not fundamentally changed even today, only that the mutual claims of supranationalisms and the particularistic nationalisms have shifted during the past decades and that the relationships between them were reformulated. Although the method and content of identity management of colonial and postcolonial states differed, the fundamental fragmentation that was born out of territorial integration in late-colonial times remained. Decolonization only added an extra degree of tension to the relationship between self-determination and the nations-state, which still exists.

Moving towards the village and ward level and far removed from the claim-making of the central state, Greg Bankoff shows a marked continuity between colonial and postcolonial times. In the rural Philippines, the weak state presence had given rise to local mutual-help organizations or networks since the onset of colonialism, if not earlier. These associations provided important security in times of natural disaster, poor harvests and state violence. The story is characterized in many ways by the absence of the state, rather than by the impact of political changes upon village life in the Philippines, urging us to reconsider the impact of global and national political changes to the temporal perception of the local communities.

Not only in the villages but also in urban societies much calls for an analysis of decolonization over time. Evidently the project of independence was tied up with the city (Betts 2004:58). Its schools and universities were breeding grounds for the nationalist movement; its streets were the stage for anticolonial rallies. But not all urban masses participated in decolonization in similar ways. In his article on the political use of urban space in South Asia, Jim Masselos views the city as both the battleground and subject of political struggles between the governed and the government. Masselos distinguishes different spatial levels: a 'territorial imaginary' that was dramatically affected by the arrival of independence, and by Partition in particular; the 'street corner', where spatial and to a large extent social divisions remained relatively untouched by decolonization; and the definition of historical space in postcolonial India and Pakistan. By this three-pronged analysis, Masselos shows how differently the change in regime impacted various domains.

From a different perspective, Freek Colombijn also arrives at an alternative dynamic that was strongly determined by the coming of independence, but did not necessarily follow a parallel rhythm. More importantly, the law reforms on land tenure following independence failed to curb the main legacies of the colonial land tenure system. Colombijn shows that the Indonesian land law reform of 1960 did not only come late – 15 years after the proclamation of independence – but also changed little in the basic rules of landownership and contributed only slightly to the security of tenure.

In city planning too, the continuities between colonial and postcolonial periods were strong. Bill Freund argues that in the late-colonial period, colonial governments had initiated forms of modernist planning in the African cities they ruled over. Postcolonial regimes continued the modernist impulse for some time – in some areas and some respects up to the present day, but especially since the late 1970s the effects of planning were severely limited by the enormous influx of citizens from rural areas to the cities. By analysing the dynamics of planning and the pursuit of urban modernity Freund questions the standardized chronologies of independence as a moment of overall change. He characterizes the period between 1945 and 1980 as an extended period of transition, particularly of urbanization.

An essential – if not uniform – part of the colonial urban makeup was residential 'zoning', the system by which European and indigenous urban quarters were distinguished and separated. Cathérine Coquéry-Vidrovitch investigates the transformations of social segregation in the period of decolonization, which brings her to a similar outcome as Bill Freund's narrative of planning and Jim Masselos' use of urban space: it was not the removal of European colonial rule that influenced the distribution of the social classes in the urban centres decisively, but rather the interference between urban planning, which enabled legal residential segregation, on the one hand, and urban migration and illegal squatting on the other. The vicissitudes of Asian and African cities accentuate how the transition from colonial to postcolonial societies was tied up with the broader issue of redefining state and society. This political and social reorientation may be framed as a process of modernization, which often had its roots in colonial examples and practices, but was adopted by postcolonial regimes.

Necessarily, many things remain unsaid in this volume. It is impossible to contain within the covers of one volume the startling variety of experiences on two continents comprising many dozens of states and hundreds of millions of people who witnessed or were part of the history of decolonization. Together the articles in this volume constitute a justification for research into important mid-twentieth-century transformations from another perspective than simply as a change of rule. They demonstrate clearly that changes in political power do not always adequately represent the rhythms of society and of everyday lives. In most countries, gaining independence from colonial rule was certainly not a negligible event, but it was not an all-encompassing juncture either. It was one inevitable step in a process of social and governmental transition, which is often assimilated into the confusing denominator of modernization. In many ways, the political events of decolonization were the backdrop of the larger, more ambitious and bewildering – and endlessly more diverse – process of reorientation that swept across most of the world in the middle decades of the twentieth century.

## References

Betts, Raymond F.
2004        *Decolonization*. Second edition. New York/London: Routledge. [The Making of the Contemporary World.] [First edition 1998.]
Chakrabarty, Dipesh
2000        *Provincializing Europe; Postcolonial thought and historical difference.* Princeton, NJ: Princeton University Press.
Le Sueur, James D.
2003        'An introduction; Reading decolonization', in: James D. Le Sueur (ed.), *The decolonization reader*, pp. 1-6. New York/London: Routledge.

ELS BOGAERTS AND REMCO RABEN

# Beyond empire and nation

Writing history is a political activity. Generally speaking, history follows power, and the history of decolonization is no exception to this rule. Whether told from the perspective of colonizer or colonized, popular narratives of decolonization often reflect national historical frameworks, geographical boundaries, and chronologies, though motivation, logic, morality, and much else likely differ. Former colonizers had to adjust to the changed political geographies, which involved forgetting the nascent and hybrid identities of the late imperial era. The colonies that had been understood as part of the national destiny gradually became foreign. Decolonization, accompanied by the loss of colonial clout and sometimes as well by military and diplomatic defeat, set in motion a process at times characterized as wilful forgetting or selective memory. The most common word in the analyses of postcolonial memory in the metropolitan countries is 'silence'.[1]

In the newly-founded countries too, a kind of wilful forgetting was at work, sometimes voluntarily, sometimes encouraged by policy. Public representations in the postcolonial states tend to conceive of decolonization as a common struggle against foreign rule or as the consummation of a national destiny. The coming of independence constituted a rupture, both in political discourse and in leadership; this often resulted in imposing a rigid national framework that eschews the confusing dynamics of societies in the period up to and during decolonization. To a large extent, nationalist leaders have encouraged the veiling of historically and morally unpalatable realities such as institutional continuities, collaborations, and violence. In former colonized and colonial countries alike, it was in many national politicians' interests to see independence as a new start, a clean slate, more the fulfilment of a promise than a process that would mark an enduring legacy.

---

[1] The literature on the remembrance of empire is large and growing. For France, see, for instance, Stora 1991; Blanchard, Bancel and Lemaire 2005a, 2005b; for the Netherlands: Raben 2002; Oostindie 2010; for Italy: Pinkus 2003; Andall and Duncan 2005; interestingly, historiography of British postimperial images puts much less stress on amnesia and silence, but more on persistence and reenactment: Ward 2001.

*Languages of decolonization*

National histories strongly endorse the narrative of decolonization as a clear rupture. But coming into one's own was less determined and trouble-free than was often assumed in the public representations of the time. Not only were there uncomfortable legacies and continuities of colonial practices, but the acceptance of and adaptation to the new political realties did not occur as the new leaders had hoped for or planned. To capture the nuance, complication, and contradiction as lived by those who went through decolonization, we have to turn to arts and letters. A dip into the literary output of Africa and Asia produces a wide array of visions based on hopes and dreams, but also on the awkwardness and disillusionment of decolonization. Poets and novelists explore perspectives and point to ambiguities that politicians and historians have tended to obscure or neglect. As novelist Chinua Achebe (2009:39) (born 1930) put it in his recent memoirs: 'Nigerian nationality was for me and my generation an acquired taste – like cheese'. In order to capture the decolonization process and to describe how the 'consciousness of self' (Fanon 1961) was obtained, many literary authors have analysed the phases they went through in order to mentally unravel double loyalties and to overcome the intellectual and emotional ambiguity between two or even more worlds. They testify to the dilemmas of the postcolonial era and often disclose the feelings of disappointment when expectations remained unfulfilled.

Naturally, the changes of power deeply affected the lives of writers and intellectuals. With only few exceptions, most indigenous authors welcomed the end of colonial rule. But the political changes also constituted a source of confusion. Toety Heraty (born 1933), an Indonesian philosopher and poet of Javanese descent, offers insight into the different stages of the complicated process of dissociation from the former colonizer. She belonged to a small, modern, educated elite of about one-and-a-half million people, who in the 1950s represented the less than two percent of the Indonesian population who had been educated in Dutch – a result of Dutch policy deliberately not introducing Dutch on a large scale (Groeneboer 1998:7). Reflecting on her memories of historical events over the past fifty years, she gives an account of the way she herself experienced decolonization 'since personal and public events are closely intertwined' (Heraty 1996:71). She labels the process of untying the threads between Indonesians and the former colonizers as amnesia. This loss of memory was caused by the traumatic rupture between the Netherlands and Indonesia, which started during the Japanese occupation of Indonesia when the use of Dutch was forbidden, and was galvanized at the declaration of independence in August 1945. Later the fissure deepened. Compelled by the circumstances and under social pressure, in the 1950s the Dutch tongue became 'a language to be forgotten, a mentality to be forgotten' (Heraty

1996:68). Indonesian was the language of the new nation and its institutions, the unifying tool to realize the new ideals: Dutch and regional vernaculars were no longer tolerated in the schools or in the press.

Thus, untying and being untied, in a continuous reorientation to the changing political, economic, and social fabric, Toety Heraty gradually detached herself from the Dutch and their influence, while growing into Indonesian surroundings. But this process could never be complete: however conscious the distancing, traces of the past remained. Many years later the author opted for further study in the Netherlands, as the country and the language were familiar to her (Heraty 1996:68-9). It proved impossible and ultimately not desirable to completely expunge the intellectual and cultural legacy of colonialism, but its meaning in daily life changed and its power diminished considerably.

If Toety Heraty only gradually accommodated to the new nation, others 'forgot' more abruptly. Kenyan novelist, essayist, playwright, journalist, editor, academic and social activist Ngũgĩ wa Thiong'o (1986:xiv, 9, 12) (born 1938) made a radical decision in 1977 to abandon writing in English and only compose in his native tongues: 'From now on it is Gĩkũyũ and Kiswahili all the way', he explained, since '[l]anguage was the means of the spiritual subjugation' and English was 'the official vehicle and the magic formula to colonial elitedom'. According to Ngũgĩ (1986:xii), 'Africa needs back its economy, its politics, its culture, its languages and all its patriotic writers' in order to decolonize the mind. Ngũgĩ was neither the first author to realize that the choice of language was a political position nor to make such a radical break with the colonial tongue. In the intellectual wave of 'Africanization', Chinua Achebe had already decided to publish in his native language from 1962 onwards, and earlier in the twentieth century Rabindranath Tagore (1861-1941) chose to write in Bengali and urged his compatriots to do the same.

These accounts demonstrate the significance of language in the development of new identities in the twentieth century, showing how the colonial past had taken root through language and engendered feelings of a deep ambivalence in colonial days, but also thereafter. The colonial heritage could not easily be discarded, as much of the changing lifestyles, cultural forms, and the language of modernity had entered under the cloak of colonialism. The Indonesian foreign minister Subandrio characterized the conflict between the colonial heritage and the new nationalism as 'two souls, two minds in one person' (Dolk 1993:11). Interestingly, in a recent book on Indonesian intellectuals' memories of their youth in colonial times, Rudolf Mrázek (2010:xii, 125-86) likened the colony to 'a big classroom' where the brightest Indonesian boys, and a few girls, were educated and where they were imbued with certain visions of modernity. An entire generation of Indonesian intellectuals faced this 'cultural and historical hybridity' (Goenawan Mohamad 2002:184), which was above all a product of the introduction of the colonizers' language as the instrument not just of administration and trade, but of learning and education (D'haen 1998:10). As such, it became the chief means of expression for the educated elites. It was in a sense a borrowed language, the language of the foreign oppressor, but at the same time it was internalized (D'haen 2002 I:439-440), and had become part of Indonesians' 'colonized selves', just as the French language had penetrated the brains and spirit of the Martiniquans (Chamoiseau 1997:37).

In actual fact, the situation was often even more complicated, as colonial and nationalist linguistic pressures added to the polyglossia that characterizes most societies. For instance, Senegalese film director and literary author Ousmane Sembène (1923-2007) learned to speak French at a French school and Arabic at a Koran school, while Wolof was his mother tongue, one of the about 36 vernaculars of Senegal. Bilingual or more often multilingual environments typify colonial and postcolonial societies, each language constituting a window to different worlds. Like the language, the colonial experience had become part of the confusing postcolonial present, which often was less 'post' than the vagaries of political change dictated.

### The people that are never mentioned

Literary authors have brought attention to the richly diverse perspectives of the people, often doing this in a much more subversive way than historians, who have focused on the events at a national level and settled into the moulds of national chronology. The African and Asian writers make us aware of the innumerable tensions created by the twentieth-century transition to independence. Their plots, topics, and concerns are innumerable, but some subjects recur: the relations to the West, visions of modernity, the intrusions or ineffectiveness of the central state, and social inequalities and tensions connected to political independence and the task of reordering society. The appearance and popularity of social themes and the attention given to the lower classes in the writings of Asian and African authors – and in the works of other artists – illustrate changing world views in the mid-twentieth century. These concerns were not the product of independence; they occurred earlier but gained in force after colonies achieved self-rule. Moreover, because of their attention to the development of labour organizations, to strikes and demonstrations, to protests against injustice and oppression by fellow countrymen and the new elites, these literary works represent realities that differ widely from the world of 'homogenized people' (Duara 2004:7), the kind of people nationalist ideologies of the new authorities were propagating. Tunisian-French author Albert Memmi (1957:121, 123) (born 1920) stated the following:

La carence la plus grave subie par le colonisé est d'être placé *hors de l'histoire* [...] 'il est hors de jeu. En aucune manière il n'est plus le sujet de l'histoire; bien entendu il en subit le poids, souvent plus cruellement que les autres, mais toujours comme objet. Il a fini par perdre l'habitude de toute participation active à l'histoire et ne la réclame même plus.

The colonized had not been allotted their due place in history, nor had the people in postcolonial states. For accounts of their everyday lives, the works of literary authors and film makers are more relevant than those of historians. In their stories and films, the artists paid attention to 'l'héroïsme au quotidien' and 'ces gens dont on ne parle jamais et qui font bouger l'Afrique'.[2]

Bearing witness to 'people that are never mentioned', many novelists have engaged in describing the fate of the lower social classes. For instance, Indian-Pakistani author Saadat Hasan Manto (1912-1955) in his short stories (1987, 1991), written in Urdu, looks at the changing world through the eyes of those directly involved, and depicts the devastating disillusion and confusion brought about by Partition. India's and Pakistan's inhabitants did not only have to adapt their mental map to the new situation, but also had to learn how to make sense of the sudden appearance of two different worlds that before Partition belonged to one country with multiple cultures and languages. In *Les bouts de bois de Dieu*, Ousmane Sembène (1960) gave a gripping account of West African railway labourers' fight for justice during the 1947-1948 railway strikes on the Dakar-Niger line. And Indonesian novelist Pramoedya Ananta Toer (1925-2006) portrays life at the lowest rungs of society in many of the short stories he wrote in the 1950s, and shows how the poor struggle and toil for basic food and shelter in a hostile and threatening metropolis (1957). The novelists' penchant for addressing social issues preceded independence, and reflected the hopes for social emancipation, the mass mobilizations, and the discourses of social justice that circulated in the late colonial period. They demonstrate how closely visions of independence were connected to ideals of equality and social justice, and therefore had a strongly modernist slant. Pramoedya also criticized his fellow Javanese for maintaining the feudal tradition. 'Mahluk dibelakang rumah' (Creatures behind houses), for instance, is an indictment against the new elite's attitude towards servants.

After independence, the social agenda of intellectuals and artists often brought them into conflict with the national regimes, demonstrating the sensitivities of the new leadership. Postcolonial regimes have been particu-

---

[2] Ousmane Sembène in an interview, published 14-5-2004 on http://www.afrik.com/article7295.html.

larly distrustful of their intellectual elites. Authorities often responded to the criticism, satire, or political preferences by trying to mute their voices, ban their works, and jailing them or driving them into exile. In Indonesia, novelist and journalist Mochtar Lubis (1922-2004) was jailed in 1956 for criticizing President Soekarno's inclination towards communism and again by Suharto in 1974 for denouncing the mismanagement of Indonesia's state oil company (Lubis 1980). Pramoedya Ananta Toer, who had a leftist orientation, was imprisoned three times: once by the Dutch for assisting the revolutionary effort, once by Soekarno for criticizing the discrimination of ethnic Chinese in Indonesia, and again by President Suharto for his alleged communist sympathies. This was the fate of many artists in the decolonized world (but not only there). In Kenya in 1977, Ngũgĩ wa Thiong'o was imprisoned by the government, which was enraged by the performance of his play *Ngaahika ndeenda* (I will marry when I want). Addressing the concerns of the local poor and performed in Gĩkũyũ by members of the local community, the popular production led to Ngũgĩ's arrest and imprisonment by Kenyan authorities. In 1982 he was forced into exile. Likewise in Cameroon, the colonial administration and, later, the independent regime tried to silence Mongo Beti (1932-2001) for his critical attitude. His novel *Le pauvre Christ de Bomba* (1956) was banned by the French governor of Cameroon. After a long exile, Mongo Beti returned to Cameroon in 1972. His *Main basse sur le Cameroun; autopsie d'une décolonisation* was again banned, both in Cameroon and France for its biting criticism of politics in his land of origin, and the continuing French influence there (Arnold 1998:356).

The tensions between intellectuals and the state and the ambiguous benefits of independence point to the fundamental characteristics of many decolonizing societies – the unfulfilled hopes, the complexities of identity, and the problems of governance. The lives and works of the novelists and artists exemplify the profound insecurities that beset a large part of the world in the middle decades of the twentieth century. Colonial powers had introduced or incited the creation of novel forms of organization, but they did so in pursuit of their own interests, not to build an integrated state or a harmonious nation – those are tasks for state and nation-builders. The national regimes that succeeded the colonial ones were often unable to create legitimacy and adequately include all sectors of society in the new national project. The decolonization that novelists have chronicled was much more chequered, diverse, and contentious than the history offered by nationalist accounts. In ways that official accounts cannot, imaginative writing explores the nuances of history, the complex richness of daily lives, and reveals the deeply ambivalent rewards of decolonization, how life improved for elites but for many people little changed, except for the worse.

*Histories of retreat and retrieval*

On both sides of the colonial divide, among the political elites decolonization was represented either as a sudden closure or as an epiphany. The term decolonization was minted in the West and continues to stress the concerns of the West. It emphasizes the undoing of the colonial relationship and is usually described in these terms, as a withdrawal and a dispossession. Indeed, the study of decolonization started as a problem of the West. This Western trope of decolonization is one of a retreat, the 'last call' sounding, the lowering of one flag and the raising of another. It signals the end of empire. Seeing decolonization as 'the process whereby colonial powers transferred institutional and legal control over their territories and dependencies to indigenously based, formally sovereign, nation-states' (Duara 2004:2) is the predominant perspective in the study of decolonization (see, for instance, Rothermund 2006; Shipway 2008; Thomas, Moore and Butler 2008). For colonial powers, the departure from the colony created a sudden shift of focus, a reformulation of the metropolitan position in the world.

However, from the newly independent regimes beams the image of restoration of an indigenous order, typically propped up by the nationalist successor governments. Retreat by the colonial powers meant a retrieval of national destiny for the indigenous peoples. In few countries has the image of total reversal been as absolute as in Indonesia, where history has been reformulated around the creation narrative of the 1945 Proclamation of Independence (Frederick 1999). But even if independence elsewhere came with less of a bang, there too the birth of independence or at least the advent and triumph of nationalism have become the umbilicus of national history.

Nationalist visions of independence have dominated the production of history in the decolonized world. Understandably, nationalist representations of the process of independence have often thrived on an organized amnesia. As Benedict Anderson (1991:199-201) explains, the formation of a national identity was based on forgetting as much as on remembering. In order to create the image of a unified nation and a common struggle against the colonial regime, alternative visions of the new society under construction and discomforting continuities had to be obscured. The need for a new start stimulated the image of a clear break with the past. Thus, both in the colony and the metropole, the perception of a rupture gave logic to the new situation. The process of distancing from colonial times was both political and moral as colonialism had ceased being an acceptable form of political organization. Now it was commonly associated with economic exploitation and inequality, and understood as incompatible with the principle of self-determination and the ideal of the nation-state.

The colonial image of decolonization as a retreat, and the nationalist representation of independence as national destiny both emphasize the event as a rupture, and both have dominated the debate on decolonization. But there are some good reasons to look beyond Western temporalities, which, in an inverse way, became those of the nationalists, and to move away from the strict breaks and established chronologies of the state.

*Whose decolonization?*

One reason to look beyond accepted temporalities concerns the old question of whose history is being told. If decolonization is primarily a change of guard, colonial power structures being appropriated and continued by the new nationalist leaders, we might ask what was in it for the majority populations. In the words of Southeast Asian historian Wang Gungwu (2004:268): 'What did those who found themselves decolonized actually get?'. What did national freedom mean? In the actual reality of being decolonized, freedom was followed by an increasing sense of discontentment. In many aspects of life, decolonization did not bring the sea changes that historical traditions and nationalist discourses have assumed. One poignant example is the continuing reliance of many rural Filipinos on mutual assistance organizations (Greg Bankoff in this volume). Likewise, slum dwellers in Bombay or Abidjan, although joining the festivities after achieving national independence, often experienced little difference in their livelihoods, or even a downward turn.

Indonesians in the 1950s almost collectively vented their frustration with the failure to fulfil the promises of emancipation. Indonesia's President Soekarno received innumerable letters from concerned citizens complaining about the state of affairs in the country, and especially the new government's failure to enforce safety, guarantee legal security, fight poverty, and establish democracy.[3]

Not only in Indonesia, but also in many other new states, the people were confronted with inefficient rule, failing economies, and a repression of labour movements and other instruments and media of the people's voices. In many places, the countryside remained unsafe after the formal ending of the revolution, wages stagnated at colonial levels, and labour organizations were reined in. In his recent analysis of the fruits of decolonization, Albert Memmi (2004:17) wrote about what he called the 'great disillusionment' of decolonization:

---

[3]    Arsip Nasional Republik Indonesia, Jakarta, Archives Kabinet Presiden, contains hundreds of letters by Indonesian citizens to their president, complaining about the lack of justice, democracy, safety, and wages, among many other things.

La fin de la colonisation devait apporter la liberté et la prosperité [...] Hélas, force est de constater que, le plus souvent, dans ce temps nouveau si ardemment souhaité, conquis parfois au prix de terribles épreuves, règnent encore la misère et la corruption, la violence sinon le chaos.

It is impossible to write a history of decolonization without referring to its main failure: to bring about peaceful, stable, and thriving societies. This is not only accounted for by corrupt or incompetent successor regimes. Much of an explanation may be found in the historical transition into modernity: the peculiar exploitative and uneven character of colonial rule; the divergence of the pace of transformation in different parts of the country; the dominance of European business interests; and the social and political instability created by the liberation process. Often colonial legal frameworks remained in force, indigenous entrepreneurs had difficulties getting a foothold, and the activity of labour unions was restricted in postcolonial times almost as much as during European rule. All these issues have provoked debates since the late colonial period and have affected the process of disentanglement and the experiences of the peoples involved.

## Times of decolonization

A second issue concerns the time frame of decolonization. That decolonization takes longer than lowering one flag and raising another is generally acknowledged, although most histories of decolonization take a fairly limited time frame. A 'light-switch view' of decolonization, as Frederick Cooper (2005:19) has called it, is not a feasible and is indeed a rarely used approach. Britain's escape from India may seem to come close to a turn of the switch, but even there the story of decolonization can only be told within a longer span. In most other cases, political decolonization was a drawn-out process, involving lengthy negotiations, intermediary stages of institutional reform, and experiments with autonomy, or sustained conflict. Periodization and temporal demarcation remain an uncertain business. Even if the completion of political decolonization is often easy to mark, its start is hard to date. Was it the first expression of the will to achieve independence, or the start of nationalist movements? Was it the onset of the Second World War that discredited Western imperial power and stirred up international principles of self-determination of all peoples? And was the formal achievement of independence the end of decolonization? Or the eradication of the European business interests? For this reason alone, it seems more logical to think in terms of a process of reorientation than of a clearly demarcated period of the colonial endgame.

Taking the issue to an extreme, Frey, Preussen, and Tan have emphasized the necessity to see decolonization as an extended process, starting already in the late-nineteenth century and stretching beyond the formal transfer of power (2004:viii). For them, it seems, decolonization forms a linear process from dependency to emancipation. But even if they account for the need to take a long-term perspective, they ignore the wider social changes that accompanied – and were partly triggered by – the expansion of state intervention since the early decades of the twentieth century. Here we invoke a more complicated vision of decolonization, not by looking at the transfer of power, at the intrinsic impossibility of an interventionist late colonial welfare state, or at the permutations of governance, but at a wide array of developments in society spanning from the late-colonial period to well after independence. In this comfortably undefined period, societies were being reshaped in response to increasing mobility and communication media, social and political tensions, changing living environments and infrastructure. These dramatic transitions triggered novel expectations and scenarios among the colonized that show a great continuity between late colonial and early independence years. This continuity was also evident in the survival strategies of the common people and their reliance on local and non-governmental networks to provide basic needs such as a home, health care, and security.

*Reorientations*

Our third reason to question the standard perspective on decolonization is connected to our conception of what constituted colonialism and therefore also decolonization. If colonization was about more than the political ramifications of foreign rule – which is undeniable – then decolonization too should be viewed in a broader perspective. In the background of the political changes looms a much larger and much more diffuse movement of reorientation and reorganization of society, which continued after the formal achievement of independence. It is not our aim, nor would it bring much clarity, to let decolonization correspond with a concept of modernization. But there is a strong functional relationship between the two concepts. Political decolonization, we would argue, was part of a much larger and profound process of reorientation and change, of an invention of oneself in a rapidly changing world. Decolonization was not the driving force behind the societal changes occurring in most of the world in the mid-twentieth century, but one of the results – if doubtlessly the one most prominently displayed and most loudly heralded – of this process under pressure of intensifying governance, expanding institutionalization, widening horizons, and increasing mobilization.

The moment of political emancipation was, in other words, one point in the dynamics of social transition. This change was for a great part induced by Western agents – and colonial governments taking a predominant role – but the indigenous strata were as instrumental in picking up the seeds of change and shaping society according to their developing needs and visions. Colonial societies – especially urban environments – have experienced an astoundingly swift change since the early 1900s, when urbanisation took off and modernist urban planning emerged (Freund 2007:65-101; Heitzman 2008). New types of organizations, such as housing associations and health care agencies, became involved with people's daily lives. In this period too, the mobilization of labourers started, beginning at the turn of the century in the major colonies in Asia, and a bit later in Africa (Chandarvarkar 1998; Ingleson 1986; Cooper 1996). Streets became stages for demonstrations by political parties but also by other organizations representing the communal interests of workers, women, and others. Although often limited to urban areas, public discussions arose, and increasing numbers of people were mobilized for ideological or political purposes. The convergence of these major transformations had an enormous impact on people in the colony, who in a myriad ways responded to the challenges of 'modern' times, and not necessarily in terms of adherence to a nationalist ideal.

Colonial states faced increasing difficulties in channelling the mounting complexities. In the words of John Darwin (1999), the late-colonial polity gradually evolved into a 'dense' state, characterized by the proliferation of parapolitical institutions, centralizing tendencies, and an increasingly interventionist government, and ultimately into a 'self-destruct' state, which envisaged and prepared the transition to self-rule. Colonial governmentalities found themselves challenged by the rising volume of demands by society. Though not inevitable, it is evident that the forces of change and the limited possibilities of colonial occupation made political independence desirable and possible. The change of regimes cannot be seen in isolation from the fundamental transformation of colonial societies. Only by viewing decolonization in this basic perspective of urgent renewal and adaptation can we account for the meandering routes of change, the range of options open, the variety of outcomes possible, and the fundamental continuities between colonial and postcolonial times.[4] It also explains why debates and experiments – as well as protests and violence – continued after independence, and why processes of change were so similar in colonized and noncolonized countries (such as Thailand, China, and Ethiopia).

---

[4] For Indonesia, this has been the ambition of the research programme 'Indonesia across orders: The reorganization of Indonesian society', run by the Netherlands Institute for War Documentation in Amsterdam over the years 2002-2008. Some major publications coming from this project are Bogaerts and Raben 2007; Lindblad 2008; Colombijn 2010; Keppy 2010.

One problem we encounter concerns the use of the term decolonization. If decolonization is to be understood as the disengagement between colonizer and colony, the question what was being decolonized remains. Because colonization was not only about a power relationship, but about a large range of interventions varying from administrative institutions to businesses, education, and lifestyles, we should look for a wider framework of analysis. Political decolonization becomes part of a large and complicated complex of social change, up to a point that the term decolonization becomes a misnomer. It might well be that, by using such a broad approach, according to Wang Gungwu (2004:270) 'the word "decolonization" might be overworked and made to do too much'. Wang's caution is certainly justified, but rather than proposing a neologism, it may be rewarding simply to avoid the restricted views of the colonialist or nationalist interpretations. If one agrees that decolonization involves more than a fairly abrupt political transition from colony to independent state, one is simply left searching for a better term, but the processes remain the same.

*References*

Achebe, Chinua
2009        *The education of a British-protected child; Essays.* New York: Knopf.
Andall, Jacqueline and Derek Duncan (eds)
2005        *Italian colonialism; Legacy and memory.* Bern: Lang.
Anderson, Benedict
1991        *Imagined communities; Reflections on the origin and spread of nationalism.*
            Revised edition. London/New York: Verso. [First edition 1983.]
Arnold, Stephen H.
1998        'The new Mongo Beti', in: Stephen H. Arnold (ed.), *Critical perspectives on Mongo Beti*, pp. 355-66. Boulder, CO: Rienner.
Blanchard, Pascal, Nicolas Bancel and Sandrine Lemaire (eds)
2005a       *Culture post-coloniale 1961-2006; Traces et mémoires coloniales en France*, pp. 53-68. Paris: Éditions Autrement.
2005b       *La fracture coloniale; La société française au prisme de l'héritage colonial.* Paris: La Découverte.
Bogaerts, Els and Remco Raben (eds)
2007        *Van Indië tot Indonesië.* Amsterdam: Boom.
Chamoiseau, Patrick
1997        'Un rapport problématique', in: Lise Gauvin, *L'écrivain francophone a la croisée des langues; Entretiens*, pp. 35-47. Paris: Karthala.
Chandavarkar, Rajnarayan
1998        *Imperial power and popular politics; Class, resistance and the state in India, c. 1850-1950.* Cambridge: Cambridge University Press.

Colombijn, Freek
2010        *Under construction; The politics of urban space and housing during*
            *the decolonization of Indonesia, 1930-1960.* Leiden: KITLV Press.
            [Verhandelingen 246.] [Indonesia across Orders.]
Cooper, Frederick
1996        *Decolonization and African society; The labor question in French and British*
            *Africa.* Cambridge: Cambridge University Press. [African Studies
            Series 89.]
2005        *Colonialism in question; Theory, knowledge, history.* Berkeley, CA:
            University of California Press.
Darwin, John
1999        'What was the late colonial state?' *Itinerario; European Journal of Overseas*
            *History* 23-3/4:73-82.
D'haen, Theo (ed.)
1998        *(Un)Writing empire.* Amsterdam/Atlanta: Rodopi.
2002        *Europa buitengaats; Koloniale en postkoloniale literaturen in Europese talen.*
            Amsterdam: Bakker. Two vols.
Dolk, Liesbeth
1993        *Twee zielen, twee gedachten; Tijdschriften en intellectuelen op Java (1900-*
            *1957).* Leiden: KITLV Uitgeverij. [Verhandelingen 159.]
Duara, Prasenjit
2004        'Introduction: The decolonization of Asia and Africa in the twentieth
            century', in: Prasenjit Duara (ed.), *Decolonization; Perspectives from now*
            *and then,* pp. 1-18. London/New York: Routledge.
Fanon, Frantz
1961        *Les damnés de la terre.* Préface de Jean-Paul Sartre. Paris: Maspéro.
            [Cahier Libres 27-28.]
Frederick, William H.
1999        'Reflections in a moving stream; Indonesian memories of war and the
            Japanese', in: Remco Raben (ed.), *Representing the Japanese occupation of*
            *Indonesia; Personal testimonies and public images in Indonesia, Japan, and*
            *the Netherlands,* pp. 16-35. Zwolle: Waanders, Amsterdam: Netherlands
            Institute for War Documentation. [Originally published as *Beelden van*
            *de Japanse bezetting van Indonesië; Persoonlijke getuigenissen en publieke*
            *beeldvorming in Indonesië, Japan en Nederland.* Zwolle: Waanders,
            Amsterdam: Nederlands Instituut voor Oorlogsdocumentatie, 1999.]
Freund, Bill
2007        *The African city; A history.* Cambridge: Cambridge University Press.
            [New Approaches to African History 4.]
Frey, Marc, Ronald W. Pruessen and Tan Tai Yong (eds)
2004        *The transformation of Southeast Asia; International perspectives on*
            *decolonization.* New York: Sharpe. [An East Gate Book.]
Groeneboer, Kees
1998        *Westerse koloniale taalpolitiek in Azië; Het Nederlands, Portugees, Spaans,*
            *Engels en Frans in vergelijkend perspectief.* Amsterdam: Koninklijke
            Nederlandse Academie voor Wetenschappen. [Mededelingen van de
            Afdeling Letterkunde, Nieuwe Reeks, 61, 2.]

Heitzman, James
2008        *The city in South Asia.* London/New York: Routledge. [Asia's
            Transformations, Asia's Great Cities.]
Heraty, Toety
1996        'Dekolonisatie, amnesia en anamnese', *Indische Letteren* 11-2/3:64-73.
Ingleson, John
1986        *In search of justice; Workers and unions in colonial Java, 1908-1926.*
            Singapore: Oxford University Press. [Asian Studies Association of
            Australia, Southeast Asia Publications Series 12.]
Keppy, Peter
2010        *The politics of redress; War damage compensation and restitution in Indonesia
            and the Philippines, 1940-1957.* Leiden: KITLV Press. [Verhandelingen
            263.] [Indonesia across Orders.]
Le Sueur, James D.
2003        'An introduction; Reading decolonization', in: James D. Le Sueur (ed.),
            *The decolonization reader,* pp. 1-6. New York/London: Routledge.
Lindblad, J. Thomas
2008        *Bridges to new business; The economic decolonization of Indonesia.* Leiden:
            KITLV Press. [Verhandelingen 245.] [Indonesia across Orders.]
Lubis, Mochtar
1980        *Catatan subversif.* Jakarta: Sinar Harapan.
Manto, Saadat Hasan
1987        *Kingdom's end and other stories.* Translated from the Urdu by Khalid
            Hasan. London/New York: Verso.
1991        *Partition: Sketches and stories.* New Delhi: Penguin India.
Memmi, Albert
1957        *Portrait du colonisé; Précédé du portrait du colonisateur.* Paris: Buchet/
            Chastel.
2004        *Portrait du décolonisé arabo-musulman et de quelques autres.* [Paris]:
            Gallimard.
Mohamad, Goenawan
2002        'Forgetting; Poetry and the nation, a motif in Indonesian literary
            modernism after 1945', in: Keith Foulcher and Tony Day (eds), *Clearing
            a space; Postcolonial readings of modern Indonesian literature,* pp. 183-212.
            Leiden: KITLV Press. [Verhandelingen 202.]
Mrázek, Rudolf
2010        *A certain age; Colonial Jakarta through the memories of its intellectuals.*
            Durham, NC/London: Duke University Press.
Ngũgĩ wa Thiong'o
1986        *Decolonising the mind; The politics of language in African literature.* London:
            Currey. [Studies in African Literature, New Series.]
Oostindie, Gert
2010        *Postkoloniaal Nederland; Vijfenzestig jaar vergeten, herdenken, verdringen.*
            Amsterdam: Bert Bakker. [Postkoloniale Geschiedenis in Nederland
            3.]
Ousmane Sembène
1960        *Les bouts de bois de Dieu; Banty mam yall.* [Paris]: Livre Contemporain.

Pinkus, Karen
2003          'Empty spaces: Decolonization in Italy', in: Patrizia Palumbo (ed.), *A place in the sun; Africa in Italian colonial culture from post-unification to the present*, pp. 299-320. Berkeley, CA: University of California Press.
Pramoedya Ananta Toer
1957          *Tjerita dari Djakarta; Sekumpulan karikatur keadaan dan manusianja.* Djakarta: Grafica. Translated as *Tales from Djakarta; Caricatures of circumstances and their human beings.* Jakarta/Singapore: Equinox 2000.
Raben, Remco
2002          'Koloniale Vergangenheit und postkoloniale Moral in den Niederlanden', in: Volkhard Knigge and Norbert Frei (eds), *Verbrechen erinnern; Die Auseinandersetzung mit Holocaust und Völkermord*, pp. 90-110. München: Beck.
2007          'Hoe wordt men vrij? De lange dekolonisatie van Indonesië', in: Els Bogaerts and Remco Raben (eds), *Van Indië tot Indonesië*, pp. 13-29. Amsterdam: Boom.
Rothermund, Dietmar
2006          *The Routledge companion to decolonization.* London/New York: Routledge.
Shipway, Martin
2008          *Decolonization and its impact; A comparative approach to the end of the colonial empires.* Malden, MA: Blackwell.
Stora, Benjamin
1991          *La gangrène et l'oubli; La mémoire de la guerre d'Algérie.* Paris: La Découverte.
Thomas, Martin, Bob Moore and Larry Butler
2008          *The crises of empire; Decolonization and Europe's imperial states, 1918-1975.* London: Hodder Education.
Wang Gungwu
2004          'Afterword; The limits of decolonization', in: Marc Frey, Ronald W. Pruessen and Tan Tai Yong (eds), *The transformation of Southeast Asia; International perspectives on decolonization*, pp. 268-73. New York: Sharpe. [An East Gate Book.]
Ward, Stuart (ed.)
2001          *British culture and the end of empire.* Manchester: Manchester University Press. [Studies in Imperialism.]

RAYMOND F. BETTS

# Decolonization
# A brief history of the word

*The scope and chronology of decolonization*

'They shot up like volcanic lava', dramatically wrote the former French colonial administrator, Robert Delavignette (1977:137), of the independence movements that had occurred in the European colonial possessions. The metaphor seems at first glance to be most appropriate, suggesting that decolonization was a force gathering from deep causes and bursting forth uncontrollably onto the international scene. The metaphor, moreover, had a timeliness about it, appearing in 1968 when the several European empires had been largely replaced by dozens of new nation-states.

The series of erupting facts to which the word decolonization had been applied by Delavignette were considered to be primarily political. The British scholar John D. Hargreaves (1996:244) said of decolonization that 'its central theme' was 'the creation of self-governing nation-states'. The American historian David Gardinier in his 1967 article defining 'decolonization' stated that it was initially a political phenomenon soon extended in meaning to include all elements incurred in the colonial experience, 'whether political, economic, cultural or psychological'.[1] Delavignette (1977:131) went further, arguing that decolonization fundamentally meant the 'rejection of the civilization of the white man'.

Like many globally-embracing terms, such as 'imperialism' and 'postcolonialism', 'decolonization' was seldom restricted in application to a particular political activity or a neatly defined era. Moreover, as a binary activity, decolonization was interpreted to be both a calculated process of military engagement and diplomatic negotiation between the two contending parties: colonial and anticolonial.

Many authors, of whom Gardinier is one, understood decolonization to be best defined as a process that began before the dramatic occurrences of which

---

[1]    Gardinier 1968:269. Gardinier suggests that the first use of the word 'decolonization' was probably made by Moritz Joseph Brown (1932) in his article 'Imperialism', appearing in the *Encyclopedia of the social sciences*.

Delavignette wrote. Not using the word but clearly subscribing to the idea of decolonization, the British scholar H.M. Kirk-Greene (1982:575), for instance, saw an early 'metropolitan initiative' toward the devolution of empire not only in the work of Lord Hailey, famous for his *African survey,* but also in a lecture Hailey gave at Princeton University in 1943 titled 'The future of colonial peoples'. The metropolitan drive for decolonization reappears in many studies. Recently, Dutch authors Gert Oostindie and Inge Klinkers (2004) in their *Decolonising the Caribbean* wrote of two forms of decolonization. First, there was the 'classic model' of armed conflict ending around 1960. Then the second phase began; it was characterized by negotiation toward independence between the contending parties, as in the Caribbean when both the Dutch and the British determined that their possessions there were no longer of value and sought the means to retreat from them (Oostindie and Klinkers 2004:9, 216-7).

Sharply dissenting from such interpretations of voluntary or negotiated decolonization were two French authors. The Marxist historian Jean Suret-Canale (1982:476) plainly wrote: 'The empires did not deliberately decide upon decolonization, did not desire it, and did not really prepare for it'. Henri Labouret (1952:20), a former French colonial administrator and one of the first persons to attempt an analysis of decolonization, went further than most in describing the development of the occurrence. According to him, 'modern colonization necessarily led fatally to this ineluctable end that historic circumstances only sped up or slowed down'.

Subscription to this conclusion in which human intervention could do little against accumulated forces was found in book titles bearing qualifying nouns such as 'eclipse', 'collapse', and 'dissolution'. Describing the situation in Africa in 1960, the then British Prime Minister Harold Macmillan offered the most memorable of metaphors: 'the winds of change'. As with few other major events, decolonization seemed to many to occur with the force of inevitability. Starkly put in the words of British historian John Darwin, 'the colonial order fell to pieces'.[2]

Although the majority of authors writing on the subject restricted their analysis, as did Delavignette, to the widespread upheaval beginning with the end of World War II, others reached further back in time. The first major disruption of the European order of things was marked by World War I, with enormous losses in manpower, finances, and confidence, while anticolonial resentment grew and was widely expressed in literature and strikes. The famous words of the Irish poet William Butler Yeats summed up the condi-

---

[2]　Darwin 1988:4. Darwin's introductory essay on decolonization, which extends beyond the British case, is one of the best available. Two anthologies of essays on the subject are worth mentioning: Le Sueur 2003 and Duara 2004.

tion in 1921: 'Things fall apart; the centre cannot hold.'[3]

Some scholars have continued the march for causes back to the beginning of modern imperialism when 'pacification' in the colonial world really meant military action against restive populations and resistance writing appeared in many colonial regions. Oostindie and Klinkers (2004:9), concentrating on the Caribbean, write of two stages of decolonization, one occurring in 1791 when Haiti declared its independence from France and in an armed revolt gained its independence; the second came in the 1960s and 1970s.

Whatever its assigned chronology, decolonization was foremost considered a global-scale political change, most intense and successful in the three decades following World War II. As Edward Said (1994:xii) wrote in the preface to his *Culture and imperialism*, the dominance of the West 'culminated in the great movement of decolonization all across the Third World'.

*Decolonization as political change*

The rapidity of the retreat from modern colonial empire impressed all as it was happening. Yet few among those who assessed the colonial situation immediately after World War II expected such a swift outcome. Introducing both administrative and political changes that they assumed would redefine and reinvigorate the colonial system, those still favouring empire anticipated a long run ahead, as certainly did those British who anticipated that Nigeria would reach independence at the end of the twentieth century. Fewer, however, were as optimistic as the organizers in 1941 of a Dutch symposium on that nation's colonial rule in the East Indies. One of the two editors of the papers that appeared in their English-language edition under the title *Mission interrupted* was W.H. van Helsdingen, who, before the war, had been chairman of the People's Council in the Netherlands Indies. He wrote that this book 'expresses the confidence that in future more "great things" will be done in the Indies and that they will be done by the Dutch. May the Mission Interrupted become a Mission Fulfilled!' (Van Helsdingen and Hoogenberk 1945:viii).

It did not. The Dutch, after four years of bitter fighting, left the East Indies in 1949. They were not the first of the colonial powers to leave this part of the world. The Americans, belated imperialists, left the scene first: they had

---

[3]    Chinua Achebe's novel *Things fall apart* (1958) is entitled after a line from W.B. Yeats' poem 'The second coming', and bears as motto the first four lines:
'Turning and turning in the widening gyre
The falcon cannot hear the falconer;
Things fall apart; the centre cannot hold;
Mere anarchy is loosed upon the world.'

planned for independence in the Philippines to take place in 1944, but the act was delayed until 1946 because of World War II. The British had already quit India in 1947. Then the French, after the disastrous military defeat at Dien Bien Phu, followed the Dutch in 1954.

Resistance to colonial rule grew successfully around the world when the two remaining, major colonial states had lost their status as 'Great Powers'. Britain was weakened by a war that drained its wealth and saw the quick defeat and surrender of its Far East bastion, Singapore, to the Japanese. France was defeated and with much of its colonial empire overrun. Not only was their postwar hold on empire tenuous as a result of the war but also the metropolitan population in all the European nations now questioned what had hitherto been largely treated with indifference: the purposes of colonial empire. Moreover, as Europe recovered from the war, the colonial powers increasingly vested their interests in their own continent, faced on the east by the Soviet Union and the west by the United States, the two superpowers of the new era, both publicly opposed to the colonial empires. The defensive treaty NATO (1949) was one clear indication of a new European cooperation, distinguished from the former colonial rivalry.

A considerable factor in the debate over decolonization was the United Nations. With a 51-state membership in its founding year, 1945, the United Nations grew to 99 in 1960, the year the largest number of states joined: 17, of which 16 were from Africa. That year the United Nations gathered further significance because it was then that the Declaration on Decolonization of Granting Independence to Colonial Countries and People was adopted by the General Assembly of the United Nations on 14 December. 'Believing that the process of liberation is irresistible and irreversible', the Declaration asserted that 'an end must be put to colonialism'.

Although world opinion favoured this development, sufficient vestiges of colonial domination lasted so that the General Assembly declared the 1990s 'the international decade for the eradication of colonialism'. The decade passed, but the problem in miniscule form still continues. One of the remaining 16 non-self-governing territories is Pitcairn Island, where some of the crew who precipitated the famous mutiny of HMS Bounty had settled, along with a few Tahitian cohorts. The population of the island, never more than 300, is fewer than 50 today. Seized in 1838 to become Great Britain's first Pacific colony, Pitcairn is today the last in that region. That decolonization is no longer a contemporary political issue of any consequence does not mean that the centuries-long history of Western domination of much of the world has ended. Most students of decolonization would argue that only the focus has shifted.

*Early study of decolonization*

As the colonies broke away, scholars amassed considerable literature on the subject. In the 1970s, more than two dozen studies in English carried the word 'decolonization' in their title. Grandest of the texts was Rudolf von Albertini's *Decolonization; The administration and future of the colonies, 1919-1960* (1971). This hefty volume, analysing the recent history of the colonial world by concentrating on each of the former national empires, was one of the first studies of the colonial world to appear – in German in 1966 – after the colonial empires had been largely disassembled. It was preceded, however, by the work of Henri Grimal, a French author, whose *La décolonisation 1919-1963*, more descriptive than analytical, was published in 1965. As decolonization evolved even more rapidly in the 1960s, it became a hot topic. After the first synthesizing studies, most of the scholarly work was done by examination of decolonization in a national or regional context, with the phenomenon treated most frequently as it occurred in Sub-Saharan Africa, where the action was generally the quickest and centred on states having little or no experience of unity before the Europeans 'carved up' the continent in the late nineteenth century. International conferences of comparative decolonization were frequently organized – such as the one held in Amsterdam in 2003. But perhaps the most significant conferences were organized in the years immediately following the great movement of decolonization in Africa by two American scholars, Prosser Gifford and Wm. Roger Louis. Two of the conferences were sponsored by Yale University in 1965 and 1968. The third, sponsored by the Rockefeller Foundation and held in 1977, was a retrospective analysis of the end of colonial power in Africa. 'Decolonization is one of the great themes of our age', the two editors said in the first line of their introduction to the papers emerging from the first conference (Gifford and Louis 1982:vii).

Yet the most provocative of the earliest, critical studies of decolonization appeared in 1961, the year following the disassembling of French West Africa and the outbreak of violent resistance by the National Liberation Front (FLN) in Algeria. This book, *The wretched of the earth*, written by the Martiniquan author Frantz Fanon, became one of the most widely read on decolonization. The first sentence of the book establishes the author's stark thesis: '[Decolonization is always a violent phenomenon'. He adds: 'The naked truth of decolonization evokes for us the searing bullets and blood-stained knives which emanate from it' (Fanon 1966:29-30). Clearly influenced by French writer and radical syndicalist Georges Sorel, whose *Réflexions sur la violence* (1908) found therapeutic value in violence, Fanon saw in it a cleansing effect, the expunging of the colonial experience, itself achieved through the use of violence. The disinherited or wretched, in rising against the system, become 'new men', gaining an authority and dignity previously denied to them by their colonial overlords. As Fanon insists, there is or will be a complete change in the social order with the earlier oppressed people now becoming free and in control of their own destinies.

Few studies of decolonization have been so taut, both angry and analytical. In his preface to the book, the French philosopher Jean-Paul Sartre (1966:11) lay down this challenge: 'Europeans, you must open this book and enter into it'. A reviewer for *Time*, the American weekly magazine, wrote in the 30 April 1965 issue: 'This is not so much a book as a stone thrown against the windows of the West'.


*Decolonization after political independence: The economic argument*

*The wretched of the earth* broadly described many of the characteristics that would soon appear in subsequent considerations of decolonization. The book, moreover, became part of a crowded concourse of ideas and theories that appeared as the world was being reshaped politically and on the way to being dominated by global economics. In these years, notably the 1950s and 1960s, 'modernization' and 'underdevelopment' entered the popular vocabulary.

The disparity in wealth and standard of living between the former colonial powers and the colonized areas was submitted to wide analysis. The term 'exploitation' gained severely in negative connotation and stood as a synonym for underdevelopment. The Guyanese scholar Walter Rodney (1974:205), in his provocatively titled book, *How Europe underdeveloped Africa*, described the situation ironically as that of a 'one-armed bandit', not a two-handed activity: on one hand, exploitation, and on the other, benefits to the indigenous populations. Underdevelopment, the comparative advantage of one group of nations over another, is 'a product of capitalist, imperialist and colonialist exploitation' (Rodney 1974:14). Kwame Nkrumah, first president of the new state of Ghana, had already made a similar argument in *Neocolonialism; The last stage of imperialism*. As V.I. Lenin had seen imperialism as the means of carrying on elsewhere the highest or last phase of capitalism then surfeited in the West – hence the title of his small but largely influential book, *Imperialism; The highest stage of capitalism* – so now Nkrumah found that the economic exploitation that had been carried on in the colonial period continued unabated after the European flags were taken down and sent home. Neocolonialism was the 'worst form of imperialism' because it assumed no responsibility in the new states it was exploiting. He argued that this development 'means exploitation without redress' (Nkrumah 1970:xi).

'Neocolonialism' did not gain value as currency in any way comparable to that of 'decolonization'. Furthermore, it was surpassed in significance – and in scholarly debate – by dependency theory, of which a wide variety of soon well-known critics like Samir Amin (1977) and Andre Gunder Frank (1979) are among the best known. In 1980 a series of essays on the subject and colonialism was published under the title of *Decolonization and dependency*. The editor of the book, Aguibou Y. Yansané, a professor at San Francisco State University, argues in the conclusion that the benefits of political decolonization were few among the indigenous population at large. It was the collaborative middle class 'that allowed transnational corporations to gain control of local economies and to make them part of ongoing globalization' (Yansané 1980:287-9). Fanon had already complained in *The wretched of the earth* of this national middle class as an 'under-developed middle-class'. Having no economic power itself, he claimed, it has '[t]he psychology [...] of the businessman, not that of a captain of industry'. Its chief function was to act as an intermediary 'between the nation and a capitalism [...] which today puts on the masque of neo-colonialism' (Fanon 1966:122, 124).

To many critics, then, decolonization was not solely achieved with national independence. Economic control also had to be obtained but was not. Nonetheless, '[t]he oppressed and exploited of the earth maintain their defiance: liberty from theft'. So wrote the Kenyan novelist Ngũgĩ wa Thiong'o. But Ngũgĩ's concern (1986:3) was not primarily economics; he added, 'the biggest weapon wielded and actually daily unleashed by imperialism against that collective defiance is the cultural bomb'.


*Decolonization and culture*

That bomb caused cultural destruction, the annihilation of a people's culture through the imposition of the colonial power's cultural system. The mind had to be decolonized as well. Such was the thought of Ngũgĩ (1986), well expressed in the eponymous title of his small but provocative book *Decolonising the mind*. The subject was one Ngũgĩ had long considered as it related to literature. It first aroused his interest at a 'Conference of African writers of English expression', held at Makerere College in Uganda in 1962. A few years later, in 1967, he attended an African-Scandinavian conference on contemporary African writing, held in Stockholm in 1967. There, Eldred Jones, a professor of English literature at Fourah Bay University, argued in his paper 'The decolonization of African literature' that the writer should be faithful to his imagination in whatever language or literary mode he chose to employ. Language need not constrain cultural authenticity, he asserted (Jones 1968). That argument was supported by a considerable number of African writers at the time, but not by Ngũgĩ.

Language greatly concerned Ngũgĩ. He understood that language and its uses are 'central to a people's definition of themselves' (Ngũgĩ 1986:4). Hence the system of communication should be the people's own, not the culturally alienating, imposed one of the colonial power. Writing in Gĩkũyũ, his native tongue, Ngũgĩ (1986:28) considered himself to be 'part and parcel of the anti-imperialist struggle'. With colleagues at the University of Nairobi, he called for reform in the literature department, which would dethrone English in favour of African languages. 'With Africa at the centre of things, [...] things must be seen from the African perspective', the statement read (Ngũgĩ 1986:94).

In *The empire writes back* – its title is a play on an episode of George Lucas's film *Star Wars* – the Australian academics Bill Ashcroft, Gareth Griffiths, and Helen Tiffin follow and extend Ngũgĩ's argument into postcolonial thought. They are more concerned with the instrument of writing than with the language it utilizes. As they put it, 'In many postcolonial societies, it was not the English language which had the greatest effect, but writing itself'. Both the 'seizing of the means of communication' and adaptation of the written language are 'crucial' to independence from the colonial situation (Ashcroft, Griffiths and Tiffin 1989:82).

As the title of the book also suggests, those once indigenous writers held under imperial sway can and do use Western literary devices and do effect linguistic adaptation to their own uses. Postcolonialism, essentially a literary phenomenon, defines the condition of the newly emerging body of African and Asian literature. However, 'post' is frequently taken by many literary critics to mean the reaction to the colonial presence from its first appearance on the scene. It therefore includes the literature created as an expression of opposition to colonial rule and cultural domination. David Punter (2000:4) in his remarkable book *Postcolonial imaginings* briefly describes the various approaches to postcolonialism but opts for the one accepted in *The empire writes back*.

Hyphenated or not, made coeval with colonization or considered as the set of conditions and thought about the colonial experience once it had ended, postcolonialism veers toward the vague and intrudes upon decolonization in its cultural considerations. Cleaning up and reorganizing the cultural mass – and mess – left behind by the retreating empires is the business of postcolonialism. Not only thought but also space figures in this work. The perspective of the observer to the observed has changed. The 'imperial gaze' must be replaced. The angle of vision assumed by the Europeans in the colonies was not only that of the 'master of all he surveys', it also came from the 'cultivation of facile sublimity' by novelists and painters who depicted the landscape of Africa and Asia in relentless sweeps that ignored detail (Ridley 1993:653).

Space itself was changed. Through exploration, invasion and settlement, Europeans recreated the shape and form of the world, an activity explained in one instance by Marlow, the narrator in Joseph Conrad's novella *The heart of darkness* (1902). Looking at a map of Africa hanging on a wall in a European office, he considers the geographic change. Africa had been for him, when he was young, 'a blank space of delightful mystery – a white patch for a boy to dream gloriously over'. Since then, however, 'it had become a place of darkness', filled in with European names and political boundaries (Conrad 1983:33). Here was what might now be called 'substitutive geography', a condition that David Punter (2000:38) contends figures prominently in post-colonial literature.

### Decolonization from and in the West

Decolonization roamed far from its political basis, as Ngũgĩ had shown. In recent years it figured into the intellectual effort to reconfigure the world, to 'provincialize' Europe (Chakrabarty 2000), or to 'decentre' it, to use another new term. Essentially, the former acclaimed and explained Eurocentric vision of the globe had to be replaced as a mindset. In a compelling study of early-modern European travel Mary Louise Pratt, a professor of French at Stanford University, argued that such travel led to a new and different appreciation of the world, an awakening of a 'planetary consciousness'. This was the 'con-struction of global-scale meaning', as a new discourse in which the European and non-European were compared and arranged (Pratt 1994:15, 19-30).

The discourse of modernism, in which the rhetoric of empire was formed, emphasized the rational and the orderly, praised the technological improve-ments that assured the West its only field of superiority, and rejoiced in an attitude of imagined differences that allowed terms like 'primitive' and 'back-ward' to stand as antonyms for the nouns 'progress' and 'betterment', these last two providing the themes of the meganarratives that gave unity to that age's endeavours and imposed their cultural bias on the world at large.

Nowhere are the nature and spirit of this 'modern' world better captured than in an oft-quoted statement by the intrepid nineteenth-century English traveller Margaret Kingsley. 'All I can say', she wrote, 'is that when I come back from a spell in Africa, the thing that makes me most proud of being one of the English is not the manners or customs up here, certainly not the homes or climate, but is the thing embodied in a great steam engine' (Kingsley 1899:385). One of the last expressions of that conceit was rendered poignantly by the English actor Alec Guinness in David Lean's *The bridge on the River Kwai* (1957), a cinematic interpretation of a novel by the French author Pierre Boulle. In the film, Guinness plays the role of British Colonel Nicholson, now a Japanese prisoner-of-war, required with his troops to build a railroad for the Japanese in conquered territory in Siam. Under this imposed assignment, the colonel becomes determined to build a railroad bridge that would shame, by its ingenuity and quality of construction, anything that his Japanese captors could have contrived. Released in 1957, the film displays in Guinness's character Colonel Nicholson the worst effects of the colonial situation, an imposed reality at odds with the environment and the situation.

The bridge is finally destroyed, and the colonel is killed while trying to save it. Bridges and railroads were, as the Margaret Kingsley quotation suggests, the stuff of modern empire. They were the prime examples of the geometrization of the world, an essential imperialist activity supported by a mindset respecting rationality. Chakrabarty (2000:16), however, states that the task of 'provincializing Europe' is not one of discarding European thought but of finding ways in which 'this thought – which is now everybody's heritage and affect [sic] us all – may be renewed from and for the margins'.


*Decolonization in the Metropole*


Decolonization brought in its wake one of the most significant floods of immigrants, this in reverse flow of earlier European migratory patterns. Now it was in, not out. First of the arrivals were those in retreat: European settlers and administrators who had had long residence, particularly in major colonial cities serving administrative and economic needs. Batavia in the Dutch East Indies, Algiers in Algeria, and Bombay in India are obvious examples of urban centres emptied of Europeans.

More significant in number and effect were the decolonized people themselves who, primarily desiring economic betterment but also seeking a European education, swept into the continent as it was undergoing its 'economic miracle', the quick recovery from the war, bringing with it the immigrant opportunities for employment, albeit in menial positions, in Europe. The 417 Jamaicans who arrived in one ship in the port of London in 1948, were the first of 1.5 million people from various parts of the former empire who had gone to Great Britain by 1980. More stunning in effect was the immigration of 237,000 people, roughly one third of the population of Surinam who went to the Netherlands in the 1970s. Between the years 1945 and 1990, 514,400 Moroccans went to France.[4]

Two developments accompanied this immigration, the one damaging, the other advantageous. Racism became a major problem in the 1970s and 1980s, with the emergence of new political parties, like that led by Jean-Marie Le Pen in France who claimed that France's problems were aggravated by the presence of North Africans and Indochinese who, he claimed, had no

---

[4]   This information comes from the University of Leiden International Migration site, http://www.let.leidenuniv.nl/history/migration/chapter8.html (12-1-2005).

desire to be assimilated into French culture. In Great Britain, Enoch Powell, a Conservative member of Parliament, called for the expulsion of the coloured population of the kingdom after race riots in 1980.

The second advantageous development was cultural change and enrichment, most easily measured by the number of ethnic restaurants opened in the metropoles. It has been said that the best Indonesian food can be obtained in the restaurants in the Netherlands, while Indian restaurants in London and North African restaurants in Paris have been greeted with success. One unusual development has occurred in France where the end of the nation's *vocation coloniale* has been instrumental in changing the French vision of things, as described and assessed in Kristin Ross's *Fast cars, clean bodies; Decolonizaton and the reordering of French culture* (1995).

*Decolonization as a topic today*

The Web browser Google on 1 December 2010 listed some 750,000 sites for decolonization. Subsumed under this search word appear subjects as varied as decolonization and art, the imagination, music, and film; also decolonization of the imagination, decolonization and British literary canons, and 'soul decolonization'. Many of these topics on the edge are of recent appearance, since the 1990s. Postmodernist thought, in which the commanding position of Western culture is questioned and the term 'Eurocentric' qualifies as an unsustainable conceit, has joined with postcolonialism in changing the way the world is understood and seen.

Consider entertainment, in particular tourism and movies. Tourism today plays on the imperial past and its setting. The renovation of public buildings and hotels from the colonial era has been done to attract the tourist. 'The rooms at the Imperial in New Delhi', a house brochure announces, 'retain the regal flourishes of a glorious past'. The signs in the large reception room of the town hall in Penang, Malaysia, proudly announce that scenes from the film *Anna and the King of Siam* (1946) were shot there. Here, as elsewhere, the media have found the means to evoke visions of the imperial age. In the early 1980s several British films and television productions, situated in imperial India, and of which the 14-part *Jewel in the Crown* was the most acclaimed, were greeted with success because of 'a national nostalgic gaze back to a golden age, presenting a vision of Empire as something great and glorious'.[5] Here, it might be argued, is the appearance of a cinematic form of neo-colonialism.

---

[5]    Peter McLuskie, 'Jewel in the Crown' on *The Museum of Broadcast Communication*: http://www.museum.tv/eotvsection.php?entrycode=jewelinthe (accessed 4-2-2005).

Yet postcolonial film making also sharply focuses on the unseemly and brutal aspects of decolonization. The Italian production of *The battle of Algiers* (1965) is one example, and the French production of *Indochine* (1992) is another. From the other shore, the decolonized nations, come films critical of decolonization and its effects. A widely appreciated film is Ousmane Sembène's *Mandabi* (The money order, 1968), which deals with the perplexity of an elderly Senegalese receiving a money order that he is frustrated in cashing because of his lack of personal identification and inexperience in such matters. Similar in theme is Satyajit Ray's Apu trilogy of the 1950s, which describes the double journey of a boy from countryside to city, from child to man. Ray commented that all his films are 'concerned with the new versus the old' (Seton 1971:143). The most recent and affecting film of the decolonized world centres on one of the several horrible civil wars that have occurred since the Europeans left. This much-acclaimed dramatic success is *Hotel Rwanda* (2004), based on an actual occurrence during the 1994 civil war in Rwanda in which an African hotel manager sought to save the lives of over a thousand individuals, yet a group who were but a small number among the many Tutsis threatened with and then suffering mass murder by Hutus.

The aftershocks of decolonization are still widely felt. Many centre on the nature of the modern state, others on the idea of modernity itself. In an interview recently placed on the Asia Source Website, Partha Chatterjee, a professor at Calcutta University and one of the founders of *Subaltern studies*, a publication series looking at alternate ways of dealing with problems of decolonization and postcolonialism, was asked if the political liberation of India and other states from European rule was not accompanied, as many asserted, by liberation 'from the knowledge system of the post-Enlightenment West'. Chatterjee's reply was direct: 'One of the things that is now widely recognized is how many postcolonial state forms [...] that emerged after decolonization [...] replicated quite consciously the forms of the modern state in the West'.[6]

The decolonized world, it seems, 'mimicked' the Western one. As Chatterjee said, the nationalist movements in India and elsewhere set out to establish a Western-style modern state and also 'simply [sought] to replace the personnel'. This is the same argument that Fanon (1966:126-9) made some forty years before about failed decolonization.

And yet . . .

The colonial past throws a long shadow over those states and peoples who had high hopes for decolonization. How to handle that past, as the films produced since the moment of independence have graphically shown and as

---

[6]    Chatterjee, 'Towards a postcolonial modernity'. Interview with Partha Chatterjee, on *Asia-Source*: http://www.asiasource.org/news/special_reports/chatterjee.html (accessed 5-2-2005).

much of contemporary academic analysis attempts to reveal, is a major question. 'The past is prologue' read the words carved in stone above the entrance to the American National Archives in Washington. Those words stand as the epigraph of any study of decolonization.

One event of iconic significance occurred during the preparations for the inaugural ceremonies in Pretoria of Thabo Mbeki as the second president of the Republic of South Africa in 1999. The issue was straightforward, but not with a simple resolution: whether the statues of the likes of Generals Botha and Smuts, iconic figures from the time of white domination, should be covered so as not to serve as part of the backdrop of the ceremony or be left there where they were al fresco. Put otherwise, the issue concerned history: was the past, however odious, to be obscured or openly confronted?

## References

Albertini, Rudolf von
1971        *Decolonization; The administration and future of the colonies, 1919-1960*. Translation from the German by Francisca Garvie. Garden City, NY: Doubleday. [Originally published as *Dekolonisation; Die Diskussion* über *Verwaltung und Zukunft der Kolonien, 1919-1960*. Köln: Westdeutscher Verlag, 1966.]
Amin, Samir
1977        *Imperialism and unequal development*. New York: Monthly Review Press. [Originally published as *L'Impérialisme et développement inégal*. Paris: Minuit, 1976.]
Ashcroft, Bill, Gareth Griffiths and Helen Tiffin
1989        *The empire writes back; Theory and practice in post-colonial literatures*. London and New York: Routledge. [New Accents.]
Chakrabarty, Dipesh
2000        *Provincializing Europe; Postcolonial thought and historical difference*. Princeton, NJ: Princeton University Press.
Chatterjee, Partha
            'Towards a postcolonial modernity'. Interview with Partha Chatterjee on *AsiaSource*. http://www.asiasource.org/news/special_reports/ chatterjee.html (accessed 5-2-2005).
Conrad, Joseph
1983        *The heart of darkness*. New York: Penguin. [First published 1902.]
Darwin, John
1988        *Britain and decolonisation; The retreat from empire in the post-war world*. London: Macmillan. [The Making of the 20th Century.]
Delavignette, Robert
1977        *Robert Delavignette on the French colonial empire; Selected writings*. William

B. Cohen (ed.). Chicago: University of Chicago Press. [Translated by Camille Garnier.]

Duara, Prasenjit (ed.)
2004          *Decolonisation; Perspectives from now and then*. London: Routledge. [Rewriting Histories.]

Fanon, Frantz
1966          *The wretched of the earth*. Translated by Constance Farrington. New York: Evergreen. [Originally published as *Les damnés de la terre*. N.p.: Maspéro, 1961]

Frank, Andre Gunder
1979          *Dependent accumulation and underdevelopment*. New York: Monthly Review Press.

Gardinier, David
1968          'Decolonization', in: Joseph Dunner (ed.), *Handbook of world history; Concepts and issues*, pp. 268-72. London: Owen. [First published 1967.]

Gifford, Prosser and Wm. Roger Louis (eds)
1982          *The transfer of power in Africa; Decolonization 1940-1960*. New Haven, CT: Yale University Press.

Grimal, Henri
1965          *La décolonisation 1919-1963*. Paris: Colin. [Collection U, Série Histoire Contemporaine.]

Hargreaves, John D.
1996          *Decolonization in Africa*. Second edition. London: Longman. [The Postwar World.] [First edition 1988.]

Helsdingen, W.H. van and H. Hoogenberk
1945          *Mission interrupted; The Dutch in the East Indies and their work in the XXth century*. Amsterdam: Elsevier. [Abridged English version of *Daar wèrd wat groots verricht ...; Nederlandsch-Indië in de 20ste eeuw*. N.p.: Elsevier, 1941.]

Jones, Eldred
1968          'The decolonization of African literature', in: Per Wästberg (ed.), *The writer in modern Africa*, pp. 71-8. Uppsala: The Scandinavian Institute of African Studies, New York: Africana.

Kingsley, Margaret H.
1899          *West African studies*. London: Macmillan.

Kirk-Greene, A.H.M.
1982          'A historical perspective on the transfer of power in British colonial Africa; A bibliographical essay', in: Prosser Gifford and Wm. Roger Louis (eds), *The transfer of power in Africa; Decolonization 1940-1960*, pp. 567-602. New Haven, CT: Yale University Press.

Labouret, Henri
1952          *Colonisation, colonialisme, décolonisation*. Paris: Larose.

Lenin, V.I.
1933          *Imperialism; The highest stage of capitalism*. [First published 1917.]

Le Sueur, James D.
2003          *The decolonization reader*. New York/London: Routledge.

McLuskie, Peter
      'Jewel in the Crown', *The Museum of Broadcast Communication*: http://
      www.museum.tv/eotvsection.php?entrycode=jewelinthe    (accessed
      4-2-2005).
Ngũgĩ wa Thiong'o
1986      *Decolonizing the mind; The politics of language in African literature*. London:
      Currey.
Nkrumah, Kwame
1970      *Neo-colonialism; The last stage of imperialism*. New York: International
      Publishers. [First published 1965.]
Oostindie, Gert and Inge Klinkers
2004      *Decolonising the Caribbean; Dutch policies in a comparative perspective*.
      Chicago: University of Chicago Press.
Pratt, Mary Louise
1994      *Imperial eyes; Travel writing and transculturation*. London: Routledge.
Punter, David
2000      *Postcolonial imaginings; Fictions of a new world order*. Lanham: Rowan
      and Littlefield.
Ridley, Hugh
1993      *Images of imperial rule*. London: St. Martin's.
Rodney, Walter
1974      *How Europe underdeveloped Africa*. With a postscript by A. M. Babu.
      Washington, DC: Howard University Press.
Ross, Kristin
1995      *Fast cars, clean bodies; Decolonizaton and the reordering of French culture*.
      Cambridge, MA: MIT Press.
Said, Edward W.
1994      *Culture and imperialism*. New York: Vintage.
Sartre, Jean-Paul
1966      'Preface', in: Frantz Fanon, *The wretched of the earth*. Translated by
      Constance Farrington. New York: Evergreen. [Originally published as
      *Les damnés de la terre*. [Paris]: Maspéro, 1961.]
Seton, Marie
1971      *Satyajit Ray: Portrait of a director*. Bloomington: Indiana University
      Press.
Sorel, Georges
1908      *Réflexions sur la violence*. Paris: Pages Libres.
Suret-Canale, Jean
1982      'From colonization to independence in French tropical Africa; The
      economic background', in: Prosser Gifford and Wm. Roger Louis (eds),
      *The transfer of power in Africa; Decolonization 1940-1960*, pp. 445-81. New
      Haven, CT: Yale University Press.
Yansané, Aguibou Y.
1980      *Decolonization and dependency; Problems of development of African societies*.
      Westport, CT: Greenwood Press. [Contributions in Afro-American and
      African Studies 48.]

FREDERICK COOPER

# Decolonization and citizenship
# Africa between empires and
# a world of nations

The difficulty of examining 'postcolonial Africa' in relation to 'colonial Africa' is the complexity of what lies in between. Decolonization was not simply a moment dividing a neat 'before' from a clear 'after', but a process. The possibilities and constraints of the 'after' were shaped not only by the fact of colonialism, but by the process by which it was challenged, by the responses of the colonial state to those challenges, and by hopes, fears, and traumas unleashed in the course of struggle. Just after independence, historians and political scientists looked back on recent African history as a build-up to independence: everything Africans did became part of the rise of African nationalism and the quest for a state that was truly African. Decades later, intellectuals had become disillusioned, and everything in the colonial past was now looked at as an explanation of why independence was a failure, why either the trauma of colonization or something deep in African culture prevented its people from achieving democratic polities. At the present time, postcolonial theory tends to posit a very general coloniality, located somewhere between 1492 and the 1960s, which gave rise to an equally general postcoloniality. The path between the two is easily reduced to an inevitability, missing the paths not taken, the choices made, the constraints that appeared amidst the openings.[1]

Both views subordinate the past to the future and by doing so may misread the future as badly as they misread the past. My goal in this chapter is to look at a crucial period in African history, the decade and a half after World War II in a more dynamic fashion, to look at possibilities that opened up and possibilities that shut down. In the aftermath of war, the two most powerful colonial powers, Britain and France, needed both to expand the economic utility of their African territories and to reinforce the legitimacy of holding colonies to a world in which such claims were becoming increasingly con-

---

[1] For an extended discussion of the relationship of colonial and postcolonial studies to the study of colonial history, see Cooper 2005. As stimulating a book as Achille Mbembe's *On the postcolony* (2001) is, it moves too easily from a notion of colonialism focused on the concept of *commandement* to a generic 'postcolony'.

tested.[2] For both economic and political reasons, colonized people could no longer be regarded as passive subjects. If they were to remain in the imperial polity, the basis of their belonging would have to be taken seriously: as active contributors to economic development, as people with legitimate interests in raising their standard of living and levels of education, and as participants in political institutions. The political possibilities that the postwar situation opened up were something that the French had tried to contain within narrow boundaries and the British to dismiss altogether – the colonized population as citizens of an imperial polity. If citizens have obligations to a political unit, they also have rights and they make claims. But – and here my argument differs from nationalist historiography – the claims made in the name of citizenship focused not only on would-be nations but on actual empires.

The citizenship idea was crucial to a lively period of African politics. But citizenship was not the only framework within which Africans mobilized and acted politically. The danger posed by other forms of collective action that seemed to lie outside the realm of politics as Europeans saw it – and which they could condescendingly label as 'primitive' or 'atavistic' or as demagogic or revolutionary – put colonial authorities in a bind. Hoping to encourage politics inside the familiar channels of parties and legislative elections – and fearing that Africans might not stay there – they had to ensure that making claims within those channels would to a significant extent pay off. The power of such claims threatened French and British governments with having to pay the bill: even if administrations could contain anticolonial movements and local rebellions, they would be faced with demands for social and economic resources in the same language with which France and Britain asserted the legitimacy of imperial rule.

Later, the possibility of an active, claim-making citizenry would threaten African political leaders themselves, who understood very well the force of the political movements they were trying to ride to power. In most newly independent African countries, political elites felt the temptation to shut down the possibilities that had opened in previous years. This view of African history between 1945 and, say, 1965, is a tragic one: of a democratic opening giving way to antidemocratic closures. But it is not a story of inevitability, for neither African culture nor the trauma of colonization prevented Africans, for a time, from acting as citizens. The possibility remains.

The sub-Saharan Africa that became independent since 1957 was indeed an Africa of nation-states, small, economically weak, but with the institutions and the international status of sovereignty. Yet that was not the Africa that most

---

[2]    I have limited discussion to these instances for reasons of space and because these experiences seriously affected the options of other actors, but the catastrophic decolonization of the Belgian Congo and the late and violent decolonization of Portuguese Africa complicate the picture.

African leaders looked to in 1945. Their scope was broader than that, in some cases – especially Anglophone Africa – with a strong pan-Africanist orientation, looking toward the liberation of people of colour throughout the world, but not necessarily with a clear idea of what kind of institutions that would entail. Francophone Africans in late 1945 were preparing for a major effort to bring pressure on French legislators to rewrite the constitution of the new Fourth Republic in a way that provided meaningful citizenship in a Greater France to the people of the colonies. Aimé Césaire was claiming that West Indian colonies should become integral departments of the French Republic. Algerians were divided, some already pushing for independence, while others focused on the humiliating French law that insisted Muslims give up their civil status under Islamic law in order to become French citizens. Meanwhile, in both Francophone and Anglophone Africa, people were involved in all sorts of political activities with a more immediate focus – politics of chieftaincies and other localized communities in some cases, labour issues in others, attempts to change the terms of trade of exports in still others.

If colonial subjects at the end of the war were not focusing on the nation-state as the object of mobilization, British and French officials were not thinking about giving up empire, certainly not within a time span of less than a generation. Empire was in some ways more essential than ever. Damaged economically by World War II, both powers saw in their colonies the only real hope of earning hard currency via the sale of tropical products for dollars. Both powers recognized that the legitimacy of empire was now a more salient and delicate question than it had been before.

But the rules of the game in Africa itself were already coming undone. Just before the war Britain had confronted labour unrest that erupted simultaneously in Africa and the West Indies in the form of waves of strikes and urban riots. The colonial rulers of Africa could not do what they had done before, that is, treat them as 'tribal' uprisings and deal with them by concentrating forces at the local level, hoping to push Africans back into the kind of political cage that Mahmood Mamdani (1996) describes as 'decentralized despotisms'. They were empire-wide issues and had to be confronted as such.

Economic and social policy also had to be reframed. The colonial administrations of both Britain and France had in the 1920s and 1930s considered amending the old colonial doctrine that each colony should pay for itself by instituting development plans that would use metropolitan funds to improve the long-term productivity and economic integration of the colonies. Both plans were rejected, in the name of the old doctrine of budgetary self-sufficiency and also for fear within colonial provincial administrations that too much economic initiative would upset the delicate relationship of the colonial rulers to the traditionalist authority structures on which they depended. Those ideas too would come under assault during and after the war.

The shifting political situations and positions of the postwar decade posed problems of analysis for scholars at the time and thereafter. During the period of decolonization in the 1950s and early 1960s, most scholars – and African political leaders themselves – were eager to assimilate them to European patterns. They thought or at least hoped that educated African elites would turn European ideals into African realities: elections and legitimate governments eager to participate in the world political order and the world economy. A new wave of scholarship dismissed such views as elitist and found in Africa diverse popular movements within different idioms: some to heal the land of the damage done to particular forms of community by the ravages of colonization, some to build new forms of solidarity among workers or peasants, and some to follow a messianic route to the making of a new Africa. Both schools can point to important examples. What I emphasize here is the dynamic in which different types of political mobilization intersected with colonial strategies that were themselves in flux. The threat of some kinds of politics pushed colonial regimes further down other paths than they would have liked to go, until those regimes lost control of the political process.[3]

It was on political territory that France and Britain thought they could control their effort at reshaping colonialism for a postwar world unravelled. Colonial regimes did not lose their will or capacity to repress rebellions in Sub-Saharan Africa: the British in Mau Mau or the French in Madagascar and Cameroon are cases in point, and the seemingly paradigmatic case of Algeria – as recent scholarship has demonstrated – was more of a political than a military defeat for the French government (Joseph 1977; Berman and Lonsdale 1992; Connelly 2002). But they did operate in the shadow of revolutions in Indonesia and Indochina and of the negotiated but conflict-ridden decolonization of India.

The initial reaction in Africa of both British and French governments was to deepen commitments rather than to end them: to forge a development-oriented colonialism that would allow for colonies to contribute more effectively to the recovery of imperial economies, while raising the standard of living of the colonized, sustaining a slow and carefully controlled evolution toward fuller participation of Africans in political affairs, whether at the territorial or the imperial level. It was a project that turned out to be vulnerable in its own terms, and that is why focusing on the politics of citizenship reveals a great deal about how France and Britain convinced themselves that they could and had to give up empire. The claims that were being made upon colonial regimes in terms of citizenship were certainly for political voice, but they were also quite material – about wages, benefits, access to public services

---

[3]   For a discussion of different approaches to decolonization and an interpretation of the timing and process, see the introduction to Cooper 1996a, and 2005:chapter 2.

on a nonracial basis, for education and health services equivalent to those available in the metropole. If empire were to be reformed and made into a meaningful unit of participation, then workers, farmers, students, and others might pose a claim on the resources of the empire as a whole. Such claims revealed that people working within the ideology and institutions of empire could make empire unsustainable.

The escalation of claim-making in the 1940s was framed within two sorts of discourse, both of which were the terms on which Britain and France based their postwar legitimacy and which guided postwar policy: ideas of development and citizenship. They were no less radical for their relationship to colonial ideology – basic issues of social justice, poverty, and equality have been on the table ever since. For Britain and France, devolving power to nation-states became an acceptable alternative to their other real choice, making empire into a unit in which citizenship and development were credible notions. That in turn implied facing the voting publics of the metropoles with demands for political equality and an equivalent standard of living. Nevertheless, development and citizenship have not entirely been pushed into national containers – the notions of global citizenship and global development will not quite go away.

### The French case

General Charles de Gaulle, speaking in Normandy on 16 June 1946, asserted that here 'on the soil of the ancestors the State reappeared'. After the nightmare of the defeat of 1940, the French state would now reestablish 'national unity and imperial unity'. This dualism recurred throughout the speech: the state would 'assemble all the forces of *la patrie* and the French Union'; the new constitution would then be argued over by concerned 'French people and the peoples of the French Union'; the state would unite behind it 'all the Empire and all of France'.[4]

The awkward pairing of nation and Union makes clear that the French state was not the French nation, and the nation was not the state. The state was differentiated, but the President, the legislature, and the judiciary presided over a complex combination of nonequivalent components – characteristic of empires throughout history. There was the Republic – what De Gaulle also called the nation or *la patrie*, recently augmented by the inclusion of former 'old colonies' as departments equivalent to those of the metropole. Algerian territory was also considered part of the Republic, but its people were divided into Muslims and non-Muslims, whose terms of participation

---

4    Speech at Bayeux, 16-6-1946, reprinted in *Documents élaboration constitution*1987, I:3-7.

were unequal and highly contested. Then came the 'Overseas Territories', as colonies were renamed after the war, and finally the associated states (formerly protectorates, like Morocco and parts of Indochina). France, in 1946, was not a nation-state, but an empire-state.

Between 1946 and 1962, French leaders tried a series of organizational initiatives to preserve the polity as a unitary but differentiated entity. As the 1946 constitution was being written, the structure of the French Union was the focus of long debate, and in 1958, the French Community, as the polity was renamed, was again a compelling issue, this time in the shadow of the Algerian war. The components of the Union and later the Community would be governed in different ways, but everyone in them would be a citizen, not exactly the same as a citizen of the French Republic but with equivalent rights; just what this would mean and the power of institutions at each level of territorial aggregation was what the heated debates were all about.

Equally important, the imperial entity was also crucial to the people and movements outside Europe who challenged the French government in this period. Secession and creating new nations were one strand of opposition politics, but not the only one.

Let me back up to take a longer view of empire in France after the Revolution. The idea of dividing the population of imperial France into citizens, who had political voice, and subjects, who did not, was an attempt to organize the empire as both incorporative and differentiated. The trouble was that the two principles contaminated each other – citizenship was something theoretically available but in practice withheld. The French state tried to manipulate this process, but it became a way of posing claims. In 1848, when France finally abolished slavery in its colonies, slaves became citizens rather than members of an intermediate category. In the Four Communes of Senegal, the *originaires* had the 'qualities' of citizenship, and – unlike the case in Algeria – did not have to give up Islamic civil status in order to enjoy these qualities. When France needed more from its empire, it held out the possibility of a fuller citizenship – it did so when Britain and Spain threatened French possessions in the Caribbean in 1794 and again in the cataclysm of World War I (Dubois 2000; James 1963). In the latter case, Blaise Diagne, deputy from Senegal, used France's need for people from its empires to pay the blood tax to convince France to concede a fuller citizenship to the *originaires* and to make it easier for other Africans who served in the war to gain access to citizenship rights.

Citizenship proved to be an appealing notion to many Africans and a potentially costly one to the French state. Ex-soldiers could try to make stronger claims for a meaningful form of citizenship. The expansion of claim making in Senegal, in North Africa, in Indochina, and among colonial students and workers in France was threatening. In the 1920s, the French government tried to check the citizenship process and propagate an alternative myth: the empire as the gathering together of different cultures and nation-alities, under an imperial umbrella that guaranteed peace and the ability to preserve distinct cultures and traditions. In Africa, chiefs were given an official blessing as the embodiments of authentic authority (Conklin 1998; Lebovics 1992; Thompson 2000). Interwar imperial ideology focused on a representation of France as an imperial entity, presiding over a differentiated population, whose cultural distinctiveness could be cherished, while France itself represented a distant beacon of civilization, carefully regulating access to its summits while celebrating the integrity of its components. But Paris in the 1930s was also the site of connections of people from different parts of the empire, among Vietnamese and North Africa workers, for example, as well as intellectuals like Léopold Senghor and Aimé Césaire, who challenged impe-rial authority within the space of empire.

The situation changed again after World War II. A new international climate was part of the story: the revolutionary process unleashed in Indonesia and Indochina as colonial regimes tried to reclaim colonies taken over by the Japanese and the importance of 'self-determination' to the legitimacy of the Allied cause against the German, Italian, and Japanese versions of empire gave a new immediacy to the possibility that empires could come to an end. At the same time, France – like Great Britain – needed to make more effective use of imperial resources to reestablish their economic viability. The French state at last took a firm position favouring inclusion over differentiation, hoping to make 'France one and indivisible' the sole focus of political action. In May 1946, all subjects were declared to be citizens, regardless of civil status regime. The special and invidious judicial system for subjects was abolished. Forced labour was declared illegal. Ambitious programmes of economic development and education – refused funding in the 1920s and 1930s – were at last put in place. The Empire was renamed the French Union and the 1946 Constitution, which colonial deputies helped to write, specified the relation-ship of its component parts.[5] The Overseas Ministry's political bureau told officials in Africa about the significance of the new imperial citizenship: 'the legislature wanted to mark the perfect equality of all in public life, but not the perfect identity of the French of the metropole and the overseas French'.[6]

---

[5] See the *Journal officiel* of the Assemblée Nationale Constituante, April-May, August-September 1946, for exhaustive discussions on the constitution.

[6] Archives du Sénégal, Dakar, 17G 152, AOF, Directeur Général des Affaires Politiques, Ad-ministratives et Sociales (Berlan), note, July 46. The preamble to the Constitution stated, 'France forms, with the overseas peoples, a Union founded on equality of rights and duties, without distinction of race or religion. The French Union is composed of nations and people who come together and coordinate their resources and their efforts to develop their respective civilizations, to improve their well being and assure their security.' Yet as juridical commentators soon pointed out, the preamble could be read as a 'view of the future', not a description of a current reality (Rolland and Lampué 1952:76-7).

Making French citizenship into something meaningful had long been a focus of political activists in French colonies. Now they had possibilities to make good on such demands. The law abolishing forced labour was introduced to the legislature by Félix Houphouët-Boigny, deputy from the Côte d'Ivoire. The citizenship law bore the name of Lamine Guèye of Senegal. Léopold Senghor, the other deputy of Senegal, became an eloquent spokesman for a point of view that emphasized African membership in an 'imperial community', both to assert a place for African culture within a broader conception of human civilizations and to insist that the specific benefits of citizenship be applied equally to all people under French authority.[7] In addition, the organization in 1946 of a political party in French Africa crossing the lines of territories, the Rassemblement Démocratique Africain, turned the geography of imperial control – the organization of individual colonies into larger, centralized units of administration – into a large-scale challenge to French power. The tactical cooperation of the RDA with the French Communist Party until 1950 was another dimension (Morgenthau 1964).

The state's attempt to maintain the French Union as a singular but differentiated polity was too little, too late in Algeria – where settlers continued to use their own citizenship rights to prevent Muslims from exercising theirs – but in Sub-Saharan Africa political mobilization within the framework of French citizenship proved just as dangerous as national liberation movements (Connelly 2002). What is interesting about the moment is less what the Union and the generalization of citizenship were than the possibilities they opened up for making claims. In the late 1940s and 1950s, the logic of imperial citizenship – of the legal equivalence of all citizens regardless of their status regimes and cultural practices – became the basis for claims to equivalence of an economic and social nature: for equal wages, equal benefits, equal education, equal social services, for an equal standard of living.

My own previous research concentrated on how the labour movement used this framework to make material advances. The demand for 'equal pay for equal work' emerged in 1946 as the key slogan of the labour movement in the Senegalese general strike. The strike was more than an industrial action: part work stoppage extending from dockworkers to civil servants, part a movement of the urban population as a whole, which gathered in a daily mass meeting to coordinate action. The rhetoric of strike leaders at these meetings evoked both imperial patriotism that turned into a claim

---

[7]   Senghor 1945. Senghor, born in the countryside of Senegal, followed a path through the school system and the patronage of his teachers and officials who noted his high intellectual achievement to university in France, to a reputation as one of the leading poets in the French language, to a role in a movement of intellectuals, *Négritude*, aimed at emphasizing Africa's distinct but important role in global civilization, and to a political role that included election to the French legislature in 1945 and eventually becoming the first president of Senegal in 1960.

of belonging – a reminder that 'blacks had defended the Mother Country, now they would defend their soil, where they do not want to be considered strangers' – and proletarian internationalism, 'the growing development of the working class in organization and consciousness [that] permits it to play a decisive role as the motor and guide of all proletarian forces of French West Africa'. But concretely, the strike focused on obtaining for the lowest paid African workers similar minimum wages and salary scales to those paid to workers from European France and for civil servants of all ranks the same benefits that Europeans enjoyed.[8] In negotiations, union leaders turned around the development idea by which French officials were justifying their role: 'Your goal is to elevate us to your level; without the means, we will never succeed.'[9]

Strikers did not get equal wages, but they did force officials to apply the metropolitan system of negotiations and wage setting and the basic French framework of collective bargaining agreements to Africa. The 1948-1949 railroad strike deepened the conviction of French officials that they could only manage labour disputes if they followed a strategy based on their experience of class conflict in Europe, a strategy that would hopefully contain and channel demands (Cooper 1990, 1996b). The labour officers agreed with the unions that France needed a Code du Travail in order both to guarantee workers certain rights and to specify rules of contestation, but given that any labour code could not be racially discriminatory, the stakes were so high that the debate took six years to resolve, and a West Africa-wide general strike of workers was instrumental in giving the code the final push.

In one of the many legislative debates on the code, Léopold Senghor remarked, 'As you know, Africans now have a mystique of equality. In this domain, as in others, they want the same principles to be applied from the first in the overseas territories as in the metropole'.[10] Senghor's words had quite a material significance – workers were demanding equivalent conditions to those of workers from European France. The labour movement won the 40-hour week, collective bargaining rights, and paid vacations. It turned its attention to claiming family allowances – already won in the public sector – and got them extended to wage workers in the private sector in 1956.

---

[8]  See police reports on meetings in Archives du Sénégal, K 328 (26), Renseignements, 11-1-1946.
[9]  Archives du Sénégal, K 405 (132), Transcript of interview, 15-1-1946, between representatives of the Union des Syndicats of Saint-Louis, and the Director of Personnel and the Director of Finance of the Government General.
[10]  Assemblée Nationale, Débats 22-11-1952, 5502-5. Senghor used the phrase in print as well (Marchés Coloniaux 375 [17-1-1953]: 124) and the Governor General of French West Africa and a leading French jurist used it too. 'Allocution prononcée par Bernard Cornut-Gentille, Haut-Commissaire, à la séance d'ouverture de la deuxième session 1954 du Grand Conseil de l'Afrique Occidentale Française, 13-1-1954, 20; Gonidec 1953.

One can make similar arguments about demands for education and veterans' pensions (Chafer 2002; Mann 2003:375).

The French state was caught between the radicalism of anticolonial movements, which by 1954 had already resulted in the loss of Indochina and the start of a war in Algeria, and the demands of labour unions and political organizations. The French archives reveal that officials were, by the mid 1950s, thoroughly fed up with the demands being made upon them in the language of citizenship. The costs of modernizing imperialism in Sub-Saharan Africa were high, and the promised transformation of the African economy was proving a more difficult goal than expected. An influential report on the modernization of colonial territories in 1953 warned of the danger that the process might result in the 'exhaustion of the Metropole'.[11] A French minister in 1956 put it bluntly: citizenship had come to mean 'equality in wages, equality in labour legislation, in social security benefits, equality in family allowances, in brief, equality in standard of living'.[12] But if the costs of modernizing imperialism in Sub-Saharan Africa were high, in Algeria the costs of not modernizing imperialism were even higher. In Sub-Saharan Africa, French officials were by 1956 looking for a way to back out of the endless demands of an inclusive imperialism without running into a stone wall that could become a second Algeria.

Meanwhile, political leaders in French Africa were mobilizing more diverse constituencies, especially as the voter rolls grew larger. The rhetoric of citizenship and equality resonated less with people for whom comparison with French citizens was a remote issue, and assertions of 'African unity' against the humiliations of French colonialism counted for more. Even some of the leaders who had begun their careers by emphasizing the vanguard role of the proletariat and the demand for equality for all citizen-workers of imperial France moved to a position that emphasized instead the distinct personality and quest for unity of Africans. As Sékou Touré insisted, 'Although the classes of metropolitan and European populations battle and oppose each other, nothing separates the diverse African social classes'. Such arguments divided the labour movement into those who stuck by the rhetoric of 'class' and 'equality' and those who preached 'African unity'. The top leaders – more and more interested in electoral office – took the movement in the latter direction despite misgivings from the rank and file.[13]

---

[11]   Archives Nationales Section Outre Mer, Aix-en-Provence, Commission de modernisation et d'équipement des Territoires d'Outre-Mer, 'Rapport général de la sous-Commission de l'intégration métropole Outre-Mer', 1953, PA 19/3/38.
[12]   Pierre-Henri Teitgen, Assemblée Nationale, *Débats*, 20-3-1956, 1072-73.
[13]   Archives du Sénégal, K 421 (165), Senegal, Sûreté, Renseignements, 21-2- 1956, 21G 215, Governor, Dahomey, to High Commissioner, 22-1-1957, reporting on the conference of the Union Générale des Travailleurs de l'Afrique Noire. These debates are discussed at length in Cooper

French officials were now willing to make considerable concessions to self-government as long as it stopped the cycle of demands. They called their new approach 'territorialization'. The new law of 1956 conceded something to the demands of African deputies in Paris: universal suffrage and a structure that gave some recognition to federalism. But the reality was a Faustian bargain (Atlan 1997). The first elections in French Africa under the new law, in 1957, resulted in victories for African political parties in each of the Sub-Saharan territories, and those governments had real power over the budget and real patronage to dispense. They offered tangible power and rewards to a political elite. But they also meant that claims on the resources of the empire as a whole were no longer enabled as they had been before. Each government was responsible to its taxpaying electorate. France might provide a narrower range of services and, if it so chose, aid, but the claims of citizens on their state now had to be focused on territorial entities.

Criticism of territorialization came from civil servants' unions who realized that the territorial treasury would be much less able to meet their pay claims than the French one and from Senghor, who realized that territorialization would imply 'balkanization' – the division of Africa into units too small to challenge European states. But the resources transferred to the governments elected after the passage of the territorialization legislation were real – and a strong incentive for political leaders to focus their efforts on their own territories. The reality of territorialization, however, was that it destroyed precisely what the French Union was intended to make invincible: the notion that France was the only unit in which real power was vested and toward which aspirations could be directed. Territorialization was – although no official admitted it at the time – the decisive step toward decolonization (Cooper 1996a:Chapter 11).

If imperial citizenship was too much citizenship for France, it was too imperial for many Africans, a humiliation for some who saw the French reference point held up before them. Such issues produced vigorous debate. People later termed 'fathers of the nation', such as Senghor and Houphouët-Boigny, were among the most notable for continuing to assert French citizenship, while Sékou Touré, most dramatically, shifted from a position of demanding equality within the French Union to one that specifically repudiated such demands in favour of national assertion. If in 1946, the idea of national independence was to French leaders anathema and the politics of citizenship a game they were willing to play, by 1956 the costs of social and economic equivalence had become so threatening that the alternative of claims to national autonomy was greeted by French officials with relief.

The 1956 measures made a few gestures in the direction of federalism,

---

1996a:Chapter 11.

which Senghor and others had espoused, but it represented a different vision of decolonization, one focused on a territorially narrow version of sovereignty. Senghor's leading political ally in Senegal, Mamadou Dia, expressed his 'profound and sad conviction of committing one of those major historical errors that can inflect the destiny of a people [...]. In spite of us, West Africa was balkanized, cut into fragments.'[14] He and Senghor tried to revive federalist politics across Francophone West Africa, but they soon learned that the interests that the first generation of African rulers had in the territorial units turned over to them were so strong and the fear of another politician with another base poaching on this territory were so great that the possibility of alternative modes of political organization were lost. French West Africa and French Equatorial Africa, the two federations through which France had administered Africa, were marginalized and disappeared altogether with the coming of independence in 1960. Senghor's fears of 'balkanization' came true – including the failure of his own brief but valiant attempt to unite Senegal and Mali.[15] The new states of Francophone Africa would remain divided and would have great difficulty in putting together resources to transform their economies or respond to the demands of workers and peasants. They would be brittle states, whose rulers were well aware of how few resources they commanded and the dangers that social movements would put demands on them that they could not meet.

*British Africa*

By 1939, officials in London decided that an imperial problem – the eruption of strikes and riots among the downtrodden of empire in both Africa and the West Indies – needed an imperial solution. They looked to the concept of 'development'. For the first time, metropolitan funding would be directed not just to projects of immediate economic utility to the metropole but to improving infrastructure and services. After the war, the era of colonial development began in earnest: projects to jump-start production in key domains, state efforts to provide housing and other vital urban services, considerable attention to education, and, above all, an insistence that each colony enact a plan for the systematic development of its infrastructure, services, and production, with the promise of funding under the Colonial

---

[14]   Archives du Sénégal, VP 93, Discours d'ouverture du President Mamadou Dia au premier séminaire national d'études pour les responsables politiques, parlementaires, gouvernementaux, 26-10-1959, 'sur la construction nationale'.
[15]   The recent opening of the archives of the federal government of Mali (in the Archives du Sénégal, fonds FM) allows historians to see how much effort went into this experiment in federalism. I have begun to work on these sources. For now, see Foltz 1965.

Development and Welfare Act (Cooper 1996a).

But the problem would not fit entirely into the development framework, for labour in the key communications nodes and in mines posed a specific set of problems. By the late 1940s, the British were rejecting their old policy of encouraging back-and-forth migration between workplace and village and their insistence that Africans might work but could not truly be workers. The new policy went under the name of 'stabilization' although in some places, such as the Copperbelt, it was less a policy than acceptance of the fact that Africans had come to live as well as work, that women as well as men were living in cities and rural chiefs and elders could no longer control family and gender relations (Ferguson 1999). The colonial state was becoming the architect of an African working class, paid enough to live with families in the city, encouraged to separate from a rural Africa now seen as backward, giving rise to a new generation of workers and homemakers acculturated to urban life, organized into trade unions that could provide coherence and predictability to industrial relations.[16] As recent work in social history has shown, the vision of a neatly bounded working class – and the notion of male breadwinner/ female homemaker – could not be realized in practice, but even the attempt contributed to the division of African economies into sectors each of which had its own political and social requirements (Lindsay 2003).

If the French state portrayed its empire as more unified than it was, Britain portrayed its colonies as more decentralized than they were. The ruling fiction was that each colony would progress through stages of increasing self-government following the pathway of Canada and New Zealand and other members of the 'white' Commonwealth. But the timetable was not specified, and most officials thought it would be decades at least, while the actual politicians and labour leaders with whom officials had to deal were almost invariably treated as demagogues or students who had to be taught politics. The transition that was proposed in 1947 was much more limited: from indirect rule to 'local government'.[17] That meant bringing educated people, not just 'traditional' elites into the picture, but keeping the focus on local communities, with a weak, partly appointed, legislative council the only check on the power of the governor at the level of the colonial territory.

But the attempt to contain political change within the imperial system quickly proved impossible. The riots that shook the Gold Coast in 1948 signalled that the basic demand for political voice would be directed at the central authority of each colony and at Britain itself. The events began as a consumer boycott, organized by a populist leader of chiefly origin in the

[16] This is the central theme of Cooper 1996a.
[17] Pearce 1982 is useful here, although he overestimates the importance of new colonial office thinking. A more skeptical view is outlined in Cooper 1996a.

capital city of Accra, focused on urban consumer's anger at rising prices and the apparent stranglehold of European commercial firms on imported goods. It took on a new dimension when army veterans staged a march to protest the government's sorry efforts to insure access to jobs and services to men who had undertaken one of the classic obligations of the citizen by fighting in the Empire's war. Panicky soldiers fired on the marchers, killing several, and setting off riots and looting that spread across several of the colony's major towns. The riots put on the table both the substance and the process of politics in a colony: demands for higher wages for workers, higher crop prices for farmers, less restricted commercial opportunities for businessmen, better education, and better health services along with the claim that only full African participation in political institutions could address such issues (Austin 1964).

Where Britain seemed to differ most clearly from France was in regard to the notion of citizenship: indeed, the citizenship construct was weak in Britain, for all were subjects of the King or Queen. But after the war, Britain reconfigured the relationship of British nationality to imperial membership in a new way that was not so sharply distinguished. After the war, a reinvigorated sense of the need to insure continued relations of Commonwealth and Great Britain led to the passage of nationality legislation in 1948 which gave people from the dominions rights, such as that of being able to enter the British Isles, that partook of imperial citizenship. Fearing charges that such legislation might be thought to privilege the 'white' dominions, Parliament took care to specify that it applied to the people of the colonies. This caused considerable unease when nonwhites, particularly from the West Indies, began arriving in the British Isles in considerable numbers, but officials could not find grounds to deny them access, given the imperial logic that defined them as British (Paul 1997).

What the British did not do was create institutions like those of the French Union, which provided representation in Parliament or in a special empire-wide body, the Assemblée de l'Union Française. The institutional structure of the British Empire pushed African politicians to concentrate more on the individual territory. Before the war, the cross-territorial connections among African elites, particularly those from West Africa, and above all the presence in London of students and militants from all the colonies, had given a pan-Empire orientation to anticolonial politics. But these movements, like pan-Africanist organizations that embraced West Indians and African Americans as well as Africans, had trouble translating a politics focused on the common fate of people of colour within the British Empire into concrete institutional demands, especially the kind of politics that provided rewards to followers.

After the war, the British attempt to expand political participation but confine it to local arenas quickly failed, as national political parties organized themselves in each territory and began to demand that legislative councils have a majority of elected members and that they be given real power. The pioneering movement was that of the Gold Coast, where leading politicians, including Kwame Nkrumah, used the occasion of the 1948 riots to claim that only an African government could address the problems of people of the territory and only it could hope to contain the potential for disorder.[18] The roots of politics in the Gold Coast were varied, from a relatively well-organized labour movement, to moderately prosperous cocoa farmers, to urban youth available for mobilization. Nkrumah was able to straddle a fine line of mobilizing diverse supporters, posing a radical demand for independence, and yet positioning himself as the only possible way of finding a constitutional, peaceful solution to the tension he had helped to channel. When his party, the Convention People's Party, won a legislative election in 1951, at a time when Nkrumah was in prison, the British government had to admit it was outmanoeuvred, that its attempt to find a manipulable middle had failed, and that Nkrumah was indeed the only alternative to disorder.

Nkrumah would soon learn that the quest of diverse people for improvements in their daily lives was only contingently hitched to his national cause. As leader of a self-governing territory moving toward independence, he moved to repress the kinds of social movements, from labour unions, farmers' organizations, and regional power brokers, which he had ridden to his party's victory in 1951. When the Gold Coast became independent in 1957 (changing its name to Ghana), national autonomy could be celebrated, but its basis was already in question (Allman 1993; Beckman 1976). But Ghana's problems were now Nkrumah's, and one reads in the colonial archives that British officials had a kind of grudging admiration for Nkrumah's success in repressing the labour movement – they wished they could have done such a good job themselves. Nkrumah was being reconstructed in British ideology from the dangerous demagogue to the Man of Moderation and Modernization.

The case of Kenya, notably the central region of that colony, reveals a different, more violent pattern. In that region, a large amount of land had been taken over by white settlers, who became much more attached to the territory than did the officials who rotated in and out of West African colonies, and their farms were also the site of a more tense form of exploitation of African labour than was the case in the Gold Coast, where farmers and farm labour-

---

[18]   Nkrumah, from a small ethnic group near the coast, had been educated in the United States, where he experienced first hand a particularly virulent form of racism. His early political activity was in pan-Africanist circles in London, and he was expecting to continue to work along those lines when he found himself in Accra at a delicate moment and seized the initiative in building a militant nationalist movement in the Gold Coast. He began under the shadow of the old-line, respectably middle-class leadership of J.B. Danquah, who like Nkrumah was detained after the 1948 riots, but he broke with Danquah to found a more militant party, the Convention People's Party, which led the Gold Coast to effective self-government in 1951 and independence in 1957.

ers were both African. After World War II, the settler sector achieved a break-through in agricultural prosperity, and that led in turn to the expulsion of African squatters who for decades had some access to land and grazing rights on white-owned farms (in exchange for labour) in favour of more direct and more intense supervision of wage labour. Many of those ex-squatters tried to return to parts of Central Kenya where they had family connections only to find that African farmers were also profiting from a more competitive market for agricultural commodities and were not willing to give the ex-squatters access to land. Nor was employment in cities sufficient to prevent the emergence of a disinherited subproletariat moving between urban and rural misery.

But the conflict that emerged was not a mechanical response to the economic crisis induced by the conflicts accompanying economic 'development'. The radical movement that emerged in the slums of Nairobi and the countryside of central Kenya was a specifically Gĩkũyũ movement, invoking the symbols of this ethnic group, looking back beyond the colonial era to a mythicized, purified Kikũyũ past. In 1952 with the assassination of a collaborating Gĩkũyũ chief, a shadowy movement emerged that eventually took the name of the Land and Freedom Army, but which British officials and settlers referred to as Mau Mau. A few murders of settlers took place, but the number of Africans on the rebel and loyalist sides who were killed or displaced was vastly larger. The guerilla movement emerging in the forests was attacked with ruthless brutality by the British army – especially regular troops brought in from Great Britain – and by Home Guards of loyalist Gĩkũyũ. The struggle forced a polarization on the region, which many Gĩkũyũ had long sought to avoid, many having in previous decades worked out a synthesis between Gĩkũyũ culture and Christianity. The effort at repression became a model 'counterinsurgency' operation, entailing the herding of Gĩkũyũ into camps, the use of harsh interrogation techniques to identify suspects, the forced settlement of people thought not to be too deeply involved in supervised villages, and a large number of executions of people judged guilty of 'belonging' to Mau Mau. The rebellion petered out by the mid 1950s, but the camps lasted until the end of the decade. The excesses of the repression in central Kenya – in contrast to the relative restraint in the Gold Coast or even in relation to urban conflict in coastal Kenya – suggests that this movement, by taking a form outside the seemingly 'modern' framework of political parties and trade unions, was seen as an affront by British officials convinced of their own sincerity as agents of development as well as a threat to a way of life by the racially conscious white settlers. Only in the early 1960s did British officials reverse themselves, give up on the settlers, accept that a deal had to be made with Kenyans who could be deemed moderate, and devolve power with safeguards to private property and connections to a British-dominated commercial system.[19]

Both sides of the pattern influenced other colonies: fear of radicals made once-radical alternatives look more moderate. In 1957, Prime Minister Macmillan commissioned a cost-benefit analysis that would 'estimate of the balance of advantage, taking all these considerations into account, of losing or keeping each particular territory'.[20] The conclusions of the study were mixed:

> Although damage could certainly be done by the premature grant of independence, the economic dangers to the United Kingdom of deferring the grant of independence for her own selfish interests after the country is politically and economically ripe for independence would be far greater than any dangers resulting from an act of independence negotiated in an atmosphere of goodwill such as has been the case with Ghana and the Federation of Malaya. Meanwhile, during the period when we can still exercise control in any territory, it is most important to take every step open to us to ensure, as far as we can, that British standards and methods of business and administration permeate the whole life of the territory.[21]

The goal now was not to keep colonies in the empire, but to keep them tied to a British way of life – something British colonial policy before the war had been intent on keeping Africans away from. Officials could only hope that British discourse and practice had framed the question of governance and that ex-colonies would become Western-style nations.

What Britain was not prepared to do was pay the economic and political costs that such a transformation implied. Officials had long feared that the Colonial Development and Welfare Act would become a colonial 'dole', and by the mid 1950s they had come to grips with the limits of the transformations that were economically possible, limits that the past record of neglect had made all the tighter. African colonies lacked the physical facilities – transportation and skilled labour – to absorb very much development spending even if Britain were willing to provide it. The labour question was not going away under the stabilization doctrine and labour costs moved upward in the most development-related sectors without providing the breakthroughs in production that had been sought. The Colonial Office in effect admitted that the supposed mission of 'preparing' Africans to live a British-style life

---

[19] The literature on Mau Mau is substantial, but one might begin with two recent books that emphasize the depth of repression (Anderson 2005; Elkins 2005). See also Berman and Lonsdale 1992.
[20] Public Record Office, London (PRO), CAB 134/1555, Prime Minister's Minute, 28-1-1957. This review was to be conducted through the Colonial Policy Committee.
[21] PRO, CPC (57) 30, CAB 134/1556, 5-6, 'Future constitutional development in the colonies', Report by the Chairman of the Official Committee on Colonial Policy (Norman Brook), 6-9-1957.

had not much to show for itself in the first half-century of African colonization and was not succeeding in its final phase. The Colonial Secretary said
of Nigeria in 1957 that there was danger of 'the country disintegrating', of
'administrative chaos', of 'corrupt, inept and opportunist rule'. But the British
could not prolong their supposed tutelage:

> This is the dilemma with which we are faced: either give independence
> too soon and risk disintegration and a breakdown of administration; or to
> hang on too long, risk ill-feeling and disturbances, and eventually to leave
> bitterness behind, with little hope thereafter at our being able to influence
> Nigerian thinking in world affairs on lines we would wish.[22]

East Africa – where the Mau Mau rebellion in Kenya had been put down
only a couple of years earlier – was considered in worse shape, but the
same course was followed. With Nigeria gaining independence in 1960,
Tanganyika followed in 1961, Uganda in 1962. The Colonial Secretary told the
Cabinet in 1962 that officials throughout Kenya believed '(i) That the rate of
advance to independence [...] was too rapid, (ii) They could think of no way
in which it could now be slowed down'. The economy was 'running rapidly
downhill'; Africans were, in terms of political maturity, 'far behind even the
West Africans'. The hope – as a decade earlier in the Gold Coast – was that
a 'moderate' wing of the Kenya African National Union could be split from
the 'men of violence and of communist contact'. The danger of delay was
'provoking a violent African reaction'.[23] Kenya became independent in 1963,
and Jomo Kenyatta, newly released from prison, had to be made over from
violent rebel to the great hope for peace.

The Cabinet reports from 1957 to 1959 overlooked clear evidence of
growth in exports and marketed output, of improved infrastructure and
much expanded schools systems, of better paid workers and newly functioning systems of industrial relations in at least some sectors of some colonies.
But the sense of failure has much to do with the way the problem was framed
in the first place: a single idea of 'development' bringing together the raising
of African standards of living and the reconstruction of the British economy,
of 'responsible' trade unions and respectable politicians, of 'scientific' ideas –
applied by knowledgeable experts – of public health and agronomy dissemi-
nated throughout the African continent. The kinship and clientage networks
of Gold Coast or Nigerian cocoa farmers may have been helping to bring

---

[22]   PRO, CAB 129/87, Memorandum by Secretary of State, 'Nigeria', C 57 (120), 14-5-1957. Len-
nox-Boyd wanted to postpone Nigerian demands for independence as far as possible, but not
resist 'overtly' should Nigerian politicians demand independence in 1959.
[23]   PRO, CAB 129/108, Memorandum for the Cabinet by the Secretary of State for the Colonies,
'Kenya', C (62)22, 6-2-1962; and PRO, CAB 128/36, 12th Cabinet Conclusions CC (62), 8-2-1962.

in record harvests, but they were not what officials meant by development. When British officials were forced to take stock of their progress in the late 1950s, they did not find what they meant by modern society and they tended to interpret its absence as danger. But African politicians – by virtue of the very insistence of British officials that they had to prove their popular mandates – made their connections with African society as it actually was, with all its particularisms and conflicting forms of affinity. Top officials often read this as demagoguery, corruption, and divisiveness. Such observations were not without basis – some of the social and political breakdowns that occurred in the 1960s in Nigeria and elsewhere resemble the predictions of 1957-1959 – but the expectations that Africa had failed to fulfil were those of a fantasy of imperial modernization of the 1940s.

Development had been put forward after the African West Indian disturbances of the late 1930s as an antidote to disorder. Instead, the increased tempo of change in an era of expanding markets and social engineering – from the intensified production at the expense of squatters on farms in Central Kenya to the heavy-handed interventions of agricultural experts in soil conservation projects – helped to bring about conflicts that strained the ability of the forces of order to contain. British perceptions about the preparedness of colonies for independence became irrelevant: sovereignty was what they were going to get, and with sovereignty responsibility for whatever went wrong.

## Decolonization and the making of nation-states

Let us return to the basic question of this chapter: how and why did decolonization – as it unfolded in the two decades after World War II – shape postcolonial possibilities? I see colonialism itself as unstable and uncertain, always caught between strategies of incorporating people more fully into an empire or marking the differentiation and subordination of conquered people. Routine administration required that elites, at least, be given some kind of stake in the imperial system – otherwise bureaucratic and military cost would make colonies a drain on metropolitan resources – but as economic and social situations changed, the need to coopt different categories of people and different kinds of leaders shifted as well. But many Africans – not least of them wage workers – did not fit in the tribal cages into which colonial rulers tried to keep them. The modern African that colonial rulers had once regarded as a dangerous anomaly now had to be encouraged. Officials thought they knew how to do such things – given the experience of European elites in managing cities, workers, education, health, and other social problems in Britain and France. But in the late 1940s and 1950s, Britain and France faced the escala-

tion of demands within a new but still colonial framework that they had
themselves put forward. It was the dynamic element that proved the most
vulnerable part of empire, and it is no surprise that the breakdown of empire
occurred first in the 'development'-oriented regimes of France and Britain
and not in the empire of Portugal. The attempt at 'modernizing' colonialism
did not systematically modernize the social order, but reframed struggles in
unintended ways, for both colonial powers and the social and political movements that challenged them.

For colonial officials, the development drive made it possible to imagine
Africans as 'modern' people, acting in institutions like legislatures and labour
unions – something that made no sense in the 'tribal' conception of Africa that
predominated before the war. At first, development seemed like an excuse to
stay around longer so that people with expertise and capital could tutor and
help those who had neither. But the costs of tutelage, investment, and the
containment of disorder or revolution turned out to be something neither
France nor Great Britain wanted to pay. The modernization argument instead
proved useful in convincing enough of the political elite at home that African
territories could become self-governing, that they could be brought enough
into the world economy and international institutions, that they would have
an interest in further interaction and cooperation, and that European norms
really were universalistic aspirations that Africans themselves would seek
to emulate. The development process went from something that had to be
directly controlled to something that painful implementation of which could
be passed on to African elites. The main difference was that Europeans could
now pass onto Africans responsibility for the consequences of a history in
which they had been prime actors.

For the leaders of trade unions and other social movements and for the
leaders of political parties who were so skilful in turning European fear
of disorderly masses into their own quest for power, the experience of the
labour and economic contestations of the 1940s and 1950s was a powerful
one. The terrain on which these struggles were conducted privileged certain
kinds of institutions and attitudes toward them: the idea that society could
be managed and engineered, that a strong state should enter into the realm of
family life and social organization, was one side. The other was that demands
put forward in the name of citizenship and development could be powerful.
The first generation of African rulers, Kwame Nkrumah leading the way in
Ghana and Sékou Touré in Guinea, knew from having profited from labour
mobilization just how potentially challenging organized labour could be.
They turned out to be the pioneers in destroying the autonomy of trade
unions – likewise with independent farmers' organizations, with students'
organizations, and so on. The closing off of debate and political action in
so many newly independent African states cannot simply be attributed to a

legacy of authoritarianism from colonial rule, but also to its opposite; to direct experience with the mobilization of civil society, which however partial it had been, was enough to challenge states with many more resources than the new ones of Africa. African states soon turned out to be brittle states: assertive of their power over society and dismissive of civil action that attempted to influence power.[24]

The other side of the story of the creation of fragile nation-states in Africa is the transformation of empire-states in Europe into something more national. The same process that made countries like Ghana or Senegal national also made Britain and France national. Before the 1960s, they had to think like empires, that is, as polities that at the same time were incorporative and differentiated and unequal. Empires could try to manipulate the balance of incorporation and differentiation, as France did in generalizing citizenship in 1946 or Britain did with the Nationality Act of 1948 – hoping in both cases on tying people into a polity in a unity that appeared inviolable and desirable. As both powers gave up their empires, they gave up this imperial view of the world – mediated by foreign aid regimes and efforts to play power games in former colonies. But the end of empire fostered a distinctly national conception of Britain or France – and notably of what their populations were supposed to look like. In the 1950s, immigration into France or Britain was both useful and a right – something that made sense in a logic of empire. This pattern persisted for a time after decolonization, but by the 1960s Britain was seeking to restrict it, and France cut off labour immigration in 1974. Some argued that France and Britain should think of themselves as multicultural polities, national but not homogeneous. On the right of the political spectrum, a new kind of racism entered the political arena. If imperial racism implied that colonized subjects had to be held within the polity so as to be useful, and held in a position of inequality, nationalist racism implied exclusion. The racism of Jean-Marie Le Pen in France drew on diehard attitudes of settler and military experience in the Algerian war – now definitively separated from the object of their zealotry – but also on a tradition of 'little France' xenophobia – Catholic, antirepublican, and antisemitic – and on the sense of loss of a French community that had probably never existed. One cannot understand Le Pennism simply as an imperial hangover; it emerges out of a national reconfiguration of French politics. Simon Gikandi (1996:71) makes a similar argument about the racism exemplified by Enoch Powell in Great Britain: '[I] Enoch Powell in Great Britain: '[I]n the imperial period [...] the essence of a British identity was derived from the totality of all the people brought together by empire; in the postimperial period, in contrast, we find a calculated attempt to configure Englishness as exclusionary of its colonial wards'.

---

[24]  See the pioneering study of Zolberg 1966.

*Meanings of decolonization*

Decolonization marked the end of a form of political organization – the empire – which had been of great importance for millennia – and against which the apparent domination of the nation-state appears as a short episode. No one claims to be an empire any more – whereas previous empires were frank and proud in claiming that status – and while issues of domination and inequality are far from over, they go by other names and require other means.[25] Empires were incorporative as well as differentiated; they reproduced distinction as they extended themselves. Today's powerful states are more concerned to keep people out than take people in, even as they exercise influence and power beyond their borders.

Second, the end of colonial empires raised expectations not only of change in forms of rule but in forms of livelihood. People expected that self-government would matter in their lives. Such aspirations were captured in Frantz Fanon's famous invocation of the Biblical phrase, 'The last shall be first' (1963:30).

The last are not first. And for some, the result is disillusionment. Many commentators insist that decolonization has been incomplete, a failure. For some conservative scholars the failure is attributed to formerly colonized people – they do not have what it takes to live in the modern world. But for others, the failure lies in once dominant parts of the world: global capitalism has continued to marginalize or exploit Africa and Asia so that economic decolonization has proven illusory; European political norms and structures – not least of which is the form of the nation-state itself – insured that in the end new states would end up within a world political system in which they would always lack something necessary for success; cultural imperialism continued the work of colonial civilizing missions.

Such arguments point to central issues that are very much with us. But to put the problem in terms of a transition from colonialism to neocolonialism is misleading on both sides of the transition. To make the claim that decolonization did not change all aspects of life presumes that colonialism determined all those aspects, that it was totalizing. That is not consistent with scholarship on colonial societies, in Africa or elsewhere, which emphasizes that colonial states were limited in their transformatory ambitions and capacities. Their frequent brutality was in fact a consequence of the difficulty they had in routinizing control.[26] Important as the consequences of colonial rule were, one cannot single out a 'colonial effect' that either continued or ended with decolonization.[27]

---

[25]  On misuses of the concept of empire in some contemporary debates, see Cooper 2004.
[26]  This argument on the nature of colonial situations is developed in Stoler and Cooper 1997.
[27]  This is one of the problems with the large and growing literature on 'postcoloniality'. For

Analysis of the dynamics of decolonization, as argued above, should take into account the nature of contestation before, during, and after the process itself. These are much more varied and complicated than a set of practices that can be labelled 'colonial' and opposed to another that are labelled 'national'. In colonial times and postcolonial times, political actors in Africa and Asia tried to use what political resources they had to make claims upon, to find alternatives to, or to oppose directly a colonial regime, which was trying to make use of its own arsenal of strategies, more powerful certainly but far from unlimited. Certainly many if not most leaders of newly independent African countries in the 1960s tried to mark their territory and their policies as in some sense national – national banking institutions, national strategies for development, as well as all the symbols of sovereignty, from postage stamps to United Nations delegations. But national economic or cultural action could not possibly be more purely national than colonial policy could be purely colonial.

Nowhere was this demonstrated more vividly and more tragically than in Algeria within months of its independence, where Fanon's dream of a liberated nation turned into a nightmare of civil war, with each faction accusing the other of deviating from the path of pure anticolonialism. Indeed, the assertion that there could be such a thing was one factor in rendering the struggles in independent Algeria so acute. The very idea of a national utopia, distinguished from the compromised realities of international politics and trade, turned into a technique of domination by a new elite, making it all the more difficult to address the already daunting task of negotiating with and distancing oneself from former colonial powers and new hegemons on the international scene. It is not just a case of the best being the enemy of the good, but of the insistence on a utopian project of pure nationality becoming a basis for oppression.

So the question of the extent to which decolonization was 'full' or 'real' needs to be reformulated in the light of the fact that the contents of politics – how claims for economic, social, and cultural resources could be made and responded to – were as important as the structure of politics, whether a polity was part of 'empire' or of a 'nation', that now claimed to be the 'state'.

One can think of decolonization as a bounded problem, defined in terms of self-government versus imperial domination. In such terms, nationalist elites could declare the problem over and that their presence at the helm of state constituted victory, regardless of how many people enjoyed the fruits of that victory. And French and British leaders could also declare the problem solved and congratulate themselves on having passed on power, on the institutions created, and the lessons taught – leaving the responsibility

references and critique, see Cooper 2005.

for whatever happened next in the hands of someone else.

The alternative is to think of decolonization as unbounded, as a step in a quest toward something else, something whose realization demanded more struggle and which still posited the existence of an enemy, now broadened to include neocolonialism, the intrusions of western culture and western political intrigue, and the dangers of enemies within. The idea of a continuing struggle could be inspiring, but it also could be stifling – when used by a self-serving ruling establishment to enforce discipline and conformity.

The dilemmas of rule in the small, militarily weak and economically fragile countries of Africa were serious, and most resolutions were partial. But the totalizing discourse that posited a dichotomy between true independence and a compromised neocolonialism did not make them easier to resolve. It was too easy for a ruler to portray the moderately prosperous cocoa farmer who might be seen as contributing to the generation of wealth as a comprador, as a mere instrument of colonial extraction. Such a person might well have the resources to pose a political challenge to a ruler, so the accusation was a self-serving one and it passes over serious examination of what positive and negative effects on society as a whole particular forms of economic activities had. Some African intellectuals have drawn attention to the way some oppressive rulers used a discourse of African authenticity – set against the neocolonial enemy – to legitimize their own self-aggrandizement and their failures to build more self-sustaining economic structures (Kabou 1991).

One might pose the alternatives differently: could citizenship in the 1960s and thereafter have been 'thickened'? Could a population conscious of having mobilized to demand political voice and access to state resources from a colonial regime continue to be mobilized to interact with an independent state? Could such a population demand accountability from their rulers? Could they legitimately demand that the state provide social services and define the space for a national economy? Could they aspire to mobility within a national civil service and a national social system? African states in the early years after independence were not without achievements in the area of social citizenship: the growth of school systems until the 1970s, the decrease in infant mortality, and other large-scale improvements in social welfare reflected the long-delayed intervention of colonial regimes in such domains in their final years of rule and the willingness of independent states to make such projects, for a time, the focus of intensified energy. The degree of seriousness of such efforts varied, as did the degree of success, as well as the extent to which internal conflict sapped these projects, but one should be careful about negative generalizations about Africa as a whole in the 1960s and early 1970s.

Things got much more difficult after that, thanks to the oil shocks and the worldwide depression of demand for tropical products, followed by policies of international financial institutions that placed the repayment of debt over the improvement of human capacities. The generalized economic crisis compounded the uneven political situations, making it all but impossible even for leaders who were trying to make citizenship socially meaningful to have much to show for their efforts and instead encouraging leaders to emphasize clientelism and repression in their strategies to maintain power, strategies for which resources might actually be found for a time. The end result in most African states has been the collapse of the dreams of the 1950s and 1960s, leaving in place a citizenship that is thin – providing little accountability, few services, a meagre security, using the trappings of sovereignty to gain a degree of leverage among various international and national networks, licit or otherwise.[28]

To look at the process of political mobilization in the postwar decade rather than to see it as a moment dividing colonial and postcolonial eras, offers two avenues toward fuller understanding. One is to recognize that alternative visions of the future have existed, have entertained serious support, and might do so again in the future. Africa's present did not lie at the end of a single trajectory of inevitability. The process of politics indeed entailed thick versions of citizenship: claims to equal wages for workers, fair prices for farmers, access to schools for a bigger part of urban and rural populations, universal suffrage, and participation of women in political life. Not all actors ascribed to the entire list. Early scholarship on decolonization tended to treat such claim-making as part of the story of nationalist challenge to imperialism, but the diverse forms of political mobilizations deserve to be taken seriously in themselves – as collective efforts to turn states from outside impositions into institutions responding to citizens' demands.

Second, the sequence of processes helps to explain the brittleness of the result. For a time, 'nationalist' leaders were able to put together coalitions and find common threads in hostility to colonial administration, but – as Aristide Zolberg argued back in 1966 – the nationalist mobilization was thin. The Nkrumahs, Senghors, and other party leaders of the 1950s had for a time channelled citizen grievances into a political movement, but they found themselves no better able than the colonial regimes to find the resources to meet such demands. What they understood well was the volatility of citizen demands and the danger that failure to meet them would pose to their own regimes. Nkrumah – the pioneer nationalist – was also the pioneer in dismantling labour movements and sapping any autonomy that farmers' organizations could muster. Sékou Touré followed in his footsteps. New governments were caught up by the same constraints that had made development such a difficult object for colonial states to achieve, only they neither had the external

---

[28] The chronology is analysed in Cooper 2002.

resources that colonial states could call on nor the possibility of getting out. The authoritarianism of postcolonial regimes throughout Africa reflected both the narrowness of constraints on social and economic change and the personal experience African leaders had in the kinds of mobilizations that had threatened colonial authority.[29]

One should not see decolonization as a single event that can be labelled either a success or a failure, the dawn of a new era, or the continuation of an old one. Not all politics in colonies in the 1950s can be reduced to struggles to attain the nation-state, and the issues those struggles raised are still alive. It does not help clarify the political stakes in regard to issues of economic resources and social justice to frame them as a failed or incomplete decolonization: these are ongoing problems whose parameters are being redefined and whose importance remains.

The world is not the same now that empires are gone, just as the takeover of most of Africa seventy to eighty years previously had radical effects on the continent's people. The political confrontations that turned empire from an ordinary fact into an impossibility are complex and momentous and deserve the kind of scrutiny from different vantage points that the chapters in this volume give them. Decolonization is no less worth pondering for being history – for being something that happened, has had important effects, but is not a singular phenomenon with certain determinant effects.

Many of the issues that arose during this complex process became the subjects of debate in international fora, and some of the most important of them remain there. The inequality between workers and farmers in different parts of the world and the crying need for access to basic resources faced by people in former colonies are no nearer an end than they were in the 1950s; perhaps they are farther away. The issues have not quite disappeared into formally independent sovereignties, even if they are no longer issues of empire. But for a time the raising of such issues shook the foundation of two of the world's most powerful colonial empires. The way that they did so and the ways in which imperial powers responded to them shaped a particular sort of decolonization – one that generalized sovereignty but did not generalize claims for vital economic and social resources. The fact that such claims were made and to such effect should remind us of the continued importance of collective action and of the enormous difficulty that analysing its effects and assessing responsibility for its consequences entails.

---

[29]  I have spelled out this argument in more detail in Cooper 2002, emphasizing that what colonial regimes had created was 'gatekeeper states' – strong at the nodal point between territory and external world, but with weak mechanisms of control and mobilization within the territory. New rulers were also strongest in capital cities and in communication nodes where they could control external trade and aid and dole out patronage, but they were weak in their ability to reshape social and economic structures.

*References*

Allman, Jean Marie
1993        *The quills of the porcupine; Asante nationalism in an emergent Ghana.*
            Madison, WI: University of Wisconsin Press.
Anderson, David
2005        *Histories of the hanged; Britain's dirty war in Kenya and the end of empire.*
            New York: Norton.
Atlan, Catherine
1997        'Demain la balkanisation? Les députés africains et le vote de la Loi-
            cadre', in: Charles Becker, Saliou Mbaye and Ibrahima Thioub (eds),
            *AOF; Réalités et héritages; Sociétés ouest-africaines et ordre colonial, 1895-
            1960,* pp. 359-75. Dakar: Direction des Archives du Sénégal. Two vols.
            [First published 1956.]
Austin, Dennis
1964        *Politics in Ghana, 1946-1960.* London: Oxford University Press.
Beckman, Björn
1976        *Organizing the farmers; Cocoa politics and national development in Ghana.*
            Uppsala: Scandinavian Institute of African Studies.
Berman, Bruce and John Lonsdale
1992        *Unhappy valley; Conflict in Kenya and Africa; Vol. II: Violence and ethnicity.*
            London: James Currey.
Chafer, Tony
2002        *The end of empire in French West Africa: France's successful decolonization?*
            Oxford: Berg.
Conklin, Alice L.
1998        *A mission to civilize; The republican idea of empire in France and West Africa,
            1895-1930.* Stanford, CA: Stanford University Press.
Connelly, Matthew
2002        *A diplomatic revolution; Algeria's fight for independence and the origins of
            the post-cold war era.* New York: Oxford University Press.
Cooper, Frederick
1990        'The Senegalese general strike of 1946 and the labor question in post-
            war French Africa', *Canadian Journal of African Studies* 24:165-215.
1996a       *Decolonization and African society; The labor question in French and British
            Africa.* Cambridge: Cambridge University Press. [African Studies
            Series 89.]
1996b       '"Our Strike"; Equality, anticolonial politics and the 1947-48 railway
            strike in French West Africa', *Journal of African History* 37:81-118.
2002        *Africa since 1940; The past of the present.* Cambridge: Cambridge
            University Press. [New Approaches to African History 1.]
2004        'Empire multiplied', *Comparative Studies in Society and History* 46:247-72.
2005        *Colonialism in question; Theory, knowledge, history.* Berkeley, CA:
            University of California Press.
*Documents élaboration constitution*
1987        *Documents pour servir à l'élaboration de la constitution du 4 octobre 1958.*
            Comité National chargé de la publication des travaux préparatoires

des institutions de la Ve République. Paris: Documentation Française. Four vols.

Dubois, Laurent
2000    'La République métissée; Citizenship, colonialism, and the borders of French history', *Cultural Studies* 14:15-34.

Elkins, Caroline
2005    *Imperial reckoning; The untold story of the end of empire in Kenya.* New York: Holt.

Fanon, Frantz
1963    *The wretched of the earth.* Translated by Constance Farrington. New York: Grove Press. [Originally published as *Les damnés de la terre.* N.p.: Maspéro, 1961.]

Ferguson, James
1999    *Expectations of modernity; Myths and meanings of urban life on the Zambian Copperbelt.* Berkeley, CA: University of California Press. [Perspectives on Southern Africa 57.]

Foltz, William J.
1965    *From French West Africa to the Mali Federation.* New Haven, CT: Yale University Press. [Yale Studies in Political Science 12.]

Gikandi, Simon
1996    *Maps of Englishness; Writing identity in the culture of colonialism.* New York: Columbia University Press.

Gonidec, P.F.
1953    'Une mystique de l'égalité; Le code du travail des territoires d'Outre-Mer', *Revue juridique et politique de l'Union française* 2:176-96.

James, C.L.R.
1963    *The black Jacobins;\Toussaint L'Ouverture and the San Domingo Revolution.* Second revised edition. New York: Vintage. [First edition 1938.]

Joseph, Richard A.
1977    *Radical nationalism in Cameroun; Social origins of the UPC rebellion.* Oxford: Oxford University Press. [Oxford Atudies in African Affairs.]

Kabou, Axelle
1991    *Et si l'Afrique refusait le développement?* Paris: L'Harmattan.

Lebovics, Herman
1992    *True France; The wars over cultural identity, 1900-1945.* Ithaca, NY: Cornell University Press. [The Wilder House Series in Politics, History, and Culture.]

Lindsay, Lisa A.
2003    *Working with gender; Wage labor and social change in southwestern Nigeria.* Portsmouth, NH: Heinemann. [Social History of Africa.]

Mamdani, Mahmood
1996    *Citizen and subject; Contemporary Africa and the legacy of late colonialism.* Princeton, NJ: Princeton University Press. [Princeton Studies in Culture/Power/History.]

Mann, Gregory
2003    'Immigrants and arguments in France and West Africa', *Comparative Studies in Society and History* 45:362-85.

Mbembe, Achille
2001        *On the postcolony*. Berkeley, CA: University of California Press.
Morgenthau, Ruth Schachter
1964        *Political parties in French-speaking West Africa*. Oxford: Clarendon.
            [Oxford Studies in African Affairs.]
Paul, Kathleen
1997        *Whitewashing Britain; Race and citizenship in the postwar era*. Ithaca, NY:
            Cornell University Press.
Pearce, R.D.
1982        *The turning point in Africa; British colonial policy, 1938-48*. London: Cass.
Rolland, Louis and Pierre Lampué
1952        *Précis de droit des pays d'outre-mer (territoires, départements, états associés)*.
            Paris: Dalloz.
Senghor, Léopold Sédar
1945        'Vues sur l'Afrique Noire, ou assimiler, non être assimilés', in: Robert
            Lemaignen, Léopold Sédar Senghor and Prince Sisonath Youtévong,
            *La communauté impériale française*. Paris: Alsatia.
Stoler, Ann and Frederick Cooper
1997        'Between metropole and colony; Rethinking a research agenda',
            in: Frederick Cooper and Ann Laura Stoler (eds), *Tensions of empire;
            Colonial cultures in a bourgeois world*, pp. 1-56. Berkeley, CA: University
            of California Press.
Thompson, Elizabeth
2000        *Colonial citizens; Republican rights, paternal privilege, and gender in French
            Syria and Lebanon*. New York: Columbia University Press. [History and
            Society of the Modern Middle East Series.]
Zolberg, Aristide R.
1966        *Creating political order; The party-states of West Africa*. Chicago: Rand
            McNally. [Studies in Political Change.]

ANNE BOOTH

# The plural economy and its legacy in Asia

The concept of the plural society was introduced into the development literature by J.S. Furnivall, a member of the Indian civil service who worked
in Burma for a number of years and then carried out research into the Dutch
colonial system in the Netherlands Indies in the 1930s. In his influential comparative study of Burma and the Netherlands Indies, he argued that by the
early decades of the twentieth century European colonialism had created a
very different type of society from that which existed in Europe at that time,
or had existed in precolonial Southeast Asia. He argued the following:

> [T]he western superstructure is only one aspect of a distinctive character,
> common to all tropical dependencies, that cannot fail to impress even the
> most casual observer; the many coloured pattern of the population. In
> Burma, as in Java, probably the first thing that strikes the visitor is the
> medley of peoples – European, Chinese, Indian and native. It is in the
> strictest sense a medley, for they mix but do not combine. Each group holds
> by its own religion, its own culture and language, its own ideas and ways.
> As individuals they meet, but only in the market place, in buying and
> selling. There is a plural society, with different sections of the community
> living side by side, but separately, within the same political unit. Even in
> the economic sphere there is a division of labour along racial lines. Natives,
> Chinese, Indians and Europeans all have different functions, and within
> each major group subsections have particular occupations. (Furnivall
> 1948:304-5.)

In an earlier essay, Furnivall pointed out that the plural society came into
being because the only factor common to all the ethnic groups in colonial
Southeast Asia was an economic one. This in turn was the result of the over-
whelming importance accorded to economic interests in the territories the
European colonial powers controlled (Furnivall 1945:171). In this sense the
plural society and the plural economy were one and the same thing. Furnivall
probably viewed the plural society and economy as essentially the result of
colonial economic policies, although he admitted that traces of a plural society

were evident in several societies outside the tropical world including Canada, the USA, and South Africa. He also argued that in these countries, and in Australia and New Zealand, 'when the influx of alien elements threatened national life', restrictions were placed on in-migration. By the second decade of the twentieth century, some colonial regimes in Southeast Asia, including the Dutch in the Netherlands Indies and the Americans in the Philippines, were also seeking to control in-migration from China in particular, although British policy in both Malaya and Burma was more *laissez-faire*, with respect to both Chinese and Indians. But by then main features of the plural society were already entrenched.

## The precolonial economy of Southeast Asia

Furnivall tended to contrast the plural society that had emerged in colonial Southeast Asia with a precolonial economic and social system where most people lived in rural villages, and social and religious factors were far more important in people's lives than economic ones. In his view, culture and community dominated in precolonial society, whereas impersonal market systems imposed from outside featured much more prominently in colonial society (Furnivall 1945; Rex 1959:116). But in recent years, historians have begun to view the precolonial economies of Southeast Asia in a rather different light.

Anthony Reid (1993) has called the years from 1450 to 1680 the 'age of commerce' in Southeast Asia, a period characterized not just by increased international trading links but also the growth of cities throughout both mainland and insular Southeast Asia, and a considerable expansion of domestic entrepreneurial and trading activity. The urban areas of Southeast Asia at this time were not just trading centres but also the conduits through which both religious and secular ideas from many countries filtered into domestic societies. Populations were mixed, with indigenous people associating freely with traders from the Middle East, South Asia, and China. Several of these cities including Aceh, Banten, and Brunei contained at least one fifth of the total population under the control of the states where they were located. In Southeast Asia as a whole at least five percent of the population was living in large urban trading centres. This was a larger proportion than in contemporary northern Europe, although probably not larger than in Mughal India or China at that time (Reid 1993:75).

In spite of the relatively high level of urban development in Southeast Asia in the seventeenth century, there were several areas where the region was still well behind other parts of Asia, as well as Europe. Banking in its modern form, as distinct from traditional money lending, was unknown; in addition the impersonal institutions to safeguard capital and property that were developing in Europe were 'totally absent in Southeast Asia' (Reid 1993:129). Reid argues that the close links between rulers and the marketplace that characterized much of precolonial Southeast Asia made the evolution of individual property rights difficult throughout the region, in contrast to late medieval Europe, and to Tokugawa Japan. On the one hand, many members of the political elite were involved in trade and commerce, which made them more sympathetic to such activities than their counterparts in other parts of Asia or indeed in parts of Europe might have been (Reid 1993:270). But, on the other hand, a robust independent class of indigenous traders and entrepreneurs, protected by an impartial legal system, was unable to emerge.

The reasons for the collapse of the powerful Asian trading port cities were complex, and varied by time and place. In the Indonesian archipelago, the Dutch would not have been able to destroy centres such as Banten and Makassar if there had been more trust, and greater willingness, to form durable alliances between the various indigenous kingdoms. Aceh and several trading cities in mainland Southeast Asia did not fall under Dutch control, but they disengaged from the regional and global trading system because they no longer found such activities profitable, or because their rulers wanted their populations to concentrate on foodcrop cultivation (Reid 1993:299-301). Other factors such as climate change may also have contributed towards the demise of the age of commerce in the region by the end of the seventeenth century. What does seem clear is that by 1700 the main Asian-ruled trading cities had 'lost their place both in world trade and within their societies' (Reid 1993:328). Not only did regional and global trading links become attenuated, but the outward-looking, cosmopolitan, urban centres underwent a steady decline.

## The emergence of the plural economy

The eighteenth century saw the growth of several port cities such as Batavia (now Jakarta) and Manila that were under the control of European powers, and from which the tentacles of foreign domination stretched out to the hinterlands. But the total urban population in Southeast Asia almost certainly declined, and there can be little doubt that this century saw a retreat from the market into a subsistence agricultural economy in many parts of the region. In addition it also witnessed the beginnings of an economic system where ethnicity and economic role were more tightly linked. In most parts of Southeast Asia, the emergence of the plural economy was inextricably connected to the growth of resident Chinese, and to a lesser extent Indian and Arab, populations. During the 'age of commerce', the Chinese were just one of several trading minorities active in the larger port cities, and they mixed with both indigenous and other trading groups without appearing to dominate. But by the eighteenth century their numbers had grown, mainly because economic and demographic pressures in China itself were pushing more Chinese into trading and commercial ventures in Southeast Asia, as well as into less skilled occupations such as agricultural labour (Reid 2001:50).

The European-controlled port cities held many attractions for Chinese traders in the eighteenth century. They were important sources of valuable commodities and precious metals, especially silver, which were much in demand in China, and they provided a 'stable environment in which Chinese could grow wealthy and even influential without ceasing to be Chinese' (Reid 1993:317). But probably the single most important development that led to the sharp functional separation of economic activity by an ethnic group was the introduction of tax farming, which was initiated by the Dutch in Batavia in the seventeenth century, and which spread to various native states in Java, Siam (Thailand), and Cambodia over the next century (Reid 1993:318-9). Tax farming, or the system whereby the right to collect revenues on behalf of the government is sold or auctioned off to private individuals, is as old as antiquity and was widely found in the early-modern period in both Europe and Asia (Copeland and Godley 1993). In Southeast Asia it was quite widely practiced in the eighteenth century and grew rapidly after 1820 (Butcher 1993:20-1). The system permitted rulers to withdraw from commercial concerns while at the same time giving private merchants, often Chinese, considerable economic power and social prestige without threatening the position of the rulers. Reid suggests that it was perhaps no accident that those ethnic groups in Southeast Asia where the entrepreneurial spirit best survived into the twentieth century were located in remote regions where Chinese tax farming did not penetrate or where religious and cultural hostility to tax farming made local rulers reluctant to adopt it.

The nineteenth century saw further growth of European-controlled port cities, and by the 1890s there were a number of port cities in mainland and island Southeast Asia with populations in excess of 50,000, including Rangoon and Moulmein, Bangkok, Singapore, Batavia, Semarang, Surabaya, Palembang, Saigon-Cholon, and Manila. In addition, some inland cities, several of which had been important in the precolonial era, including Mandalay, Yogyakarta, Surakarta, and Hanoi had become important centres of colonial administration and trade by the turn of the twentieth century. But the nineteenth century was a period of quite rapid population growth in much of Southeast Asia and several scholars have pointed out that it is probable that urban populations actually declined relative to total populations in many parts of the region (Reid 2001:55).

Certainly the European colonial powers were not in favour of rapid migration of indigenous populations to urban areas, and neither was the governing elite in Siam, where it has been claimed that the 'court helped to develop urban Siam as a Chinese preserve' (Phongpaichit and Baker 1995:174). But it would be false to claim that urban populations were always overwhelmingly European and Chinese or Indian. In Javanese cities, indigenous Indonesians were in the majority by 1890, and this continued to be the case until the end of colonial rule (Boomgaard and Gooszen 1991:220-1). But in Bangkok it has been estimated that by the 1850s Chinese outnumbered indigenous Thai by two to one, and Chinese immigration accelerated from the 1860s onwards as the demand for urban labour increased. The government was also an important source of employment for Chinese workers, especially on railway construction, while the port of Bangkok became 'virtually a Chinese preserve' (Phongpaichit and Baker 1995:174-5). In Rangoon where Indian immigration had accelerated since the late nineteenth century, the 1931 census found that Indians comprised 53 percent of the population. They were almost eleven percent of the population in Lower Burma as a whole. Only 32 percent of the population of Rangoon consisted of indigenous Burmans (Baxter 1941:9-21).

After 1900, the division between the newly arrived Chinese and the established families became more pronounced, not only in areas that had absorbed Chinese migrants for centuries, such as Java, but in other parts of Southeast Asia as well. Many children from the latter group began to assimilate; they ceased speaking Chinese dialects, learnt local vernaculars as well as Dutch, English, or French, and in many cases gravitated towards salaried jobs. As educational opportunities increased for Chinese, especially in the Netherlands Indies and British Malaya, they were, as Rush (1991:24) and Mackie (1991:89) have pointed out, attracted to the 'genteel professions' rather than the hurly-burly of commerce, although many who lacked the ability or the opportunity to learn the languages of the colonial powers stayed in unskilled labouring occupations. In addition, there were many new arrivals from China, mainly single men, who became coolie labourers, itinerant pedlars, and artisans. By the 1930s the Chinese in the Netherlands Indies, the Straits Settlements, the Federated Malay States (FMS), and Siam were spread across a variety of occupations; in all these territories the majority were in nonagricultural occupations, although over 40 percent were in agriculture in the islands outside Java and in the FMS, mainly as plantation labourers (Table 1).

The relative lack of interest in commercial careers on the part of the *peranakan* (assimilated) Chinese in late-colonial Netherlands Indies led Williams (1952:34) to argue that 'the Chinese in Indonesia did not achieve entrepreneurship'. His thorough survey of the evidence from the interwar years led him to the conclusion that the Indonesian Chinese were unable, or at least unwilling, to extend

Table 1. Percentage distribution of the Chinese in the labour force by sector, 1930s

| Sector | Java 1930 | Outer Islands 1930 | Straits S'ments 1931 | FMS 1931 | Thailand 1937 | Philippines 1939 |
|---|---|---|---|---|---|---|
| Agriculture | 9.1 | 44.7 | 17.2 | 41.5 | 25.4 | 1.8 |
| Manufacture | 20.8 | 19.5 | 17.6 | 27.3 | 20.3 | 14.3 |
| Transport | 2.8 | 2.6 | 12.5 | 3.4 | 3.9 | 1.3 |
| Commerce | 57.7 | 23.2 | 23.3 | 12.2 | 34.9 | 53.7 |
| Public Service | 0.5 | 0.7 | 0.2 | 0.1 | 1.2 | 0.2 |
| Professions[a] | 2.1 | 1.2 | 2.3 | 1.2 | 1.2 | 3.6 |
| Personal, etc. | 6.9 | 8.2 | 26.8 | 14.4 | 14.2 | 25.1 |
| Total | 100.0 | 100.0 | 100.0 | 100.0 | 100.0 | 100.0 |

[a] Includes clerical workers

Sources: Indonesia: Department of Economic Affairs 1936, VIII:Table 18; Thailand: Central Service of Statistics c.1946:75; Straits Settlements and FMS: Vlieland 1932:Tables 126, 134; Philippines: Commonwealth of the Philippines 1941:505-21.

their commercial and industrial enterprises beyond the 'limits imposed largely by tradition' (Williams 1952:55). Certainly there were exceptions, the most famous of whom was the 'sugar king' Oei Tiong Ham, who built up a large conglomerate based mainly on plantations in the early part of the twentieth century (Yoshihara 1989). In an official handbook listing all firms operating in the colony in 1940, the Oei Tiong Ham concern, including both sugar and banking interests, was by far the largest Chinese company, and the only Indonesian Chinese business, apart from the Overseas Chinese Banking Corporation, with assets in excess of 40 million guilders (Twang 1998:Table 2.3).

    Based on official data and interviews, Twang (1998:Table 2.3) assembled a list of the large Chinese firms operating in Java and Sumatra in 1940. Most were either in agribusiness, or in trade and banking. Few were in manufacturing, apart from agricultural processing. Several large Chinese companies were still exploiting the so-called privately-owned lands (*particuliere landerijen*), mainly in West Java, which had been in Chinese hands for many decades, in spite of Dutch attempts to expropriate the Chinese owners in the early twentieth century (Twang 1998:33). There were many medium and small-scale enterprises, some in manufacturing, and by no means all were Chinese-owned. In the 1920s, a government survey conducted in the Netherlands Indies showed that there were almost 1,700 Chinese-owned industrial firms employing more than five people, compared with 2,800 European firms and 870 owned by indigenous Indonesians (Fernando and Bulbeck 1992:254-9). But all these numbers pale into insignificance when compared with developments in other parts of Asia (especially Japan) at the same time. Prominent though the Chinese might have appeared in the commercial life of the Netherlands Indies, and in other Southeast Asian cities in the 1920s and 1930s, they were hardly laying the foundations for an industrial take-off.

## The 'problem' of native entrepreneurship

Like many other colonial administrators in different parts of Asia, Furnivall (1948:293) recognized that the 'development of native enterprise must be a chief object of policy in any dependency which is valued as a market for the products of the colonial power'. He argued that subsistence producers should be brought into the market economy, if necessary by imposing taxes that had to be paid in money, and was in favour of inducements to encourage indigenous cultivators to grow export crops, and of expanded credit to native producers, even where this meant borrowing on the security of crops. Again like other colonial administrators, Furnivall's views were at least partly motivated by a desire to create larger and more dynamic markets for metropolitan manufactures in the colonies. But at the same time he was well aware of the debates in various colonial regimes in Southeast Asia concerning the desirability of exposing indigenous producers to the full blasts of global capitalism. The great majority of colonial officials would have been unaware of the precolonial economic history of the regions they were controlling, and even if they had realized that there had been an 'age of commerce' in the sixteenth and seventeenth centuries, they would no doubt have argued that the world economy in the early twentieth century was very different from that four centuries earlier, and while the rewards of involvement in international commerce were great, so were the dangers.

The Dutch in particular debated endlessly the extent to which indigenous Indonesians were being incorporated into the 'Western sphere' of economic influence, the factors which promoted or inhibited such incorporation, and its effects on the economic and social welfare of the population. The views of J.H. Boeke (1953) on these issues were well-known in the English-speaking world, and some scholars have tended to treat them as the 'official' Dutch view of the entrepreneurial capacities of indigenous Indonesians. As such, they were much criticized in the postindependence period by writers such as Higgins

(1956) and Sadli (1971). But Boeke's views underwent considerable change in the course of his long career and certainly cannot be considered typical of the Dutch colonial establishment as a whole. Some of his earlier writings certainly shared similarities with the concept of the plural society, especially as they made a sharp distinction between the economic and social needs of indigenous Asian populations (*Indonesian economics* 1961:11). But other Dutch officials held different views: for example, Dutch agronomists working intensively in the agricultural sector of Java and other parts of the country, whose conclusions were grounded in detailed fieldwork, often viewed the problems facing Indonesian farmers as similar to those in other parts of Asia, and in precapitalist Europe (*Indonesian economics* 1961:15-7).

In his study of the formation of occidental stereotypes of the 'Malay character', Alatas (1977:112) pointed out that 'the general negative image was not the result of scholarship'. Most of those who proclaimed the indigenous peoples of Southeast Asia to be indolent, dull, treacherous, childish, and lacking any talent for, or interest in trade and commerce, were either colonial officials, planters, military people or casual tourists. And yet, as Alatas concedes, even in the high noon of Western imperialism there were some who were prepared to admit that these alleged features of the 'Malay national character' were by no means universal, and, where they were widely found, had quite rational economic foundations. By the early twentieth century, most colonial scholars and policymakers in the Netherlands Indies, and in other parts of the region as well, would doubtless have concurred with Van Gelderen (1961:144), that 'the inhabitant of the tropics is further removed from the classical homo economicus than the Westerner', but at the same time the reasons for the apparent lack of 'rational economic behaviour' on the part of the indigenous population in the Netherlands Indies were much disputed.

Some colonial officials were certainly content to ascribe this perceived lack to culture, religion, and the climate, but others thought differently. In 1941, Van der Kolff, who held the chair of economics in the Batavia Law School, published a remarkable paper that argued that to the extent that Indonesians, especially Javanese, adopted short-time horizons and were unwilling to invest in risky operations that would yield results only in the longer term, they were ignorant, poor, and insecure, rather than irrational. It was, according to Van der Kolff (1961:247), poverty and insecurity that led to practices such as *ijon* (Javanese, selling the crop while still immature), and such behaviour was perfectly rational given the constraints within which many Javanese had to make decisions on consumption, saving, and investment. Other writers also stressed the economic rationality of farmer behaviour in the more land-abundant parts of the region, such as British Malaya. It was argued that the Malay reluctance to work for wages did not reflect an aversion to effort or a lack of desire for a cash income, but rather the fact that with relatively abundant supplies of land they could earn more in agriculture than as unskilled workers in the city. As Winstedt, a prominent British official in Malaya in the interwar years, pointed out, 'because he is an independent farmer with no need to work for hire, the Malay has got an undeserved reputation for idleness, which his Asiatic competitors take care to foster' (Alatas 1977:50).

Views of Malay idleness would not have been universally held, although there would certainly have been greater agreement on a further assertion of Van Gelderen's (1961:147) that the indigenous cultivator was likely to be exploited in his or her dealings with the market economy because of the 'great difference in bargaining power between the buyer on the one hand and the seller on the other'.

> The buyer usually has both superior knowledge of the market situation and greater possibilities to reach and make use of more than one local market. This preponderance is even greater if the buyer is the only one, or one of a very small group of competitors, as against a larger number of persons offering the commodity for sale. In such a case it is very easy for a monopoly or semi-monopoly situation to develop, so that the local price of a commodity is forced downwards. Another factor producing the same effect is the vast difference in the value of the same unit of money for the two parties to the transaction [...]. In many cases, in fact, the normal situation is one in which the necessity to sell is so urgent that what takes place is actually a forced sale. (Van Gelderen 1961:147)

The underlying implication was, of course, that the monopsonistic middlemen were almost always Chinese, and it was their superior knowledge and bargaining power that led to the exploitation of the indigenous producer. Regardless of the truth or otherwise of these assertions it is indisputable that they were held by many Dutch colonial administrators, as well as by many indigenous Indonesians. Indeed, George Kahin (1952:64-74) argued that the rapid growth of the Sarekat Dagang Islam, formed by Raden Mas Tirtoadisoerjo in 1909 into a political-nationalist movement, was in large part due to 'sharp Chinese trading practices' on the part of 'aggressively competitive Chinese entrepreneurs' whose commercial power had increased as a result of the gradual lifting of travel restrictions between 1904 and 1911. The Sarekat Islam attracted 'an avalanche of members' (Kahin 1952:67) and galvanized anti-Chinese feelings to the point where, in 1912, there were anti-Chinese riots in both Surakarta and Surabaya.

Outside Java, although the Chinese presence was larger relative to the indigenous population, some indigenous business groups did emerge in the last phase of the Dutch colonial era. Peter Post (1997:93-103) has described the rise of a group of Sumatran traders who were able to establish themselves in

Java, and built up quite extensive trading links with other parts of Asia, especially Japan. Several had close ties to leaders of the independence struggle, particularly Mohammad Hatta, and accompanied him on a trip to Japan in 1933. The Japanese were keen to build up a network of indigenous traders in the Netherlands Indies for products such as textiles, especially as Japanese products were increasingly subject to boycotts by Chinese merchants. These links were strengthened during the Japanese occupation, and some of the Sumatran traders survived to play an important role in the early postindependence era.

Paradoxically in spite of the Dutch concern about the ability of the Javanese to participate in the 'modern economy', native Javanese accounted for a higher proportion of the nonagricultural labour than was the case in most other parts of the region (Table 2). Although it may have been true that many jobs in the nonagricultural labour force occupied by Javanese in the 1930s were in unskilled labour, petty trade, and cottage industry, they also outnumbered both Chinese and Europeans in professional occupations and in the civil service. Even in trade, where the Chinese were certainly important, their numbers were only around 12 percent of indigenous workers in Java and 37 percent in the Outer Islands (the islands outside Java) (Table 3). By the 1930s it would appear that many indigenous Indonesians were availing themselves of a greater range of economic opportunities than were other Southeast Asians, or indeed the indigenous populations of Japanese-occupied Taiwan and Korea. Certainly it is arguable that many were forced into nonagricultural occupations by the growing scarcity of agricultural land. But whether out of choice, or through desperation, indigenous Indonesians were moving into new occupations and accepting new challenges, both as employees and as self-employed business people. According to the 1930 census, in Java alone almost 500,000 indigenous Indonesians were employed in professional occupations and in government service, while a further 900,000 were in trading occupations (Department of Economic Affairs 1936:Table 18).

In order to get a broader picture of the development of indigenous participation in the nonagricultural labour force, it is instructive to compare developments in the Netherlands Indies with those in the Philippines. Although the Chinese were not in fact a much smaller proportion of the total population in the Philippines than in Java (Table 4), the American administration did not seem to be nearly as anxious about their economic role as were the Dutch. Certainly the Americans were keen to build up a robust indigenous entrepreneurial class in the Philippines, and viewed education as a key policy in achieving this goal. They facilitated the development of both secondary and tertiary education to a much greater extent than in any other Asian colony (Furnivall 1943:111). But other aspects of American policy were less conducive

Table 2. Indigenous labour force as a percentage of the total labour force, circa 1930

| | Indigenous workers as percentage of: | | |
|---|---|---|---|
| | Total labour force | Agricultural workers | Non-agricultural workers |
| Java (1930) | 98.2 | 99.7 | 95.5 |
| Outer Islands of Indonesia (1930) | 94.7 | 97.1 | 85.2 |
| Straits Settlements (1931) | 16.9 | 38.8 | 7.8 |
| FMS (1931) | 19.9 | 27.5 | 7.4 |
| Burma (1931) | 87.9 | 94.7 | 72.4 |
| Philippines (1939) | 98.6 | 99.7 | 97.9 |
| Thailand (1937) | 94.5 | 98.1 | 66.7 |
| Korea (1930) | 96.9 | 99.6 | 87.2 |
| Taiwan (1930)[a] | 92.3 | 99.5 | 80.1 |

[a] Refers to male labour force only.

Sources: Indonesia: Department of Economic Affairs 1936, VIII:Table 18; Thailand: Central Service of Statistics c.1946:75; Straits Settlements and FMS: Vlieland 1932:Tables 121-141; Burma: Baxter 1941:25; Philippines: Commonwealth of the Philippines 1941:505-21; Korea: Chang 1966:Table 2; Taiwan: Barclay 1954:71.

to the development of indigenous entrepreneurs. Norman Owen (1972:52) pointed out that when the Americans arrived in 1898 there was very little large-scale Filipino manufacturing. The advent of a free-trade regime with the USA, together with an overvalued peso, made investment in Philippine industry unprofitable outside export processing. Because several of the key politicians who emerged in the run-up to self-government were connected to, and dependent on, the sugar sector, there were few advocates for rapid industrialization. Much of the large-scale manufacturing industry that did emerge was controlled by foreign interests, either American, Chinese, or Spanish. This was also true of commercial banking.

The Chinese dominated internal trade in the Philippines, especially retailing, and also participated in wholesaling and importing, as indeed was the

Table 3. Indigenous and Chinese labour force by sector, Indonesia 1930

| Sector | Indigenous labour force by sector | | Indigenous as percentage of the total labour force | | Chinese as percentage of indigenous labour force | |
|---|---|---|---|---|---|---|
| | J. | O.I. | J. | O.I. | J. | O.I. |
| Agriculture | 65.3 | 81.6 | 99.7 | 97.1 | 0.2 | 2.7 |
| Industry | 11.5 | 7.7 | 97.4 | 88.2 | 2.3 | 12.4 |
| Transport | 1.4 | 1.4 | 93.2 | 89.0 | 2.5 | 9.1 |
| Trade | 6.3 | 3.1 | 87.9 | 70.1 | 11.6 | 36.6 |
| Professions | 0.7 | 0.7 | 89.1 | 87.4 | 3.6 | 7.9 |
| Government | 2.6 | 2.0 | 95.5 | 94.6 | 0.3 | 1.8 |
| Other | 12.1 | 3.5 | 98.9 | 89.0 | 0.7 | 11.5 |
| Total | 100.0 | 100.0 | 98.2 | 94.7 | 1.3 | 4.9 |

Note: Agriculture includes hunting, fishing, forestry, mining, and salt manufacture. Government service includes police, army, and navy. J=Java, O.I. = Outer Islands.

Source: Department of Economic Affairs 1936,VIII:Table 18.

case in many other parts of Southeast Asia. Foreign observers such as Kenneth Kurihara (1945:11) emphasized the lack of involvement of indigenous Filipinos in large-scale manufacturing, and argued that the 'Philippine experience was no different from that in European dependencies or in independent countries which, economically, occupy a semicolonial status'. His analysis of the 1939 census data on employment showed that most workers engaged in manufacturing were employed in traditional labour-intensive industries such as embroidery, dressmaking and tailoring, hatmaking, carpentry, native textiles, shoe and slipper manufacture, matmaking, and cigarette manufacture (1945:16-7). Many women were employed as homeworkers on a putting-out basis. Few workers were learning new skills in factories using modern technologies, and even fewer were learning how to manage large-scale enterprises, whether in manufacturing or in other sectors of industry and commerce.

While Kurihara's criticisms were broadly correct, there is evidence that Filipinos were, by the late 1930s, controlling a higher proportion of nonagricultural assets in the economy than was the case in other Asian colonies. Frank Golay (1969:Table 1) used the 1939 census data to estimate that Philippine

Table 4. Breakdown of colonial populations by ethnic background, 1930s

| Colony | Europeans/ Japanese/ Americans | Chinese | Other Asians | Indigenous |
|---|---|---|---|---|
| Taiwan (1935) | 5.2 | 1.1[a] | n.a | 93.7 |
| Korea (1939) | 2.9 | 0.2 | n.a | 96.9 |
| Indochina (1937) | 0.2 | 1.4 | n.a | 98.4 |
| Tonkin | 0.2 | 0.4 | n.a | 99.4 |
| Annam | 0.1 | 0.2 | n.a | 99.7 |
| Cochinchina | 0.3 | 3.7 | n.a | 96.0 |
| Cambodia | 0.1 | 3.5 | n.a | 96.4 |
| Laos | 0.1 | 0.3 | n.a | 99.6 |
| Thailand (1937) | n.a | 11.8 | 0.8 | 87.4 |
| Burma (1931) | 0.2 | 1.3 | 8.2[b] | 90.3 |
| Malaya (1931) | 0.4 | 39.0 | 15.8 | 44.7 |
| Philippines (1939) | 0.3 | 0.7 | n.a | 99.0 |
| Java (1930) | 0.5 | 1.4 | 0.1 | 98.0 |
| Other Indonesia (1930) | 0.3 | 3.4 | 0.3 | 96.0 |

[a] Refers to citizens of mainland China, and other foreigners.
[b] Includes Indo-Burmans

Sources: Korea: Grajdanzev 1944:76; Taiwan: Barclay 1954:16; Indonesia: Boomgaard and Gooszen 1991; French Indochina: Robequain 1944:Tables 1 and 6; Thailand: Sompop 1989:32; Burma: Saito and Lee 1999:Table 1-3; Philippines: Bureau of Census and Statistics 1947:17; British Malaya: Department of Statistics 1939:36.

citizens owned 45 percent of all nonagricultural assets; in the manufacturing industry the figure was higher (55 percent). Chinese nationals controlled around 14 percent of assets and Americans 25 percent. Of course, it is probable that many Filipinos of mixed Chinese or Spanish descent were classified as indigenous Filipinos in the census data. But even allowing for this, Golay's figures do suggest that on the eve of the Pacific War Philippine citizens already exercised considerable control over the nonagricultural sectors of the economy. The consequences of this for postindependence development are explored below.

Siam, although never a colony, also had to face the problem of considerable foreign control over important sectors of the economy. Eliezer Ayal (1969:338) pointed out that the leaders of the 1932 coup 'were imbued with Western ideas of exclusive nationalism and were therefore more sensitive to the presence and activities of unassimilated aliens in their country'. Their main motivation was to end the absolute monarchy and replace it with a constitutional government that would pursue more aggressively Thai national interests. The notion of 'Thaification' gained support, and, from 1935 onwards, laws were passed to reserve certain urban occupations for Thai, and to give preference to firms owned by indigenous Thai in allocating government contracts (Phongpaichit and Baker 1995:179; Yoshihara 1994:32). The Business Registration Act of 1936 was designed to facilitate the compilation of information on business ownership, and in 1938 a government-controlled Thai Rice Company was formed by the purchase of ten Chinese rice mills. The Liquid Fuel Act of 1939 attempted to establish government control over oil imports and distribution. Some of these policies were reversed later, but the measures of the 1930s set a precedent for 'persistent, if erratic' policies to indigenize the economy, which continued after 1945 (Ayal 1969:300-1, 338).

*Markets for land, labour and capital in the Netherlands Indies and British Malaya*

As has already been emphasized, it would be wrong to assume that the attitude of all colonial officials was one of purely paternalistic concern that the commercially incompetent indigenous population should be protected from the rapacity of the clever Chinese. By the beginning of the twentieth century it was becoming clear to at least some Dutch and French administrators, concerned about what was perceived as overpopulation in Java and Tonkin, that the living standards of the indigenous populations would only improve to the extent that they could participate more fully in the modern, nonagricultural economy. In Java, two facts were widely acknowledged by most scholars and administrators who had studied the empirical evidence: the proportion of agricultural output, including foodstuffs, which was sold on the market had increased to almost 50 percent in many parts of the island, and most rural households were diversifying their sources of income away from purely agricultural pursuits to manufacturing, transport, trade and wage labour (Van Laanen 1990:265; Boomgaard and Gooszen 1991:34-6). More broadly, D.H. Burger (1961:329), in discussing the 'government's native

economic policy' in a thesis defended in 1939, quoted several officials including J. van Gelderen, J.W. Meijer Ranneft, and J.H. Boeke to support his argument that the indigenous economy was becoming ever more monetized and
commercialized, and as a result a native business class was slowly emerging.

It was the slow speed of development of this business class that was the
source of frustration to many Dutch observers, as well as to Indonesians
themselves. Burger (1961:329) was no doubt correct when he argued that 'if
a vigorous group of native entrepreneurs had arisen, the authorities would
almost certainly not have gone so far with their welfare policies as they have
done'. Boeke (1961), in a lecture delivered in the late 1920s, in fact called for
a different type of government policy that put less emphasis on improving the general level of welfare and more on encouraging the emergence of
outstanding individuals with genuine entrepreneurial ability, a policy later
characterized by Wim Wertheim (1964:264-5) as 'betting on the strong'. Only
the emergence of such individuals could, according to Boeke, pose an effective challenge to European and Chinese domination of the economy. But the
1930s were hardly a propitious time for such a new breed of entrepreneurs to
emerge and consolidate their position within the colonial economy.

While the debate was continuing about the entrepreneurial capacities
of indigenous populations, their involvement with market institutions was
steadily increasing. By the dawn of the twentieth century, thousands of
Javanese were moving to Sumatra and Borneo (Kalimantan) to work as wage
labourers, and many thousands more were seeking opportunities as wage
labourers at home. These numbers increased steadily until the onset of the
depression of the 1930s. The increased willingness of the Javanese to move
in search of better economic prospects obviously contradicted the stereotype
of the indolent native who was unwilling to seek opportunities for economic
self-improvement. And the involvement with market institutions was not
limited to the labour market. Land also was becoming a marketed commodity, both in Java and in other parts of the archipelago. In addition, the colonial
authorities were experimenting with several credit programmes, including a network of regional banks, village rice barns, and pawnshops, which
attracted attention and admiration from both English and French colonial
officials (Henry 1926; Angoulvant 1926:282-3; Furnivall 1934a, 1934b).

Furnivall (1934a:26) was at pains to emphasize that even in the depths of
the depression the entire credit system was solvent and required no state subsidies. He argued strongly against the assertion that government-operated
institutions simply displaced private suppliers of credit, especially credit
provided by Chinese merchants and moneylenders. Certainly there appears
to be little doubt that the government pawnshop service was operated
more efficiently than the nineteenth-century Chinese pawnshops, and while
the relaxation of the laws on Chinese residence might have led to greater

Chinese activity in rural areas in the twentieth century, it cannot be argued that taxpayers' money was used to subsidize financial institutions that the private sector would have provided more efficiently. The private system did continue to expand alongside the state one, although, in the absence of data, it is impossible to tell how important privately supplied credit was compared with state provision.

Given that the people's credit system did develop so rapidly in the inter-war years, what was its impact on the indigenous economy in Java? Scholars seem very divided in their opinions. Alexander and Alexander (1991:386-7) argued that there was little evidence that the various rural credit institutions served to stimulate economic diversification, and the main effect of the government-sponsored initiatives was to institutionalize the two-tier credit market in the rural economy. The relatively wealthy could get access to credit at lower rates of interest that they could then lend at higher rates to the relatively poor, making large profits in the process. While no doubt correct, this argument ignores the basic economic point that credit markets always reflect a degree of dualism in the sense that some people will always be seen as more 'creditworthy' than others.

If the government initiatives did greatly increase the supply of loanable funds to rural areas in Java, were these funds used for productive investment or for consumption purposes? Jennifer and Paul Alexander argued that most went on consumption, ceremonial expenditures, and for tiding people over emergencies such as ill health, unusually long dry seasons, and so on. Other authors argued that the credit available from both the pawnshops and the other credit institutions was at least partly used for productive purposes; Furnivall (1934b:11) pointed out that 'a man may pawn his wife's bangles and use the proceeds as the first instalment towards buying a motor bus on the hire purchase system'. Both Furnivall and Van Laanen (1990) suggested that the pawnshops were not the last resort of the desperate (as they tended to be in Europe), but rather a convenient source of credit to many people who were far from destitute, but who kept their savings in commodities rather than in cash or bank deposits. The fact that the real value of credit advanced through government institutions dropped so sharply after 1930 indicates that borrowings were related to investment opportunities rather than to financial pressures, and when the investment climate deteriorated as a result of the depression the demand for loans fell.

In comparison with developments in the Netherlands Indies, the indigenous population of the Malayan peninsula was drawn more slowly into the cash economy in the nineteenth and early twentieth centuries. Indeed Indonesian migrants began arriving in British Malaya in large numbers from the 1870s to take advantage of trading opportunities and of the growing demand for wage labour, which the indigenous Malays were reluctant to avail themselves of (Roff 1967:37). According to W.R. Roff, the greater part of the Malaysian merchant community in Kuala Lumpur in the 1890s was said to originate from the Minangkabau region of West Sumatra, while Javanese began to arrive in considerable numbers in the Straits Settlements to work as labourers. Most Malays preferred to stay in their traditional occupations as farmers and fishermen, and the British certainly did not encourage them to move out of these roles. By the end of the nineteenth century the seeds were sown that were to develop into ever more bitter ethnic hostilities between the migrant Asian populations and the indigenous Malays. Roff (1967:54) quotes articles that appeared in a Straits Chinese newspaper in 1894 and drew attention to Malay educational and economic backwardness and attributed it to 'their slavish adherence to outmoded custom, the dissoluteness of their traditional leaders [...], their lack of industry and ambition, their hostility toward anyone who showed exceptional talents, and their inability to practice mutual self-help'. Roff points out that however unfair these accusations were, 'they came for many Malays uncomfortably near the truth'.

In the second decade of the twentieth century the British colonial authorities became more obsessed with rice self-sufficiency, and more frustrated that production was not growing fast enough to keep up with rising domestic demand. The 1913 Malay Reservations Enactment gave Residents in the Federated Malay States the power to set aside land (mainly but not only rice land) for exclusive Malay ownership. The purpose of this legislation was to prevent alienation of Malay land to foreign (both Asian and European) planters, and to encourage the Malays to grow rice rather than crops that the British considered speculative, such as rubber. The land could not be mortgaged, leased, or sold to non-Malays. Although in passing this legislation the British claimed to have been influenced by the earlier land legislation in the Netherlands Indies, in fact the Malay enactment was more stringent in that it prevented even the leasing of land to non-Malay parties. In 1917, following mounting anxiety about food shortages, more legislation was passed that empowered residents to regulate cropping patterns on Malay land, in effect preventing the cultivation of non-rice crops (Roff 1967:123; Lim 1977:121).

These draconian interventions in markets for both land and crops went well beyond Dutch measures in the Netherlands Indies, and indeed well beyond what the British did in other parts of Asia under their direct control. While one motivation was a genuine concern on the part of the colonial establishment that the growth of foreign estates could lead the Malay cultivator to become landless in his own country, it was clear that it was the official intention to keep the Malay away from the cultivation of crops other than rice. In particular, colonial officials showed themselves to be increasingly hostile to the idea that Malays should be involved in the cultivation of rubber (Lim 1977:116). After 1917, Malay smallholders were not permitted to obtain non-Malay land for rubber cultivation and, indeed, land already alienated to Malays that was found to be used for growing rubber was withdrawn.

Colonial officials appeared impervious to the fact that growing rubber afforded a better return to land and labour than growing rice, even at the increased rice prices prevailing in 1918-1920. The Stevenson Scheme, implemented in both Malaya and Ceylon in the 1920s to restrict the growth of rubber output and maintain its price, affected smallholder cultivation more severely than that of the estates (Jomo 1988:69). The main beneficiaries of this scheme were in fact smallholders in the Netherlands Indies, whose production really took off at this time. Although the Dutch colonial establishment gave the Indonesian smallholder little positive encouragement, they were not discriminated against, and their ready access to land meant they could increase output with little official harassment.

Paddy cultivation was to remain, in the words of one economic historian, 'the least profitable of all major occupations in Malaya' right up till the 1950s (Lim 1977:176; Jomo 1988:Table 3.1). This did not prevent the British from continuing to deter the rural Malays from doing anything else. Their zeal to keep the Malays in traditional occupations affected educational policy. Winstedt, an influential British official, argued that the provision of English medium schools should be restricted lest it make rural Malays restless and eager to leave the kampong for the wider world (Lim 1977:176). Roff (1967:125) quotes a Director of Agriculture in 1934 who warned against the dangers of inducing the rural Malay to 'forsake the life of their fathers for the glamour of new ways which put money in their pockets but today leave them empty tomorrow, and to abandon their rice-fields for new crops which they cannot themselves utilize and the market for which depends on outside world conditions beyond their orbit'. Although enrolments in Malay vernacular schools increased rapidly, by the late 1930s only about 20 percent of eligible children were attending school. Many parents could not see the point of education that did not lead to social mobility (Snodgrass 1980:237-43; Rudner 1994:289-90).

It is probable that many Dutch administrators in the Netherlands Indies in the interwar years had similar feelings to those of British officials about the dangers of exposing indigenous cultivators to the full blast of national and world market forces. But Dutch colonial thinking had, by the 1920s, been forced to recognize reality. As we have seen the great majority of the population in Java and in other parts of the archipelago were involved in the cash economy not just as producers of cash crops but also as suppliers of wage labour. Given the increasing density of population on restricted supplies of land they had little option but to avail themselves of whatever nonagricultural opportunities for earning money were available. The purpose of the Ethical Policy and of the interventions adopted in the 1930s was not so much to protect the peasants from capitalism as to facilitate their gradual absorp-

Table 5. Indigenous workers as a percentage of the labour force in manufacturing, commerce, professions and government service

| | Indigenous workers as percentage of the labour force | | |
|---|---|---|---|
| | Manufacturing | Commerce/Trade | Government and professions |
| Indonesia (1930) | 95.3 | 84.3 | 93.6 |
| Straits Settlements (1931) | 7.2 | 3.9 | 20.5 |
| FMS (1931) | 3.0 | 2.4 | 32.9 |
| Burma (1931) | 80.8 | 73.3 | 86.7 |
| Philippines (1939) | 97.6 | 82.7 | 96.5 |
| Thailand (1937) | 55.2 | 60.6 | 95.2 |
| Korea (1930) | 89.7 | 85.1 | 59.8 |
| Taiwan (1930)[a] | 78.5 | 86.9 | 49.2 |

[a] Male workers only

Sources: Sources: Indonesia: Department of Economic Affairs 1936, VIII:Table 18; Thailand: Central Service of Statistics c.1946:75; Straits Settlements and FMS: Vlieland 1932:Tables 121-141; Burma: Baxter 1941:25; Philippines: Commonwealth of the Philippines 1941:505-14; Korea: Chang 1966:Table 2; Taiwan: Barclay 1954:71.

tion into the market economy. In Malaysia, by contrast, the aim of colonial policy appeared to be to build ever higher fences between the kampong Malay and the market economy.

According to the 1931 census, indigenous Malays comprised less than 10 percent of the nonagricultural labour force in both the Straits Settlements and the Federated Malay States (FMS) (Table 2). This was a much lower percentage than in Java or the Outer Islands, or in Burma and Siam, although the Thai census data used a 'nationality' criterion that probably underestimated the actual number of ethnic Chinese in the labour force. It was also much lower than in Taiwan and Korea. Indigenous Malays were also a very low proportion of those engaged in trade and commerce compared with Burma and the Netherlands Indies, as well as Taiwan and Korea (Table 5). To some extent the very low ratio of indigenous Malays in the nonagricultural labour force reflected the fact that Malays were a much lower proportion of the total labour force in British Malaya than in other parts of East and Southeast Asia.

But there can be little doubt that the large influx of migrant workers into British Malaya, together with British policy aimed at keeping the indigenous population in rural areas, created a more extreme example of the plural economy than in other colonies in East and Southeast Asia. It was a legacy that postcolonial governments struggled with for the last four decades of the twentieth century.

### Indigenous entrepreneurship and economic opportunity in colonial Korea and Taiwan

The plural society and economy that attracted such attention throughout Southeast Asia in the last phase of European colonial rule took a very different form in the Japanese colonies. There was very little in-migration from China, or any other Asian country, except Japan, into either Taiwan or Korea, although the percentage of the population from the mainland in Taiwan was around one percent, which was higher than the percentage of Chinese nationals in the Philippines, and only slightly lower than the percentage in Burma and Java (Table 4). What did stand out in both Korea and Taiwan by the 1930s was the Japanese presence; Japanese citizens comprised over 5 percent of the total population in Taiwan and just under 3 percent in Korea (Table 4).

The vast majority of Japanese workers in both colonies was in nonagricultural occupations; in Taiwan the largest number of employed males in 1930 were in the professions and government, followed by commerce and manufacturing (Barclay 1954:Table 16). Many indigenous Taiwanese were in these occupations as well; in 1930 they comprised slightly less than half of all male workers employed in government and the professions. In Korea the proportion was around 60 percent. These were higher proportions than in British Malaya, although much lower than in Burma and the Netherlands Indies, where indigenous races accounted for the great majority of employed workers in the professions and government service by 1930. In the Netherlands Indies, indigenous workers accounted for a higher proportion of the manufacturing labour force than in either Taiwan or Korea, and a roughly similar proportion of the labour force in trade and commerce (Table 5).

There is little evidence that the Japanese colonial regimes in either Taiwan or Korea were much concerned with the development of entrepreneurial capacity among the indigenous populations. In the context of Taiwan, Samuel Ho (1971:323) argued the following:

> During the colonial period, the government relied primarily on its own savings and the savings of the Japanese corporate business structures it helped create to provide the capital for industry. It never encouraged the emergence of an indigenous industrialist class; in fact, its whole policy

was directed toward preventing the emergence of such a class. Until 1924 Taiwanese were not allowed to organize or operate corporations unless there was Japanese participation. Thus the modern sector became a monopoly of the Japanese capitalists. Even after this restrictive rule against Taiwanese participation was rescinded, Taiwanese were reluctant to seek entry to the modern sector because of its domination by Japanese capitalists. Through its power to regulate, and license, and by granting exclusive privileges to Japanese capitalists, the government successfully kept the Taiwanese from acquiring any economic power.

Ho's argument was that Japanese policy in Taiwan was trapped in an image of its own creation. Taiwan was to be developed as an agricultural appendage of Japan, and it was only in the 1930s when the Japanese government became more preoccupied with war preparations that these views changed. In Korea, Daniel Juhn (1977:48) pointed out that in the 1930s, when the Japanese authorities were trying to attract the *zaibatsu* (large Japanese industrial conglomerates) to invest in Korean industry, some officials did argue for a strategy that also encouraged Koreans to establish small and medium enterprises. But few policies were implemented, and Korean businesses received little assistance, compared with that granted to Japanese firms, which remained in a dominant position in virtually all sectors of industry and trade. Juhn (1973:128) argued that the activities of the industrial cooperatives that were established in Korea after 1910 were 'insignificant and ineffective' compared with small producers' cooperatives in Japan.

A figure frequently quoted for Korea is that Japanese investors accounted for around 90 percent of all paid-up capital in industry by the late 1930s (Kim 1973:110-1; Haggard, Kang and Moon 1997:871; Chung 2006:123). These authors emphasize that Japanese investors dominated light as well as heavy manufacturing, and that most skilled workers, and almost all managers, were Japanese. The figure of 90 percent has been challenged by Carter Eckert (1991:54), who claimed that it ignored joint Japanese-Korean companies that 'may well have garnered the lion's share of Korean capital'. He also argued that in any case such statistics did not capture the full extent of the transition, although often incomplete, by Korean merchants and landlords into the ranks of the industrial bourgeoisie (Eckert 1991:55). He cites the examples of the men who would go on to found the *chaebol* (the large industrial conglomerates established along the lines of the Japanese *zaibatsu*), which became famous in the post-1960 era, including Samsung, LG, and Hyundai. Most were sons of landlords who became small-scale businessmen in the 1930s and 1940s in sectors such as brewing, rice milling, textiles, and vehicle repair.

It was certainly true that a few Koreans did rise to control substantial business empires during the Japanese era. The outstanding example of an indigenous Korean industrial family that rose to wealth and power in the Japanese era were the Kim brothers who founded the Kyongsong Spinning Company. They came from a family that had accumulated substantial hold- ings of rice land in the southern part of the country, and after education in Japan, the two sons moved into industry in the 1920s. The move was fraught with difficulties, not the least being the stiff competition from better-funded Japanese firms (McNamara 1990:174-5). But by the 1930s they had managed to consolidate their position in Korea and move into southern Manchuria, where they established a spinning plant in 1937. The textile venture survived the war and liberation, and prospered under the First Republic (McNamara 1990:117; Juhn 1977:49-50).

The Kim success story was exceptional, although other large-scale Korean businesses were able to emerge and compete with Japanese firms in banking and in trade. Examples of successful entrepreneurs who are often cited include Pak Hung-sik who established a substantial wholesale and retail business, and the aristocratic Min clan who moved into banking during the Japanese era (Juhn 1973:126; McNamara 1990:Chapters 5 and 6). After the establishment of formal Japanese rule, there were few positions available to Koreans in the upper ranks of the civil service, or the military, so banking and finance became a socially acceptable occupation for those from families that had previously occupied senior bureaucratic posts. But as Dennis McNamara (1990:49) argued, all Korean business people 'had to carefully align their investments to find a niche in the development plans of the colonial adminis- tration'. Few were able to exploit such niches and build up substantial enter- prises, and most businesses remained small-scale, as indeed was the case in other parts of colonial Asia.

But however limited the development of an indigenous entrepreneur- ial and managerial class in Korea before 1945, it is arguable that more was achieved than in most other colonies in Asia, outside India, and possibly the Philippines. One would search in vain for successful industrial ventures similar in size to the Kyongsong Textile Company, owned and managed by indigenous families in Siam, British Malaya, or the Netherlands Indies before 1942. And as Eckert (1991:55) pointed out, some indigenous Koreans did own stock in both Korean and Japanese companies. This hardly ever happened in the Netherlands Indies, Siam, or British Malaya. Here the combination of foreign capital and local Chinese and Indian domination made it almost impossible for indigenous entrepreneurs to move beyond small-scale trading and manufacturing. Lack of access to credit was certainly one factor; in addi- tion, very few indigenous Thais, Indonesians, or Malays received the sort of education, either at home or in the colonial motherland, that gave the Kim brothers the knowledge and confidence to establish new industrial ventures. The small number that did receive such education went into the civil service or the military. This tradition was to continue after the advent of political independence.

## Eradicating the legacy of the plural economy: 1945-1965

The Japanese occupation from 1942 to 1945 facilitated the rise of an aggressive form of indigenism in several parts of Southeast Asia. This was due in part to the expropriation of almost all enterprises owned by European and American interests, and in part to the harsh treatment of many ethnic Chinese business people. In addition, the Japanese approach to economic policymaking was *dirigiste* in the extreme and relied on a range of economic controls embracing most aspects of production and distribution. Even if this controlled economy proved incapable of supplying basic needs to the great majority of the population across Southeast Asia, it still presented nationalists across the region with an alternative model to the apparently more *laissez-faire* approach of the colonial powers (Golay et al. 1969:455-6). In spite of the increasing economic dislocation in the last phase of the Japanese period, some shrewd and determined indigenous business people were able to turn a chaotic situation to their own advantage and establish viable enterprises (Twang 1998:Chapter 3).

On the political front, the fierce devotion to emperor, armed forces, and nation, which obviously inspired the Japanese military, made a deep impression on many young people in Southeast Asia, and this intense nationalism inevitably affected the way they viewed economic problems. After 1945, the relationship between indigenous business groups, the Chinese, and foreign businesses, especially those originating from the colonial power, could never be the same as it was before 1942. The forces of indigenism were stronger in some former colonies than in others. They were probably strongest in the Netherlands Indies, but even in the Philippines, where Chinese nationals were a very small proportion of the population in the late 1930s, some nationalist legislation was enacted in the decade after independence such as the Retail Trade Nationalization Law that prohibited those not holding Philippine nationality from owning retail trade outlets (Yoshihara 1994:28-32). Nor were nationalist policies entirely absent in Siam, which was the only Southeast Asian country to have escaped direct colonial control. As Ayal (1969:338) argued, for much of the twentieth century successive Thai governments were concerned with foreign control over the economy, although it was only after the 1932 coup that 'concrete measures for Thaification were introduced'. From 1935 onwards, laws were passed to reserve certain urban occupations for Thai and to give preference to indigenous Thai firms in allocating government contracts (Phongpaichit and Baker 1995:179). The purpose of the legislation was to curtail the economic role of aliens, especially Chinese.

An important implication of these measures was that the military leaders who dominated most governments in Siam (Thailand) from 1932 until the late 1950s were hostile to private enterprise and supportive of state capitalism. These attitudes were encouraged by the sojourns of several leading military figures in Italy, Germany, and Japan in the interwar years. But the Thai found, as most of the former colonies were also to find in the decades after 1945, that there were no shortcuts to greater indigenous control of the economy. The main problem was the acute shortage of managerial expertise among indigenous Thai; few had any idea at all of how to run large-scale productive enterprises, and many of the state corporations were financial failures. Many managers were former army officers and treated the enterprises they were supposed to be running as sources of personal enrichment and patronage. Ayal (1969:338-9) pointed out that even before 1940, the Thai experience confirmed the basic correlation between premature indigenism and corruption, a correlation that was to become more obvious in many other parts of the region after 1950.

In both Burma and Indonesia, indigenism in the postindependence years was the driving political force behind the adoption of inward-looking policies described by Myint (1967). In both former colonies, the independent governments wanted to eradicate what they saw as the pernicious legacy of the plural economy, with its apparent tight relationship between ethnicity and economic role. It has been suggested that the drive towards rapid indigenism was essentially an elite phenomenon, 'originating with and promoted by politicians seeking power for other ends and by members of a narrow indigenous entrepreneurial element who are motivated by avarice to expropriate alien wealth' (Golay et al. 1969:447). While this was probably true in both Indonesia and Burma, it could hardly be denied that in both countries there was considerable grassroots antagonism against the role of the Chinese and the Indians respectively. In Burma this antagonism was in large part due to the Indian expropriation of indigenous cultivators. In Indonesia it resulted from the role of the Chinese in rural areas as traders and moneylenders, together with the widespread perception among nationalists that Chinese businesses had received preferential treatment under the Dutch.

In both Burma and Indonesia, the decade after independence witnessed much political rhetoric about socialism and popular control over the means of production. In Burma, there was a strong government push during the 1950s, even before the military regime assumed power, to take over both British and Indian firms and to establish new state enterprises in manufacturing. By 1960 it was estimated that over 90 percent of industry was Burmese-owned. It was clear that many were poorly managed and that government industrial policy suffered from a lack of coordination. The Revolutionary Government which assumed control in the early 1960s, after a brief period of apparent openness to both domestic and foreign private enterprise, abruptly reversed its policy and after 1963 prevented the establishment of any new private enterprise in manufacturing industry (Pfanner 1969:231-2).

In Indonesia, the struggle to break free of the legacy of the plural economy took a rather different form. The 1945 constitution enshrined the 'family principle' of economic organization and some nationalist leaders regarded cooperatives as an 'excellent expression of Indonesian social ideals' in spite of the fact that the peasant economy in Indonesia had, during the latter part of the colonial era, been increasingly based on private ownership of land and production for the market, whether domestic or foreign (Mackie 1971:44-5). Perhaps because the spirit of private enterprise was so strong in rural areas, little was achieved with agricultural cooperatives during the 1950s in spite of several government initiatives. There was little pressure for the establishment of collective farms, even on the part of the Indonesian Communist Party (Mortimer 1974:288). Instead, in the early 1950s government policy was more directed to the fostering of indigenous entrepreneurs in the nonagricultural economy. The so-called 'Benteng' programme, established immediately after independence, was at first directed mainly to getting more indigenous Indonesians involved in the lucrative import and export trade, which had been dominated in colonial times by the big Dutch trading houses and to a lesser extent by the Chinese.

Ralph Anspach (1969:168-79) discussed the failings of the programme in detail. As he pointed out, there was concern, even among some nationalist politicians, at the blatant racial bias of the 'Benteng' measures, and the unwillingness to encourage Chinese businesses even when their owners had adopted Indonesian nationality. In addition, the lingering support for cooperatives, especially strong with Vice-President Mohammad Hatta, meant that some key politicians tended to oppose any plan to encourage private enterprise, whatever the ownership. The distaste of the Hatta camp for hothouse development of indigenous entrepreneurs was no doubt strengthened by the growing evidence that many of the so-called indigenous businesses that got access to import licences were simply fronts for more experienced Chinese companies. Chinese companies also in some cases filled the gap left by the Dutch companies that were either closed or nationalized in 1957-1958.

It was the frustration of the failed indigenist policies of the 1950s which President Soekarno exploited after he brought the period of constitutional democracy to an end in 1958 and ushered in the Guided Economy. From then on, indigenist policies became intertwined with the aim of implementing Indonesian socialism, although as Anspach (1969:126) pointed out, for most of the Indonesian political elite, socialism meant little more than 'an emotional predilection, a vestigial sentiment from the revolutionary struggle against the capitalistic Dutch'. In fact, the decades of the 1950s and the 1960s almost certainly witnessed an attenuation of the role of government in the Indonesian economy. Government expenditures relative to GDP were already low in Indonesia in comparison with several other former colonies in the late 1950s (Table 6). After 1960, in spite of the increased rhetoric about Indonesian socialism, they fell further relative to GDP. In 1960, output from government enterprises including those expropriated from the Dutch amounted to only about 20 percent of total output (Booth 1998:Figure 4.1, Table 4.9).

In several respects, British Malaya in the late 1950s offered a stark contrast to the situation in both Burma and Indonesia, as well as that in Thailand. Given that the Chinese and, to a lesser extent, the Indian presence was so large, and that non-Malays were so dominant in the nonagricultural labour force, it might have been expected that indigenist policies would have been stronger there than in other parts of Southeast Asia. But according to Golay et al. (1969:454), the forces of indigenism were comparatively weak, and there was little or no socialist content to such indigenist policies as were implemented. Pressures on foreign, and especially British, enterprise were at best minor. Indeed, White (1996:269) has argued that by 1957 the British had achieved something approximating 'neocolonialism' or 'informal empire'. The Alliance government maintained open economic policies, a competitive exchange rate, and a friendly attitude to foreign investment. In 1962, Malaya was the sixth largest recipient of direct foreign investment from Britain. Estate companies that had been established in the colonial era, far from being threatened by the government, were encouraged to undertake replanting and expansion of their activities. Although Malaya's share of world rubber production, both natural and synthetic, was only 18.2 percent in 1960 compared with 44.5 percent during the 1930s, the Alliance government recognized that both rubber and tin would continue to be important earners of foreign exchange over the 1960s, and that investment in both industries should be encouraged, whatever its provenance.

At the same time the government of what was still British Malaya was urged by international development agencies to assume more responsibility for encouraging manufacturing industry. The report by the International Bank for Reconstruction and Development (as the World Bank was then known) published in 1955 recommended a two-pronged approach. On the one hand, the government should provide infrastructure including water, electric power, and roads while, on the other hand, it should 'foster individual enterprise' through measures such as provision of technical and market research for secondary industry, investment in appropriate education and training programmes, support for foreign investors in those sectors where their technical know-how could be crucial and also the judicious use of tariff protection. On this last point the report stressed that the tariff should be used as a means of encouraging development and not as a way of supporting

Table 6. Government expenditures and revenues as a percentage of GDP and investment and defence expenditures as a percentage of total expenditures, 1957

|  | As percentage of GDP government: | | | As percentage of gov. expenditures | |
|---|---|---|---|---|---|
|  | Expenditures | Revenues | Investment | Investment | Defence |
| Taiwan | 30 | 20 | 10 | 32 | 34 |
| Burma | 25 | 20 | 10 | 39 | 28 |
| Korea (South) | 22 | 11 | 9 | 40 | 30 |
| Malaya | 19 | 17 | 3 | 25 | 16 |
| Thailand | 16 | 12 | 5 | 29 | 22 |
| Indonesia | 15 | 12 | 2 | 11 | 15 |
| Cambodia | 14 | 12 | n.a | n.a | 28 |
| Philippines | 12 | 11 | 3 | 22 | 14 |

Source: United Nations ECAFE 1961:Tables 22, 24, 25, 32, 33.

'hopelessly high-cost industries' (International Bank for Reconstruction and Development 1955:123).

Tariff protection was an especially difficult issue because those parts of British Malaya that had developed as free ports, especially Singapore and Penang, were fearful that with independence their free-port status would be removed, and their consumers forced to pay high tariffs on imported goods, or buy high cost manufactures from other parts of Malaya. These fears were in part the reason for Singapore's departure from the Federation of Malaysia in 1965. But the Malay political elites who dominated policymaking in the run-up to independence were themselves ambivalent about encouraging rapid industrialization because they knew that it would be the Chinese who would seize the opportunities provided by tariff protection. Some were also concerned about the impact of industrial protection on the urban-rural terms of trade, and about the welfare effects on small rural producers, the great majority of whom were Malay. As Frank Golay (1969:346) argued, the insecurity felt by the Malay leadership also caused them to accept, and even encourage, the continuing large Western stake in the economy.

The situation in the Philippines was different again. By the late 1930s, almost 45 percent of the assets of nonagricultural enterprises in the Philippines were owned by Filipino citizens (Golay 1969:Table 1). This was a far higher proportion than in any other colonial territory in East or Southeast Asia. Certainly many of the large owners of both agricultural estates and nonagricultural enterprises were of mixed Filipino and Chinese or Spanish descent, but the ethnicity issue was less politically fraught in the Philippines after 1945 than in many other parts of the region. Many among the governing elite had some Chinese or Spanish ancestry. They harboured little overt hostility to American or other foreign enterprises, and had virtually no sympathy for socialist policies, or even for government taking an activist role in the economy. Land-reform policies made little progress in the period from the late 1940s to the late 1960s (Putzel 1992:Chapter 3). In the late 1950s, government expenditure relative to GDP was the lowest in the region (Table 6). By and large the political forces that had come to power in the last phase of the American period remained in control after 1946, and became over time a barrier to further structural transformation of the economy. In this sense, American colonialism was as David Kang (2002:27) has argued, 'pervasive and yet, ultimately, nontransformative'.

This is not to say that the Philippines did not experience substantial growth in the two decades or so after 1945. As Golay (1969:33) pointed out, after the implementation of high levels of protection through extensive import and foreign exchange controls after 1949, the manufacturing sector grew rapidly, and by 1960 manufacturing accounted for a higher proportion of GDP than in any other former colonial territory in Asia. Export growth slowed as a result of the overvaluation of the peso, and gradually the export sector was taken over by Philippine interests. It was these interests that ultimately pushed through the removal of exchange and import controls in 1962 and the substantial devaluation of the peso. It was much easier for the government of the day to undertake such measures once the export sector was seen to be in Philippine hands. At this point it might have appeared that pressures of indigenism were driving the Philippines in the direction of a more open and competitive economy. But in spite of these policy changes, it proved impossible for the Philippines to move into the same kind of high-speed industrial growth as was achieved by Taiwan and South Korea after 1960. The benefits of the devaluation of 1962 were rapidly eroded by high inflation (Power and Sicat 1971:52), thus providing only a transitory boost to both existing and new export industries.

In both Taiwan and South Korea, forces of indigenism were weaker than in much of Southeast Asia mainly because the dominant Japanese presence had left virtually no room for any other foreign participation in either economy. There was no equivalent of the large migrant Indian or Chinese presence, and neither was there any foreign investment apart from that of the Japanese. Thus, the abrupt departure of all citizens of the colonial power in 1945-1946 left large holes in both economies, and policy debates revolved around what was going to fill them. In Taiwan, the administration that took over from the departing Japanese was imbued by the 'statist economic ideas' used in Guomindang circles to interpret Sun Yat-sen's doctrine of fostering the people's livelihood (Lai, Myers and Wei 1991:84). The administration led by Ch'en-I was in part concerned with building up a patronage network for migrants from the mainland, but was also imbued with an ideological bias in favour of a planned economy. Publicly owned firms soon controlled over 70 percent of all industrial and agricultural enterprises; in addition, a new Monopoly Bureau controlled the supply and marketing of salt, camphor, opium, matches, liquor, and tobacco. The government also imposed strict regulations on private trade.

By the end of 1946, the Ch'en I administration probably controlled 'even more economic activity than had the Japanese' (Lai, Myers and Wei 1991:87). Even before the wave of refugees from the mainland in 1949, many mainlanders were employed in the bureaucracy, including the state enterprises. Steinhoff (1980:61) estimates that the numbers of mainlanders employed by state enterprises more than doubled between 1946 and 1949; in 1949 they accounted for more than one third of the total. Many lacked experience in the jobs they were allocated, and a process of rationalization of employment began in the early 1950s. Numbers of both mainlanders and Taiwanese working in the state enterprises fell. It is probable that some moved into private sector activities. In addition, the Taiwanese landlords received compensation for the land they had surrendered in the form of government bonds and stock in former Japanese companies; some of them at least used these assets to build up new enterprises (Steinhoff 1980:59).

In North Korea, the adoption of a strict socialist model led to the elimination of most forms of private enterprise by the end of the 1950s. In South Korea, most scholars have viewed the postarmistice years as characterized by rampant cronyism where Japanese properties, and aid dollars, largely from the USA, were distributed to business groups friendly to the Rhee regime at very low prices. It was thus possible for firms with the right connections to make 'massive profits with no further effort than a bit of paper work in ordering imports' (Jones and Sakong 1980:277). In addition, businesses with good political and bureaucratic connections received low interest loans, tax benefits, and other privileges. This was a situation not unlike that which the Benteng programme created in Indonesia, although in the Korean case large inflows of foreign aid greatly added to the opportunities for rent-seeking. Jones and Sakong (1980:41) have drawn a parallel between the charismatic political talents of Rhee and those of Soekarno, and argued that both were better suited to the creation and integration of a new nation than the development of an existing one.

Jones and Sakong (1980:276) pointed out that the situation changed with the advent of the Park government. Under Park, firms were expected to make a convincing argument that the privileges conferred on them would be used productively. Good connections with the bureaucracy were still important, but as the supply of potential entrepreneurs increased, an element of competition was introduced into the process of securing the necessary government-controlled inputs. In addition, the introduction of a more open and competitive market for foreign exchange, and a decline in aid flows, eliminated an important cause of rent-seeking behaviour. The policy reforms implemented by Park would serve as a model for other governments in the region in later years.

Many of the policy debates in the former colonial territories in the decade after 1945 revolved around issues of ownership of productive assets (foreign or local, state or private, indigenous or migrant Asian). But it was clear at least to the more thoughtful nationalists that, whatever their ultimate ownership, if assets were to be properly managed, it would be necessary to develop a class of professional managers and technically trained workers. Throughout the region, whether in the former Japanese colonies or in Southeast Asia, colonial educational legacies, especially at the tertiary level, were at best modest and at worst nonexistent. The main exception to the shortage of skilled workers was the Philippines where, in the mid 1950s, numbers of graduates in science and technology per 100,000 people were roughly the same as in Japan, and substantially higher than elsewhere in Asia (Table 7). This, of course, was the result of the high secondary and tertiary enrolments there in the late-colonial era. But in Taiwan and South Korea, gross enrolment ratios at the primary level (numbers of children enrolled as a percentage of total numbers in the seven to twelve age groups) had already caught up with the Philippines by the mid 1950s, and in South Korea gross enrolment ratios at the secondary level were higher (Table 7). The growth in educational enrolments in South Korea from the 1950s onwards meant that by the 1970s, almost half the male labour force had at least secondary education (Booth 2003:153).

Even in those economies, such as South Korea and Taiwan, where, by the late 1960s and early 1970s the nonagricultural sectors of the economy were growing rapidly, it was not always easy to match the output of the educational system with the requirements of the labour market. A labour-force survey carried out in South Korea in 1974 found that although open unemployment was only around 6.5 percent, a further 13 percent of workers were 'under-utilized' in the sense that there was a mismatch between their qualifications and the work they were doing. In the Philippines, where growth was slower over the 1960s, a 1968 survey found that around 10 percent of employed workers were underutilized using the mismatch criterion. Many

Table 7. Educational enrollments and science and technology graduates in Asia, circa 1955

| | Gross enrolments ratios | | Science and technology graduates per 100,000 people |
|---|---|---|---|
| | Primary | Secondary | |
| Japan | 64 | 94 | 34.9 |
| Philippines | 54 | 25 | 34.2 |
| India | 27 | 18 | 18.1 |
| Korea (South) | 54 | 36 | 17.2 |
| Taiwan | 54 | 24 | 14.3 |
| China | 36 | 8 | 4.8 |
| Thailand | 51 | 14 | 3.3 |
| Vietnam (South) | 21 | 4 | 0.6 |
| British Malaya | 49 | 18 | n.a |
| Indonesia | 39 | 8 | n.a |
| Burma | 24 | 9 | n.a |

Sources: United Nations Unesco 1963:103-5; United Nations ECAFE 1962:34.

were also working quite short hours (Hauser 1977:Table 5). While rapid expansion of access to education for the indigenous population was viewed by many postindependence politicians as one means of eradicating the legacy of the plural economy, finding productive jobs for the output of the education system proved more difficult than many had realized. These problems were to continue in many of the former Asian colonies to the present day.

*Conclusions*

Furnivall argued that by the early twentieth century, European colonialism had created societies in much of Southeast Asia where ethnicity and economic function were tightly linked and where the different races only came together in the marketplace and were never able to integrate in any other human activity. This chapter has argued that this rather stark view of Southeast Asian colonies should be modified in some respects. Although

Furnivall put forward his views in the context of Burma and the Netherlands Indies, by the 1930s the racial division of labour was most pronounced in British Malaya, where migrant Chinese and Indians accounted for over half of the total population. It is not surprising that when British Malaya attained full independence in 1963 as the Federation of Malaysia, the island of Singapore, where the Chinese were in a large majority, did not remain long in a state where the federal government was dominated by ethnic Malays. After Singapore left the federation in 1965, Malays were in a majority, but after serious race riots in 1969 the Malaysian government felt compelled to embark on a 'new economic policy', which was in essence a government-led affirmative action programme designed to get more Malays into the secondary and tertiary education system, and into nonagricultural employment. It is beyond the scope of this essay to evaluate the success of this policy; suffice to say that almost four decades after its inception, policies favouring ethnic Malays, and thus discriminating against Chinese and Indians, are still in place. Inevitably some Chinese and Indian professionals with skills in demand in other parts of the world have left the country.

In Burma, the increasingly xenophobic military government led by General Ne Win drove many residents of Chinese and Indian descent back to their homelands or to third countries from the early 1960s onwards. After the reunification of Vietnam in 1975, many Vietnamese of Chinese descent also left the country, a considerable number as refugee 'boat people'. In Indonesia, the nationalist and anti-Chinese policies of the Soekarno era were largely abandoned after 1966, but resentment against the role of the Chinese in the economy continued to simmer throughout the Suharto era. Many indigenous business people believed that large Chinese conglomerates, some of whose owners were known to be close to the Suharto family, received unfair advantages from the government in the form of preferential access to government contracts and other privileges. Anti-Chinese feeling was one motivation in the popular protests that led to Suharto's resignation in 1998.

Probably the most peaceful and least discriminatory resolution of the problem of the plural society can be found in the Philippines and Thailand in the decades after 1960. In the Philippines, almost all Chinese migrants had taken Philippine citizenship by 1960. Their assimilation into broader Philippine society was helped by their adoption of Christianity; children of Chinese families were educated alongside Filipinos in government or church schools and shared both a language and cultural attitudes. In addition, some prominent politicians such as President Cory Aquino had some Chinese ancestry. In Thailand also, since the late 1950s, many politicians and senior government officials have been partly or largely of Chinese descent, and many Sino-Thai families have embraced Thai Buddhism. Although Sino-Thai business people continue to dominate most sectors of the nonagricultural economy, this apparently causes less popular resentment than in either Malaysia or Indonesia.

## References

Alatas, Syed Hussein
1977        *The myth of the lazy native; A study of the image of the Malays, Filipinos and Javanese from the 16th to the 20th century and its function in the ideology of colonial capitalism.* London: Cass.
Alexander, Jennifer and Paul Alexander
1991        'Protecting peasants from capitalism; The subordination of Javanese traders by the colonial state', *Comparative Studies in Society and History* 33:370-94.
Angoulvant, Gabriel
1926        *Les Indes Néerlandaises; Leur rôle dans l'économie internationale.* Paris: Le Monde Nouveau. Two vols.
Anspach, Ralph
1969        'Indonesia', in: Frank H. Golay, Ralph Anspach, M. Ruth Pfanner and Eliezer B. Ayal, *Underdevelopment and economic nationalism in Southeast Asia*, pp. 111-201. Ithaca, NY: Cornell University Press.
Ayal, Eliezer B.
1969        'Thailand', in: Frank H. Golay, Ralph Anspach, M. Ruth Pfanner and Eliezer B. Ayal, *Underdevelopment and economic nationalism in Southeast Asia*, pp. 267-340. Ithaca, NY: Cornell University Press.
Barclay, George W.
1954        *Colonial development and population in Taiwan.* Princeton, NJ: Princeton University Press.
Baxter, James
1941        *Report on Indian migration.* Rangoon: Government Printing and Stationery.
Boeke, J.H.
1953        *Economics and economic policy of dual societies, as exemplified by Indonesia.* Haarlem: Tjeenk Willink.
1961        'Objective and personal elements in colonial welfare policy', in: *Indonesian economics; The concept of dualism in theory and policy*, pp. 263-99. The Hague: Van Hoeve. [Selected Studies on Indonesia 6.] [Translated from the Dutch by James S. Holmes.] [Originally published as 'Het zakelijke en het persoonlijke element in de koloniale welvaartspolitiek', *Koloniale Studiën* 11, 1927, pp. 157-9.]
Boomgaard, P. and A.J. Gooszen
1991        *Changing economy in Indonesia; Volume 11: Population trends, 1795-1942.* Amsterdam: Royal Tropical Institute.

Booth, Anne
1998        *The Indonesian economy in the nineteenth and twentieth centuries; A history*
            *of missed opportunities.* London: Macmillan. [A Modern Economic
            History of Southeast Asia.]
2003        'Education, equality and economic development in the Asia-Pacific
            economies', in: Martin Andersson and Christer Gunnarsson (eds),
            *Development and structural change in the Asia-Pacific*, pp. 148-69. London:
            RoutledgeCurzon.
Burger, D.H.
1961        'The government's native economic policy', in: *Indonesian economics;*
            *The concept of dualism in theory and policy*, pp. 319-29. The Hague:
            Van Hoeve. [Selected Studies on Indonesia 6.] [Translated from the
            Dutch by James S. Holmes.] [Originally published as the section 'De
            economische overheidszorg' in *De ontsluiting van Java's binnenland voor*
            *het wereldverkeer.* Wageningen: Veenman, 1939, pp. 230-40.]
Butcher, John
1993        'Revenue farming and the changing state in Southeast Asia', in: John
            Butcher and Howard Dick (eds), *The rise and fall of revenue farming;*
            *Business elites and the emergence of the modern state in Southeast Asia*, pp.
            19-44. Basingstoke: Macmillan Press.
Central Service of Statistics
[1946]      *Statistical yearbook of Thailand no 21: 1939-40 to 1944.* Bangkok: Central
            Service of Statistics.
Chang, Yunshik
1966        *Population in early modernization; Korea.* PhD thesis, Princeton University.
Chung, Young-Iob
2006        *Korea under siege, 1876-1945; Capital formation and economic transformation.*
            Oxford: Oxford University Press.
Commonwealth of the Philippines, Commission of the Census
1941        *Summary for the Philippines and general report for the census of population*
            *and agriculture, 1939.* Manila: Bureau of Printing.
Copeland, Ian and Michael R. Godley
1993        'Revenue farming in comparative perspective; Reflections on taxation,
            social structure and development in the early-modern period', in: John
            Butcher and Howard Dick (eds), *The rise and fall of revenue farming;*
            *Business elites and the emergence of the modern state in Southeast Asia*, pp.
            45-68. Basingstoke: Macmillan Press.
Department of Economic Affairs
1936        *Volkstelling 1930 / Census of 1930 in Netherlands India; Volume VIII.*
            *Overzicht voor Nederlandsch-Indië / Summary of the volumes I-VII.* Batavia:
            Departement van Economische Zaken.
Department of Statistics
1939        *Malayan year book 1939.* Singapore: Government Printing Office for
            the Department of Statistics, Straits Settlements and Federated Malay
            States.
Eckert, Carter J.
1991        *Offspring of empire; The Koch'ang Kims and the colonial origins of Korean*

*capitalism, 1876-1945*. Seattle: University of Washington Press. [Korean Studies of the Henry M. Jackson School of International Studies.]

Fernando, M.R., and David Bulbeck
1992        'Chinese economic activity in Netherlands India; Selected translations from the Dutch', in: *Sources for the economic history of Southeast Asia.* Singapore: Institute of Southeast Asian Studies. [Data Paper Series 2.]

Furnivall, J.S.
1934a       *Studies in the social and economic development of the Netherlands East Indies; Volume IIIb: State and private money lending in Netherlands India.* Rangoon: Burma Book Club.

1934b       *Studies in the social and economic development of the Netherlands East Indies; Volume IIIc: State pawnshops in Netherlands India.* Rangoon: Burma Book Club.

1943        *Educational progress in Southeast Asia.* With supplement on training for native self-rule, by Bruno Lasker. New York: Institute of Pacific Relations. [Inquiry Series.]

1945        'Some problems of tropical economy', in: Rita Hinden (ed.), *Fabian colonial essays*, pp. 161-84. London: George Allen and Unwin.

1948        *Colonial policy and practice; A comparative study of Burma and Netherlands India.* Cambridge: Cambridge University Press.

Gelderen, J. van
1961        'The economics of the tropical colony', in: *Indonesian economics; The concept of dualism in theory and policy*, pp. 111-64. The Hague: Van Hoeve. [Selected Studies on Indonesia 6.] [Translated from the Dutch by James S. Holmes.] [Originally published as *Voorlezingen over tropisch-koloniale staathuishoudkunde.* Haarlem: Tjeenk Willink, 1927, pp. 1-73.]

Golay, Frank H.
1969        'The Philippines', in: Frank H. Golay, Ralph Anspach, M. Ruth Pfanner and Eliezer B. Ayal, *Underdevelopment and economic nationalism in Southeast Asia*, pp. 21-109. Ithaca, NY: Cornell University Press.

Golay, Frank H., Ralph Anspach, M. Ruth Pfanner and Eliezer B. Ayal
1969        *Underdevelopment and economic nationalism in Southeast Asia.* Ithaca, NY: Cornell University Press.

Grajdanzev, Andrew J.
1944        *Modern Korea.* New York: Institute of Pacific Relations.

Haggard, Stephan, David Kang, and Chung-In Moon
1997        'Japanese colonialism and Korean development: A critique', *World Development* 25-6:867-81.

Hauser, Philip M.
1977        'The measurement of labour utilization – More empirical results', *Malayan Economic Review* 22-1:10-25.

Henry, Yves
1926        'Le crédit populaire agricole et commercial aux Indes Néerlandaises, *Bulletin économique de l'Indochine* 29:69-124.

Higgins, Benjamin
1956        'The dualistic theory of underdeveloped areas', *Economic Development and Cultural Change* 4-2 (January):99-112.

Ho, Samuel Pao-san
1971      'The development policy of the Japanese colonial government in Taiwan, 1895-1945', in: Gustav Ranis (ed.), *Government and economic development*, pp. 287-331. New Haven, CT: Yale University Press.
*Indonesian economics*
1961      *Indonesian economics; The concept of dualism in theory and policy.* The Hague: Van Hoeve. [Selected Studies on Indonesia 6.]
International Bank for Reconstruction and Development
1955      *The economic development of Malaya.* Baltimore: Johns Hopkins University Press.
Jomo Kwame Sundaram
1988      *A question of class; Capital, the state and uneven development in Malaya.* New York: Monthly Review Press.
Jones, Leroy P. and Il Sakong
1980      *Government, business, and entrepreneurship in economic development; The Korean case.* Cambridge: Harvard University Press for the Council on East Asian Studies, Harvard University.
Juhn, Daniel Sungil
1973      'The development of Korean entrepreneurship', in: Andrew C. Nahm (ed.), *Korea under Japanese colonial rule; Studies of the policy and techniques of Japanese colonialism*, pp.113-27. Michigan: Center for Korean Studies, Western Michigan University.
1977      'Nationalism and Korean businessmen', in: C.I. Eugene Kim and Dorothea E. Mortimore (eds), *Korea's response to Japan; The colonial period 1910-1945*, pp. 42-52. Michigan: Center for Korean Studies, Western Michigan University.
Kahin, George McTurnan
1952      *Nationalism and revolution in Indonesia.* Ithaca, NY: Cornell University Press.
Kang, David C.
2002      *Crony capitalism; Corruption and development in South Korea and the Philippines.* Cambridge: Cambridge University Press. [Cambridge Studies in Comparative Politics.]
Kim, Kwang Suk
1973      'An analysis of economic change in Korea', in: Andrew C. Nahm (ed.), *Korea under Japanese colonial rule; Studies of the policy and techniques of Japanese colonialism*, pp. 99-112. Michigan: Center for Korean Studies, Western Michigan University.
Kolff, G.H. van der
1966      'Brown and white economy; Unity in diversity', in: *Indonesian economics; The concept of dualism in theory and policy*, pp. 215-50. The Hague: Van Hoeve. [Selected Studies on Indonesia 6.] [Translated from the Dutch by James S. Holmes.] [Originally published as 'De economie van bruin en blank anders en eender', *Koloniaal Tijdschrift* 30, 1941, pp. 413-45.]
Kurihara, Kenneth
1945      *Labor in the Philippine economy.* Stanford, CA: Stanford University Press.

Laanen, J.T.M. van
1990        'Between the Java Bank and the Chinese moneylender; Banking and credit in colonial Indonesia', in: Anne Booth, W.J. O'Malley, and Anna Weidemann (eds), *Indonesian economic history in the Dutch colonial era*, pp. 244-66. New Haven, CT: Yale University Southeast Asian Studies, Yale Center for International Area Studies. [Monograph Series 35.]
Lai, Tse-Hai, Ramon H. Myers and Wei Wou
1991        *A tragic beginning; The Taiwan uprising of February 28, 1947*. Stanford, CA: Stanford University Press.
Lim, Teck-Ghee
1977        *Peasants and their agricultural economy in colonial Malaya, 1874-1941*. Kuala Lumpur: Oxford University Press. [East Asian Historical Monographs.]
Mackie, J.A.C.
1971        'The Indonesian economy, 1950-1963', in: Bruce Glassburner (ed.), *The economy of Indonesia; Selected readings*, pp. 16-69. Ithaca, NY: Cornell University Press. [First published 1964.]
1991        'Towkays and tycoons; The Chinese in Indonesian economic life in the 1920s and the 1980s', *Indonesia* 51:83-96
McNamara, Dennis L.
1990        *The colonial origins of Korean enterprise, 1910-1945*. Cambridge: Cambridge University Press.
Mortimer, Rex
1974        *Indonesian communism under Sukarno; Ideology and politics, 1959-1965*. Ithaca, NY: Cornell University Press.
Myint, Hla
1967        'The inward and outward-looking countries of Southeast Asia', *Malayan Economic Review* 12 (April):1-13.
Owen, Norman G.
1972        'Philippine economic development and American policy: A reappraisal', *Solidarity* 7-9:49-64.
Pfanner, M. Ruth
1969        'Burma', in: Frank H. Golay, Ralph Anspach, M. Ruth Pfanner and Eliezer B. Ayal, *Underdevelopment and economic nationalism in Southeast Asia*, pp. 203-65. Ithaca, NY: Cornell University Press.
Phongpaichit, Pasuk and Chris Baker
1995        *Thailand; Economy and politics*. Kuala Lumpur: Oxford University Press.
Post, Peter
1997        'The formation of the pribumi business elite in Indonesia, 1930s-1940s', in: Peter Post and Elly Touwen-Bouwsma (eds), *Japan, Indonesia and the war; Myths and realities*, pp. 87-110. Leiden: KITLV Press. [Verhandelingen 173.]
Power, John H. and Gerardo P. Sicat
1971        *The Philippines; Industrialisation and trade policies*. London: Oxford University Press.
Putzel, James
1992        *A captive land; The politics of agrarian reform in the Philippines*. New York: Monthly Review Press.

Reid, Anthony
1993        *Southeast Asia in the age of commerce, 1450-1680; Volume 2: Expansion and crisis.* New Haven, CT: Yale University Press.
2001        'South-East Asian population history and the colonial impact', in: Ts'ui-jung Liu, James Lee, David Sven Reher, Osamu Saito and Wang Feng (eds), *Asian population history*, pp. 45-62. Oxford: Oxford University Press. [International Studies in Demography.]

Rex, John
1959        'The plural society in sociological theory', *British Journal of Sociology* 10-2:114-24.

Robequain, Charles
1944        *The economic development of French Indo-China.* London: Oxford University Press.

Roff, William R.
1967        *The origins of Malay nationalism.* New Haven, CT/London: Yale University Press. [Yale Southeast Asia Studies 2.]

Rudner, Martin
1994        *Malaysian development; A retrospective.* Ottawa: Carleton University Press.

Rush, James
1991        'Placing the Chinese in Java on the eve of the twentieth century', *Indonesia* 51:13-24.

Sadli, M.
1971        'Reflections on Boeke's theory of dualistic economies', in: Bruce Glassburner (ed.), *The economy of Indonesia; Selected readings*, pp. 99-124. Ithaca: Cornell University Press.

Saito, T. and Lee Kin Kiong
1999        *Statistics on the Burmese economy; The 19th and 20th centuries.* Singapore: Institute of Southeast Asian Studies.

Snodgrass, Donald R.
1980        *Inequality and economic development in Malaysia.* Kuala Lumpur: Oxford University Press. [Harvard Institute for International Development.]

Sompop Manarungsan
1989        *Economic development of Thailand, 1850-1950; Response to the challenge of the world economy.* PhD thesis, State University of Groningen.

Steinhoff, Manfred
1980        *Prestige and profit; The development of entrepreneurial abilities in Taiwan, 1880-1972.* Canberra: Development Studies Centre, Australian National University. [Monograph 20.]

Twang, Peck Yang
1998        *The Chinese business élite in Indonesia and the transition to independence, 1940-1950.* Kuala Lumpur: Oxford University Press. [South-East Asian Historical Monographs.]

United Nations ECAFE
1961        *Economic survey of Asia and the Far East, 1960.* Bangkok: United Nations Economic Commission for Asia and the Far East.
1962        *Economic survey of Asia and the Far East, 1961.* Bangkok: United Nations Economic Commission for Asia and the Far East.

United Nations UNESCO
1964           *UNESCO Statistical Yearbook 1963*. Paris: United Nations Education,
               Scientific and Cultural Organization.
Vlieland, C.A.
1932           *British Malaya; A report on the 1931 census and on certain problems of vital
               statistics*. London: Crown Agents.
Wertheim, W.F.
1964           'Betting on the strong', in: W.F. Wertheim, *East-West parallels; Sociological
               approaches to modern Asia*. The Hague: Van Hoeve.
White, Nicholas J.
1996           *Business, government and the end of empire; Malaya, 1942-1957*. Kuala
               Lumpur: Oxford University Press. [South-East Asian Historical
               Monographs.]
Williams, Lea
1952           'Chinese entrepreneurs in Indonesia', *Explorations in Entrepreneurial
               History* 5-1:34-60.
Yoshihara, Kunio (ed.)
1989           *Oei Tiong Ham concern; The first business empire of Southeast Asia*. Kyoto:
               Center for Southeast Asian Studies, Kyoto University.
1994           *The nation and economic growth; The Philippines and Thailand*. Kuala
               Lumpur: Oxford University Press. [South-East Asian Social Science
               Monographs.]

W.G. WOLTERS

# Decolonizing money
# Central banks in the Philippines
# and Indonesia

When the Pacific War ended in August 1945, the former colonies in Asia found themselves in a new domestic and international situation. On the home front, nationalist sentiment had grown stronger and dissatisfaction with the prewar political dispensation spread as people clamoured for independence. Internationally, the global balance of power had changed with the United States emerging as the hegemonic power at the onset of the Cold War.

Nationalists were aware of the fact that independence implied more than formal sovereignty; the economic might of the colonial rulers had to be broken as well. This entailed a reorganization of the monetary system, an aspect of the decolonization process that remains little known even today. After the war, every former colony in Asia had to confront this problem, which was at once a highly technical matter and the focus of nationalist passions. Economist Ralph Anspach (1969:137) described its importance:

> [C]ontrol of money and credit is generally recognized as an essential ingredient of sovereignty. Newly-independent, underdeveloped countries seeking to modernize and industrialize inevitably turn to their inherent power to create money and credit to mobilize resources for these purposes.

In this respect, Indonesia and the Philippines provide interesting and contrasting cases for comparison (Higgins 1957:161). On the face of it they have much in common. They are neighbouring archipelagos with similar climates. Both have mountainous islands and are home to a variety of ethnic and linguistic groups. One significant difference between them is population size; in 1955 the Philippines had 22 million inhabitants, compared to Indonesia's 82 million. However, there are even more similarities. Both countries achieved independence after World War II, following more than three centuries of colonial presence. Economically, too, the likenesses were notable, in that both countries had a capital-intensive plantation sector producing cash crops for export and a labour-intensive peasant agricultural sector that was technologically less developed and low in productivity and income. When independence came in the late 1940s, both countries faced the challenge of changing and diversifying their economic structures and channelling investment towards industry. To meet this challenge they had to achieve economic as well as political sovereignty.

This chapter compares the monetary systems of the Philippines and Indonesia and the establishment of central banks in both countries. The aim of this comparison is not to arrive at a causal analysis of broad economic developments such as inflation, but rather to highlight particular aspects of each country's financial policies and woes. Monetary organization and economic development took divergent paths in the two countries. While Indonesia succumbed to economic chaos and runaway inflation in the late 1950s and early 1960s, the Philippines saw a much more orderly monetary and economic development during the 1950s.

*From the gold standard to managed currency systems*

By the late nineteenth century the gold standard had become the model for most European countries, the USA, and Japan. Under the gold standard, the money in circulation is not limited to full-bodied coins of gold or silver, but gold is kept in a reserve as the state's means of guaranteeing the value of the token coins and paper money in circulation. Countries without a sufficient amount of gold in their treasury applied the gold-exchange system under which foreign currency and debt paper with gold value was kept in the state fund. From the early 1900s until the mid-1930s the US government endeavoured through diplomacy to propagate the gold standard in other parts of the world. There was an element of self-interest in these efforts, as American investors, facing uncertain conditions in a world of fluctuating and variable silver currencies, preferred a reliable international system of gold-based currencies. This would create a dollar bloc in which their dollar-based investments would be safe.

For many years the gold standard acted as a regulator of international exchange with a stabilizing effect on international trade and investment. However, the system had serious drawbacks, particularly for agricultural countries. Money circulation under the gold standard was closely tied to the balance of payments, and there was little space for the creation of credit to stimulate economic development. Agrarian economies are generally susceptible to both seasonal and cyclical fluctuations. In monsoon climates, the seasonal nature of agricultural production is especially pronounced. Exports bring in foreign exchange during and after the harvest season. This means that both the country as a whole and the cash-crop producing regions in particular experience alternately incoming and outgoing flows of money and goods.

This requires a highly flexible monetary system, as British economist John Maynard Keynes observed in India. The gold standard held an advantage over a purely metallic system in that paper money could be produced and brought into circulation much more quickly than metallic coins. However, paper money had to be backed by the precious metal fund, which limited the potential to create credit. This was even more strongly felt during cyclical depressions, when foreign exchange earnings dropped significantly. The disruption of the balance of payments caused an outflow of gold and a subsequent contraction of domestic money circulation at the very moment when a credit injection was most necessary. Critics of the gold standard system, such as Keynes in the 1930s, therefore advocated a managed currency system in which governments could increase the amount of money in circulation to encourage economic growth.

Such a system was created under the Bretton Woods scheme in 1944. The US dollar was the only currency directly denominated in gold. Other currencies were linked to the dollar with fixed exchange rates. However, gold no longer reigned absolutely, as countries could alter the exchange values of their currencies. In order to support their currencies, countries could borrow from the International Monetary Fund (IMF).

The Bretton Woods scheme became the new international monetary system after World War II. To cope with this new situation, many countries had to reorganize their monetary system. The newly-independent countries had to establish central banks. They were supported in these efforts by economists working with the IMF and the US Federal Reserve that in the years 1943-1946 had been advising Latin American countries on monetary reforms and central bank policies. The economists involved in missions to these countries included Robert Triffin, John Exter, Henry Wallich, and David Grove. During this period they had come into contact with Latin American economists who held more nationalistic views, such as Raul Prebisch.

The main lesson learned from the economic depression of the 1930s was that the mechanisms assumed in the classical theory of international balance had failed. According to this theory, price and cost level disparities within a single country would cause a disruption of the balance of payments and thus lead to readjustment through currency devaluation. Through this mechanism the country's competitive position in the world market would be restored. If international cost and price disparities had been the main cause of economic fluctuations during the 1930s, some countries would have lost and others gained. For several years, however, both exports and imports fell in practically all countries. Total world trade dropped more than 60 percent between 1929 and 1932. The mechanisms that appeared to be at work in individual countries apparently did not lead to an adjustment of the whole system (Triffin 1947:56, 79).

There was a growing conviction that automatic mechanisms in monetary systems should be discarded, particularly the link between domestic monetary policy and the balance of payments. Under the old system it was considered necessary to keep a reserve fund for the stabilization of both the external and domestic value of the currency. Experience had shown, however, that such reserve requirements were of little or no value in central bank policy. During the Depression of the 1930s many countries had reduced the minimum requirements. Under the new concept central banks were only required to keep enough reserves to satisfy the country's international debts. Policymakers would manage the domestic currency volume with regard to the needs of the economy and the stability of prices. Triffin and his colleagues helped implement these ideas in the monetary reforms in Paraguay (1943-1945) and Guatemala (1945), and after the war they promoted this model in other countries as well. In 1947-1949 they had a hand in the recommendations for the outline of the Philippine Central Bank. One finds these principles discussed in Cuaderno's monograph on the Philippine Central Bank (1949).

*The gold exchange standard in the Philippines*

The foundation of the Philippine currency system under the American colonial administration (1898-1941) was laid down in the Philippine Coinage Act of 1903, which established a form of the gold standard in the country. The plan entailed the introduction of a theoretical gold peso, of a certain weight and degree of fineness, as the unit of value. This unit was equivalent to one-half of the American gold dollar. For actual circulation, the gold dollar was represented by a silver peso, which had the same value as the gold peso, although the pure silver content had a lower value. The value of the currency was guaranteed by a gold reserve, called the Gold Standard Fund, which served to maintain the gold value of the currency in transactions abroad. The government issued paper money, called silver certificates, against which an equal amount of silver pesos was held in reserve. In this gold standard system, the silver coins and the paper money were token coins.

The Gold Standard Fund was composed partly of silver coins in the Treasury in Manila and partly of dollar deposits in US banks. When an adjustment was needed, the Insular Treasurer could sell drafts on dollar deposits of the Gold Standard Fund in New York in exchange for pesos in Manila, or the depository banks in the US could sell drafts on the Manila part of the Fund in exchange for dollar payments in the States. This was conceived as an automatic adjustment of the amount of money in circulation. If drafts on the US were bought in Manila, the peso circulation was automatically reduced by the amount paid to the Treasurer. If drafts of Manila were bought in the US, the payment of these drafts in pesos in Manila increased the money in circulation. It soon became clear that this monetary system had its limitations. It linked circulation too closely to the balance of payments and was not conducive to the creation of credit for economic development.

The Philippine system was both conservative and inflexible (Jenkins 1954:112). Under the new arrangement, the currency reserves in the Philippines were excessive. According to the law, Treasury certificates (paper money) had to be backed by a 100 percent dollar reserve. In addition, the Gold Standard Fund, which was the adjustment mechanism, had to hold in reserve at least 15 percent of Philippine currency. At the end of 1932, for example, the total amount of currency available for or in circulation was 101.5 million pesos, of which 72.2 million was actually in circulation. Total cash reserves amounted to 123 percent of money in circulation. American dollar reserves amounted to 102 percent of money available for, or in, circulation, and 143 percent of money actually in circulation.

The economic depression of the 1930s caused a significant degree of price deflation in the country as well as a contraction of the money in circulation. Since 1930 the price level had fallen, indexing 1926-1928 prices as 100, to 66 in 1933, 58 in 1934, and 69 in 1935. A downward spiral had set in; prices for export products, rural income, and purchasing power plummeted while poverty grew widespread. Nationalists and socialists clamoured for government intervention to boost the economy. In Europe, Keynes criticized the gold standard as an unduly restrictive monetary system.

In the 1930s Philippine political leaders and their advisers were confronted with a host of problems, ranging from economic stagnation, unemployment, and widespread poverty to increasing inflation. They considered it wise to increase the amount of money in circulation in the Philippines. However, issuing new coins and notes was prohibited under existing laws and impossible in practice because there was no foreign exchange support. The existing colonial arrangement provided no means of divorcing the peso from the dollar. These problems in the mid-1930s proved to Philippine financial experts and government officials that the Insular Treasury was incapable of managing the currency system. They realized that a central bank would be the most effective means of adjusting the supply of credit and currency to the demands of trade. It would clearly be impossible to develop a more viable economy as long as the country had an inflexible currency system and a decentralized banking system that stymied the creation of credit (Cuaderno 1960:2).

In 1938 the National Assembly passed a bill reducing the required level of reserves behind the insular currency. The aim was to free up funds to meet the government's current expenditures, particularly those aimed at development. When this act was presented to President Roosevelt, he rejected it.

The American government tactfully suggested to President Quezon of the Philippines that the bills be withdrawn from the Assembly. This was done by resolution in 1939 (Golay 1997:396-7). In 1939, Philippine Finance Secretary Manuel Roxas proposed formal legislation to establish a central bank. Under the existing political arrangement, the law required the approval of the US president, and again the president refused. To Filipino nationalists, this was proof that as long as the Americans remained in control there could be no independent monetary and economic policy.

In December 1941, Japan launched its surprise attack on the US fleet at Pearl Harbor, and within a few months Japanese troops had occupied most of Southeast Asia, including the Philippine Islands and the Netherlands Indies. In the Philippines, the occupation lasted until the US reconquered the islands three years later. The Japanese occupation had created havoc in the Philippines; in 1946 the total economic output was 35 percent of its 1940 level, while the Philippine peso lost most of its value.

*Independence and the central bank*

The US granted the Philippines independence from the 4th of July 1946. However, Washington imposed economic and security measures that put serious constraints on the new state's sovereignty. Shortly before granting independence, the US Congress had passed the Philippine Trade Act of 1946 (also known as the Bell Trade Act). At the time of independence the Philippine government accepted the act as a trade agreement, mainly because it was accompanied by promises of financial assistance. The Bell Trade Act provided for an eight-year period of free trade between the two countries and ruled out tariff increases as a means of reducing imports.

The act also stated in Article 5 that the Philippine peso would remain pegged to the US dollar:

> The value of the Philippine currency in relation to the US dollar shall not be changed, the convertibility of the Philippine peso into the US dollar shall not be suspended and no restriction shall be imposed on the transfer of funds from the Philippines to the United States except by agreement with the President of the United States.

In 1946, the exchange rate of the peso was reset at its prewar parity of 2 pesos to 1 US dollar, which gave the peso an implicit value of $7\,^{13}/_{21}$ grains of gold 0.900 fine, equivalent to the US dollar parity of the peso (Republic Act No. 265 in Cuaderno 1949:103). In fact, this amounted to an overvaluation of the peso.

Manuel Roxas was elected president of the Philippines in 1946, and he held office until his death in 1948. His top priority was the rebuilding of the country's productive capabilities that had been destroyed during the Japanese occupation. He appointed Miguel Cuaderno as secretary of finance. Cuaderno (1890-1975) studied law in Manila and pursued a career in the civil service of the colonial administration in the 1920s. He served for many years as a high-ranking official and later became president of the government-owned Philippine National Bank (PNB). In 1938 he started a commercial bank. During the 1930s, Cuaderno was an adviser to the then-secretary of finance in Quezon's cabinet, Manuel Roxas. It was in this period that Cuaderno developed nationalistic ideas on the Philippine economy. He was critical of the gold standard system and advocated strong government intervention in the economy. He pointed out to President Roxas that it would be a mistake to reconstruct the Philippine economy along prewar lines and that earnings from agricultural exports alone would not meet the needs of an independent country (Cuaderno 1960:1). He therefore advocated a policy of balanced economic development based on agricultural development and industrialization. Cuaderno (1952:323) pointed out that in 1948, 23 percent of the national income was spent on imports, some 70 percent of which consisted of consumer goods. The basic pattern of the Philippines required an economic transformation, in particular the promotion of an import substitution industry.

In 1947 the Joint Philippine-American Finance Commission concluded its work assessing the financial and budgetary problems of the Philippines. The main Filipino members were Cuaderno and economist Andres Castillo. Among the American members were economists from the US Treasury Department and the Federal Reserve System (the American central bank). An important question the commission had considered was the need for a central bank. The American members of the commission were initially opposed to this idea; there were angry exchanges between them and Secretary Cuaderno. In his memoirs, Cuaderno (1960:9-12) wrote that 'an influential New York banker' had asked the American Treasury to instruct its representatives in the Joint Commission to vote against the establishment of a central bank. Cuaderno attributed this resistance to doubts among American bankers about the capabilities of the Filipinos, but the real cause was probably the American banking sector's fear that the operations of American business in the Philippines would be curtailed under a Philippine central bank. Cuaderno (1960:10) argued 'that it would not look well for the United States, now that the Philippines was a free country, to give the impression that she still wanted to control our economy'. When President Roxas, during a meeting with the leaders of the Commission, threatened to have a separate Philippine report written, the American members suddenly declared that they fully agreed with the Filipino commissioners on the central bank question (Cuaderno 1960:10). The final report of the Joint Commission stated that '[t]he Commission regards the present Philippine monetary system as an unsuitable permanent system for an independent Philippines' and recommended 'that the Philippine Government adopt a managed monetary system in which the monetary authority and responsibility would rest with the central bank'.

### The Philippine central bank

The commission's conclusions led Cuaderno and Castillo to make extensive preparations in 1947 and 1948 for the foundation of the new central bank. They studied the innovative charters of the central banks established in Guatemala and Paraguay in the early 1940s. They also consulted with economists who had been advising Latin American governments on the establishment of central banks. Among them were Belgian economist Robert Triffin (1946, 1947) who after the Second World War worked for the newly-created International Monetary Fund (IMF), and David Grove who was on the Board of Governors of the US Federal Reserve System.

Cuaderno (1960:88) and his colleagues modelled their draft charter of the Philippine Central Bank on its Guatemalan counterpart. The charters for Latin American countries were specifically designed to meet the problems of relatively small agricultural countries that were particularly vulnerable to disturbances in international trade. The problem was that in countries where the money volume was rigidly linked to gold or foreign exchange reserves, and the issuing of money was largely restricted to the conversion of foreign exchange surpluses and deficits, the national money supply was vulnerable to international business cycles.

The new concept of central banking was to separate the two purposes, namely the regulation of currency and credit, and the stabilization of the external value of the currency. This was based on the view that in developing countries, the first purpose should not be linked with the balance of payments. While the external value of the currency should be based on a currency reserve directly linked to the balance of payments, the internal circulation should not be managed in accordance with the needs of the economy. The charter should not provide for any required ratio between the bank's international reserves and its currency issue. Currency issue should respond directly to the country's trade and business needs.

The Philippine government adopted the charter of the central bank as Republic Act 265 on 15 June 1948. The bank was opened on 3 January 1949. Miguel Cuaderno was appointed governor. The Central Bank Act made the Philippine Central Bank responsible not only for monetary management, supervision of the banking system and preservation of the international value of the peso, but also for promoting economic production in the country. This was a wide mandate that gave the Central Bank governor far-reaching powers of management and intervention.

To complement the Central Bank Act, the Philippine Congress adopted the General Banking Act (R.A. No. 337) on 24 July 1948, which gave the central bank complete control of private bank reserves, loans, and credit. A series of other acts gave the central bank control over property loans and domestic and foreign insurance companies. The Central Bank Act stated that the central bank was responsible for maintaining the peso's par value. It was under the authority of this provision that the central bank took over the administration of exchange and import controls (Golay 1969:60).

Organizationally the relationship between the Philippine government and the central bank was a balancing act. Overall supervision of the bank resided with a Monetary Board consisting of seven members including the bank governor, the secretary of finance, and the president of a large Philippine state bank, all appointed by the government. So it is clear that, on the one hand, the central bank legislation did not make central bank policy completely independent of the government's national economic policies. On the other hand, however, the bank governor had the power to keep the government at bay, as it was explicitly stated that the secretary of finance participated in, but did not dominate, the formulation and execution of monetary policy (Cuaderno 1949:18-9, 92-3).

Independence and the foundation of a central bank did not put all monetary issues to rest. One remaining problem was American legal control over the Philippine currency. In 1954, the Philippine government sent a mission to Washington to negotiate a revision of the conditions arranged under the Bell Trade Act. The mission was headed by Senator José Laurel, who had been president of the Philippine puppet government under the Japanese occupation. In spite of his tainted past, Senator Laurel was received well in the United States. One of the mission's tasks was to seek the elimination of Article V of the agreement, which gave the US president control over the Philippine monetary system. Initially the American negotiators resisted the revision. Cuaderno argued again that the Philippines had become an independent country and that the US government could not justifiably demand that the Philippine government surrender its right to manage the currency. After long and difficult negotiations, the final Laurel-Langley Agreement stated that Article V would be eliminated.

*A system of controls*

In the Philippines, 1949 was an election year, and the incumbent President Elpidio Quirino, who as vice president had assumed the presidency after the death of Manuel Roxas in 1948, spent large sums of money on his reelection campaign. Inflation rose sharply and the ensuing flight to dollars raised fears that the peso would collapse. In consultation with the president, central bank governor Cuaderno sent an urgent request to the US president asking him to approve the imposition of exchange controls. An IMF mission arrived in the Philippines to study the situation. The urgency of the situation was compounded by the fact that the communist Huk rebellion was expanding rapidly, bringing the possibility of a communist victory within sight. In December 1949, the White House gave consent to impose exchange controls. The central bank governor immediately ordered domestic and foreign banks to cease the sale of foreign currency (Cuaderno 1960:23-4). In May 1950 this was followed by tighter import controls, which lasted until 1953. In subsequent years the Philippine Central Bank issued a large number of circulars, with very precise instructions concerning the various exchange rates of the peso and the character of goods that could be imported under various categories.

   After 1953, exchange controls were deliberately used as an instrument of nationalist economic policy to bring about import substitution industrialization and a Philippinization of the economy. The government discouraged the import of finished products and consumer goods, and promoted the import of raw materials and machinery.

   The exchange and import controls of the 1950s strengthened the state's role in determining who could get dollar allocations. The state used this instrument to promote an import substitution industrialization programme. The state offered other incentives as well, such as tax exemptions, liberal credit facilities and profits from an overvalued peso. Together these incentives created a protective barrier for domestic entrepreneurs who manufactured import substitution products. As a result, a large number of Filipino entrepreneurs established industrial enterprises.

   Statistics show that the controls brought about structural economic change. Manufacturing saw an annual growth of 12.1 percent in the period 1951-1955 and 7.7 percent in 1956-1960 (Doronilla 1992:55). The growth rate of the gross national product (GNP) was 8.1 percent in 1951-1955 and 5 percent in 1955-1960. In 1949 consumer goods constituted 64.4 percent of imports, raw materials 26.2 percent, and capital goods 9.4 percent. By 1957 a dramatic change had taken place; finished goods were down to 21.9 percent of all imports, while raw materials jumped to 58.5 percent and capital goods to 19.6 percent (Castro 1960:177-8).

Monetary policy was relatively successful during the 1950s; the amount of money in circulation grew slowly, and inflation was mild. The central bank was able to prevent balance of payment problems from getting out of hand. Unlike the gold-exchange system, the managed currency system did not automatically limit the money supply in the country. That opened up the possibility of pursuing a flexible domestic monetary policy that was responsive to the needs of the Philippine economy. However, the monetary authorities had to keep a watchful eye on rising inflation. While the creation of credit was healthy for an expanding economy, excessive creation of bank credit could lead to rising prices.

In the mid 1950s, during the presidency of Ramon Magsaysay (1954-1957), a 'great debate' on fiscal and monetary policy was raging in government circles and among the informed public in the country (Cuaderno 1960:138). While Governor Cuaderno and his advisors advocated restraint with regard to credit creation and foreign exchange, a number of Philippine politicians demanded a rapid increase of bank credit to boost economic development, even if this meant deficit spending. This expansionary or 'cheap money' school was supported by agricultural exporters, particularly the 'Sugar Block'. Their representatives in the Magsaysay cabinet were Salvador Araneta, secretary of agriculture and advocate of pump-priming measures, Oscar Ledesma, secretary of commerce and industry, and Alfredo Montelibano, head of the Office of Economic Coordination. These politicians proposed an ambitious economic development programme calling for an expenditure of two billion pesos over a period of five years. They argued that economic development should be pushed by strong credit creation (Cuaderno 1960:127-30).

Cuaderno warned the president that such a programme would cause inflation and wreck the economy; he announced that he would resist pressure to change policy. President Magsaysay wavered between the two camps. He was attracted to the prospect of rapid economic growth that deficit spending would promote. However, he feared the inflationary effects of such a policy. Throughout 1955 President Magsaysay was apparently influenced in his views by the expansionary school. He asked the US to send two central banking experts to review the operation of the Philippine Central Bank. In early 1956 these economists submitted a report that spoke favourably about the central bank's policies. President Magsaysay decided in favour of the restrictive school (Cuaderno 1960:127-50; Abueva 1971:341-52; Doronilla 1992:341-52).

Throughout his period as governor of the central bank, Cuaderno battled with powerful politicians and business people. He continued to fight for limited credit creation in order to combat inflation. In this struggle, he was relatively successful. However, in the late 1950s the system of controls became less effective. Import substitution industrialization seemed to have lost its momentum and entrepreneurs were clamouring for a loosening of controls.


## Monetary liberalization

Since the late 1940s, monetary policy in the Philippines had followed the prevalent economic model of 'embedded liberalism', particularly with the 'managed currency' view propagated in the 1920s and 1930s by economists such as Keynes. The idea was to unlink the money supply from the balance of payments and to assign the central bank the task of managing this supply in accordance with the needs of the domestic business community. This view had strong proponents in Miguel Cuaderno and his colleagues in the Philippines. It also found some support among high officials in the US Federal Reserve System.

In the late 1950s, state-led development faced a growing challenge from the neo-liberal views on monetary and economic policy that were gaining ground in the United States. Its most prominent spokesman was American economist Milton Friedman (1962:67), who advocated an international system of free trade based on free-floating exchange rates, determined in the market by private transactions without government intervention. Friedman argued that import controls and other types of trade restriction stifled economic development. A fixed exchange rate combined with unlimited imports would sooner or later lead to the depletion of foreign reserves, forcing governments to impose controls to stop the outflow. In the name of freedom, Friedman therefore advocated abolishing fixed exchange rates and switching to flexible exchange rates. Friedman argued that this would be a self-equilibrating system. Under freely floating exchange rates, excessive imports would lead to a devaluation of the currency in accordance with market forces, until imports became so prohibitive and exports so attractive that the balance of payments would reach a new equilibrium (Lichauco 1988:192-4). In the late 1950s and early 1960s these ideas gained general acceptance in the US Treasury and the IMF. In 1960 the US government and the IMF exerted pressure on the Philippine government to devalue the peso and to abolish import controls. Friedman's ideas became the dominant monetary theory in 1971 when the US government took the dollar off gold. Since then all the world's currencies have been irredeemable or fiat currencies, freely floating against each other.

In 1946, the exchange rate had been fixed at two pesos to the dollar. Over the course of time, the official exchange rate came under pressure. By the late 1950s there was a growing disparity between the legal value and the free-market value, which had risen to three to four pesos to the dollar. Under these conditions, control could no longer be effectively maintained. The country was losing dollars through widespread evasion of controls and the smuggling out of dollars.

In 1960 the central bank started gradually lifting exchange and import controls. The first step was to limit the type of goods that could be imported under the two-to-one exchange rate and to restrict foreign exchange. In 1962 the peso exchange rate was officially changed to 3.90 to $1. In 1970 a free-floating exchange rate was adopted, leading to a further depreciation of the peso in subsequent years (by 1987 it was 20 to $1). At the end of 1960, Miguel Cuaderno, who did not agree with this decontrol program, resigned as governor of the central bank.

As a result of Cuaderno's balanced monetary policy, the Philippines had experienced relatively stable economic development in the 1950s. Although monetary policy was liberalized to some extent in the following decade, the ideology of state intervention to promote economic development remained very strong. When President Marcos proclaimed martial law in 1972 and established an authoritarian regime, he used 'development' as the legitimizing slogan.

For Indonesia, the late 1950s and 1960s were much more turbulent. Monetary policy in Indonesia was far less effective in curbing inflationary tendencies. This was mainly due to the structure of the Indonesian central bank. In the late 1950s Indonesian politics fell into the grip of authoritarianism, and the New Order regime established by Suharto in the late 1960s had much in common with Ferdinand Marcos's New Society.

*The colonial monetary system in Indonesia*

Prior to the Second World War, the monetary systems of the Dutch East Indies and the Netherlands were closely interwoven. The East Indies system was based on the Indies Currency Law (*Muntwet*) of 1912, which was repealed by the Indonesian Republic in 1951. Under this system the monetary unit was the guilder, equal to the Dutch guilder, with an unlimited one-to-one convertibility. The coins that constituted legal tender were completely identical in the two countries. Bank notes were different, but they were freely interchangeable and transferable between the Indies and the Netherlands at a virtual one-to-one rate. Companies operating in both countries made no distinction between the Dutch guilder and the Dutch East Indies guilder in their accounts (Van Eck 1970:295).

With the exception of a few short periods the monetary system of the Netherlands and the Dutch East Indies had been based on the gold standard since the mid 1870s. In 1875 the Netherlands adopted gold as legal tender. It designated the gold ten-guilder coin (consisting of 6.048 grams of fine gold) as the standard coin and proclaimed it equal in value to ten silver guilders. In 1877 this system was introduced in the Dutch East Indies. Because the gold value of silver declined significantly in the late nineteenth century, the silver coins circulating in both the mother country and the colony became fiduciary or token money. Silver coins and small change were the only coins in circulation among the Indonesian population.

The Javasche Bank (established in 1827) had a central function in the financial system of the colony. It was a private bank structured as a joint-stock company. It had a dual purpose. As a commercial bank it was engaged in general banking. At the same time it was a bank of issue with a monopoly on the issuing of bank notes. The Javasche Bank (also known in some sources as the Java Bank) resembled a central bank in that it issued currency, performed services for the state, kept the cash reserves of the commercial banks, and stored and managed the country's reserves of international currency. Given such operations, the Javasche Bank could have developed into a 'bankers' bank' or central bank, a financial institution that provides liquidity to other banks and has a certain responsibility for the whole money and credit system. However, this did not happen.

The Javasche Bank maintained the gold value of the Dutch East Indies guilder in international exchange through its readiness to exchange the intrinsically inferior silver guilders at all times for gold coins or for bills of exchange on the Netherlands or England at a fixed price of 1,653.44 guilders per kilogram of gold. As the value of the Dutch East Indies guilder was maintained through the sale of bills of exchange on foreign countries, the proper name for this system is the gold-exchange standard. Interestingly, when the Americans constructed this system for the Philippines in 1903, they claimed they had invented it, while in fact the Dutch had been using it for more than a quarter century.

Only twice was the gold-exchange standard suspended. It had to be abandoned from 1914 to 1925, during and after World War I, when the export of gold and silver was prohibited. The same happened from 1936 until the Japanese invasion. In the early depression years of the 1930s, the Netherlands had strictly adhered to the *gave gulden*, the stable gold value of the guilder, even though other countries had already abandoned the gold standard. In September 1936, the Netherlands left the gold standard and devalued the guilder.

Although the Javasche Bank did perform some functions typical of a central bank, its role was limited by two factors. Firstly, the bank was not the end point or apex of the Netherlands Indies' money and banking system (Scheffer 1951b:21-4). This was due to the special structure of Dutch businesses in the colony. Almost all Dutch enterprises in the Netherlands Indies had their headquarters in the Netherlands and these companies had the habit of sending all excess funds back home. Profits on exports automatically went to headquarters. For their financing, the companies received funds directly from the Netherlands, via either the Dutch banks or the Javasche Bank. This is the main reason why the Javasche Bank did not become a central bank. A true central bank is the apex of the banking system in a country and is able to exert some control over the other banks, to function as lender of last resort, and to influence the money volume. The banks and Dutch enterprises active in the Dutch East Indies did not fall back on the Javasche Bank, but directly on the money market in the Netherlands. If transfers passed via the Javasche Bank, the bank only executed transfers from the monetary system of the Netherlands to that of the Dutch East Indies (Scheffer 1951b:22-3). Secondly, the Javasche Bank did not play the role of controlling the Indies' banking system.

In addition to the Dutch-owned Javasche Bank, seven commercial banks were licensed to handle foreign exchange: three of them Dutch, two Chinese and two British. Two government institutions catered to the financial needs of the indigenous population: a pawnshop service and the People's Credit Bank, a government-run money lender.

After the Germans occupied the Netherlands in May 1940, the Dutch East Indies guilder could no longer be defined in relation to the Dutch guilder. Foreign payments could no longer be passed through the mother country. At this point, the Javasche Bank took on some of the tasks of a central bank. The government of the Dutch East Indies felt that 'an independent Indies currency' had come into being and that the country had a 'monetary system of [its] own' (Van Eck 1970:298).

Within a few months after starting the Pacific War in December 1941, the Japanese had conquered most of Southeast Asia. They occupied the Dutch East Indies in March 1942 and controlled the territory until they were defeated by the Allied forces in August 1945. On August 17, a few days after the Japanese surrender, Indonesian nationalists proclaimed the independent Republic of Indonesia. From 1945 until 1949 the Dutch fought their last colonial war in the archipelago, a conflict that was ended through diplomacy.

The monetary situation during these years was confusing and chaotic. The Japanese military government had put large amounts of rupiah-denominated 'invasion money' into circulation. The allied occupation authorities had also issued rupiahs while the provisional government of the Republic and the returning Dutch government had issued their own currencies (the URI, *Uang Republik Indonesia* and 'Red money', respectively). From 1946 until the war ended in 1949, two centres of government vied for power. In March 1946, the Dutch tried to reestablish the old Dutch East Indies guilder at the prewar one-to-one exchange rate. However, transfers between the Netherlands and Indonesia were no longer free, but regulated by strict licenses and quota.

The government of the Republic issued large amounts of its own Indonesian Republic money, but outside Java it was valid only in the territories of issue. After December 1949 an estimated 3.3 billion guilders of Dutch currency were in circulation in addition to about 6 billion rupiah in different types of Republican money. The Indonesian government declared all 'Red money', all prewar Javasche Bank notes and all URI notes to be legal tender. The two denominations, guilder and rupiah, were considered equal, as the two names had been used interchangeably in the past. In early 1950 the Indonesian government embarked on a money purge in an attempt to remove surplus money from the economy and to stabilize prices.

December 1949 marked what the Dutch call 'the transfer of sovereignty' to Indonesia and what the Indonesians refer to as the 'recognition of sovereignty'. Either way, political sovereignty did not immediately bring the Indonesians monetary sovereignty. The 1949 Round Table Conference Agreement stipulated that the Netherlands would have to be consulted before any changes were made in the Bank Law regulating the position of the Javasche Bank and the extension of credits by the Javasche Bank to the Indonesian government. The agreement also required consultation with the Dutch government prior to any personnel changes on the bank's board of directors.

*Disentangling the colonial monetary system*

From the recognition of independence in December 1949 until the 'takeover' of Dutch-owned business property in December 1957 there was a period of political struggle and increasing political radicalization. The conflicts of this period can be analysed in various ways: as struggles between left and right, liberalism and socialism, moderate and radical nationalist politics, the political elite and the masses, or economists and developers. Economist Glassburner (1971:76-83) points to the basic, twofold problem underlying these different interpretations: the 'continued existence of an entrenched Dutch economic interest' in the country and 'the economic impotency of the Indonesian elite in general'. Indonesian politicians were aware of this situation but could not agree on how to deal with it. The task faced by the government in 1950 was to stabilize and expand an economy that was foreign-dominated and privately owned.

After 1949 the Javasche Bank appeared likely to become the new central bank of Indonesia. But disputes soon emerged, with rival economic powers taking opposite sides. The Dutch wanted to retain control over the Javasche Bank and, via the bank, over Indonesian central banking activities. They were strongly opposed to credit expansion to finance indigenous development, as this would undermine Dutch economic interests in Indonesia and reduce the real value of remaining Dutch financial claims against the new state (Anspach 1969:137). Apparently the Netherlands hoped to maintain indirect control of the Indonesian monetary system through the central bank's Dutch personnel (Anspach 1969:137).

Both the Ministry of Finance and the Javasche Bank still employed a large number of Dutch officials and civil servants. In 1949 the board of directors of the Javasche Bank counted only one Indonesian member. The top executive positions of the central office were Dutch, as were all but one of the branch offices' chief agents. In the words of American economist Anspach (1969:138): 'The Indonesian nationalists doubted whether these bankers, no matter how competent, would interpret national interests as Indonesians would'. Indonesia had too few trained economists to take over the new central bank, the Ministry of Finance and the banking system. The *indonesianisasi* of the Javasche Bank, that is the replacement of Dutch civil servants by Indonesians, was a slow process (Lindblad 2004).

The Dutch officials still in place represented Dutch economic interests indeed. In the first annual report of the Javasche Bank published after 1949 (*Verslag Javasche Bank* 1951:11, 43-4), President A. Houwink expressed his satisfaction at the continuing 'independence' of the Javasche Bank. He remarked that the bank should not exercise control over the credit policies of the other banks in the country. Houwink asserted that these banks, most of which were Dutch, should 'be left unrestricted in their extension of credit'. However, he did propose that the bank impose licensing restrictions on new Indonesian firms wishing to enter the field of banking and foreign trade. In other words, Houwink openly advocated a policy shielding foreign banks from control and preventing the rise of Indonesian competitors.

On 30 April 1951, Minister of Finance Joesoef Wibisono announced the government's intention to nationalize the Javasche Bank. The cabinet headed by Prime Minister Soekiman submitted the proposal to parliament, and in July a committee was established to prepare the nationalization. On the committee's advice, the government decided to purchase the shares from the shareholders. The government offered 120% of the price listed in Dutch guilders and 360% of the listed rupiah value. By late 1951 the Indonesian government had acquired most of the shares. The nationalization became law on 6 December (Saubari 1987:120-1). The bank was no longer a joint-stock company, but a corporate public body (*badan hukum*). Bank president Houwink, who had not been informed in advance of the government's nationalization plans, tendered his resignation and was discharged on 12 July 1951. He was succeeded by Sjafruddin Prawiranegara (Saubari 1987: 121).

Sjafruddin Prawiranegara (1911-1989) had graduated with a law degree from the Rechtshogeschool in Batavia in 1939. He became a civil servant, served under the Japanese government and joined the Indonesian Republic after the Japanese capitulation. Sjafruddin was a member of the Masjumi party and belonged to the party's religious socialist wing. Before his appointment as bank president he had served as minister of finance and prime minister. Politically, he was moderate. He did not believe, for instance, that the nationalization of the Javasche Bank and other Dutch companies was a prerequisite for economic development. Glassburner (1971:81) compares him with other Indonesian economists at the time: 'Of this group, Sjafruddin was the one most clearly inclined to accept the circumstances and willing to make the necessary accommodation'. Sjafruddin's economic and monetary views were very close to those of the Dutch. In his 'recollections' Sjafruddin (1987:103) says that he agreed to become bank president 'because of the pressure from the Dutch who had the greatest trust in me! Houwink himself approved of my becoming his successor'.

*Debates about monetary policy*

In his first report (*Report Java Bank* 1953:19-21) Sjafruddin argued against the principle that a central bank should be a 'banker's bank' only. In his view, there were good reasons for the bank to continue its commercial banking activities: the absence of a money and capital market in Indonesia, and a paucity of capital in the Indonesian banking system that rendered it incapable of satisfying all applications for credit facilities (Ali Wardhana 1971:347).

A small number of economists, both Indonesian and Dutch, disagreed with Sjafruddin's views. Among them was professional economist Soemitro Djojohadikoesoemo (1917-2001), who had studied at the Netherlands School of Economics in Rotterdam. There he had defended his doctoral dissertation, entitled *Het volkscredietwezen in de depressie* (The people's credit system during the Depression), in 1943. During the revolution, Soemitro served as deputy chief of mission of the Indonesian delegation to the United Nations, and from 1950 to 1956 he was trade and industry minister and finance minister in several cabinets. In 1950 he was also appointed professor of economics at the newly-established Faculty of Economics at the University of Indonesia. Soemitro was well-versed in the main economic theories of the 1930s and 1940s.

In 1951, differences of opinion about monetary policy clearly came to the fore in a public polemic between Soemitro and H. Teunissen, a member of the board of directors of the Javasche Bank. In a public lecture on 13 November 1951, Teunissen had explicitly argued that the bank's main task was to implement a monetary policy aimed at maintaining stability of purchasing power and prices. To this end money circulation should be limited, he stated, adding that although the gold standard system was no longer in place, the bank should still adhere to the principles enshrined in it.

In a paper that circulated in Jakarta and was later published in a business journal, Soemitro disputed Teunissen's monetary analysis, questioned his expertise and criticized him for adhering to an obsolete economic theory. In Soemitro's view, Teunissen was guilty of nostalgia for the old and discredited gold standard policies. Teunissen's statement that the gold standard had in the past maintained price stability was historically incorrect, according to Soemitro. Experience of the last fifty years had shown that price stability was an illusion, as prices had continually risen. The gold standard policy had successfully maintained parity between currencies, but not stability of domestic purchasing power and prices. On the contrary, the gold standard had provided the mechanism for transferring the price and conjunctural trends from abroad into the domestic sphere, Soemitro argued.

Soemitro's main objection was that Teunissen advocated monetary stability as the primary task of the future Indonesian central bank. In Soemitro's view it was not the central bank but the government that should determine the volume of money in circulation. He saw this as a matter of political decision-making rather than a purely technical issue (Teunissen 1951; Soemitro Djojohadikoesoemo 1951; Scheffer 1951a). In his paper Soemitro made a case for separating the central bank's domestic function from its role in preserving international parity.

In 1953, when parliament discussed the draft bill on the Bank of Indonesia's new charter, the then Finance Minister Soemitro went public with his view that the bank should discontinue its commercial banking operations because these might come into direct conflict with its role as a 'bankers' bank'. He felt the success of a central bank depended largely upon the support and cooperation of the commercial banks, and that this could only be ensured if the central bank refrained from competing with smaller banks in commercial banking (Soemitro Djojohadikoesoemo 1953:98). Despite his efforts, however, the Bank of Indonesia maintained its commercial banking department when the draft bill became law.

Even though he was minister of finance, Soemitro was unable to effectively counteract influential lobbies within the Indonesian monetary establishment, particularly the Dutch civil servants in the Javasche Bank and Finance Ministry. Most of these civil servants had earned degrees in 'Indologie', a course of administrative studies and Indonesian languages at Leiden University. They had a poor grasp of economics. Soemitro's description speaks volumes: '[T]o me their technical competence was very dubious. [...] Those people who posed as economists had their training in Leiden as "indologs"!' (Soemitro Djojohadikoesoemo 1986:35-6) The Indonesian politicians and civil servants who created the framework of the central bank appear to have been poorly informed about international developments in central banking. They were advised by Dutch officials and had no opportunity to consult with experts from the IMF or the US Federal Reserve System.

Unlike the policymakers, Indonesian and Dutch economists working in the newly-established Faculty of Economics at Universitas Indonesia were well-informed. One of them was C.F. Scheffer (1911-1979), an independent Dutch economist who had begun working at the Indonesian finance ministry in 1949. He was named to sit on a committee that was to study the Indonesian banking system. Although the committee never got off the ground, it provided Scheffer (1951b) with enough research material for his PhD dissertation. In his dissertation he analysed the dual position of the Javasche Bank and argued in favour of a supervisory role for the future Indonesian central bank. In 1951, when he was still employed at the Ministry of Finance, Scheffer became a lecturer in the University of Indonesia's economics faculty. When Scheffer gave his inaugural address as full professor in 1953, he defended strong state control over the banking sector. Scheffer (1951b) was aware of the recent work of IMF economists such as Triffin, as one of the theses in his PhD dissertation shows: 'The new monetary legislation in the Philippines, Guatemala and some South American states has not received the interest from the discipline of economics that such innovative legislation deserves'. However, Scheffer and a handful of other economists were not able to influence the structure and policies of the Indonesian central bank (Soemitro Djojohadikoesoemo 1986:35) described the relationship between policymakers and economists at that time as follows: 'Those Dutch people – like Kraal and Schaffer [sic] – who were good economists were ostracised in the Ministry of Finance, and I got them in the Faculty of Economics'.

## The Indonesian central bank

On 10 April 1953 the Indonesian parliament passed legislation establishing the Bank of Indonesia, a new central bank meant to replace the Javasche Bank. The law, which went into effect on 1 July of that year, explicitly stipulated that responsibility for monetary policy resided with the government. The bank was completely subordinate to the government. The Bank of Indonesia's charter did not set aside an important role for the president and directors; they were not given the power to make monetary decisions. Decision-making power rested with the Monetary Council (Dewan Moneter) made up of the bank president, the minister of finance, and the minister of economic affairs.

Remarkably, it was not the Indonesian-established Bank Negara Indonesia (BNI) but the Javasche Bank that was made the central bank. The BNI had been the official bank of the national revolutionary government in Yogyakarta during the independence war (1945-1949). Some Indonesian nationalists would have preferred to see it become the central bank because, as Soemitro (1986:34) wrote, 'it was our bank'.

The purposes of the central bank were similar to those of the Javasche Bank, namely to issue bank notes, manage gold and foreign currencies, and advance funds to the central government. The Monetary Council was responsible for formulating monetary policy, for regulating the value of the currency, and for setting the interest rate. At first, the Bank of Indonesia did not take on the role of lender of last resort to the banking system, nor did it act to control credit in accordance with the needs of business (Charlesworth 1959:30-1). The Bank lacked the power to control other banks' foreign exchange operations. Likewise, it had no voice in determining the exchange rate of the rupiah (Irvine 1953:151).

Although the postwar monetary system was no longer based on the gold standard, one feature of the old system was maintained in the central bank's charter: the relationship with the balance of payments. The architects of the new banking system ensured that the volume of rupiah was tied to the central bank's foreign exchange holdings. In theory, when foreign reserves fell, this would bring about an immediate contraction of the money supply, which would deflate the economy, encourage exports, and discourage imports. The aim was to restore the balance of payments.

The designers of the Bank of Indonesia Statutes, particularly Sjafruddin, anticipated that the management of reserves would play an important role in monetary policy. The Bank Act imposed a statutory requirement that the bank retain a minimum reserve of gold and foreign exchange against its note issue to the value of 20 percent of its advances (Article 16 of the Bank Act). Finance Minister Soemitro had criticized this old-fashioned reserve requirement. In fact, it was clear to observers at the time that the reserve requirement would be irrelevant or ineffectual in fulfilling its intended purpose (Higgins and Hollinger 1960:75).

Indonesian economist Ali Wardhana has explained why the Javasche Bank could not fully develop an independent policy for Indonesia even after the recognition of independence in 1949. A full-fledged central bank must have a mandate to create and contract credit, functioning as the ultimate source of money supply in a country. Such a bank can exert tight control on the country's need for money. The Javasche Bank did not have these powers. The bank could not control the funds of Dutch enterprises because their earnings from Indonesian exports went directly to the enterprises' headquarters in the Netherlands. In addition, these businesses also transferred all excess funds to the Netherlands. This meant that the money market for Indonesian funds was in the Netherlands. Ali Wardhana (1971:341) writes, '[I]n Indonesia [...] the financial and business world would fall back on the Netherlands' money market, thus reducing the activities of the Java Bank to a mere intermediary'.

In the years 1955-1958, the central bank acquired more powers through a number of government ordinances and Monetary Board decrees. In 1955 a government ordinance authorized the Bank of Indonesia to award licenses to banking institutions. In 1957 a Monetary Board Decree imposed a system of reserve requirements on banking institutions under the discretionary administration of the Bank of Indonesia. In 1958 the government removed the reserve requirement from the Statutes.

From the transfer of sovereignty until the late 1960s Indonesia experienced high inflation. From 1949 until the end of 1956, inflation was a persistent and serious problem, but it seemed possible to curb it. The growth of the money supply and the rise of prices resulted mainly from the government's cash deficit. The Javasche Bank, and later the Indonesian central bank, could not resist the pressure from the Indonesian government to create money and to lend it to the government (Charlesworth 1959:9). Table 1 shows index figures of the money supply.

In 1957 President Soekarno began introducing a series of radical changes to the Indonesian political system including the sidelining of parliament and the proclamation of Guided Democracy in 1958. The sudden nationalization of Dutch enterprises, banks, and estates in December 1957 was an attempt to wrest control of the Indonesian economy from Dutch hands. The move ushered in a period of political conflict and rampant inflation. Money and prices had already been increasing much more rapidly since early 1957. In the years 1961-1964 inflation got completely out of hand.

*Conclusion*

The Philippines and Indonesia show both similarities and contrasts with respect to monetary development in the 1950s. Both countries went through a political struggle to disengage their monetary systems from colonial control, while both the American and Dutch governments tried for several years to maintain some monetary sovereignty in their former colonies. After a number of years the Philippines and Indonesia succeeded in freeing their systems from this control. In both countries political leaders held sharply nationalistic views and were striving for economic nationalism, advocating various forms of 'managerial indigenism' (Anspach 1969:133). The buzzwords of that time were 'philippinization' and 'indonesianisasi'. Another shared feature was that both countries adopted a managed currency system in keeping with the prevailing economic wisdom. But here the similarities end.

The Philippines followed a tight money policy, domestically keeping inflation in check by strictly controlling the money supply and credit creation while internationally defending the value of the peso (until 1958) by main-

Table 1. Money supply index for the Philippines and Indonesia (M1)
1949-1957

|      | The Philippines | Indonesia |
|------|-----------------|-----------|
| 1949 | 100             | 100       |
| 1950 | 118.7           | 130.2     |
| 1951 | 112.1           | 152.2     |
| 1952 | 115.7           | 199.4     |
| 1953 | 118.2           | 226       |
| 1954 | 118.5           | 335.3     |
| 1955 | 129.1           | 368.5     |
| 1956 | 144.8           | 404.8     |
| 1957 | 154.4           | 571       |

Note: Money supply is the sum of currency in circulation (notes and coins) and demand deposits, excluding government and inter-bank deposits (technical term: $M_1$). For both countries the 1949 money supply is set at 100.

Sources: Palafox 1958:244 and *Report Bank Indonesia* 1958:53 (index figures computed).

taining a positive foreign exchange balance. The latter measure was achieved through a rigorous system of foreign exchange and import controls. The Philippines central bank governor withstood government pressure to loosen the reigns of money supply and credit creation. This monetary policy strongly contributed to the growth of a manufacturing (import substitution) sector in the economy, significantly changing the country's economic structure.

By contrast, Indonesia's rapidly growing money supply went hand-in-hand with high inflation, which by the mid 1960s had reached unmanageable proportions. The government made heavy demands on the central bank for cash to cover budget deficits. The central bank president was not able to effectively resist these demands and this led to a steadily growing money supply. Table 1, which shows the money supply index for both countries from 1949 to 1957, illustrates the differences between the Philippines and Indonesia.

This article argues that the divergent monetary and economic developments in the two countries are partly caused by differences in the design and organization of their central banks. The Philippine Central Bank was set up by experienced and competent civil servants who had the support of several economists from the US Federal Reserve System and the newly-established

IMF. These economists had broken with the liberal outlook of their prewar counterparts and had adopted views more in line with those of politically-oriented nationalists in the developing world. Manila's central bank was able to impose exchange and import controls and to maintain a relatively stable exchange rate for the Philippine peso throughout the 1950s. The central bank governor had the power to resist political pressure from the government and to formulate a relatively independent monetary policy.

By contrast, Indonesia was plagued by a lack of trained personnel. Dutch officials retained influence through the Javasche Bank and the Ministry of Finance of the young republic. Initially, the Indonesian central bank did not have the teeth to supervise the country's banking system or to impose controls. The central bank president was structurally too weak to stand up to the government and therefore could not implement an independent monetary policy.

Of course, not all the monetary and economic differences between the two countries can be attributed to the design and organization of their central banks. These features were important, but not decisive. Other factors had a greater impact. The Philippines still had a small central state apparatus with limited financial needs. Its president and his entourage respected the experts in the bank. The army, too, made modest demands even though it had to fight an armed communist rebellion in Central Luzon. In this political setting the central bank was able to stand its own ground.

For Indonesia the 1950s began in turmoil and ended in chaos. As a result of the independence struggle, the political mood was far more nationalistic. To ensure that it had mass support, the Indonesian government decided to ease the tax burden on the peasant population. As a result all revenue had to come from export taxes. The government strongly opposed cutting imports. Like President Soekarno, most of the country's other political leaders were uninterested in the nitty-gritty of economics. In the late 1950s and early 1960s the political scene was dominated by a contest for power and control over the course of the Indonesian revolution. This jostling between President Soekarno, the army and the communist party created a political atmosphere that was not conducive to economic development. In such a setting, the central bank was a paper tiger.

*References*

Abueva, Jose V.
1971             *Ramon Magsaysay; A political economy.* Manila: Solidaridad Publishing
                 House.

Ali Wardhana
1971            'The Indonesian banking system; The central bank', in: Bruce Glassburner (ed.), *The economy of Indonesia; Selected readings*, pp. 338-58. Ithaca, NY/London: Cornell University Press.
Anspach, Ralph
1969            'Indonesia', in: Frank H. Golay, Ralph Anspach, M. Ruth Pfanner and Eliezer B. Ayal, *Underdevelopment and economic nationalism in Southeast Asia*, pp. 111-201. Ithaca, NY: Cornell University Press.
Castro, Amado A.
1960            'Central banking in the Philippines', in: S. Gethyn Davies (ed.), *Central banking in South and East Asia*, pp. 171-82. Hong Kong: Hong Kong University Press.
Charlesworth, Harold Karr
1959            *A banking system in transition; The origin, concept and growth of the Indonesian banking system*. Djakarta: The New Nusantara Publishing Coy.
Cuaderno, Miguel
1949            *Central bank of the Philippines (A monograph)*. Manila: The Central Bank.
1952            'The Bell Trade Act and the Philippine economy', *Pacific Affairs* 25-4:323-33.
1960            *Problems of economic development; The Philippines. A case study*. Manila: n.n.
Doronilla, Amando
1992            *The state, economic transformation, and political change in the Philippines, 1946-1972*. Singapore: Oxford University Press.
Eck, D. van
1970            *Juridische aspecten van geld met name in het vroegere Nederlands-Indië*. Deventer: Kluwer. [PhD thesis, University of Leiden.]
Friedman, Milton
1962            *Capitalism and freedom*. Chicago: University of Chicago Press.
Glassburner, Bruce
1971            'Economic policy-making in Indonesia, 1950-1957', in: Bruce Glassburner (ed.), *The economy of Indonesia; Selected readings*, pp. 70-98, Ithaca, NY/London: Cornell University Press.
Golay, Frank
1997            *Face of empire; United States-Philippine relations, 1898-1946*. Quezon City: Ateneo de Manila Press.
Golay, Frank H., Ralph Anspach, M. Ruth Pfanner and Eliezer B. Ayal
1969            *Underdevelopment and economic nationalism in Southeast Asia*. Ithaca, NY/London: Cornell University Press.
Higgins, Benjamin
1957            'Development problems in the Philippines; A comparison with Indonesia', *Far Eastern Survey* 26-11:161-9.
Higgins, Benjamin H. and William C. Hollinger
1960            'Central banking in Indonesia', in: S. Getyn Davies (ed.), *Central banking in South and East Asia*, pp. 53-77. Hong Kong: Hong Kong University Press.

Irvine, Reed J.
1953        'New central banking legislation in Indonesia', *Far Eastern Survey* 22-11:19-52.
Jenkins, Shirley
1954        *American economic policy toward the Philippines*. With an introduction by Claude A. Buss. Stanford, CA: Stanford University Press.
Lichauco, Alejandro
1988        *Nationalist economics; History, theory and practice*. Quezon City: Institute for Rural Industrialization, Inc.
Lindblad, J. Thomas
2004        'Van Javasche bank naar Bank Indonesia; Voorbeelden uit de praktijk van *Indonesianisasi*', *Tijdschrift voor Sociale en Economische Geschiedenis* 1-1:28-46.
Palafox, Liria A.
1958        'Movements of money supply and consumer prices in the Philippines from 1949 to 1957', *Economic Research Journal* 5:243-7.
*Report Bank Indonesia*
1958        *Report of the governor of Bank Indonesia for the financial year 1957-58*. Djakarta: Bank Indonesia.
*Report Java Bank*
1953        *Report of the President of the Java Bank (de Javasche Bank) and the board of directors for the 124th financial year 1951-1952*. Batavia: The Java Bank.
Saubari, Moh.
1987        'Reflections on economic policy making: 1945-51', *Bulletin of Indonesian Economic Studies* 23-2:118-21.
Scheffer, C.F.
1951a       'Kommentaar; theorie en praktijk rond de controverse Teunissen-Soemitro', *Madjalah Dunia Ekonomi* 3 December.
1951b       *Het bankwezen in Indonesië, sedert het uitbreken van de Tweede Wereldoorlog*. 's-Hertogenbosch: Zuid-Nederlandsche Drukkerij.
1953        *Enige aspecten van de verhouding tussen de staat en het algemene bankwezen*. Djakarta: Noordhoff-Kolff. [Inaugural speech Universitas Indonesia, Djakarta.]
Sjafruddin Prawiranegara
1987        'Recollections of my career', *Bulletin of Indonesian Economic Studies* 23-3:100-8.
Soemitro Djojohadikoesoemo
1943        *Het volkscredietwezen in de depressie*. Haarlem: Bohn.
1951        *Monetair evenwicht, Centrale Bank en economische constellatie*. Djakarta: Sekretariat Fakultet Ekonomi Djakarta.
1953        'The central bank of Indonesia', *Ekonomi dan Keuangan Indonesia* 6-2/3:94-8.
1986        'Recollections of my career', *Bulletin of Indonesian Economic Studies* 23-3:27-39.
Teunissen, H.
1951        *Taak en werkkring van de Javasche Bank versus Dr. Sumitro Djojohadikusumo: Monetair evenwicht, Centrale Bank en economische constellatie*. [Jakarta]: Sekretariat Fakultet Ekonomi Djakarta.

Triffin, Robert
1946        *Monetary and banking reform in Paraguay.* Washington: Board of Governors of the Federal Reserve System.
1947        'National central banking and the international economy', in: Lloyd A. Metzler, Robert Triffin and Gottfried Haberler (eds), *International monetary policies*, pp. 46-81. Washington: Board of Governors of the Federal Reserve System.

*Verslag Javasche Bank*
1951        *Verslag van de President van de Javasche Bank en van de Raad van Commissarissen over het 122e boekjaar 1949-1950.* Djakarta: Kolff.

KARL HACK

# Decolonization and violence in Southeast Asia
## Crises of identity and authority

How far did Southeast Asia's experience of colonialism and decolonization contribute to severe postcolonial problems, notably: high levels of violence and endemic crises of authority? There can be no denying that colonialism left plural societies in countries such as Malaysia and Singapore, and that countries such as Indonesia and the Philippines attempted to bolt together very different regions and groups of people. These divisions were to breed violence as far apart as Myanmar and New Guinea, and Aceh and Mindanao. Much of Southeast Asia also experienced an intense period of Japanese era and occupation in the years just before independence. The Japanese conquest of 1941 to 1945 propagandized and mobilized people, promoted quasi-militaristic values, and left in its wake large groups, some with military training or even weapons. In many cases the use of force, or threat of force, also expedited decolonization, further legitimizing the use of violence in resolving disputes over national authority and identity.

It is easy to establish that there were traumas and violent experiences in colonialism and in decolonization. But demonstrating how these fed through to the postcolonial period is difficult in the extreme. Was the legacy a region-wide one of visceral divisions that demanded, and still demand, either fissure or authoritarian government? Are the successor states, as governments as varied as Singapore and Myanmar claim, young, fragile creations where authority remains fragile even after five decades or more?

This chapter reflects on a number of approaches to explaining the persistence of crises and their links to the colonial and decolonizing eras. These include historical and political science modes of analysis. Rather than arguing for one approach or the other, it will suggest we take some of the most potent tools of historical and political science approaches and combine them by conceptualizing the problem as one of identity management. A major part of the challenge of decolonization was precisely that colonial societies had many layers of identity – peasant, class, ethnic, religious, regional – that were not in the first place 'national', and often resisted subjection to the leadership of postcolonial as well as colonial elites.

Some regional states never really overcame the legacies of fractured iden-

tities, of colonization, and of Japanese occupation, continuing to rely on high
levels of coercion to enforce state authority, as in New Order Indonesia and
in Burma/Myanmar. But the chapter is not unremittingly negative. Looking
at Malaysia and Singapore as a case study will show how two states have
managed to dampen violence and achieve a degree of cohesion despite the
legacies of colonialism, Japanese occupation, and decolonization. It argues
that to fully understand identity management we also need to accept – as
Malaysia and Singapore do implicitly in their policy, though not explicitly in
their propaganda – that most Southeast Asian states originated not so much
as nation-states, but rather as *nations-states*. In each case an overarching
supranationalism has been in a constantly shifting relationship with more
localized or particularistic identities.

### *In search of Southeast Asian patterns; peasant wars*

The first problem to confront anyone attempting to analyse Southeast Asia
as an area is what can so diverse a group of territories have in common?
The most obvious answer when it comes to crises of authority is that almost
all territories have experienced significant peasant wars and peasant conflicts. This is a common-sense starting point since, with the exception of
Singapore, all Southeast Asian countries have consisted mainly of peasants.
It is therefore scarcely surprising that peasant revolts and village wars have
been geographically wide-ranging across time and space: these have constituted a huge if not the major challenge to central authority for much of the
twentieth century. There has been everyday resistance to tax and landlord
demands in most of the countries. In particular, the 1920s and 1930s were
characterized by a move towards modern styles of peasant organization.
This included communist organization in Indochina, peasant unions in the
Philippines, and Burmese peasant mobilization in 10,000-plus village-level,
nationalist-linked *wun-tha-nu* or village associations. The form varied, but
the move away from the merely localized, or local religious leader-led reac-
tive and millenarian revolts, and towards modern organization was clear.
There was a continuous thread, with prewar peasant-based organizations
becoming radicalized, armed, and extended during anti-Japanese wartime
organization. This pattern led to severe insurgency in Indochina (1945-1954),
the Philippines (1948-1954 and post-1960s), Malaya (1948-1960) and Burma
(from 1948 onwards) (Tandrup 1995).
    Postwar developments in Indochina, Malaya, and the Philippines also
have similarities rooted in these rural-based conflicts. In each case a leftist
movement – the Indochina Communist Party and Malayan Communist Party,
and the peasant unions and later the armed Hukbalahap in the Philippines –

claimed leadership before and during the Pacific War. Each fought the Japanese during the occupation, and then fought back after the war against state attempts to reimpose power using people who had collaborated with the Japanese. In each case the postwar fight-back defended peasants' models of a 'moral economy'. Hence, in the Philippines the government supported land-lords returning from the cities or exile abroad to demand back rents, or higher rents than peasants now thought fair. Having enforced 'just rents' during the Japanese period, peasant leaders had no intention of being muscled aside. The British Military Administration of 1946-1948 in Malaya (dubbed the Black Market Administration) likewise used Malay police, fresh from wartime collaboration, to squeeze Chinese squatters off jungle fringe land. Again, having enforced a rough social justice by taking land to farm, squat-ters who had supported anti-Japanese guerrillas during the Pacific War were reluctant to go quietly. Not surprisingly a spiral of violence followed, with Tim Harper (1999) claiming that the Malayan Communist Party (MCP) was virtually forced by this to prepare an insurrection in 1948. In Vietnam mean-while, the Indochina Communist Party – under the guise of the Viet Minh united front – drew on wartime experience, and its role in freeing food sup-plies and declaring a Republic in September 1945 to fight the postwar French attempt to regain control of the administration. Again, the attempted reimpo-sition of urban rule, in the form of French colonialism, on peasants featured the use of wartime collaborators with the Japanese, in the form of Vichyite French administrators whose nominal independence the Japanese had only cast aside in March 1945 (Hack 2001; Kerkvliet 1977). The Huk revolt, the Malayan Emergency, and the Indochina Wars all represented continuations of peasant conflict across the colonial, decolonizing, and postindependence periods.

Peasant wars and tensions between central state and rural areas loomed large but with limitations. Although one movement, communist, claimed to speak for all peasant conflicts, only in Indochina did it succeed in seizing power. Elsewhere, villagers and urban youth – unleashed by the Japanese in 1942-1945 – could choose between different 'imagined decolonizations'. In arming and training militias across the region, the Japanese gave varied groups the power to express themselves violently. Thus, in Indonesia young Muslims were as likely to end up in Islamic and largely independent *lasykar* or armed groups as in broader Republican units. In such circumstances, the secular nationalists could not claim to be the sole legitimate leaders of peasants.[1] In Burma, hilltribes remained loyal to the British, in contrast to the young Burman *thakins*: radical student nationalists who rejected mere internal self-government in the 1930s. From 1942 until March 1945 the latter

---

[1]    For the latest summary of these events, see Abu Talib Ahmad 2006.

worked with the Japanese, who helped them raise a Burmese National Army (Taylor 2006:195-210).

*Ethnic, regional, and religious wars*

The attitude of Burmese hilltribes points to the most prevalent challenge to postwar states: ethnic and regional revolt. Ethnic and religious divides have afflicted the majority of the region's postindependence states, notably in ongoing tensions between Christians and Muslims in Indonesia's Sulawesi and Maluku, in Mindanao and Sulu in the southern Philippines, and in Burma/Myanmar's perennial struggle between core and periphery, plain and hill (Christie 1996; Brown 1994:112-57). Since regional and ethnic identities have played so large a part in successive crises, it is important to be clear about their nature. Do they reflect many 'nations': distinct groups with the desire if not right to self-determination?

The question arises because regional identities sometimes seem to accommodate state-level identities and sometimes to resist them. Take the case of Aceh. Is Acehnese nationalism – in as much as it is more than mere parochialism – a phenomenon with deep roots in precolonial times, something manipulated into being by local elites, or are its more separatist inclinations a more recent response to post-1945 Indonesian policy? Acehnese have at times passionately supported 'Republican' visions of Indonesia. They supported the Republic in its 1945-1949 struggle for independence, and Acehnese resistance to Dutch rule of 1873-1903, 1941, and 1945-1949 became integrated into a Republican story of historic 'Indonesian' nationalism. Yet a few years after Indonesian independence Aceh was in revolt. How can this be (Christie 1996:chapter 7)? Aceh all along had the elements necessary to constitute an Acehnese nation. It had a vividly remembered history as an Islamic sultanate, which had acted as a bridge between the Arabic and Malay worlds, and a tradition as a seventeenth to eighteenth-century centre of Malay learning. It was still in the nineteenth century an independent sultanate. But the tidying instinct of nineteenth-century imperialism had doomed Aceh. An 1824 Anglo-Dutch understanding prevented the Dutch from interfering with Aceh. An 1871 Treaty permanently removed this restriction. The Dutch invasion of 1873 was followed by three decades of murderous war, first led by the sultan, and later by religious leaders. 'Peace' was punctuated by another revolt in the 1920s, then by the rise of Persatuan Ulama Seluruh Aceh (PUSA, Islamic Union of Scholars) in the 1930s. In 1941 PUSA-influenced Acehnese threw out the Dutch before the Japanese arrived. In 1945 to 1946 they again liberated themselves from Dutch-supported aristocrats.

There was a clear Acehnese identity: nationalism. But it was not a zero sum game between Acehnese or Indonesian nationalism. In the 1940s each was seen as buttressing the other, and in 1945-1949 the Acehnese had no problem supporting the overall Republican struggle, as opposed to Dutch proposals for a federal Indonesia.

This discussion of Aceh leads to an important point about 'nationalism' in Southeast Asian states: it needs to be conceived of as existing at different levels. First, nationalism consisted of those communities – often part-based on an 'ethnic' identity – with a clear geographic concentration. These communities hoped for some level of local control, desired the preservation of their identity, and also sought a degree of influence in shaping a shared future for the overall state and 'supra-nation': the latter seen as something sitting above and binding the more local identities. Second-level nationalism was thus what we might call supranationalism. This emerged to link the inhabitants of an entire colonial territory, including inhabitants of more localized 'nations' or communities.

This distinction between local identity and nation, and state-level supranationalism, does not imply a simple opposition between ethnic and imagined, organic and artificial, or natural and official communities. Both levels of nationalism could use the full range of tools, such as myths of ethnic consanguinity, language, shared memory, symbols, and more. Both could also use negative nationalism – by fixing on a threat, such as the colonial ruler, or powerful foreigners or immigrant settlers, or even globalization or secularism.

Seen in the above terms, the relationship between Aceh and Indonesia was not merely between regionalism and nationalism, or local elites seeking advantage and centralizing elites, but between two levels of nationalism. The Acehnese were amongst the most avid early Republicans because Indonesian supranationalism then seemed the most viable route for a potent anti-Dutch identity. But just because they bought into the anticolonial, negative vision and the accompanying idea of Indonesian unity does not mean they shared an 'imagined decolonization' or image of what the postcolonial state would be. It seems that for many Acehnese and their *ulama* or religious leaders, their 'imagined decolonization' envisaged a higher level of local autonomy, and a more distinctly Islamic state than Republican elites were going to allow.

Looked at this way, we avoid the danger of a pathological state-centred view, that local 'nationalism' is not authentic, but merely a form of local protest at inefficiencies in the state, such as inadequate development, overcentralization, unjust distribution of resources, or oppressive security action. We can also see that subsequent Acehnese actions were an attempt to realign the relationship between a regional, primary level nationalism and state supranationalism so as to conform to their imagined state of decolonization.

At first, in 1949, integration into supranationalism and its politics seemed possible, through the likes of reformist Islamic parties such as the Muhammadiyah-influenced Masjumi. Masjumi was open to influence by local Islamic figures from Aceh. But out of disappointment with Masjumi's declining influence and with the secular tone of the state Aceh joined the Darul Islam (House of Islam) revolt in 1953 as a way of pressurizing the central state to take more notice of Acehnese demands and needs. Though the wider Darul Islam revolt achieved little, it did achieve something for Aceh. The Acehnese part of the revolt ended with the restoration of special status as a region in 1960, and with allowing elements of Islamic law from 1962. These were concessions to Acehnese nationalism in order to realign it with Indonesian supranationalism.

In the 1960s to 1970s Suharto's New Order then tried to build a class of local collaborators in Aceh – technocratic figures committed to development – who would link region to centre by means of developmental ideology, and through the Suharto-controlled Golkar party. The *ulama* could also gravitate towards the Partai Persatuan Pembangunan (PPP, or United Development Party), an amalgamation of Islamic parties brokered by the regime. It took anger over the siphoning of most liquefied natural gas and petroleum profits from the 1970s, frustration at the low level of development locally, and increasing realization that Acehnese could exert little influence through Golkar or PPP to help reignite regionalism by 1976. It took army counteraction – including destroying villages thought to support GAM (Gerakan Aceh Merdeka – the Free Aceh Movement) – to create widespread sympathy for GAM's idea that Acehnese nationalism might be incompatible with Indonesian supranationalism.

By the dawn of the twenty-first century these repeated failures to ensure local interests could exercise sufficient influence on both local and central policy had rendered Acehnese nationalism more separatist in sentiment than ever. Only the tsunami of 26 December 2004 convinced both sides that peace was vital if the level of international aid necessary to rebuild the region was to be forthcoming. Hence, the October 2005 agreement by which GAM accepted reintegration and a decommissioning of weapons, in return for 'special autonomy', increased percentages of oil and gas revenues, and a rundown of Indonesian troops to normal garrison levels. The increases in local autonomy and control of resources as arranged by the 1999 and 2005 autonomy laws could yet reconcile Acehnese nationalism with a looser Indonesian supranationalism (Reid 2005:346-50).

*Colonialism, decolonization and the continuity of violence*

The presence of different levels of nationalism, or identities, is not enough in itself to explain the level of violence used in Southeast Asian crises of authority. This raises the question: did the colonial state in some way entrench the use of violence for political means, or entrench groups and attitudes likely to encourage such violence?

The first place to look is at the discourses of colonial states themselves. These include narratives of a centralizing state imposing order over chaos, and over societies couched in Machiavellian terms as naturally disordered and underdeveloped. These include narratives of Dutch *rust en orde* and Ethical Policy, of British *Pax Britannica*, and of French or Portuguese colonialism, but also of Indonesian New Order and Myanmar and Singapore government claims to be protecting society from its own tendency to dissolve into mutually warring primordial groups. The colonial state variously claims that its mission is 'civilizing', peacemaking, framework-providing, assimilatory, or developmental.[2]

Opposed to this are the various anticolonial, radical, and minority claims that it was the colonial state that divided groups against each other and suffused violence throughout society. We might characterize this as a division between opposing claims that colonialism had a 'civilizing', or alternatively a fracturing, impact on their territories.[3]

The civilizing claim was commonplace for colonial era administrators and historians. Take scholar-administrator Frank Swettenham, whose career spanned from before 1874 to being governor of the Straits Settlements (1901-1904). For him, Britain imposed a *pax*, paving the way for development, over Malay states where the sultans held a man's life cheap, piracy was rife, and running *amok* was a way of avenging the inherent injustice of society (Gullick 1987:238-57). Imperialism equalled peace, and peace allowed British-driven development. It meant imposing an 'iron framework', binding together inherently plural societies – of hilltribes, Burmans, and Indians in Burma; of Malays and Chinese workers invited in Malaya; and of myriads of linguistic and *adat* groups in Indonesia. In Burma, Malaya and Indonesia the colonial powers attempted to raise minorities and outsiders – Indians and hilltribes in Burma, Indians as police and military in Malaya, and Ambonese to leaven Javanese colonial troops in Indonesia – to ensure this 'framework' remained reliable (Hack and Rettig 2006:1-72).

---

[2]    Vickers 2005:9-32; for Dutch expansion as driven by ideas of bureaucratization and 'good government', see Locher-Scholten 1994:91-112.
[3]    The classics are Furnivall 1939, 1948. He argued colonial policy's rapid development and immigration produced 'plural societies' where people met in market but did not mingle.

This version sees fast economic and glacial social development under European tutelage disrupted by the Pacific War that produced chaos and unrealistic expectations. It implies that postindependence violence was the consequence of war, and of the premature throwing off of the colonial framework. The adoption of liberal democracy by societies not yet ready for it, and of central and unitary authority over fractured territories, provoked regional rebellion. Hence, the Dutch attempt to construct a Federation of Indonesia in 1945 to 1949 appears as sincere and the Indonesian reneging on the agreed federal framework for a Republic in 1950 as disastrous (the 1949 agreement was for an Indonesian Republic inside a federal United States of Indonesia).

Some postindependence states have continued the imperialist discourse, emphasizing the need to keep diverse societies bolted together by demonstrations of force and a strong unifying central state. Hence Indonesian generals and officials sometimes echoed colonial-era claims about the uncivilized, disordered nature of subjects. The Myanmar army's 'iron framework' is supposedly as vital now as British *pax* or Dutch *rust en orde* was then.[4]

On the other hand, it is possible to argue that pervasively divisive and violent colonialism was the problem. This goes beyond arguing that colonial rulers divide in order to rule, and foster 'plural societies'. Lacking the legitimacy accorded to indigenous regimes, the colonial state supposedly required displays of violence. In this mode, we could also argue that the colonial state self-consciously kept local political organization premodern, while encouraging, almost ossifying, regionalism and *adat* differences, and creating or importing 'martial races', and what the imperialists felt were 'capitalist races', notably Chinese and Indians. For instance, the Dutch encouraged the use of Acehnese vernacular in schools in the 1930s precisely as they were encouraging local *adat* (customs) and identity elsewhere. This was in part the result of an academic trend towards taking cultural identities seriously, but it was also in convenient contrast to growing pan-Indonesian nationalism.

Imperial states' combination of informal and indirect rule – giving greater freedom to outlying areas and enlisting local toughs and robber bandits – also entrenched violence. Hence, Britain's recruitment of Burmese hilltribes provided excellent models and means of violence.[5] In Burma, faced with growing Buddhist and nationalist organization, the colonial state tolerated the 1930s formation of volunteer corps, such as conservative, trusted politician U Maung Gyi's Ye Tat or All Burma Volunteers.[6]

---

[4]   See Frey 2003:93 for the 'orientalizing' of Indonesians by military actors, such as supreme commander General S.H. Spoor, and Colombijn and Lindblad 2002:8-9, for a rejection of essentialist approaches. For the argument that restricting 'colonial' analysis to Western-Asian relations overlooks their continuation, see Hack 2003:122-6 and vii-xiv.

[5]   The British story is in Hack 2001:107-65, 2006:239-65.

[6]   Taylor 2006. *Letyon* in Burmese is the arm below the elbow.

A related explanation, therefore, does not emphasize the strong state but to the contrary a thin state. Henk Schulte Nordholt (2002) suggests that the myriad ways in which the Netherlands Indies practiced violence – from colonial conquest and labour discipline, through police action, to the alliances of rural headmen with *jago* (a local fighter or underworld figure) – entrenched violence in the rural world. The colonial state as a weak or thin state left a lethal legacy by its whole panoply of indirect rule methods. Southeast Asian historiography might be thought to be mirroring a prior trend in South Asian historiography, where academics turned away from the idea of a strong Raj, seeing instead a surface-thin state that coexisted with, co-opted or left scarcely-touched local power groups.[7]

There is, however, a danger in accepting that a thin state entrenched local level power groups and violence. This is the danger of underplaying times of peace and of underplaying changes over time. Take British relationships with *panglima* (bandit captains) in the outer reaches of the Malay States. Cheah Boon Keng has traced how these were prevalent in frontier zones (ecological and national) of the Malay States between 1874 and 1914, when *panglima* had relationships with local *penghulu* (village heads), or were appointed *penghulu* themselves. Some posed as 'Robin Hood' types, but many were feared bandits or enforcers for local notables. Their prevalence fell from the late 1920s as police expanded into outlying areas. This reflects a general pattern of the British imperial state as it became more entrenched, becoming more direct and bureaucratic (Cheah Boon Kheng 1988; Trocki 1990). We also need to ask questions about the tangent of change in Indonesia in the 1930s. Were relationships between *jago* and others and the state fixed or declining as state-building gathered steam? Just how thin the colonial state was, where, and at what points, remains open to debate.

On the other hand, there clearly were elements in Indonesia that threatened any attempt at a centralistic imposition of order. One of these was the persistence of *jago*. Another was Islamic boarding schools (*pesantren*), with their dormitories, charismatic leaders, and sometimes businesses too. These formed semi-autonomous centres, and potential sources for crises of authority, from the seventeenth century to their production of modern-day radicals. Thus, colonialism did tolerate, and sometimes encourage, these potential repertoires and reservoirs of violence.

Hence various scholars have suggested that postcolonial patterns of violence are partly due to a continuous presence of militias and informal groups, not just from the Japanese period, but across colonial Japanese occupation, and postcolonial times. For scholars such as Robinson dealing with East Timor,

---

[7]   In the case of Harper 1999, a book arguing for the primacy of social forces in Malaya emerged from a thesis supervised by Christopher Bayly, a South Asianist of the 'weak Raj' mould.

Elsbeth Locher-Scholten with colonial era police, and Budi Agustono dealing with Sumatran labour, precolonial and colonial era repertoires of violence have persisted (Robinson 2006; Locher-Scholten 2002; Budi Agustono 2002). William H. Frederick has talked of Indonesia's decolonization process further legitimating violence through the various, partly autonomous Republican militias and their 1945-1949 insurgency against the Dutch. Colombijn and Lindblad talk of violence being institutionalized over time in Indonesia, and legitimized as a 'good thing' in certain circumstances (Frederick 2002; Colombijn and Lindblad 2002:15-6; Cribb 2002). Robinson, using the language of the political scientist, talks of violent practices being sustained or added to during colonial times, leading to 'repertoires' of violence: bankable sometimes by rebels and sometimes by regimes (2002, 2006). Such arguments were further reinforced by the post-1998 upsurge of violence in Indonesia after Suharto's fall. But in a way they represented an inversion of a much older, colonial argument that Southeast Asian societies were naturally disordered.

There is, however, still a problem. Repertoires of violence and reservoirs of violence could be quiescent, potential rather than active sources of conflict, across times of relative normality and of crisis. They pattern crises when these arise. But can they be said to create crises? In other words, how can we bridge culturally and historically-transmitted patterns on the one hand, and sporadic events and politics on the other? How can we bridge the models of the political scientist and the untamed events of the historian?

Geoffrey Robinson has suggested one way of doing this. He sees repertoires (and we might add to this, reservoirs) of violence providing fuel cells, whose latent powers are activated by political leaders. Thus, he argues that specific militias were the products of Indonesian army tactics to use them in the 1975-1999 occupation of East Timor. The TNI has a long history of using militias and informal groups, stretching from the 1965 massacre of communists to contemporary Aceh. But Robinson also argues that militias' availability and modes of behaviour followed local traditions reaching back to the practice of local chiefs in the seventeenth and eighteenth centuries of levying local men, and their style of combat: with long hair, a medley of modern and traditional weapons, and demonstrative violence. The Portuguese in Timor had continued to use these, stipulating 30 days of military service a year. Some chiefs maintained personal militias up to 1975 (Robinson 2006:269-301). Like the *lasykar* or informal militia groups of the Indonesian revolution, these provided remembered 'repertoires of violence', which various players – Portuguese, Indonesian, and even Fretilin insurgents – could call upon.[8] Robinson thus joins the approaches of the historian and the political scientist,

---

[8]   Singh 1996, in giving a rather pro-Indonesian view of events, does nevertheless raise the question of how far Fretilin, too, might be seen in this light.

the latent cultural models available, and the specific motives that call them into action.

The political scientist thus simplifies, providing heuristic models such as 'repertoires of action'.[9] Another political-science model invoked to explain entrenched violence in Southeast Asian politics is that of neopatrimonialism. This models many Southeast Asian polities as working on the basis of vertical linkages from villager to local elite, and from local elites to central elites. These vertical linkages, which seek to secure patronage to distribute to clients, characterize political parties. The Philippines is usually seen as a strong example of such patrimonial politics persisting from colonial to postcolonial times. Landé and McCoy thus see postcolonial Philippine political parties as empty vessels, coalitions of such vertically linked groups.[10] Hence, individuals can freely switch parties or form new ones. The implication is that such patrimonial systems are inherently flawed. Given that governments command loyalty not because of the legitimacy of a process – of elections and government, or because of party programmes – but due to rewards, groups feel free to turn to nonconstitutional means when excluded from patronage. Here, it is not so much 'reservoirs of violence' as the whole basis of political organization (notably in pre-1998 Indonesia and the Philippines) that is seen as unstable.[11]

So we have two political science models that help explain Southeast Asia's postindependence condition, suggesting underlying reasons for a continuity of violence across colonial, decolonizing, and postcolonial periods. Neopatrimonialism suggests that patronage continued to be the critical factor across periods – for instance, Philippine independence leaving the same elites and patronage linkages in place. Hence, politics have not replaced violence, but just remained another tool for obtaining patronage. Robinson's approach, meanwhile, marries both the political scientists' preference for models and the historians for contextualization by showing the potential for violence in historical patterns, in repertoires of violence, but also its contingency, based on political manoeuvrings. Both approaches suggest ingrained potential for political violence across our period of time. But there is a roadblock to concluding from this that such political-science models can easily explain the persistence of crises and violence across periods. That impediment is the Japanese occupation, a period so dramatic as to raise the question whether

[9]    Steinberg 1994:3-8 is a good example.
[10]   Landé 1965; McCoy 1981. These ideas are discussed as a form of orientalism and imperial knowledge in Ileto 1999.
[11]   Brown offers other models as well, for example, the ethnocratic state in Burma, which allows its apparatus – army, civil service, enforced curricula – to increasingly favour one ethnic or linguistic group, and at the same time tries to increase interference in areas previously experiencing more autonomy. See Brown 1994:33-65.

it, rather than continuities from the colonial era, played the bigger part in preshaping the terrain for postcolonial politics and violence.

## The Japanese occupation

Was the Japanese occupation of 1942 to 1945 just another cumulative step in building tensions, conflicts and repertoires and reservoirs of violence? Did it do little more than extrapolate colonial-era entrenchment of social divisions and patterns of violence, notably by fostering militias? Or was it something more, throwing decolonization off its gradualist path and catapulting under-developed supranationalisms such as the 'Indonesian' into premature power?

It could be argued that nothing qualitative changed, that colonialisms – Western and Japanese – all tolerated or raised local groups with coercive power – from village strongmen to Ambonese with military traditions – but without entrenching the legitimacy of processes for reconciling local differences. Local assemblies tended to be blunted by the slow devolution of power, and tainted by the aura of colonial and later pro-Japanese 'collaboration'. The Japanese, with their militias such as the volunteer PETA forces (37,000 strong for Java and Bali alone), and auxiliaries such as the *heiho*, and Malaya's and Sumatra's *giyugun* (volunteer army) or *giyutai* (volunteer corps) extrapolated existing tendencies. Hence, the Japanese occupation represented acceleration rather than a qualitative shift.[12]

That said, there is still a case for seeing the Japanese period as the starkest example of a historically significant external shock, other notable shocks being the 1930s depression and the 1997 Asian economic crisis. By this I mean an event or series of events that reshapes history, creating new organizations, forces, and possibilities, and destroying some older forces and patterns. To what extent was the Japanese occupation a destructive and creative force? At the least, it involved dramatic changes. There was the crushing defeat of Western forces in 1941 to 1942. Then there was the Japanese emphasis on *seishin*, on martial spirit and discipline overcoming all odds. Finally, there was the impact of the interregnum, the period between Japanese surrender and the arrival of British Southeast Asia Command (SEAC) in September 1945. Throughout Southeast Asia, that power vacuum allowed *pemuda* (youth) and nationalists to arm and entrench themselves. In Indonesia and Indochina it actually saw new, independent governments declared.

---

[12]   PETA is the acronym of Tentara Pembela Tanah Air (Defence Army of the Homeland). The Malayan *giyugun* was around 2,000 in three battalions. The 5,000 odd *giyutai* were more like a supra-police unit. Lebra 1977:116-19; Reid 1979; Abu Talib 2006. Other classics include McCoy 1980.

We must turn to literature to grasp the impact of this period. When telling of the events in Surabaya in October to November 1945, Idroes's story ('Surabaja') relates that, in response to the tumult of war, to recently released Eurasian internees trying to raise the Dutch flag on the Oranje Hotel, and to British attempts to restore 'order' by returning Dutch administrators, Indonesian victories against British Indian troops left them 'intoxicated'. The Republican *pemuda* 'fell in love with carbines and revolvers as if they were beautiful girls: they caressed them, kissed them' (Idroes 1968). British tanks could force physical retreat, just as Dutch organization could conquer towns in the 'police actions' of 1947 and 1948 to 1949, but the respect for armed violence unleashed in 1942-1945 could not be tamed. The innumerable militia and local 'boss'-led gangs, whether of Republican youth, tough *jago* linked to the underworld, or Muslims in Hizbullah – whether in Surabaya or Rangoon, or on the forest fringes of Malaya – and whether they wanted a secular-free Indonesia or some local or Islamic regime, remained vital forces into the 1950s, and powerful memories afterwards. In the context of prewar foot-dragging by colonial authorities, and the example of Japanese military prowess, decolonization could be conceptualized as the violence necessary to remove oppression. In such circumstances, violence in the pursuit of 'national' salvation was legitimized (Frederick 2002; Idroes 1946, 1968).

The Japanese occupation had an even more transforming effect on Burma. There had been a vigorous village association movement from the 1920s, together with strikes, antitax movements and occasional revolts, notably the peasant Saya San revolt in 1930. The British relied on police and prisons, rather than legitimacy, to suppress protests and strikes. But up to 1941 large-scale violence was not a sustainable option for Burmese nationalists (Taylor 2006:198). Instead, the main split in Burma (as in then Netherlands Indies) was between parties that cooperated in the Legislative Assembly – separated from India and enjoying partial self-government by 1937 – and those not cooperating. Then came Japan's rise. The thirty Yebaw (Comrades), of the noncooperating Thakin nationalist group escaped British pressure for Japan. There and in Hainan and Taiwan the Comrades helped train a Burmese Independence Army. Numbers swelled as Japan surged through Burma from January 1942. In early 1945 it became the Burma Army, which switched sides to the British in May 1945. Under the leadership of the Anti-Fascist People's Freedom League (AFPFL) its veterans then helped pressure Britain to grant independence by January 1948.[13]

---

[13]    Violence in Burma afterwards was thus fuelled not so much by *jago* and prewar legitimating of violence in politics, as by two divisions: between mainly Burman wartime BIA/BNA forces and the national army they later fed into, at least at leadership and political level, and the hill-tribes who were the prewar majority in the Burma Army and Field Force; and between the communist components of the BNA (even Aung San having had communist sympathies) and the noncommunists.

In both Indonesia and Burma these events, with mobilization reaching down into the village, showed it was (in the words of a Malay saying) time for 'the frog to come out of the coconut shell'. Villagers and town dwellers were forced to opt for what sort of perpetrators of violence and disturbance they should align with (Hack 2001:46). Once mobilized, how could these people – notably if mobilized in semi-autonomous groups – *laskyar*, Hizbullah, along interest and identity lines – be persuaded to put down their weapons and give to the state a measure of forbearance?

In summary, the Japanese occupation acted on the plural societies, or nascent nations-states created by late colonialism, in two main ways. First, it contributed to preexisting fissures, with communications between different areas reduced, and militias both Japanese-raised and anti-Japanese strongly linked to local areas or particular communities. Secondly, it led to the accelerated, if not premature, birth of these 'nations-states'. By premature we mean their negative anticolonial glue was strong, but their capacity to mediate between supranationalism and more localized nationalisms was underdeveloped. Only where decolonization was relatively peaceful (Malaysia) or a very long struggle unified groups more strongly (northern Vietnam) might this problem be alleviated. But where the war unleashed relatively rapid or violent decolonization, as in Indonesia and Burma, the results were dangerous. As distance from independence weakened the negative glue, states such as Indonesia struggled. In this way, the Japanese occupation provides not so much a divide but a pivot between the colonial and postcolonial parts of our longer period of study, adding to colonial repertoires and reservoirs of violence, and accelerating the birth of nations-states with underdeveloped legitimacy and inadequate apparatus for conflict resolution.

Clive Christie has further developed this case for a link between nationalism, radicalization in the war, and later problems. His *A modern history of Southeast Asia* (1996) argues that common experience of prewar anticolonialism, and accelerated and violent decolonization from Japan's invasion onwards, created a common regional dynamic. This resulted in the definition of nationalisms – what we have termed supranationalisms – broad enough to support the newly intensified decolonizing struggles, but not flexible enough to satisfy all groups. Disappointments were inevitable given the way colonial states had shackled together different peoples. To make matters worse, key elites often viewed proposals for dividing the colonial state, or for significant federalism – as a continuation of colonial divide and rule tactics.

In general, colonial states kept their territorial integrity, only a few breaking up in the process of decolonization (notably including Indochina and India), but given most Southeast Asian colonial states contained distinct, numerous minorities, it was inevitable that still-evolving supranationalisms would create losers. Some Muslims were disappointed that the Indonesian

Republic's ideology from 1945 – *Pancasila* or five principles – named belief in one god rather than Islam as one of the five pillars of national ideology. These losers, especially people in areas peripheral to the core state, such as Aceh, Maluku, Mindanao, Southern Thailand, and the Burmese hills, frequently turned to revolt. Meanwhile, those Muslims who wanted a more Islamic state in Indonesia began a Darul Islam (House of Islam) revolt in West Java in 1948, with Aceh joining in 1953. These revolts were suppressed by military action, but their causes were not removed. In areas such as the Burmese hills, revolts periodically flashed back into life.

Christie also highlights the forces arrayed against the break-up of the postindependence states. Quite apart from the natural propensity of states to support the territorial integrity of other states, the Cold War, especially after the Korean War started in 1950, caused Western and Southeast Asian governments to rally together for state integrity and against separatism. From the late 1950s there was little sympathy for anything that might weaken central authority, and so make it easier prey for communism. The fall of Cambodia, Laos, and southern Vietnam to communism in mid 1975 redoubled this defensiveness about territorial integrity. Southeast Asian states' resort to security and developmental nationalism thus enjoyed sustained Western sympathy. It took the end of the Cold War and of the Soviet Union in 1989 to 1991, and the disintegration of central and southeastern European states such as Czechoslovakia and Yugoslavia, to encourage the idea that minorities again stood a chance of breaking out of nations-states.

By implication, the 1990s and the new millennium were likely to see a decline in international support for and sympathy with the policing of identities and states by excessive or extraconstitutional force (Christie 1996). The decolonization-period tensions between supranationalism and disappointed regional, ethnic, and cultural identities – more particularist nationalisms – seemed to be reemerging. It was as if the Cold War had put the genie in the bottle, and its end had let it out again.

How far we see this reemerging 'genie' as historical, part of an overarching story, depends on how we conceptualize the problem. What are contemporary crises of authority about, or, more precisely, what sorts of identities are causing the problems? Are we dealing more with regional demagogues invoking local nationalism to bolster their search for a bigger share of power and resources? Or regional attempts to shake off states they perceive as failing or as representing some kind of unwanted meddling? To what extent are we dealing with historically-rooted and continually-existent 'nations': states-in-waiting, able to draw on historical reservoirs and repertoires of violence to support their claims?

*Political science models and the question of continuity*

If we take three scholars' explanations for recent conflicts, we will see that three very different notions of identity underlie them, with very different implications for linkage across our colonial, decolonizing and postindependence periods.

First, David Brown's *The state and ethnic politics in Southeast Asia* (1994) sees the politicization of local identities – the move from regionalism (an affiliation with a region as a subordinate unit of a larger state) to regionally-based nationalism – as a result of a breakdown in state-periphery relations. Crises are seen in pathological terms, as symptoms of polity failure. He looks at different types of state-periphery (and majority to dispersed minority) relations in each country. Hence, for him Acehnese supported the Republic when they associated it with an Indonesian nationalism within which they could maintain regional identity, and from which neo-patrimonial politics could secure them benefits. So long as their religious leaders could influence the central religious party Masjumi, and the latter could aspire to power, they had a stake in the system. But when they failed to secure the benefits they wanted from the centre (such as a more Islamic state), and Masjumi declined, they turned to violence. First, they attempted to coerce the centre through revolt, successfully gaining renewed recognition as a province in 1960. Later, when they grew dissatisfied with New Order centralization and its appropriation of Aceh's oil and gas wealth, they resorted to separatist revolt.

Yet Clive Christie's *A modern history of Southeast Asia* hints at more rooted identities, with localized groups linked by culture, language, and a negative history of their relations with core populations. These rooted nationalisms might ultimately demand recognition despite generous treatment in the distribution of resources or light rule from the centre. Furthermore, in an age of globalization, when efficiency matters as much as size and most states claim to base rule on consent, secession Timor Leste-style or very loose federalism might complete decolonization, while simultaneously helping core states to modernize (see also Hack 2003). These thoughts echo Basil Davidson's *The black man's burden* (1992), where he argued postindependence states reflected the colonial powers' cobbling together of different tribes. In short, postindependence states are not postcolonial because they replicate the artificiality in boundaries of the colonial. They perpetuate premodern conflicts about ethnicity, preventing the development of more modern notions of civic and inclusive nationalism. In this model, the curse for Africa and Southeast Asia is that postindependence states refuse to complete decolonization via separation, or Swiss-style federalism, or granting more substantial measures of autonomy, or more equal, civic- rather than ethnically-based citizenship. Self-determination remains incomplete, and rule is therefore based on coercion as much as on consent.

But a third type of analysis warns us against overhasty embrace of disintegrationist conclusions. This is Mahmood Mamdani's reworking (1996) of an old idea, that politicized ethnic identities are themselves a legacy of colonial rule. Writing after ethnic cleansing had wracked the Balkans and Rwanda, he argued that the colonial state – especially when practicing indirect rule – had entrenched in law both race and indigeneity/ethnicity. It instituted race hierarchies, for instance white, nonnative and native – and divided natives into ethnicities each coming under so-called customary law, and native chiefs. These were not just 'natural' customs, however. The colonial state gave despotic power to just one source of authority, the chief, ignoring alternative sources of customs, age-groups, women, religious groups, and ignoring checks and balances in precolonial society.

Mamdani characterizes nationalists' response as being at two levels. First, they sought to deracialize politics, getting rid of European supremacy. But on ethnicity there was a split between radical nationalism, seeking equal rights for all members of new nations based on residence, and conservative nationalisms, which sought to preserve ethnicities: between ethnic citizenship and rights, and territorial.

The conservative nationalists sought to use ethnicities as mobilizing badges, to justify privileging the indigenous over so-called settlers and their descendants, or collect regional support. Yet giving in to such ethnicized politics runs counter to both the supranationalism of the postindependence state, and the freedom to belong to a wider territory and grouping. In Indonesia, increasing indigenization would clash with the post-1920s movement that produced Indonesian identity over Javanese, Sumatran, Balinese, and other identities. It was precisely the modernization of Indonesia, with new travel for education, jobs, and business, and an increasingly pervasive and universal colonial state that made elites feel Indonesian, stressing Malay as a lingua franca. In an ever flatter, more globalized world, the notion that additional barriers be erected again to trade or movement between, say, Aceh and Bali runs counter to economic logic, to the need for greater counterweight to global forces and multinationals, and to the wider freedom an archipelago-wide, inclusive citizenship brings.

*Malaysia and Singapore as case-studies in an integrated approach to identity and authority*

What are the options for Southeast Asian states that want to maintain territorial integrity, and their supranationalisms, without excessive reliance on restrictions and coercion? In at least two cases, plural societies or 'nations-states' appear to have achieved some balance between an emerging supranationalism, and the particularist demands of individual communities. This has been accompanied by rapid development and relatively low levels of state violence. These 'success' stories are for two states with large but dispersed minorities, namely Malaysia and Singapore. In both cases, their decolonization and postindependence periods were characterized by severe crises of authority and extremely plural societies.

These achievements have been made possible, in part at least, through their development of effective approaches for managing authority and identity. In order to understand their achievement we therefore need to understand decolonization not just as a political process but as a series of battles over identity.

This section uses the example of one key figure in Malaysian and Singapore history, Chin Peng, as a window on competing 'imagined decolonizations', on competing visions of postcolonial identity, and on how these states successfully managed these. By focusing on the Malaysia and Singapore case study, and by beginning this with one individual, I hope to render abstract talk of decolonization, identity, and authority concrete.

Chin Peng became Secretary General of the Malayan Communist Party (MCP/CPM) in 1947. He was born in 1924, when the nine Malay states of British Malaya were sovereign Malay territories, and only Malays were considered citizens. A final wave of Chinese immigration made the Chinese a majority in the tin-producing west coast states of peninsular Malaya, as they already had been in Singapore. As a second generation immigrant, Chin Peng had a number of ways of narrating his identity. Businessmen often resorted to Chinese clan or dialect associations, or Chambers of Commerce. Mobilization along such traditional or commercial lines was possible for Chin Peng as well, as was return to China. In the 1940s the former, traditional approach to identity would manifest as the Malayan Chinese Association (MCA). This originated from the efforts of Chinese business and clan leaders. It transformed into a political party around 1951, and formed an Alliance with the United Malays National Organisation (UMNO) in 1952. This Alliance, with the Malayan Indian Congress added, went on to dominate the 1955 federal elections and lead the country to independence on 31 August 1957.

UMNO's model of Malay predominance (later expanded to the concept of the *bumiputra,* or son of the soil), managed through elite accommodation of other communal-based parties, won. After 1970 it was broadened to include other parties, becoming the Barisan Nasional (BN). Elite accommodation meant creating a framework that balanced divergent identities, albeit with one predominant. It also involved (neo)patrimonialism, in that Alliance/BN members remained representatives of vertical alliances reaching down into the towns, based on their ability to deliver resources, and to preserve space for Indian and Chinese cultures, languages, and businesses. What made this workable was that UMNO's foundation in 1946 was a response to an acute threat as the British tried to remove the Malays' special place and grant equal Chinese citizenship in the Malayan Union of 1946-1948. This would have undone Malay claims to special rights and political position as indigenous. UMNO's success in reversing this, and the resulting spirit of Malay unity, ensured Malay splits were afterwards fought out mainly within UMNO. This made UMNO a reliable partner for minority elites needing patrimonial resources since they were not threatened with the possibility of exclusion from power should UMNO lose control. By comparison, no Thai or Indonesian political party could offer such stable access to central resources and policy.

Had Chin Peng chosen the Chinese association or business (MCA) route, he could have preserved his particularistic identity. Chinese had such opportunities because UMNO developed a strategy not of negating alternative identities, but of coopting them as junior partners and leaving them space, for instance allowing primary education in vernacular languages.

The model offered benefits to everyone, but by the late 1960s it was coming under severe strain. The failure of rural development initiatives by the 1960s caused the Malays to feel aggrieved. There were no Malay secondary schools until the 1950s, and in most of the nonelite sections of the civil service into the early 1960s non-Malays remained preponderant. These tensions boiled over on 13 May 1969 following victories by non-Alliance parties such as the multiracial Gerakan whose supporters paraded in Kuala Lumpur. Feeling the promise of independence – which to them meant restoration of Malay dominance and improving conditions – in danger, some Malays exploded in anger and riot. After these 1969 racial riots, a New Economic Policy (NEP) was introduced in 1970 in response in order to complete decolonization as Malays saw it, by increasing preferences for Malays, and pump-priming a Malay middle class by further preferences in shares, contracts, and education. Media questioning of Malay rights was banned, Malay culture was lauded as the root of national culture, and ultimately school history began to present modern-day Malaysian institutions as a culmination of Malay history. Slowly, Islam achieved a more prominent place in public culture and government attentions. Even then the plan was not to decrease the proportion of Chinese capital, but to increase Malay participation at the expense of foreign capital, and by buying up percentages of new share issues for Malays.[14]

The young Chin Peng could have continued the family business, entered the MCA, and shared in that party's access to government through the Alliance and later the Barisan Nasional. But young Chin Peng was not inter-

---

[14]   Von Vorys 1976 is the classic work. The most recent are Cheah Boon Kheng 2004 and the relevant chapters in Wang Gungwu 2005.

ested in merely continuing the family bicycle and motor workshop, or traditional identity. By the mid 1930s two alternative narratives were opening up: Guomindang (GMD) and Communist. In the 1920s Guomindang branches had been established. In 1930 the Malayan Communist Party (MCP) was formed. What made increasing numbers of Chinese turn towards these two parties was pride in China's awakening, and then support for China in the long Pacific War from 1937. Chin Peng considered joining the GMD to help the fight against Japan in China, but was already reading communist material, notably Mao Ze Dung's *On protracted war*. He decided the communists were the most effective anti-Japanese organizers, with strikes and boycotts by their AEBUS (Anti-Enemy Backing-Up Society), and a theory of guerrilla warfare.

The teenage Chin Peng took up positions in anti-Japanese organizations, finally entering the MCP as a full member in 1940. In this pro-China, anti-Japanese drive, he was typical of his generation. His subsequent rise also reveals the ambivalent relationship between reservoirs of potential violence and the state. British tactics were to keep the MCP penetrated, isolate it from Malays, and periodically cripple it with arrests (Ban Kah Choon 2001). Malays remained mostly loyal to their sultans. In Malaya and Singapore, then, it was the external impact, the Japanese occupation, that turned prewar communist strikes and plots into postwar armed opposition. The story is well known. The humiliating fall of Singapore on 15 February 1942 prompted changes. First, the British increased the Malay Regiment from one battalion to two, and in the 1950s to several. Secondly, they recognized the MCP and GMD, and from December 1941 enlisted their help. Communists were trained in guerrilla tactics and formed the nucleus of the wartime Malayan People's Anti-Japanese Army (MPAJA), supported by jungle fringe squatters. GMD supporters were recruited into Britain's Force 136 and infiltrated into Malaya as liaison officers with the MPAJA. Force 136 supplied the MPAJA with weapons and training so it could become the local eyes and ears of Britain's Southeast Asia Command: its intelligence gatherers ahead of any potential British landing.

But the war was as much a disaster as a triumph for Chin Peng's comrades: a triumph because they gained heroic status as mountain rats; a disaster because Japanese raids killed off much of their leadership. This last paved the way for Chin Peng's rise to power as the new secretary general in 1947. By that time he had switched his personal narrative from pro-China, anti-Japanese, to Malayan anti-British, and communist. Indeed, the MCP's resort to united front tactics of 1946-1948, seeking broad alliances and to build power through unions, paralleled the world communist line of the time, just as the resort to violence of 1948 also paralleled a resort of communists to violence in Burma, Indonesia, and the Philippines. In June 1948 the government declared an Emergency, eventually taking sweeping powers of preventive detention, banishment, and food and movement controls.

Chin Peng's Malayan National Liberation Army (MNLA) peaked at almost 8,000 in 1951, before the resettlement of squatters into New Villages forced the MCP onto the defensive. By 1954 most forces had retreated to the Thai border.[15] Chin Peng found himself directing a small-scale movement now based mainly in southern Thailand. He himself moved to Beijing in 1961. After Chinese support waned from the late 1970s, the MCP signed peace agreements with the Thai and the Malaysian government in December 1989.

Put bluntly, Chin Peng never had any real chance of success in Malaya, as identity narratives arrayed too heavily against him. First, within the Chinese community, the MCA, GMD, and traditional organizations were strong amongst what was by origin an immigrant-settler-sojourning community. For too many MNLA troops, many of whom spoke little except Chinese, the nationalist Malayan discourse remained a forced one compared to pro-China, class-based, and anti-Japanese motivations. Secondly, the main Malay narrative emerged from a combination of increasing cultural identity of the 1930s, defensive awakening in the war against the mainly-Chinese MPAJA and its pretences to power, and a stand against Britain's Malayan Union plan of 1946. From 1946 the MCP leadership repeatedly instructed cadres to increase Malay recruitment, but it was a thankless task. The *semangat* (spirit) of 1946 – the fount of UMNO's identity amongst its divisional teachers, journalists, and *penghulu* – was defensive against the mainly Chinese radicalism that the MNLA represented, and against Chinese economic dominance.

In these circumstances, both British and postindependence governments found a solution to the communist challenge that involved the management of several identities. The Singapore Government varied this formula after its grant of internal self-government in 1959; hence, it is worth taking each approach in turn.

The Malayan model involved a dominant Malay UMNO elite using elite accommodation of other communal groups, and neopatrimonialism. The MCA and Malayan (later Malaysia) Indian Congress needed access to secure resources, contacts, contracts, and negotiated economic and cultural space. The Alliance/Barisan Nasional model, even after 1970, meant holding the identities its constituent parties represented in balance. It simultaneously involved a gradual increase in the dominance of public discourse by an indigenous Malayan – later Malaysian identity based on Malay language, moderate Islamic forms and practice, and to a lesser extent Malay cultural norms. This dominance became more marked from the 1970s onwards. To be

---

[15]   The best succinct introduction to the Emergency is Chin and Hack 2004. This work is the source for this section's comments on Chin Peng and his context.

classified as 'indigenous' (*bumiputra* or son of the soil) and share in privileges one had to speak Malay, profess Islam, and accept Malay custom. Yet indigenization was balanced by acceptance of pluralism. Only in states run by PAS (Parti Islam Se-Malaysia) in the East has there been the suggestion that Islam might more radically reshape the country, and even then supposedly only for Muslims. Alongside this, the state has chosen to negate by coercion only those narrative streams that directly threaten this elite accommodationist, neopatrimonial structure, notably but not solely communism (Cheah Boon Kheng 2004).

The coercive aspects of the model were mostly kept in reserve in normal times. During the first Malayan Emergency (1948-1960) they had emphasized tight population control (through Emergency laws allowing detention without trial, food controls, and resettlement of much of the rural Chinese population into wired areas), along with civic measures such as provision of medical care. Simultaneously, communal identities were allowed to flourish. The overall model thus emphasized not just crude coercion, or winning hearts and minds, so much as winning confidence by creating a system of control that offered a combination of reasonable security, progress without revolt, and some minority influence on politics. Outside of Emergency periods, coercive measures such as detention without trial were used sparingly, with society for the most part regulating itself to avoid crossing unseen out of bounds markers. In short, embodying ethnic narrative flows – internal nations – into politics and law made it possible to manage dissent with low levels of state coercion and minimal levels of state violence.

For Islam, there was a similar attempt to marginalize the main opposition party, PAS, by balancing rather than totally negating its power (reducing petroleum taxes available in states it controlled, cutting government funding to select madrasahs), while incorporating respected Islamic leaders, notably with Anwar Ibrahim (a leader of Islamic and university youth groups) and, after his fall in 1998, the rise within UMNO of Abdullah Ahmad Badawi. The latter – the son of a PAS founder – became first deputy prime minister after Anwar's fall, prime minister in 2003, and then set out a concept of Islam Hadhari or modern, moderate, tolerant Islam.

The Malaysian 'success' story thus lay in defeating British attempts to deconstruct the ethnic politics and ethnicized identities of the colonial period. Ironically, Malaysian success in managing identities is based on defeating late colonialism's 'unite and quit' tactics in order to perpetuate the previous colonial tendency to differentiate by ethnicity. It also replicates the colonial modus operandi of allowing representation of different interests within a controlled arena so that only low-level coercion is required to police remaining dissidence. This means interests are now represented through the Barisan Nasional, where before it meant through a governor appointing representatives as unofficials to an Executive or Legislative Council. It has also moved towards supporting the idea of an overarching supranational identity – a *bangsa Malaysia*, though one which implicitly accepted the separateness of different communities or ethnicities. This is clearly a success, delivering measures of development, legitimacy and stability, but it is not clear whether the result is unproblematically postcolonial. Indeed, the cost of this success is, to a degree, the perpetuation of late-colonial communal divisions.

The Singapore state, like the post-1965 Malaysian state, retained the use of internal security legislation, including detention without trial, and attempted to negate communist narratives. But Singapore adopted a different approach to handling other identities. Whereas Malaysia balanced the most fundamental communal identities through its Alliance/BN structures with their neopatrimonial elements, the Singapore state opposed virtually all alternative forms of narrative – communist, radical, and communal. From its first year in office, upon the grant of full internal self-government in June 1959, the People's Action Party (PAP) required released leftwing detainees to make statements supporting democracy and eschewing communism. Use of detention without trial, control of the media through licensing laws, removal of trial by jury, and government determination to limit the terms of debate all ensured hegemony for their narrative. By the 1980s newspaper coverage of major Singapore events seldom carried analysis from the viewpoint of any alternative party or interest group. A state-sponsored Singapore Story or discourse was integrated into education through history teaching, through the integration of National Education across the curriculum, and through special events (National Harmony Day, National Defence Day) (Lau 2005; Mauzy and Milne 2002).

Singapore squeezed out the space available for any political mobilization around ethnic identity or class. Chinese-language education declined. The Chinese-speaking Nanyang University founded in 1956 found its degrees not recognized at first, and graduates who supported the Barisan Sosialis opposition were barred from some jobs. By 1981 it had been integrated with the main English language university to form the National University of Singapore. English was made compulsory for teaching school subjects such as mathematics by the 1970s, and gradually English-medium schooling outstripped the vernacular. Asian languages were then encouraged under a policy of bilingualism, with children eventually obliged to learn their mother tongue. But this was not primarily about preserving organic identities, but rather a pragmatic maintenance of economically useful skills, and later an attempt to instil 'Asian' (in fact politically authoritarian and patriarchal) values. Chinese dialects – which the majority of Chinese spoke at home – were for a time barred from the media to encourage Mandarin. It was made clear that mobilization along ethnic lines was out of bounds of the state's meritocratic ideology and would provoke a PAP backlash, if not detention.

It is true that certain, basic communal sensibilities were respected, Islamic *madrasah* continued, and Muslim marriage and death practices allowed for. But this did not extend to toleration of pressure group politics for these interests. So, if integrating representatives of such identities and groups into the body politic, or providing them with space, was vital to crisis avoidance in Malaysia, how has Singapore avoided an explosion?

In part the answer is by good governance and meritocracy, combined with an extremely successful export-oriented and multinational-friendly development programme. This delivered nonpatrimonial benefits to all on the basis of merit and work ethic, as well as subsidized housing, and a tax system that leaves many not paying any tax.[16] But it also integrates people on an atomized basis, incorporating them into the PAP's narrative of meritocratic development. Community centres, grassroots leaders and meet-the-people sessions ensure continuous feedback to the government. Key individuals were sought, especially where they showed dissent within constitutional bounds. The PAP wooed procommunist unionist Devan Nair, who became president in the 1980s. It courted dialect-speaking Chinese and Malays as PAP MPs, and institutionalized this in 1988 by instituting Group Representation Constituencies, in which at least one of a three-member team must be from a minority. Feedback is formalized in feedback panels and in institutions such as the Housing Development Board. This is a form of control reminiscent of George Orwell's *1984*, but it is also a form of bureaucratized democracy and atomized integration. It means identities and aspirations are atomized, channelled to the PAP-state, sifted, and those deemed acceptable aggregated and used. Simplistic liberal criticism of Singapore as authoritarian all too often fail to engage with this bureaucratic or information-bureaucracy aspect of Singapore by which knowledge of individual needs and desires is fed into the system.

Malaysia and Singapore are thus examples of sophisticated systems for dealing with identities that threatened the state. Yet how they integrated – and continue to integrate – identities is very different. They are also success stories at the cost of never becoming fully postcolonial and totally decolonized. The Malaysian model entrenches the pluralism of mature colonialism. Singapore's model entrenches newly created, cultural categories of Malay, Chinese and Indian, though through education rather than privileged citizenship. In both cases the assumption that society is dangerous and must be

---

[16]   Poorer households will receive not only reductions on utilities and other bills, but credits to cover a fraction of the percentage they earn under a minimum. This is part of a wider attempt to entrench the notion of shared citizenship by giving, for instance, 'Singapore shares'.

policed limits the scope for civil society to develop wider consensus and processes that would allow self-adjustment. Controls reproduce the conditions that justify their existence.

*Conclusions*

We have looked at a number of approaches to linking present-day crises to the colonial and decolonizing past, several of which come close to seeing Southeast Asia as inherently unstable, as an area requiring strong government – military, corporatist or other – to counterbalance divided societies.

Hence we can talk of the legacy of the colonial period, the way divide-and-rule strategies politicized differences, ossifying plural societies. We can also recognize the way the colonial states were collections of differing areas and groups – hilltribes in Burma, the Malay/non-Malay divide in Malaysia and Singapore, or the outer islands in Indonesia, and the Muslim south in the Philippines. In short, independence generally bequeathed an immature nations-state, rather than a nation-state, with recurrent tension between state supranationalism and the more particularistic nationalisms.

Worse still, relatively weak colonial empires had sometimes relied on almost feudal arrangements, leaning on local power brokers to exert force on the state's behalf. Hence, *jago*, *penghulu*, hilltribe chiefs, *adat* and religious leaders, and in the Philippines private militias lurked in the background. The habit of leaning on these, or at least the example and related 'repertoires of violence' and 'reservoirs of violence' was too much for postindependence elites to resist. At the least, colonial states had usually resorted to stratagems, such as deportation, harsh press-licensing regimes, and emergency laws, which if repeated would undermine civil society.

Clearly the potential for crises existed, but equally obviously these countries were not in permanent crisis. So there is the suggestion that external impacts, or shocks to the system, have played a vital part in determining when and how crises break out, and creating pulses of crisis across the region. World War II was particularly critical in force-marching states to independence while the relationship between supranationalism and particularist nationalisms was still immature, in further legitimating the use of force, and in extrapolating and adding to preexisting, localized repertoires and reservoirs of violence.[17]

If that suggests region-wide state vulnerability, there is the contrasting

---

[17] The most recent discussion of attempts to see the ASEAN-10 as spanning some kind of region rooted in more than 'nots' (not India, not China) is by Kratoska, Raben, and Schulte Nordholt 2005.

suggestion that skilful management of identities has helped some states to tame their history, although at a price. Admitting that most Southeast Asian states were not nation-states at birth, but nations-states, may be a starting point. This does not mean that there was no potent, overarching state nationalism, imagined nation, or supranationalism. Rather it puts the focus on the relationship between this supranationalism and other, smaller identities or 'nations' in each country: Acehnese, Malukan, Papuan, Karen, Sulu and Patani, or major, dispersed minorities (Chinese in Malaysia) or identity groups (*santri* Muslims in Indonesia). It makes it more important to understand the former as sometimes constituting nationalisms or quasi-nationalisms in their own right, rather than merely as pathological reactions to state failure: to poor distribution of resources, heavy-handed policing, or not having the right level of autonomy.

Nations-states remain as prevalent in Southeast Asia today as in the period of postwar decolonization. But after the Cold War the component 'nations' have been more demanding, making it more vital to get the right balance of social justice, distribution of powers, and a broadly acceptable ideological glue, or alternatively to accept that decolonization may mean, in some cases, further secessions. Further fragmentation is inherent in the logic of decolonization as bestowing freedom through self-determination for those territorially concentrated groups who demand it. But membership of larger nations-states, despite increasingly fractured authority, can still have value for some smaller 'nations' and identity groups when dealing with an ever more globalized world. Not every 'nation' need break out of a nations-state and achieve separate statehood. Globalization and economic development increase mobility, and so the need to restrict ethnic ghettoization. The privileging of local 'indigenous' groups, and the concomitant dangers of increasing fragmentation – and at worst of ethnic cleansing – sharply contrast to needs and dynamics of globalization. So there remains an inherent tension between decolonization as extending statehood and self-determination to all territorially concentrated groups who claim national status, and decolonization as the creation of wider supranationalism.

One central Southeast Asian problem of decolonization and in reaching a 'postcolonial state' therefore remains, that of identity management in nations-states. In times of relative stability – as in Malaysia and Singapore for much of the period – each state pursued its own mix of authoritarian negation of select alternative identities (previously communism, now mainly jihadist political Islam), while producing an effective model for integrating other major identities at the group or individual level. Finding such a working model remains an acute challenge in Myanmar, Indonesia, and to a lesser extent the Philippines and Thailand.

## References

Abu Talib Ahmad
2006        'The impact of the Japanese occupation on colonial and anti-colonial
            armies in Southeast Asia', in: Karl Hack and Thomas Rettig (eds),
            *Colonial armies in Southeast Asia*, pp. 213-38. London: RoutledgeCurzon.
            [Routledge Studies in the Modern History of Asia 33.]
Ban Kah Choon
2001        *Absent history; The untold story of special branch operations in Singapore,*
            *1915-1942.* Singapore: Raffles.
Brown, David
1994        *The state and ethnic politics in South-East Asia.* London: Routledge.
            [Politics
            in Asia Series.]
Budi Agustono
2002        'Violence on North Sumatra's plantations', in: Freek Colombijn and
            J. Thomas Lindblad (eds), *Roots of violence in Indonesia; Contemporary*
            *violence in historical perspective*, pp. 133-141. Leiden: KITLV Press.
            [Verhandelingen 194.]
Cheah Boon Kheng
1988        *The peasant robbers of Kedah, 1900-1929: Historical and folk perceptions.*
            Singapore: Oxford University Press. [East Asian Historical
            Monographs.]
2004        *Malaysia; The making of a nation.* Singapore: Institute of Southeast Asian
            Studies.
Chin, C.C. and Karl Hack
2004        'The Malayan Emergency', in: C.C. Chin and Karl Hack (eds), *Dialogues*
            *with Chin Peng; New light on the Malayan Communist Party*, pp. 3-37.
            Singapore: Singapore University Press.
Christie, Clive
1996        *A modern history of Southeast Asia; Decolonization, nationalism and*
            *separatism.* London: Tauris, Singapore: Institute of Southeast Asian
            Studies.
Colombijn, Freek and J. Thomas Lindblad (eds)
2002        *Roots of violence in Indonesia; Contemporary violence in historical perspective.*
            Leiden: KITLV Press. [Verhandelingen 194.]
Cribb, Robert
2002        'Explaining Indonesian military violence in East Timor', in: Freek
            Colombijn and J. Thomas Lindblad (eds), *Roots of violence in Indonesia;*
            *Contemporary violence in historical perspective*, pp. 227-72. Leiden: KITLV
            Press. [Verhandelingen 194.]
Davidson, Basil
1992        *The black man's burden; Africa and the curse of the nation-state.* New York:
            Times Books.
Frederick, William H.
2002        'Shadows of an unseen hand: some patterns of violence in the
            Indonesian revolution, 1945-1949', in: Freek Colombijn and J. Thomas

Lindblad (eds), *Roots of violence in Indonesia; Contemporary violence in historical perspective*, pp. 143-72. Leiden: KITLV Press. [Verhandelingen 194.]

Frey, Marc
2003     'The Indonesian revolution and the fall of the Dutch empire; Actors, factors and strategies', in: Marc Frey, Ronald W. Pruessen and Tan Tai Yong (eds), *The transformation of Southeast Asia; International perspectives on decolonization*, pp. 83-104. Armonk: Sharpe. [An East Gate Book.]

Frey, Marc, Ronald W. Pruessen and Tan Tai Yong (eds)
2003     *The transformation of Southeast Asia; International perspectives on decolonization*. Armonk: Sharpe.

Furnivall, J.S.
1939     *Netherlands India; A study of plural economy*. Cambridge: University Press.
1948     *Colonial policy and practice; A comparative study of Burma and Netherlands India*. Cambridge: University Press.

Gullick, J.M.
1987     *Malay society in the late nineteenth century: The beginnings of change*. Singapore: Oxford University Press.

Hack, Karl
2001     *Defence and decolonisation in Southeast Asia; Britain, Malaya and Singapore, 1941-1968*. Richmond, Surrey: Curzon.
2003     'Theories and approaches to British decolonization in Southeast Asia', in: Marc Frey, Ronald W. Pruessen and Tan Tai Yong (eds), *The transformation of Southeast Asia; International perspectives on decolonization*, pp. 105-26. Armonk: Sharpe.
2006     'Imperialism and decolonisation in Southeast Asia; Colonial forces and British world power', in: Karl Hack and Tobias Rettig (eds), *Colonial armies in Southeast Asia*, pp. 239-65. London: RoutledgeCurzon. [Routledge Studies in the Modern History of Asia 33.]

Hack, Karl and Tobias Rettig (eds)
2006     *Colonial armies in Southeast Asia*. London: RoutledgeCurzon. [Routledge Studies in the Modern History of Asia 33.]

Harper, T.N.
1999     *The end of empire and the making of Malaya*. Cambridge: Cambridge University Press.

Idroes (Idrus)
1946     *Soerabaja*. Jakarta: Merdeka Press
1968     'Surabaya', *Indonesia* 5:1-28. [Translated by S.U. Nababon and B. Anderson.]

Ileto, Reynaldo C.
1999     *Knowing America's colony; A hundred years from the Philippine War*. Honolulu: University of Hawai'i.

Kerkvliet, Benedict J.
1977     *The Huk Rebellion; A study of peasant revolt in the Philippines*. Berkeley, CA: University of California Press.

Kratoska, Paul H., Remco Raben and Henk Schulte Nordholt (eds)
2005        *Locating Southeast Asia; Geographies of knowledge and politics of space.*
            Singapore: Singapore University Press.
Landé, Carl H.
1965        *Leaders, factions and parties; The structure of Philippines politics.* New
            Haven, CT: Yale University.
Lau, Albert
2005        'Nation building and the Singapore story', in: Gungwu Wang (ed.),
            *Nation-building; Five Southeast Asian histories*, pp. 221-50. Singapore:
            Institute of Southeast Asian Studies. [History of Nation-building
            Series.]
Lebra, Joyce C.
1977        *Japanese trained armies in Southeast Asia.* Kuala Lumpur: Heinemann
            Educational Books (Asia).
Locher-Scholten, Elsbeth
1994        'Dutch expansion in the Indonesian archipelago about 1900 and the
            imperialism debate', *Journal of Southeast Asian Studies* 25-1:91-112.
2002        'State violence and the police in colonial Indonesia circa 1920', in: Freek
            Colombijn and J. Thomas Lindblad (eds), *Roots of violence in Indonesia;
            Contemporary violence in historical perspective*, pp. 81-104. Leiden: KITLV
            Press. [Verhandelingen 194.]
Mamdani, Mahmood
1996        *Citizen and subject; Contemporary Africa and the legacy of late colonialism.*
            Princeton: Princeton University Press.
Mauzy, Diane and R.S. Milne
2002        *Singapore's politics under the People's Action Party.* London: Routledge.
McCoy, Alfred W. (ed.)
1980        *Southeast Asia under Japanese occupation.* New Haven, CT: Yale
            University. [Yale University Southeast Asia Studies, Monograph Series
            22.]
McCoy, Alfred W.
1981        'The Philipines; Independence without colonisation', in: Robin Jeffrey
            (ed.), *Asia; The winning of independence; The Philippines, India, Indonesia,
            Vietnam, Malaya*, pp. 23-65. London: Macmillan. [Macmillan
            International College Editions.]
Reid, Anthony
1979        *The blood of the people; Revolution and the end of traditional rule in Northern
            Sumatra.* Kuala Lumpur: Oxford University Press.
2005        *An Indonesian frontier; Acehnese and other histories of Sumatra.* Singapore:
            Singapore University Press.
Robinson, Geoffrey
2002        'The fruitless search for a smoking gun; Tracing the origins of violence
            in East Timor', in: Freek Colombijn and J. Thomas Lindblad (eds), *Roots
            of violence in Indonesia; Contemporary violence in historical perspective*, pp.
            234-76. Leiden: KITLV Press. [Verhandelingen 194.]
2006        'Colonial militias in East Timor from the Portuguese period to
            independence', in: Karl Hack and Tobias Rettig (eds), *Colonial armies*

*in Southeast Asia*, pp. 269-301. London: RoutledgeCurzon. [Routledge Studies in the Modern History of Asia 33.]

Schulte Nordholt, Henk
2002            'A genealogy of violence', in: Freek Colombijn and J. Thomas Lindblad (eds), *Roots of violence in Indonesia; Contemporary violence in historical perspective*, pp. 33-61. Leiden: KITLV Press. [Verhandelingen 194.]

Singh, Bilveer
1996            *East Timor, Indonesia, and the world; Myths and realities*. Kuala Lumpur, Malaysia: ADPR Consult (M). [First published Singapore Institute of International Affairs.]

Steinberg, David Joel
1994            *The Philippines; A singular and plural place*. San Francisco: Westview Press.

Tandrup, Anders
1995            'World war and village war; Changing patterns of rural conflict in Southeast, Asia, 1945-1955', in: Hans Antlöv and Stein Tønnesson (eds), *Imperial policy and Southeast Asian nationalism, 1930-1957*, pp. 170-90. Richmond, Surrey: Curzon, [Copenhagen]: Nordic Institute of Asian Studies. [Studies in Asian Topics 19.]

Taylor, Robert H.
2006            'Colonial forces in British Burma; A national army postponed', in: Karl Hack and Tobias Rettig (eds), *Colonial armies in Southeast Asia*, pp. 195-210. London: RoutledgeCurzon. [Routledge Studies in the Modern History of Asia 33.]

Trocki, Carl
1990             *Opium and empire; Chinese society and colonial Singapore, 1800-1910*. Ithaca, NY: Cornell University Press.

Vickers, Adrian
2005            *A history of modern Indonesia*. Cambridge: Cambridge University Press.

Vorys, Karl von
1976            *Democracy without consensus; Communalism and political stability in Malaysia*. Kuala Lumpur: Oxford University Press.

Wang, Gungwu (ed.)
2005            *Nation-building; Five Southeast Asian histories*. Singapore: Institute of Southeast Asian Studies. [History of Nation-building Series.]

GREG BANKOFF

# 'For the good of the *barrio*'
# Community associations and the state
# in the rural Philippines 1935-1965

The men and women of Barrio Canderia described themselves in the early 1950s as being closely tied, that they were 'bound as one, moved as one'.[1] The same sentiments were expressed in Puncan, the adjacent *barrio* (neighbourhood) where the whole population was said to possess 'a spirit of cooperation for the good of the barrio' (HDP, Puncan, Nueva Ecija Roll 47:5). People in small rural communities across the Philippines are usually tied to one another either through descent, marriage, or fictive bonds of kinship, so it is not surprising that they tend to help one another. Yet this sense of neighbourliness extends well beyond the family to encompass a wider, mainly territorially defined group. There is a long history at the local level of formal and informal associations and networks committed to individual and extrafamilial welfare that enhance people's capacity to withstand the magnitude and frequency of hardship as experienced in their daily lives. Moreover, the attainment of nationhood did not significantly alter the situation for most rural people to whom the state often represents more of a threat than a source of benefaction.

The relative lack of state presence at the village (*barangay*) or subvillage level across the archipelago has existed for most of the historical period and still persists in varying degrees today. If, as James Scott contends, the state 'sees' in its own particular way, that certain forms of knowledge and control require a narrowing of vision that 'brings into sharp focus certain limited aspects of an otherwise far more complex and unwieldy reality' (1998:11), so the *barrio* 'sees' in its own way, too, with a look that often bears little relation to the march of grand events on the national scale. To premise the notion of change based around political benchmarks such as decolonization, therefore, may have little immediate relevance to rural communities. People are not necessarily unaware of the larger picture, but it may make little difference to their everyday lives and the way in which they face adversity and cope with misfortune whether personal or from external causes. Moreover, the whole question of independence is one characterized by a great deal of ambiguity

[1]   HDP, Canderia, Nueva Ecija Roll 47:31. Research for this chapter was partly funded by the Netherlands Institute for Advanced Study (NIAS) as a fellowship-in-residence 2003/2004.

over when the event actually took place and so what period actually constitutes decolonization. The Philippines has formally declared its independence
at least three times: from the Spanish on 12 June 1898, under Japanese tutelage on 14 October 1943, and by American fiat on 4 July 1946.[2] According
to the implied assumptions of the modern state, the whole period of U.S.
administration is often represented in national historiography as part of a
gradual process of 'tutelage' towards decolonization. As the principal argument of this chapter stresses continuity more than change (though without
overstressing the importance of the former or denying the existence of the
latter), its temporal framework encompasses roughly a thirty-year period
from the inauguration of internal self-rule under the Commonwealth government in 1935 to the presidency of Ferdinand Marcos in 1965, who was to
dominate Filipino politics until his flight in 1986. It should be noted, however,
that while these dates may constitute significant yardsticks in the history of
the nation, they are far less noteworthy in the narrative of the community. To
the latter, the real milestone during this period was the Japanese occupation
(1941-1945) and the disruption to lives and livelihoods caused by constant
low-intensity conflict, widespread migration, and the permanent abandon-
ment of some settlements.[3] Throughout these years, rural people mainly
relied on their communities and the various forms of associations that operated within them for the extrafamilial services that they required to provide
food, shelter, and support. While the political complexion of the state may
have changed according to the fortunes of war or the advent of nationhood,
the socioeconomic nature of the *barrio* did not or did so only according to its
own internal logic and rhythm.

### Associations and rural communities

The Philippines sit at a geographical and cultural crossroads that through
its Hispanic legacy link Asia across the Pacific to the Americas. It also shares
with its neighbours a rich history of community associations that reflects its
'Malay' heritage.[4] The prevalence of 'traditional' self-help organizations has

---

[2]    Ambeth Ocampo argues that there have actually been a further three declarations of Philippine independence in addition to the ones already mentioned: by Andres Bonifacio in the
Pamitinan Caves on 12-4-1895, the 'Cry of Pugad Lawin' on 23-8-1896, and in the decrees of the
Revolutionary Committee signed by Emilio Aguinaldo on 31-10-1896 (1993:74-5).
[3]    On the Japanese occupation of the Philippines, see Agoncillo 2001. On the wartime experience of communities, however, it is necessary to look through the relevant entries in the national
oral history project instigated in the early 1950s and known as the Historical Data Papers held in
the Philippine National Library.
[4]    The term 'Malay' is used in this sense to denote a commonality of cultures between people who
predominantly share an Austronesian linguistic heritage and who inhabit maritime Southeast Asia.

long been recognized in Indonesia where anthropologists such as Clifford Geertz (1962) and Shirley Ardener (1964) have debated how organizations like rotating credit associations needed to be understood in terms of modernization and the introduction of a monetary economy. Mutual benefit societies existed in urban areas from at least the last quarter of the nineteenth century and were common among wage labourers and their families in the workplace and *kampong* (neighbourhood) by the first decades of the twentieth. Their relationship to organized labour has also been documented, as is their contribution to the nationalist movement by way of the unions. While they are not seen as being pivotal to either, serving more to blunt potential (communist) radicalism among artisans than to foster political consciousness among workers, self-help organizations of every persuasion 'all helped to improve the material conditions of urban workers and gave them at least a modicum of security in a society lacking even a basic social welfare system' (Ingleson 1996:585). Less is known historically about village society, though informal associations that assist people in times of need have probably long existed in one form or another (Ingleson 1996:578). Certainly they still are important groupings within contemporary village communities (Warren 1993).

Just as significant as this Malay influence on the Philippines was the Hispanic heritage brought across the Pacific principally from New Spain. Mutualism in Mexico has its origins in the agrarian communal practices of pre-Columbian societies and the clan-like birthrights that held communities of small property holders together. In urban areas, this custom melded with guild forms derived from a European artisan tradition that gradually became more democratized during the colonial era with broader memberships until they emerged as essentially mutual saving and assistance associations by the second half of the eighteenth century (J. Hart 1996:589-90). In rural areas, indigenous and Hispanic notions combined to produce a state-endorsed form of community-based mutualism known as the *caja de comunidad* (community chest). The dues paid by individual holders of community property were given out as personal loans to meet health, educational, or bereavement needs and were used in the construction of civic utilities or agricultural development.[5] This colonial blueprint was then introduced into the Philippines in 1565 as part of the basic state structure where it seemingly blended well with indigenous forms of rural cooperativeness.

Evidence that mutualism and cooperation were very much part of rural cultures in the Philippines dates back to the charitable activities of the village religious associations or *cofradías* and to the manner in which extrafamilial

---

[5] Hart 1996:589. A conscious effort was made to recreate this 'traditional' rural social structure with the introduction of the *ejido* system following the Mexican Revolution (1910-1911).

work was organized through informal customary practice.[6] The ensuing structures had much in common with the organizations that assisted people in times of need in Indonesia and with the mutualism of the *gremios* or guilds so characteristic of Mexico. All three also share a tradition in which it is difficult to profitably distinguish the divide between mutual benefit societies and early unionism.[7] Nor were the more formal types of these associations in the Philippines completely separate from political movements: the Katipunan, the secret society that instigated the revolt of 1896 against the Spanish, was also a multipurpose organization being at the same time a political grouping, a religious brotherhood, and a form of mutual benefit association. The multiple purposes that these kinds of associations often served were evident in the kinds of organizations that thrived during the Revolution (1896-1898) and the Philippine-American War periods (1899-1902). While the Americans were 'unable to learn of any associations of Filipino working people for mutual benefit or self-help', deeming them not to have reached 'a stage of development favorable to the success of such enterprises' (Clark 1905:850), the new colonial authorities were keen to instil the virtues of Jeffersonian democracy in the peoples of their far-flung outpost of empire. They enacted a Rural Credit Law to organize small farmers into self-help cooperatives officially known as rural credit associations (Act No. 2508 of 1915) and created agricultural credit cooperative societies that were envisaged as 'village banks' able to make small loans for farming-related improvements (Census 1921, IV, Part 1:16, 37 and Balmaceda 1924:18-9). The question remains, however, whether such rural credit associations were altogether new or were, in fact, superimposed on an existing network of more informal mutual benefit organizations.

*Village cooperation prior to 1946*

Apart from these formal officially-inspired organizations, reciprocal exchanges of a more informal nature continued to be practised in rural areas throughout the latter years of the American period. Misfortune and particularly death were occasions that elicited expressions of solidarity and support: 'The good neighbour spirit of the people is best expressed when death comes to a member of a family. Upon being informed of the death of a certain person, the people in the *sitio* [locality] come to the house of the bereaved family,

---

[6]    Bankoff 2004, 2007. Need or sometimes lot determined the order in which a person or family received help, the notion of succession suggested by the Tagalog term *turnuhan* derived from the Spanish word *turno* meaning 'a turn'. Testifying to the widespread nature of these practices throughout the archipelago, reciprocal forms of labour were known by a wide number of terms and often by more than one in the same province (Balmaceda 1927).
[7]    Bankoff 2005:72-6. On unionism, see W. Scott 1992; M. Kerkvliet 1992; Carrol 1961.

not only to console them, but also to offer whatever help they are capable of giving' (HDP, Putting Tubig, Nueva Ecija Roll 47:95). In Nueva Ecija, this was referred to as the *abuluyan* system, and people showed their sympathy and solidarity by contributing as much money as they could afford, an act that was 'considered a must by each and every family of the neighbourhood' (HDP, Kababao, Nueva Ecija Roll 47:38). Help was not only forthcoming at times of distress but also on more joyous family occasions such as baptisms and weddings when 'people gave their share to the family concerned' (HDP, Saguing Talugtug, Nueva Ecija Roll 47).

The spirit of cooperation included working together. Farmers across the archipelago adhered to loose customary practices that involved contributing labour for the benefit of others or for the community at large (HDP Santicon, Albay Roll 1:266 and HDP Maniango, Pampanga Roll 36:27). The elders of Polangui, Albay, reported the following:

> It is a custom of the people that when a certain family plans to build a house, they [...] but only pass a word to their neighbours that on a certain day they will start building their house. On that day everybody in the neighbourhood offers his helping hands [...]. In planting season, one doesn't hire planters to plant palay [unhusked rice]. He only let his neighbours and relations know that on a certain day, he will plant his kaingin [swidden field] with palay and on that day everybody will be there doing their shares. (HDP Santa Cruz, Albay Reel 1:141)

Called by various names and undoubtedly with regional or even local variations, the basic structure of the system was the same: 'Most of their work especially in plowing, planting, harvesting, and building of houses [is] done by the *tagnawa* system. In the tagnawa the labour is free but the host feeds the workers' (HDP Cabugbugan, Tarlac Roll 72:17). More precisely, communal labour during the planting and harvesting seasons was performed under the *pinta* system, while working together on the repair or construction of each other's homes was known as *tagnawa* (HDP Caanamongam, Tarlac Roll 72:11). Cooperation was even more pronounced in areas of new settlement such as on the central Luzon plain where 'working cooperatively was their virtue in any undertaking to make work faster and livelier. In clearing a certain place they work together in cutting down the trees to let them dry and later on [burn]'.[8] This sentiment sometimes found expression in the place name given to a new community. Barrio Caanamongam was so called at its establishment in 1935 after an Ilocano word denoting togetherness 'as a

---

8    HDP Saverona, Nueva Ecija Roll 47:3. On agricultural expansion in central Luzon, see McLennan 1980; Lataillade, Dumontier and Grondard 2002.

symbol of the people's cooperative spirit in grouping together and forming a [settlement]' (HDP Caanamongam, Tarlac Roll 72:10). Not that communal labour necessarily always brought forth success. Joint efforts to establish a water supply and build irrigation canals by the inhabitants of Pajo and Rangayan, *sitios* founded in 1907 by homesteaders in Nueva Ecija were not successful as 'the place where they built the dam was destroyed and became very wide' (HDP Rangayan, Nueva Ecija Roll 47:1-2).

Attention also needs to be paid to the role and function of local Parent Teacher Associations (PTAs) as these soon became the most visible *barrio* organizations after their foundation in 1926 (Rivera and McMillan 1952:167). The ostensible focus of their activities was schools and raising the voluntary contributions of money, material, or labour needed for their erection, maintenance, and reconstruction. However, the location of clinics and other community services at these sites and the allocation of communal fields for their support inevitably widened the range of services they provided (HDP La Purisima, Albay Reel 1:257; HDP Dela Paz, Pampanga Reel 36). Much as earlier *barrio* organizations had cloaked their activities in a religious guise as *cofradías* under Spanish colonialism, so now they sought official approval as PTAs given the emphasis placed by American authorities on educational attainments. Given the common Hispanic heritage, there is an interesting comparison between the role of associations in village schools in the Philippines and those on the *ejidos* or collective farms established in Mexico after the Revolution of 1910-1921. Henrik Infield described how such schools introduced new plants through cultivating vegetable gardens and provided communities with collective washing facilities, libraries, adult education courses, and sport activities but required the cultivation of communal plots for their maintenance (1947:88). The dual nature of these organizations has not completely disappeared in rural areas of the Philippines where they are now sometimes known as Parent Teacher Community Associations or PTCAs.[9]

Living conditions in rural areas began to deteriorate during the 1920s and 1930s, especially in the more densely populated regions of Luzon where the effects of the Great Depression and growing landlessness caused unprecedented degrees of hardship (B. Kerkvliet 1979:26-60). Organizations that complemented their social activities with more overtly political aims seeking redress for rural grievances began to appear such as the Tagulan Katipunan Pambangsa, a farmer's organization that recruited *barrio* folk in Pampanga and elsewhere in central Luzon (HDP Baliti, Pampanga Reel 36:29). There were even sporadic peasant uprisings, among the best known of which were

---

[9]   Interview with Danilo Atienza, Program Supervisor, Integrated Community Disaster Planning Program. Red Cross, Bonifacio Drive, Manila, 22-10-2002.

the Kapisanan Makabola Makasinag (1924-1925), the Tayug uprising (1931), and the Sakdalista movement (1934-1935) (Sturtevant 1972; Guerrero 1967; Ileto 1979).

Many of these new peasant organizations still strongly displayed characteristics that stressed reciprocity and mutual assistance. The Kapatiran Magsaka (Farmer's Brotherhood), for instance, a militant anti-landlord peasant union in central Luzon was essentially a millenarian nationalist society whose affiliates bore triangles branded on their shoulders, wore the omega or yoke symbol on their hats, and marched in uniform at each other's funerals. Members swore a blood oath not to betray the names of their associates, to resist eviction, to refuse to pay exorbitant rents or accept the tenancy of anyone evicted, and to support those in trouble with the landlord especially when the latter tried to enforce his rights to a share of the harvest or collect debts. The Kapatiran had many features in common with mutual benefit societies but also reorganized reciprocal farm labour on a morally euphoric and more militarized basis. Each affected village appointed a *kabisilya* (headman) who kept a book for each farm and its family. Farm work was organized in turns: each day of labour contributed by a family and their buffalo (together representing one day's labour) was entered as a credit and each day of labour performed by another was entered as a debit. At the end of a season, the credits and debits for each family were totted up and any difference between the two made good by payment in *palay*. Farm work was organized in teams, the start and finish signalled by the *kabesilya* blowing a *tambuli*, a buffalo-horn bugle.[10] There were specific bugle calls for fires, to summon help to resist to the landlord's thugs, and to warn of the arrival of the owner or his overseer. Such organizations were a source of concern to landowners and government officials who viewed them as potentially if not actually seditious. During the Great Depression of the 1930s, the Commonwealth government under Manuel Quezon even approved the passing of the 'Tambuli Ordinances' all over Luzon that made it an offence to use a bugle in such a manner.[11]

Though mutual assistance and millenarianism remained significant aspects of these movements, increasingly many rural associations fell under more socialist or even communist influences. The Aguman ding Malding Talapagobra (AMT or General Workers Union) that had a following of 70,000 in Pampanga and southeastern Tarlac was an organ of the Socialist Party; the Kalipunang Pambansa ng mga Magsaka sa Pilipinas (KPMP or National Society of Peasants in the Philippines) founded in 1919 by the

[10]   The sounding of the *barrio* lieutenant's horn was also a signal for all able-bodied men to report for advising on needed community work that required collective labour (Rivera and McMillan 1952:168).
[11]   Brian Fegan, personal communication, NIAS, Wassenaar, the Netherlands 2003. See also Connolly 1992:94-6.

communist leader Jacinto Manahan claimed a membership of 60,000 by the time it merged with the AMT in 1939 mainly in Nueva Ecija and Bulacan (B. Kerkvliet 1977:45). Political considerations have always been important in leadership circles if not among the rank and file membership of civic associations dating back to the Katipunan of the 1890s and the early union movement whose initial founders, Isabelo de los Reyes and Dominador Gómez clearly had reformist agendas. However, as misfortune and mishap in the Philippines increasingly came to be seen as having its roots in human activity as much as in natural causes, to be as much the product of the social structure as it was of hazard or misfortune, so mutual assistance increasingly came to take on political overtones.

The Japanese occupation in 1941 only further encouraged communities faced by adversity to help themselves. Many people were forced to relocate to safer locations to escape the fighting where they were not only welcomed but often greeted royally by *barrio* folk who showed their hospitality by serving them with roasted pig, chicken and even slaughtering *carabao* (HDP Mangandingay, Nueva Ecija Roll 47:2). Organizations were established in communities with the express aim of helping their members to promote mutual relationship between each other and to advance agriculture such as the one known as Kalaoman in Polangui. 'Much was [sic] the accomplishments of this organization that it may be the reason why not a single life and property was damaged during those tumultuous days', the local history of the town recounts (HDP La Purisima, Albay Roll 1:257). In other cases, however, it was the Japanese occupation forces themselves that instigated such neighbourhood associations 'to have the civilians cooperate with them in their fight against the guerrillas' (HDP Bularit, Tarlac Roll 72:69). There were particular attempts to enlist young people in this respect with the formation of the Junior Kalibapi and the Melchora Aquino sisterhood in villages, organizations created by the occupation administration in 1942 as supposedly nonpartisan and dedicated to the social, spiritual, cultural, moral and economic advancement of the nation under suitable Japanese tutelage.[12] The consequences, however, were not always those intended by the occupying forces. As one village respondent remembered: 'The Japanese soldiers did not know that the members of the neighbourhood associations were guerrillas themselves' (HDP Bularit, Tarlac Roll 72:69).

---

[12] HDP Mangandingay, Nueva Ecija Roll 47. The parent organization, the Kalibapi or Kapisanan sa Paglilingkod sa Barong Pilipinas (Association for Service to the New Philippines) had chapters in every province, its 'tentacles reached into almost every home' (Agoncillo 2001:367).

*Village cooperation after independence*

Far from being a recent manifestation, then, there is a long history of formal and more informal associations among the peoples of the archipelago. The advent of independence did not constitute a discrete break in the consideration of these organizations; the status of the Philippines in the immediate decades following 1946 remained largely neocolonial as a result of tariff and military agreements favourable to the USA and the heightened tensions of the Cold War period. The element of continuity in form and substance remains very pronounced at least until the long presidency of Ferdinand Marcos that began in 1965. During his presidency, there was a concerted attempt to curtail the power of the traditional elites and modernize the socioeconomic basis of society, culminating in his introduction of a corporatist model for the country under martial law, the 'New Society' (Stauffer 1977). An important development during the first postwar decades, however, was the increasing prominence paid by government to the political ramifications of community welfare. The years following independence were largely dominated by events connected to the outbreak of a large-scale peasant rebellion in central Luzon known as the Huk Rebellion (named after Hukbong Mapagpalaya ng Bayan – the People's Army of Liberation) and the full-scale military operations involved in its suppression from 1946-1954.[13] In the ensuing climate of fear, all associations not sanctioned by the state or church were regarded with suspicion as harbouring communist sympathies and subject to repeated repression by police and military agencies.

As part of a counterinsurgency strategy to thwart the spread of communist influence, the national government and the Catholic Church placed increasing emphasis on rural development and introduced policies aimed at decentralizing government and promoting cooperative organizations at the grassroots level. The establishment of *barrio* councils with the passage of the Revised Barrio Charter of 1963 (RA3590) and the Decentralization Act of 1967 (RA5185) led to the progressive emergence of elected local government empowered to promulgate ordinances and implement public works and was paralleled by attempts to sponsor more functional community organizations such as 4-H Clubs, farmers' associations, cooperatives and women's rural

---

[13]   The Huks had their origins in the prewar peasant unions of the 1930s. These became the mass basis for the rural united front formed by the communist and socialist parties of central Luzon to wage guerrilla warfare against the Japanese and were known as the Hukbalahap or People's Army against the Japanese. Peasant radicalism was heightened in the postwar period by: the reimposition of traditional agrarian systems; the harassment, arrest and assassination of Huk cadre and their outlawing in 1948; and the refusal of the national government to allow seven peasant-supported elected representatives of the Democratic Alliance to take their seats in Congress (Lachica 1971; B. Kerkvliet 1977).

improvement clubs.[14] An attempt was also made to mobilize farmers with the formation of Farmers Cooperative Marketing Associations in 1953 and to coordinate the government's approach to community organizing through the creation of a Presidential Arm on Community Development in 1956 (Clarke 1998:58).

The Catholic Church, too, was actively engaged in organizing rural associations. In 1953, the Federation of Free Farmers (FFF) was established by a group of Catholic laymen affiliated with the Jesuit-inspired Institute of Social Order. The FFF sought to achieve land redistribution and improve agricultural production through promoting peaceful reforms, mass bargaining and the formation of cooperatives. Though initially strongly anticommunist, many of its more youthful membership began to advocate a form of social action influenced by the new liberation theology of the 1960s.[15] At the height of its popularity in the early 1970s, the FFF claimed a membership of around half a million people.[16] A comparable programme of mass mobilization of the peasantry was also attempted by the Philippine Communist Party (Partido Kuminsta ng Pilipinas or PKP) with the founding of Malayang Samahang Magsaka or Free Farmers' Union (MASAKA) in 1964. Despite the union's rapid growth in membership to 68,000 by 1968, it only really functioned more as a pressure group and never undertook collective projects or attempted to strengthen group cohesiveness at the *barrio* level (Po 1980:54-8). These forms of community programmes were imposed on communities from the outside mainly as a response to the formation of the national government's attempt to restore law and order in rural areas and were of questionable efficacy (Romani 1956:236).

With the inauguration of internal self-rule under the Commonwealth in 1935 and especially after independence in 1946, certain local associations and even some grassroots ones became associated with one or other of the principal political parties of the period, the Nationalistas and the Liberals, even in some instances delivering votes en bloc in return for material benefits or patronage (Lewis 1971:142-3). Such political affiliations were clearly apparent in the municipality of Hulo, Bulacan (studied by Mary Hollnsteiner during the 1950s), although the associations here were ones whose leader-

---

[14]  Po 1980:31-2. While a measure of functional *barrio* government was achieved with these reforms, local government continued to remain chronically under-funded. 4-H Clubs were initiated in 1952 with the aim of providing young people (15-18-year olds) with opportunities to learn through individual, group and community projects that enhance self-reliance, instil a spirit of voluntarism, and promote cooperation and fellowship. They are still active today with a membership of over a 100,000 youths distributed across the archipelago in 3,881 clubs.

[15]  These members were later expelled during the purges that followed the declaration of martial law in September 1972.

[16]  Po 1980:39-54. An urban-based Federation of Free Workers was also established (Constantino-David 1998:31-2).

ship was dominated by local elites.[17] At the *barrio* level, however, evidence suggests that village cooperation and the formal and more informal forms of associations that were prevalent there continued to provide communities with their only reliable form of social security. Fieldwork studies conducted in the 1950s and 1960s show the persistence of arrangements based upon an exchange of labour or for mutual advantage. Henry Lewis points to the continued importance of *zangjeras* or cooperative irrigation societies in the Ilocos area of northwestern Luzon. These associations existed to provide a stable and reliable supply of water to increase crop production. To achieve this end, the associations employed a wide variety of organizational means. Membership might include landowners as well as tenants and even, in some cases, involved investing outright ownership of the land in an association. In the main, membership was determined more by the hydraulic engineering necessary to distribute water.[18] People contributed their labour to maintain a network of dams and canals in return for water. Water was then 'sold' to non-members and the money used to purchase materials required for the upkeep of the works and to hold an annual fiesta. Associations cooperated with one another as need or topography dictated and even formed loose kinds of federations to mediate disputes between their members or act on their behalf on matters of political importance (Lewis 1971:128-30). One association even had a written agreement dating from 1937 that claimed to be a copy of the 'original' constitution dating from 1793 and written in Spanish despite the fact that no one in the community could read or write that language. Ilocanos who migrated to the Cagayan valley at the turn of the twentieth century took with them this form of mutual-benefit association, and though such organizations did not prosper in quite the same way as in Ilocos, they were still a notable feature in some communities at the time of Lewis's research (Lewis 1971:135-8). The operation of less formal types of contractual labour arrangements were also observed by Donn Hart in the Visayas where it was known as *bolhon* and by Mary Hollnsteiner in Bulacan (Hart 1955:431-3; Hollnsteiner 1968:22-31).

In other parts of Luzon, *puroks* or small neighbourhood associations persisted, concerned with overall municipal improvements, that in one incidence were responsible for the construction of a new public plaza and recreation area almost entirely funded through donations of labour and materials (Rivera and McMillan 1952). Many of these activities were accomplished in

---

[17] Thus the Knights of Columbus and the Daughters of Isabela were identified with the Nationalistas, while the Lions Club and the Hulo Women's Club were associated with the Liberals (Hollnsteiner 1963:112, 116).

[18] Rivera and McMillan (1952:168) attribute the success of *zangjeras* to the fact that the majority of their members held plots of commensurate size, were of similar backgrounds and had long been resident in the community.

cooperation with local Parent Teacher Associations. Practically all the postwar rebuilding of damaged schoolhouses, the construction of new ones and the provision of equipment for both were carried out by PTAs (HDF Cabiao, Nueva Ecija Roll 47:9; Romani 1956:235). John Romani and M. Ladd Thomas (1954:133) estimated that between 50-60 percent of all the schools they visited had been built through this means. Meanwhile, community-centred school movements promoted literacy, better health, economic development and civic character at the local or *purok* level (HDP Cabanatuan, Nueva Ecija Roll 47:21). In more remote areas, access roads and other public constructions were built in a similar fashion, with municipal authorities sometimes setting aside funds for the purchase of materials and loaning equipment as their contribution to the programme (Romani and Thomas 1954:132). Outside observers saw these voluntary projects as a necessary result of the failure of local government and the need for unofficial groups to assume the *barrio*'s 'normal functions'. At the same time, however, these mainly American anthropologists assessed them to be of only limited efficacy due to their 'shortage of human and material resources' (Romani 1956:235-6). Such views, of course, reflect the lack of any real appreciation of the role such organizations have played in local communities.

Equally interesting is the evidence that shows the operation of rotating credit associations in Ilocos. According to Lewis, the essential features of these types of financial savings associations or *ammong* were their fixed regular contributions. Participants agreed to a schedule of collections (often weekly) with the order of pay-out usually determined by lot. According to 'the luck of the draw', the first recipient obtained an entire week's collection but continued contributing till all participants had received their share, at which point the association dissolved or formed anew with the same or different members. There was also the added attraction of chance as to who would receive the first payment but without any of the corresponding risks associated with gambling (Lewis 1971:147-9). Similar forms of enforced savings were observed in the central Philippines where they were known as *bu-bu-ay* on the island of Leyte (Pal 1956:408). There is evidence that money saved in this manner was 'often loaned to needy members' (Rivera and McMillan 1952:168). The approximately 500 members belonging to Ang Uliran (The Paragon or Model of Excellence), an association dedicated to the improvement of *barrio* life through unity and cooperation were supporting several families who had fallen on hard times in 1951 (HDP San Josef, Nueva Ecija Roll 47:88). Lewis noted the existence of other forms of organizations associated with social as opposed to financial savings. In these *arayats*, whose membership was exclusively female, payments were made in the form of food but were unscheduled and occurred only as individual need arose. An organizer recorded all such contributions and was charged with informing the members of an upcoming event (such as baptism, wedding or funeral) and the time and place at which their payments were due. Contributing members were likely to be guests at these functions. Lewis concluded that these *arayats* were a form of social investment that used economic goods to reinforce established social ties (Lewis 1971:149-50).

## The nature of social services 1935-1965

The evidence suggests, then, that the formal processes of decolonization between 1935 and 1965 did not materially affect the manner in which the provision of social services in rural communities remained largely dependent on local-level networks of reciprocity and mutual assistance. The nature of these informal associations, however, and the services they provided (and continue to provide) people with defies easy definition. On the one hand, they were recognizable groups in their own right that appealed, if not to an abstract sense of community consistent with a politically or geographically defined area, then at least to identification with a more socially circumscribed one like a neighbourhood. As the elders of Sitio Taluate in Gapan, Nueva Ecija described the formative process that generated their associations: 'Group activities began in the family, spread to neighbours and then to the whole village' (HDP Taluate, Nueva Ecija Roll 47:131). The inhabitants in nearby Sitio Balante confirmed this, adding: 'Little by little people associated themselves into a bigger and stronger group, until they voluntarily assembled in connection with their industrial, religious, political or social interest' (HDP Balante, Nueva Ecija Roll 47:20). On the other hand, evidence suggests that the operative mechanism at work here was one that involved more dyadic bonds, a concept of reciprocity that existed on an individual or family basis that was both temporary and shifting. In fact, what often constitutes an association was not a group with a bounded and stable composition so much as a temporary set of people, each with dyadic exchange obligations to other individuals. In cases of labour reciprocity, for instance, a farmer needed to assemble a large team of men who brought with them their buffalo and gear as well as the women and boys required to harrow and carry out transplanting. A person needed to build up sufficient 'credits' and reciprocal obligations that permitted him to organize this and pay off all his outstanding 'debts'. It was more of tit-for-tat reciprocity than a form of group solidarity.

Agaton Pal identified different types of cooperative labour exchange in his anecdotal study of social organizations in Barrio Esperanza on the southwestern coast of Leyte in the postwar years. *Sangga* was characterized by a joint investment of labour and the sharing of resultant income or produce and was usually closely related to subsistence activities such as farming, fishing or forest-harvesting and rarely necessitated an exchange of money. Outright labour exchange or *ayon* involved the accumulation of respective workdays for others by each member of a group that could then be called upon when required. Not everyone's workdays, however, were assessed in the same way, so a carpenter's labour was held equivalent to two days weeding, and ploughing was assigned a higher value than transplanting rice as it involved the use of a *carabao* (Pal 1956:402-5). Brian Fegan also described a number of reciprocal arrangements he encountered in rural parts of central Luzon in the early 1970s that were known collectively as *gantihan* (where the root *ganti* means to reciprocate, while the suffix indicates a form of payment).[19] First, there was *lusungan* (to go out to the fields) or *suyuan* (ingratiation) in which groups of farmers discussed their ideal planting schedules, decided when each would plant and in what order, and arranged a schedule to avoid any clashes of interest. Then there was a form of reciprocity known as *bataris* or *batarisan* in which the farm holder repaid labour on the spot through providing food, drink, and cigarettes. *Tulungan* was more generalized help that was not restricted to farm work and covered all forms of tit-for-tat reciprocity. Amounts given were meticulously recorded and set the standard of reciprocity each family had to meet when called upon on a similar *okasyon* or in case of need. There was even a more sinister form of reciprocity known as *purga* derived from the Spanish word for a purge to force someone into providing help. On the eve of threshing, widows and old women might press a gift of pork or chicken on a farmer's wife in order to put that family under an obligation to repay her generously with paddy the next day.

Pal, however, also specified another form of labour exchange that, though still dyadic in nature, was manifestly more altruistic. *Alayon* was a form of worker bee where people offered their labour to those in need of assistance. Help was rendered to avoid the criticism of unneighbourliness but also with the expectation that it would be repaid if and when the giver found him or herself in similar circumstances. Only *tagbu* was labour contributed completely free of obligation and involved work on community improvements such as the repair of the *barrio* chapel, the construction or maintenance of school buildings, and the upkeep of bridges. Even here, though, the motives might still be of a rather personal nature: avoiding the displeasure (and cash fines) of local authorities, earning *panalangin* or merit from the saint to whom the house of worship was dedicated, or maintaining thoroughfares used by one's family (Pal 1956:404-7). According to Fegan, only *bayanihan* (from the root *bayan* meaning people or nation) appealed to a more abstract sense of community welfare and was a form of emergency labour rendered in the face of a disaster such as fire, flood, or typhoon when everyone nearby

19   Brian Fegan, personal communication, NIAS, Wassenaar, the Netherlands 2003.

contributed. Events such as these could happen to anyone and so could not be anticipated. They were not a matter of reciprocity, but those who refused assistance in such circumstances were noticed and might find it difficult to obtain help in the future.[20] In the main, Generoso Rivera and Robert McMillan (1952:168) concluded that forms of community cooperation were most successful when the number of people involved were few, the organization simple, and the objectives clearly defined.

The various forms of community assistance were subsequently categorized by anthropologists in the 1960s who divided them neatly between contractual and quasi-contractual forms of reciprocity. However, they reserved a special place in their typology for those forms of dyadic bonds that were reified under the rubric of *utang na loob*, a debt from within, where favours or services were rendered to one outside the immediate family and that were expected to be repaid with interest so as to ensure that one did not remain in another's debt. This somewhat romanticized view of society was said to characterize social relations among Filipinos creating respectively temporary or permanent superordinate or subordinate relationships that in effect lasted indefinitely as neither party could ever be entirely sure that the debt had been fully discharged. Those who wilfully ignored its precepts and did not reciprocate in kind on the appropriate occasion were said to be *walang hiya*, literally without shame, a derogatory term that was considered to place someone below that of a beggar or a dog.[21] Many of these notions were championed by a Christian sociology that espoused voluntarism and pushed modernization theory.

Such romanticized notions of indigenous pre-Hispanic society were later taken up by President Marcos to form the core values of his martial-law New Society, an attempt to find a Filipino third way and exemplified by his suggestion that the country be renamed *Maharlika* (the noble or aristocratic one).[22] Similar ideas were pursued in Indonesia where President Soekarno modelled his vision of the indigenous state on an idealized village society writ large. State propaganda for Guided Democracy claimed the *desa* (village) as a cradle of consensus (*musyawarah* and *mufakat*), mutual aid (*gotong royong*), and reciprocity (*tolong-menolong*) (Lev 1966:46-59). Despite the somewhat clumsy political rhetoric that accompanied such state-championed visions of society, there was at least some recognition of the people's intrinsic resilience to cope with hardship and an appreciation of their multifaceted abilities to manage risk that is somehow lacking from contemporary perspectives.

---

[20]   Brian Fegan, personal communication, NIAS, Wassenaar, the Netherlands 2003.
[21]   Hollnsteiner 1968:28-31. 'A beggar prays for the good health of whoever gives him alms, and a dog barks for his master': a person without shame does not acknowledge the giver in any way.
[22]   See the multi-volume history of the Philippines, *Tadhana* (Fate), supposedly written by Ferdinand Marcos (Marcos 1976-1980).

Unfortunately, all these postcolonial attempts at reform became hopelessly mired in cronyism and nepotism and proved of little lasting benefit to folk in the *barrios*. They can be said, however, to mark the real beginning of the decolonization process in that government policies attempted to employ non-Western, community-based models for the first time as a basic framework of society and the provision of social services.[23]


## Conclusion

Social security is usually defined as the totality of public measures that provide some form of protection for the members of a particular society in specified situations of need and distress.[24] The main issue of debate concerns those institutions established by the state to fulfil these public services and pays only scant attention to the sets of customary practices that also operate, though not exclusively, in this sphere (De Swaan 1988). State provision is regarded as modern and progressive, a function of specialized agencies in the formal sector of the economy. Provision, however, based on indigenous cultural mechanisms that obligate individuals, groups, or communities to provide assistance is seen as traditional and regressive to capital formation, ill-defined and part of the informal sector of the economy (Midgley 1984). Accordingly, the latter is supposed to gradually give way to the former as societies become more urbanized, their economies more industrialized, and an increasingly larger percentage of the population is included within the provision of the state sector. Despite the manifest failure of such a process to eventuate in many non-Western societies over recent decades, attention has still largely been focused on the shortcomings of the former rather than on the potentialities of the latter (F. von Benda-Beckmann and K. von Benda-Beckmann 2000). Yet not only do customary practices extend the only form of social security coverage that most of the world's rural populations actually experience, indigenous welfare systems may actively contribute to realizing the so far elusive goal of universal provision (Midgley 2000:224-5). The

---

[23]    These types of strategies comprised an enormous variety of possible recourses including land utilization and conservation strategies, crop husbandry and diversification practices, exploitation of geographical complementarities in ecosystems, symbiotic exchanges between communities, the development of patronage relationships, migration, the redeployment of household labour, and complex dietary adjustments (Drèze and Sen 1989:1–75).

[24]    The International Labour Organisation defines social security as 'the protection which society provides for its members, through a series of public measures against the economic and social distress that otherwise would be caused by the stoppage or substantial reduction of earnings resulting from sickness, maternity, employment injury, unemployment, invalidity, old age and death; the provision of medical care; and the provision of subsidies for families with children' (Social security 1984:2-3).

current emphasis on the importance of local knowledge to tackle intractable social, economic, and environmental problems is a belated recognition that non-Western peoples have historically developed sophisticated strategies and complex institutions to reduce the constant insecurity of their lives.

As the case of informal associations and networks in the Philippines shows, there has been a long history of non-state provision of individual and community welfare that stretches back for as long as the written record exists. In this it has much in common with its nearest regional neighbour, Indonesia. However, the shape and form those organizations took derived as much from its transpacific heritage as it did from its 'Malay' origins, and especially from Mexico and perhaps even more latterly from the United States of America as well. There is ample evidence that informal groupings continued to play an important role in the period between 1935 and 1965. Independence, whether determined to have occurred in 1898 or in 1946, offered no real change in how community associations worked or in how they provided a form of social security to people in rural areas. Nor did the decades immediately following the establishment of self-government or a national government substantially change matters; only the increasing incorporation of these associations into the structure of national politics appears to have been a relatively novel development. This politicization only accelerated in the 1970s and 1980s as leftward-leaning, 'progressive', nongovernment organizations began to emerge with a more direct focus on education, community-based primary care, the promotion and protection of civil and political rights, and providing material support for the activities of grassroots organizations (Silliman and Noble 1998; Clarke 1998:72-7). While the role of the state in rural areas also increased substantially during these decades, particularly its policing and military writ during the long presidential tenure of Ferdinand Marcos, it is debateable whether its greater presence has always been to the advantage of local people or 'for the good of the *barrio*'.

*References*

Agoncillo, Teodoro
2001        *The fateful years; Japan's adventure in the Philippines, 1941-45*. Manila: University of the Philippines Press. Two vols.
Ardener, Shirley
1964        'A comparative study of rotating credit associations', *Journal of the Royal Anthropological Institute of Great Britain and Ireland* 94-1/2:201-29.
Balmaceda, Julian
1924        *Agricultural credit cooperative associations in the Philippines*. Manila: Bureau of Printing. [Bureau of Agriculture Bulletin 40.]

1927            '"Turnuhan" as practised in various provinces', *Philippine Agricultural Review* 20-4:381-421.
Bankoff, Greg
2004            'Local associations and the provision of social services in the rural Philippines, 1565-1964', *IIAS Newsletter* 34:19.
2005            'Wants, wages and workers; Laboring in the American Philippines, 1899-1908', *Pacific Historical Review* 74-1:59-86.
2007            'The dangers to going it alone; Social capital and the origins of community resilience in the Philippines', *Continuity and Change* 22-2: 327-55.
Benda-Beckmann, Franz von and Keebet von Benda-Beckmann
2000            'Coping with insecurity', in: Franz von Benda-Beckmann, Keebet von Benda-Beckmann and Hans Marks (eds), *Coping with insecurity; An 'underall' perspective on social security in the Third World*, pp. 7-31. Yogyakarta: Pustaka Pelajar.
Carrol, John
1961            'Philippine labour unions', *Philippine Studies* 9-2:220-54.
Census
1921            *Census of the Philippine Islands, 1918.* Manila: Bureau of Printing. Four vols.
Clark, Victor
1905            'Labor conditions in the Philippines', *Bulletin of the Bureau of Labor* 58 (May):721-905.
Clarke, Gerard
1998            *The politics of NGOs in South-East Asia; Participation and protest in the Philippines.* London and New York: Routledge.
Connolly, M. John
1992            *Church lands and peasant unrest in the Philippines; Agrarian conflicts in 20th-century Luzon.* Quezon City: Ateneo de Manila University Press.
Constantino-David, Karina
1998            'From the present looking back; A history of Philippine NGOs', in: G. Sidney Silliman and Lela Noble (eds), *Organizing for democracy; NGOs, civil society, and the Philippine state*, pp. 26-48. Quezon City: Ateneo de Manila University Press.
Drèze, Jean and Amartya Sen
1989            *Hunger and public action.* Oxford: Clarendon Press.
Geertz, Clifford
1962            'The rotating credit association; A "middle rung" in development', *Economic Development and Cultural Change* 10-2:241-63.
Guerrero, Milagros
1967            'The Colourum uprising', *Asian Studies* 5-1:65-78.
Hart, Donn
1955            *The Philippine Plaza complex; A focal point in culture change.* New Haven, CT: Southeast Asian Studies, Yale University. [Southeast Asian Studies, Cultural Report 3.]

Hart, John
1996        'Mexican mutualism in historical perspective', in: Marcel van der Linden (ed.), *Social security mutualism; The comparative history of mutual benefit societies*, pp. 589-607. Bern: Lang.
Hollnsteiner, Mary
1963        *The dynamics of power in a Philippine municipality.* Manila: Community Development Research Council, University of the Philippines.
1968        'Reciprocity in the lowland Philippines', in: Frank Lynch (ed.), *Four readings on Philippine values*, pp. 22-49. Quezon City: Ateneo de Manila University Press, Quezon City. [Institute of Public Administration Papers 2.]
Ileto, Reynaldo
1979        *Pasyon and revolution; Popular movements in the Philippines, 1840-1910.* Quezon City: Ateneo de Manila University Press.
Infield, Henrik
1947        *Co-operative communities at work.* London: Kegan Paul, Trench, Trubner.
Ingleson, John
1996        'Mutual benefit societies in Indonesia', in: Marcel van der Linden (ed.), *Social security mutualism; The comparative history of mutual benefit societies*, pp. 577-88. Bern: Lang.
Kerkvliet, Benedict
1977        *The Huk Rebellion; A study of peasant revolt in the Philippines.* Berkeley, CA: University of California Press.
Kerkvliet, Melinda
1992        *Manila Workers' Union 1900-1950.* Quezon City: New Day.
Lachica, Eduardo
1971        *Huk; Philippine agrarian society in revolt.* Manila: Solidaridad Publishing House.
Lataillade, Camille, Alexandre Dumontier and Nicolas Grondard
2002        *L'Agriculture des Philippines; La plaine centrale; Histoire et perspectives.* Paris: Les Indes Savantes.
Lev, Daniel S.
1966        *The transition to Guided Democracy; Indonesian politics, 1957-1959.* Ithaca, NY: Modern Indonesia Project, Southeast Asia Program, Cornell University.
Lewis, Henry
1971        *Ilocano rice farmers; A comparative study of two Philippine barrios.* Honolulu: University of Hawaii Press.
Marcos, Ferdinand
1976-1980   *Tadhana; The history of the Filipino people.* Manila. 4 vols.
McLennan, Marshall
1980        *The central Luzon plain; Land and society on the inland frontier.* Quezon City: Alemar-Phoenix Publishing.
Midgley, James
1984        'Social assistance; An alternative form of social protection in developing countries', *International Social Security Review* 84:247-64.
2000        'Social security policy in developing countries; Integrating state and traditional systems', in: Franz von Benda-Beckmann, Keebet von

Benda-Beckmann and Hans Marks (eds), *Coping with insecurity; An 'underall' perspective on social security in the Third World*, pp. 219-29. Yogyakarta: Pustaka Pelajar.

Ocampo, Ambeth
1993            *Looking back*. Pasig City: Anvil Publishing.
Pal, Agaton
1956            'A Philippine barrio; A study of social organisations in relation to planned cultural change', *University of Manila Journal of East Asiatic Studies* 5-4:333-473.
Po, Blondie
1980            'Rural organization and rural development in the Philippines; A documentary study', in: Marie S. Fernandez (ed.), *Rural organizations in the Philippines*, pp. 1-123. Quezon City: Ateneo de Manila University Press.
Rivera, Generoso and Robert McMillan
1952            *The rural Philippines*. Office for Information, Mutual Security Agency, Manila.
Romani, John
1956            'The Philippine barrio', *The Far Eastern Quarterly* 15-2:229-37.
Romani, John and M. Ladd Thomas
1954            *A survey of local government in the Philippines*. Manila: Institute of Public Administration, University of the Philippines.
Scott, James
1998            *Seeing like a state; How certain schemes to improve the human condition have failed*. New Haven and London: Yale University Press.
Scott, William
1992            *The Union Obrera Democratica; First Filipino labor union*. Quezon City: New Day.
Silliman, G. Sidney and Lela Noble
1998            *Organizing for democracy; NGOs, civil society, and the Philippine state*. Quezon City: Ateneo de Manila University Press.
Social security
1984            *Introduction to social security*. Geneva: International Labour Office.
Stauffer, Robert
1977            'Philippine corporatism; A note on the "New Society"', *Asian Survey* 17-4:393-407.
Sturtevant, David
1972            *Agrarian unrest in the Philippines; Guardia de Honor – Revitalization within the revolution and Rizalistas – Contemporary revitalization movements in the Philippines*. Ohio University. [Center for International Studies, Papers in International Studies Southeast Asia Series 8.]
Swaan, Abram de
1988            *In the care of the state; Health care, education and welfare in Europe and the USA in the modern era*. Oxford: Polity Press.
Warren, Carol
1993            *Adat and Dinas; Balinese communities in the Indonesian state*. Kuala Lumpur and New York: Oxford University Press.

*Archives*

HDP

Historical Data Papers, National Library of the Philippines, Manila.

Albay, HDP Historical Sketch of the Town of Polangui, La Purisima. Historical Data Papers, Albay Roll 1 (Officially Roll 3).

Albay, HDP Historical Sketch of the Town of Polangui, Santa Cruz. Historical Data Papers, Albay Roll 1 (Officially Roll 3).

Albay, HDP Historical Sketch of the Town of Polangui, Santicon. Historical Data Papers, Albay Roll 1 (Officially Roll 3).

Nueva Ecija, HDP Historical Sketch of the City of Cabanatuan. Historical Data Papers, Nueva Ecija Roll 47.

Nueva Ecija, HDP Historical Sketch of the Town of Cabiao. Historical Data Papers, Nueva Ecija Roll 47.

Nueva Ecija, HDP Historical Sketch of the District of Carranglan District, Barrio Canderia. Historical Data Papers, Nueva Ecija Roll 47.

Nueva Ecija, HDP Historical Sketch of the District of Carranglan District, Barrio Puncan. Historical Data Papers, Nueva Ecija Roll 47.

Nueva Ecija, HDP Historical Sketch of Peñaranda, Barrio San Josef. Historical Data Papers, Nueva Ecija Roll 47.

Nueva Ecija, HDP Historical Sketch of Gapan, Sitio Balante. Historical Data Papers, Nueva Ecija Roll 47.

Nueva Ecija, HDP Historical Sketch of Gapan, Sitio Kababao, Barrio San Cristo. Historical Data Papers, Nueva Ecija Roll 47.

Nueva Ecija, HDP Historical Sketch of Gapan, Sitio Putting Tubig. Historical Data Papers, Nueva Ecija Roll 47.

Nueva Ecija, HDP Historical Sketch of Gapan, Sitio Taluate. Historical Data Papers, Nueva Ecija Roll 47.

Nueva Ecija, HDP Historical Sketch of the Guimba District, Barrio Saguing Talugtug. Historical Data Papers, Nueva Ecija Roll 47.

Nueva Ecija, HDP Historical Sketch of the Guimba District, Barrio Saverona. Historical Data Papers, Nueva Ecija Roll 47.

Nueva Ecija, HDP Historical Sketch of Muñoz, Barrio Mangandingay. Historical Data Papers, Nueva Ecija Roll 47.

Nueva Ecija, HDP Historical Sketch of Muñoz, Sitio Rangayan. Historical Data Papers, Nueva Ecija Roll 47.

Pampanga, HDP History and Cultural Life of the Municipality of Minalin, Sitio Maniango. Historical Data Papers, Pampanga Roll 36 (Officially Roll 52).

Pampanga, HDP Historical Data of the Town of San Fernando, Barrio of Baliti. Historical Data Papers, Pampanga Reel 36 (Officially Reel 52).

Pampanga, HDF History and Cultural Life of the Town of San Simon, Barrio of Dela Paz. Historical Data Papers, Pampanga Roll 36 (Officially Reel 52).

Tarlac, HDP Historical Sketch of Gerona, Barrio Bularit. Historical Data Papers, Tarlac Roll 72.

Tarlac, HDP Historical Sketch of Sta Ignacia, Barrio Cabugbugan. Historical Data Papers, Tarlac Roll 72.

Tarlac, HDP Historical Sketch of Sta Ignacia, Barrio Caanamongam. Historical Data Papers, Tarlac Roll 72.

JIM MASSELOS

# Decolonized space
# The reconfiguring of national
# and public space in India

One of the great moments in the twentieth century was the achievement of
independence on the Indian subcontinent. Along with independence went a
reconfiguring of national space and of how it was perceived, understood, and
utilized. This chapter examines some of the implications of the changes in
attitudes following on the creation not of one but two nations on the subcontinent. The discussion tracks through three terrains: the first is the transformation of territorial imaginaries as a result of independence and Partition; the
second is that of the streetside locality, the space inhabited by people in their
daily lives before and after independence; and the last is the historicizing of
a spatial past, a continuum of a rethought past provoked by new national
identities. Decolonization created new national spaces that affected behaviour and influenced perceptions in a variety of ways and in different places.
The impact of the intersection between the levels, between the configuring,
for instance, of street-level and national space, was variable and often limited,
and thus problematizes the affects of decolonization. That the street corner
continued to retain spatial integrity – a sense of separateness within increasingly wider city, state, and national circles of organization – much as it had
done under the predecessor regime challenges notions of the pervasiveness
of decolonization in bringing about encompassing and qualitative structural
change.

*'When the world went topsy-turvy.'*[1]

Decolonization did not bring any change in the physical space and topography of South Asia: the same rivers continued to flow through the same
terrain past the same cities and villages. The magic moment of independence
of course could not affect the physical form of the land, but it could – and
did – affect how the former colonial space was categorized and perceived.
In this sense, there were significant spatial changes in consequence of the

---

[1]    Manto 1987:39.

moment when Britain gave up its raj over the subcontinent.

The free space long desired and struggled for by nationalists, the idea of the free nation's territory that had underscored the drive for political freedom, received physical reality on the assumption of independence. Yet the transfer of power to two independent nations failed to satisfy either of the parties that had pushed for the creation of successor states: the imagined national space behind the freedom struggles did not conform to the physical realities of the partition of British India into Pakistan and India. Neither the Muslim League with its push for Pakistan received the extended territorial areas that it had at some point wanted, nor did the Indian National Congress, the leading organization of the freedom struggle, fulfil its dreams of a subcontinental India as the proper, the logical, successor nation. There was thus ambiguity and contradiction in the new national territories. Hence, while in the celebrations at the independence hour there was jubilation over what had been won, there was also a sense of loss, perhaps failure, even if part of what had been wanted, freedom from British political rule, had been achieved. Nehru in his 'Tryst with destiny' speech at the midnight hour on 15 August 1947 in parliament noted that at that moment when India was achieving independence, the tryst with destiny, the pledge to obtain freedom, had eventuated – but only partially (Norman 1965, II:336-7). His underlying point was that while political independence was a reality the space of the nation had fallen short of what they had struggled for.

And what had been the idea of nation behind the struggle? Nehru, who had spent much of the 1920s and 1930s travelling around India in his work for the nationalist cause, discovered during his tours an India with an underlying unity that drew from the land and was expressed through its people:

> Though outwardly there was diversity and infinite variety among our people, everywhere there was that tremendous impress of oneness, which had held all of us together for ages past, whatever political fate or misfortune had befallen us. The unity of India was no longer merely an intellectual conception for me: it was an emotional experience […].[2]

In speeches during his tours, Nehru used the three terms India, Hindustan, and Bharata to describe the territory of which he spoke (Nehru 1946:39). He wrote that he tried to make his audiences 'think of India as a whole', a notion already present in their minds through popular pilgrimage circuits and the all-India spread of the settings of the great epics and myths.

Nehru's audiences sometimes greeted him with a shout, *Bharat Mata ki Jai* – Victory to Mother India – which gave him the opportunity to question

[2]    Nehru 1946:39. See also the perceptive analysis of these meetings by Pandey 1988.

what they meant by Mother India. For a time during the struggle for independence Bharat Mata had been personified as a goddess whose form was that of the subcontinent. The idea had emerged prominently in the agitation against the first partition of Bengal in 1905 and remained fixed in national consciousness through the rallying song, *Vande Mataram* (Hail to thee, O Mother), which Congress used as a prime song of protest against the raj and to promote the idea of national unity during its *satyagraha* (nonviolent) campaigns from the 1920s. The hymn came from the nineteenth-century Bengali novelist Bankimchandra's account of an uprising of *sanyasis* (Hindu holy men) and their chant as they made their way to battle. The song to the Mother celebrated the confluence of two ideas, a national space which was that of the Mother, and a national space combining with national community: it was that confluence that was used to justify demonstration, action, and battle. As Gandhi pointed out to a Bengali audience in 1927, 'Shall we not then live up to it and sing with all our hearts and say we are sons of Mother India, not merely sons of Bengal?'[3] *Vande Mataram* provided a lineage that justified the struggle by locating it within a continuous history of the territory of the motherland and thus extended it from Bengal to all of India to assert a metaphysic unity of belief and space (Masselos:2002).

Nehru himself had a somewhat different perception of Mother India, one which brought diverse social and geographical complexity into the notion of a subcontinental entity. This is evident in his campaign through the villages of northern India for the 1937 elections. His style of electioneering was to begin by throwing questions at his audiences. When he asked them what was Mother India, someone might answer: the good earth of India; Nehru would probe: Which earth, the farm, the village, the province, all of India? Finally his audience would impatiently ask him to tell them. He answered as follows:

> India was all this that they had thought, but it was much more. The mountains and the rivers of India, and the forests and the broad fields, which gave us food, were all dear to us, but what counted ultimately were the people of India, people like them and me, who were spread out all over this vast land. *Bharat Mata*, Mother India, was essentially these millions of people [...]. (Nehru 1946:40.)

At the time of independence at that midnight hour in 1947, the territory Nehru had perceived was divided and the link between land, people, and culture broke with the creation of Pakistan and India. Later each would estab-

---

[3]  M.K. Gandhi, 'After the Congress', speech at Comilla, 5-1-1927, published in *Young India* 13-1-1927, in Prasad 1929:30.

lish new linkages as part of the process of creating new national identities. But that was to be in the future.[4]

Before 1947 the general objective of the Indian National Congress had been to win political freedom for a nation covering the entire subcontinent. The imagined space of the nation was that of the total territory of the British raj and political freedom would apply to all of it. After 1947, however, the truncated and separated nations on the subcontinent created a reality that was not in conformity with the earlier imagined nationalist space of the Congress, nor even of the Muslim League that had wanted a larger and more extensive Pakistan.

Immediately, both Congress and the League were faced with the fact of the truncation of what they had long considered national space, though for each it was different. The process of coming to terms with what they had, rather than what they had aspired to, was made even more traumatic by the surgical division of the two border provinces, Bengal and Punjab, with each divided into two parts. The division of Bengal was the less difficult. Punjab posed greater problems, given the intermixing of Muslims, Hindus, and Sikhs throughout the provinces. Since the Congress and the Muslim League were unable to agree on how the provinces were to be partitioned, the task of ensuring a fair division was assigned to an independent arbiter, Cyril Radcliffe. He was to determine the precise boundary that both sides were required to accept, sight unseen. The moment of independence on 15 August, however, was not spoilt since Radcliffe's decision was handed down only afterwards, on 17 August. Inevitably difficulties arose over the decision. The line of separation between India and Pakistan was painful. The line cut through villages and fields that had before always been a single unity, and massive numbers of people had to relocate in order to place themselves within their preferred nation. The communal antagonism that had exploded during the Great Calcutta Killing in August the preceding year and had spread throughout the subcontinent now intensified and drove large numbers of people away from their ancestral villages. By the time order was largely restored in 1948, perhaps ten to twelve million people had become refugees in great, sweeping movements of population across the new borders. Perhaps over half to a million people died in the rioting and civil conflagration that accompanied the uncoordinated interchange of people and what was, though the term was not then current, the ethnic cleansing of the districts that straddled the borders.[5]

The pain of what had happened was intense. At the emotional level,

---

[4]    For a discussion of the way this applied in the context of national celebrations, see Masselos 1990, 1996.
[5]    As Gyanendra Pandey has pointed out, any set of figures is *per se* questionable both for methodological as well as practical reasons, 2001:88-91.

Mother India had been dissected, whether she was perceived as the combining of people and land in civilizational unity as in Nehru's case, or as a pervasive quasi-religious mystical entity, as among more right-wing opinion within the country. As Butalia notes, the *Organiser*, the mouthpiece of the Hindu cultural body, the RSS (Rashtriya Swayamsevak Sangh), had a front-page illustration on 14 August of Mother India – a map of the country and a woman lying on it. One of her limbs was cut off. Nehru stood beside her holding a bloody knife. Butalia (1998:141, 143) continues, '[T]he severing of the body of the country recalled the violation of the body of the nation-as-mother'. It was for what was seen as his pro-Muslim and pro-Pakistani attitudes that Mahatma Gandhi was assassinated not much later, on 30 January 1948.

A large literature has appeared over the past decade around these events.[6] The studies attempt to explain a hurricane of destruction and murder unparalleled in the history of the subcontinent. Whatever the social, political, religious, and psychological reasons for the massacres, in the hunting out of victims and in the exodus were new underlying territorial mindsets about what was one's own territory and what was alien territory. It was one's own territory that was being asserted in the attacks on people who were viewed as other, people who after the Partition belonged to, and were part of, another space, another and opposed nation. Though ideas of the nation's space had been under challenge and were in a state of flux from the time of the appearance of Pakistan on the League's political horizon, the consequences of the policy and the realities of what it would mean had remained unclear and were not at all apparent at the ground level. Only from late August 1947 did the practicalities become the unavoidable stuff of daily life and the consequences painfully evident in chaos and killing. Apart from a range of alternate explanations for the behaviour, the attackers and their forays can also be interpreted as imposing the new spatial order of the new nation on those who were viewed because of their religion as not belonging to it. The victims were seen as inhabiting a space not theirs anymore and, therefore, were the object of exclusion and persecution. That there was so much chaos in the process derived from the very confusion and uncertainty caused by the seemingly irrational partition of what had previously been undividable and complete.

Clearly a major rethinking of the space of the nation was needed. The enormity of what happened around Partition has been caught in numerous short stories; outstanding among them are those by Saadat Hasan Manto. His focus is on individuals caught up in events. Manto captures the feeling

---

[6]    They include Pandey 2001; Butalia 1998; Low and Brasted 1998; and Talbot 1996: section 2. Of course, all scholars owe major debts to the memoirs and studies that appeared in the first decades after independence and for the major collection of articles and reminiscences put together in Philips and Wainwright 1962.

of weirdness and strangeness, of alienation, that set in overnight around what had been a continuous and familiar place. How could something that had been a whole become a fragment and be something different because its political status had changed? How could it no longer be home or become so unfamiliar? In a short memoir he described his own bewilderment:

> My wife and children were in Pakistan, but they had gone there when it was still the India that I knew. I was also familiar with the occasional riots which broke out between Hindus and Muslims. But now that piece of land which I had once known as India had a new name. Had this changed anything? I didn't know. What self-government was going to be like, I had no idea, not that I hadn't tried to think it out.[7]

The difficulty in grasping the sundering of what had only recently been a whole is handled metaphorically in one of his best-known stories, 'Toba Tek Singh'. A couple of years after Partition the two governments decided to exchange the inmates of lunatic asylums, people who had been left high and dry on the wrong side of the border. They were to be returned to their putative nations, but they did not understand:

> As to where Pakistan was located, the inmates knew nothing. That was why both the mad and the partially mad were unable to decide whether they were now in India or in Pakistan. If they were in India, where on earth was Pakistan? And if they were in Pakistan, then how come that until only the other day it was India?[8]

The story focuses on a Sikh inmate who had become known as Toba Tek Singh, from the small town in the Punjab that had been his home. Nobody knew where it was, whether it was in Pakistan or India. Everyone was confused about where places were or if and where they had moved to.

> Those who had tried to solve this mystery had become utterly confused when told that Sialkot, which used to be in India, was now in Pakistan. It was anybody's guess what was going to happen to Lahore, which was currently in Pakistan, but could slide into India any moment. It was also possible that the entire subcontinent of India might become Pakistan. And who could say if both India and Pakistan might not entirely vanish from the map of the world one day? (Manto 1987:14.)

---

[7] Part of the memoir is reprinted in Hasan 1987.
[8] Manto, 'Toba Tek Singh' in Manto 1987:12.

On the day of the exchange, the Sikh was taken to the no man's land separating the two nations' borders but when told that Toba Tek Singh was in Pakistan he refused to move but remained standing there through the night till he collapsed, dead. Manto (1987:18) concludes the story: 'There, behind barbed wire, on one side, lay India and behind more barbed wire, on the other side, lay Pakistan. In between, on a bit of earth which had no name, lay Toba Tek Singh'.

Such stories and the events of 1947 and 1948 themselves highlight how ideas of the nation and the nation's territory on which the freedom struggle had been predicated were badly out of kilter with the new realities that followed the breaking up of British India. The mental maps through which people had operated – their sense of place and of where they were – had been contradicted by the division of the country and had become obsolete and useless. Likewise nullified was the previous national imaginary, the nation's imagined space of the pre-independence struggles, by the creation of the two new nations – and the new paper maps they engendered. Yet, the new did not easily replace the old. Often old ideas of place survived subliminally. To use a favoured analogy of the day, what was happening resembled the way in which writing survived on a palimpsest, never quite totally obliterated or replaced by later writing, but visible underneath it.[9]

At best the realities of separation were slow to sink in and it took time for new localities and national templates to develop. The uncertainties and adjustments demanded by separation were to continue for years.[10] People had lost the core of their identity – their farms and villages, their religious places and shrines, their ancestral houses and all that was familiar.[11] The bewilderment is caught by Urvashi Butalia (1998:80) in an interview with Rajinder Singh who describes the feelings of reaching safety: 'When we got to Dera Baba Nanak they said to us, you have come home. But we thought, our home was over there. We have left it behind. How can this be home?'.

For many the sense of loss would never entirely go away, but would remain, a permanent scar in the memory. And for the children of such migrants there could be a paradoxical twitch of memory. Urvashi Butalia (1998:25) describes her feelings on entering Pakistan for the first time:

---

[9]  Nehru (1946:38-9) considered that India was 'like some ancient palimpsest on which layer upon layer of thought and reverie had been inscribed, and yet no succeeding layer had completely hidden or erased what had been written previously. All of these exist together in our conscious or subconscious selves, though we may not be aware of them, and they had gone to build up the complex and mysterious personality of India.'

[10]  A prime example of the continuity of dispute is provided by Kashmir, a princely state whose territory was outside the purview of Radcliffe's arbitration. After some wavering Kashmir acceded to the new India shortly after independence but its placement continues to be a matter of contention between Pakistan and India to the present time.

[11]  The sense of loss a half century later pervades interviews with former refugees. See those reproduced in Butalia 1998 and Talbot 1996:section 2.

I felt – there is no other word for it – a sense of having come home. And I
kept asking myself why. I was born five years after Partition. What did I
know of the history of pain and anguish that had dogged the lives of my
parents and grandparents? Why should this place, which I had never seen,
seem more like home than Delhi, where I had lived practically all my life?

Yet in the chaos of the time for those who fled just as those who attacked, a
new order did begin to emerge, created on the ground, through these very
actions and in the global confusion that beset the Punjab. Those who went or
fled were heading for a sanctuary whatever their specific reasons for fleeing,
whether driven by terror or national patriotism. In the movement of people
towards sanctuary there were different drives: for safety, security, escape; for
reaching home, the homeland, one's nation. The two clusters of ideas con-
verge since in the atmosphere of the times only the space of one's own nation
could be safe.

Sanctuary could thus in those times have different sets of meanings –
or could encompass both. The place for sanctuary became a space for the
coalescing of new territorial associations, for a new spatial-national identification and for the realization that the new place could be – and ultimately did
become – home. The old place that had been home was being replaced by a
new space that over time would garner its own mindset of associations and
identification. The sanctuary would become home. What was home was thus
determined by the new lines superimposed on the physical map of the Punjab
and Bengal – and by people in consequence moving to one side or other of
the line. The physical realities of division not only affected the specific, the
physical place of abode or refuge, but also promoted a new mindset, a new
mental template, of the location of home in a context equated with the space,
organization, and place of the new nation. This was of course never total or
complete. The palimpsest analogy continued to apply and to be reflected in
the ways in which people still continued to think longingly of what they had
left – and some of those who moved across the borders did so more than
once. Some Muslims went to Pakistan in 1947 or early 1948, returned to India
when the situation settled, but then decided it was Pakistan they preferred
and finally settled there. Initially they had not understood the permanence
or totality of the creation of two sovereign nations, but saw the Partition and
the events of 1947 as merely an exaggerated version of the limited outbreaks
of communal rioting that had happened before. It took time for the full realization to sink in that 1947 was entirely different – and that the change was
permanent. Others took more time to leave and more time to deliberate over
what space they could consider their own. As Manto wrote, 'I found it impossible to decide which of the two countries was now my homeland – India or
Pakistan' (Hasan 1987:6). He was not alone in his uncertainty, nor was he

unique. Others were surer and stayed where they were: a significant proportion of Hindus remained in East Pakistan (East Bengal), while many more Muslims stayed in India than fled as refugees or, in more ordered fashion, chose to migrate.

## Controlling city space

The decolonization of the subcontinent created two new nations and, in imposing borders between them, truncated regions whose immediate postcolonial history was disfigured by waves of mass killings. In the process, new perceptions of regional and national space perforce emerged and nullified preindependence ideas of the nation-space and the entity of the affected regions. Such factors did not apply in the major towns and cities many kilometres away from the epicentres of disruption. There decolonization linked into preexisting perceptions of city space and did not alter them as dramatically.

The city had played a critical role in the freedom struggle as a key locus for organizing resistance to the raj. The space of the city had assumed symbolic importance in the great Congress-led agitations before independence. While the *satyagraha* campaigns were about political confrontation, about the massing of individual wills and bodies against the force of the raj, the form that they assumed was often about contestation of space, about the right of *satyagrahis* to offer nonviolent resistance on the streets and in open spaces, all in places denied to them by the government. At issue in such fights to control or have access to public urban space were at least two ideas. The first lay in the power of the government to control all such space – its streets and lanes, its parks and the open sands of the beaches that were common recreation and meeting spots. The second concerned city space, which symbolized the power of the raj: this covered such prominent and distinctive sites as government buildings – secretariats, legislative assemblies, municipal offices, court buildings. It also covered specific localities, the places where such buildings were concentrated, where Europeans mainly lived, where European businesses and offices were located.

The Indian city in colonial times was characterized by the way in which space was demarcated according to function and activity. Certain parts were predominantly commercial or financial in character; other parts were the location of industry or of trade. Some parts were the locus of British administration, the area from which the raj operated its nexus of power and control. In this sense there were clearly British and Indian areas, though Indians lived and worked in raj areas, just as the converse could apply. The distinctive example of spatial separation and power appeared in the final decades of

British power with the formal inauguration of New Delhi in 1931 (Frykenberg 1986; Gupta 1981). It was a city replete with the symbolism of British domination – the palatial Viceroy's House at the end of a long avenue, the Kingsway, which challenged the Champs Élysées in size and grandeur; the flanking monumental Secretariat buildings at one end, and an arched war memorial at the other. It was an entirely planned city embedded in a green belt intended for the siting of British authority and for those who worked the machines of imperial power. New Delhi was a tailor-made imperial city, polarized and distinct from the numerous earlier and ancient cities that had once flourished in the area, the last being Shahjahanabad, built by Emperor Shah Jahan in the 1640s. It had been the centre of the Mughal Empire at its greatest, and the centre also in its twilight. It managed to hold on to its symbolic importance and was a focus for the great uprising of 1857 and even retained much of its identity after the British defeated the last Mughal emperor, subjugated the city and reestablished their paramountcy over northern India.

Shahjahanabad survived the late nineteenth century despite the physical inroads the British made on its urban form. Soon after their conquest, the British razed a whole city quarter, from the Jumma Masjid (the Great Mosque) to the Red Fort, where had been located the palace of the last Mughal emperor.[12] Later, a railway line truncated another part of the old city. Nevertheless, the city retained a symbolic potency that was consciously manipulated by the raj in order to take on to itself some of that aura while it was also the place where British rule had been unequivocally reestablished through the conquest of Delhi in 1857. Both strands of meaning were at play in the way the raj used Delhi as the site for grand imperial set-piece durbars.[13] At the first of them Queen Victoria was proclaimed empress of India in 1877. Other equally grandiloquent ceremonials followed. At the durbar of 1911 the King-Emperor, George V, in person proclaimed that the British capital of their Indian Empire would move from Calcutta to Delhi. In moving to Delhi, a new city was built and in consequence thereafter Shahjahanabad became Old Delhi. While it still retained its unique character, the symbolic centre of the Indian Empire was located outside it, in New Delhi. Near neighbours and separated by only a few kilometres, the one became the antonym of the other.

In long–established colonial port cities like Madras, Calcutta, and Bombay,[14] the contrast was not as stark, and though some areas were considered essentially European and distinct from Indian localities, they were

---

[12]   For a photograph of the quarter before it was razed see the cover of Masselos and Gupta 2000.
[13]   British durbars were an appropriation of the great ceremonial audiences staged by Mughal emperors at which the emperor received pledges of allegiance from the subordinate nobility and thus maintained and re-asserted his preeminence (Cohn 1983).
[14]   Though each of the cities was renamed in the 1990s, the old names are used here as they reflect the usage of the day.

not exclusive. Wealthy Indians also lived there, for example in Malabar and Cumballa Hills in Bombay, as indeed did a whole panoply of Indians who provided the services necessary for residents to live in the luxury and comfort they expected. Similarly, large Indian business firms clustered where their European counterparts gathered, as in the Fort area of Bombay. Such localities were commonly viewed in terms of dominance in function and power as being raj in character while the areas where the wealthy and powerful did not live, were on occasion referred to with terms like the 'native town', the 'Indian town', the 'market' or 'bazaar' areas and so on. Though less distinct than the polarity between Old and New Delhi, in the great port cities there was an equivalent mental antonym of spatially distinct areas.[15]

Before independence it was a template of power and function that provided the locale for the great agitations. They challenged British spatial control and symbolism in a variety of ways. Parades and marches through the streets asserted rights of spatial accessibility and challenged British control, while at the same time they rallied wider public support. Meetings in the *maidans* (parks) of the city and in accustomed gathering places on beach sands as at Bombay's Chowpatty Beach also asserted the same point, particularly when the government banned such meetings. When the Congress flag, the then national flag, a tricolour of white, saffron, and green with a spinning wheel superimposed in the middle, was raised at such meetings and such spaces, it served the same purpose. There was added symbolism: the action asserted the public space was not British but was proper and inalienable national space: it was the nation's and of all who lived in and were part of it. When nationalists managed to hoist the flag on public buildings during the campaigns, the point was emphasized even more powerfully, the clear defiance of public authority in an action that tweaked the nose of the raj by symbolically appropriating the locations of its power.

The marches and demonstrations usually started in the 'Indian' quarters of the city and wended through them towards the power centres. In Bombay they might start from Girgaum or Kalbadevi or other localities, and meander through similar areas to gather supporters and publicize the immediate issue (such as the salt laws) and the wider cause, national freedom. Finally they would move on towards the Fort area, the city's business and financial hub, and the nearby concentration of government buildings. They were usually stopped before they could reach their destination, sometimes in the 'Indian' parts, sometimes closer to the key locations of British power. In the Salt Satyagraha and Civil Disobedience Campaign from 1930 there were great confrontations. Processions of *satyagrahis* would head to Bori Bunder, a vast traffic interchange of six main roads with the grand Victoria Terminus

---

[15] For templates and different mental maps of the city, see Masselos 1991.

(present-day Chhatrapati Shivaji Terminus) of the then G.I.P. Railway on one side, and the Bombay Municipal Corporation headquarters on the other. In one notable confrontation on 1 August 1930, which began in the evening peak hour, *satyagrahis* occupied much of the square and the streets leading to it, and stayed there on the road overnight until the police charged the next morning and arrested them (Masselos 1987:81-2). Other demonstrations on other occasions managed to push through into the European business area, on towards government buildings and beyond to the Gateway of India (the spot where George V had landed in all pomp in 1911). Various marches ranging from 5,000 to 50,000 people surprised Europeans sipping their gins and tonic in the exclusive Europeans-only Royal Yacht Club nearby, something that had not happened before, and something which, as a British officer noted, 'caused much irritation'.[16] There were similar incidents in other spaces over the years and in different campaigns. All highlight the importance space played in the nationalist movement and in the demonstrations through which the movement expressed its opposition to the raj.

Contesting the space of the raj was an obvious way to assert the right of Indians to the symbolic and organizational centres of raj power. In addition, access to public space was necessary for demonstrators to voice their views and garner wider support. It paralleled the armoury of tactics that workers used in more tightly focused agitations. When workers went on strike, they demonstrated outside the workplace and even at times marched to the head office. Such action too reflected the idea of mental templates of power and function and of how contestation was couched in terms of challenging the physical space represented or controlled by dominant power, whether political or material. Where their aims differed from the nationalist campaigns discussed above was that strikes and workers' demonstrations lacked the overall ideological implications of nationalist commonality that underlay the Gandhian campaigns and were directed at issues of direct concern: working conditions, hours of work, salaries. The targets were Indian industrialists, not British imperialists. On occasion, industrial labourers did make common cause and participate in the nationalist agitations as, conversely, nationalists supported workers' causes. When they did so, they asserted their presence and political beliefs through the use of city public space.

The last of the great nationalist campaigns was Quit India in 1942, a campaign for immediate independence. Wholesale arrests of Congress leaders on the night before the campaign was to begin largely nullified any detailed implementation of whatever planning had been completed. Nevertheless, there was a massive response – a spontaneous revolution, as one historian

---

[16]  Handwritten minutes of conversation with Brigadier Charles, 16-5-1930, Mumbai, Government of Maharashtra State Archives, Home Dept. Special Br 1930 File 750(26), f.9.

described it (Hutchins 1971). The initial reaction, before moving into extensive sabotage in the countryside, was widespread street-level protests and a determination on the part of the Congress to go ahead with such meetings as were already scheduled. The first, around 8 a.m. on 9 August shortly after the arrests, was at Gowalia Tank in Bombay where the first session of Congress had been held in 1885. The government tried to stop the understudy leadership from making speeches, singing the national song and raising the national flag, but the leaders went on regardless until they were forcibly stopped and tear gas was fired at the 4,000 people present. The soldiers who encircled them wore 'hideous' gas masks, like creatures from outer space (Sahai 1947:82). Aliens were in power.

The next major set-piece battle early in the campaign had an equally potent spatial element. It was held a few days later in the suburbs of the city – at Shivaji Park in Dadar, a middle-class and Marathi-speaking area. Police stopped people from entering the park from around 4 p.m., but they forced their way through. People tried to make speeches, sing songs and raise the flag, but police attacked them with tear gas and charged them with *lathis* (metal-tipped bamboo staves). From the residential apartments that formed a semicircle around the park, residents cheered on the thousands of demonstrators and provided them with rags and buckets of water to counteract the tear gas. This was serious confrontation, 'a regular pitched battle'[17] over occupying the park that lasted until the demonstrators retreated around 8 p.m. It had been a battle about access to and possession of open space. The day became embedded in the nationalist armoury of memory and was used in Congress propaganda over the following months. As with other demonstrations, this one in Shivaji Park exemplifies the congruence of issue and space jointly deployed against the power of the raj, and Congress's assertion of its right of access just as conversely it displayed raj repression in its most highly developed form.

Over the following weeks, demonstrations centred as much in the 'Indian' parts of Bombay as in the British-dominant parts. Crowds formed in streets, lanes, and alleyways and charged out to confront police determined to quell them by using as much force as was necessary, *lathi* charges, tear gas, and even gunfire. When attacked, the crowds retreated into their streetside localities, sometimes referred to as *wadis* where mainly Hindus and Jains lived, or as *mohollas* for Muslim areas. There they would regroup and come out charging in a different direction. The confrontations were direct, violent, and often bloody – and there was a significant death toll. Sixteen people died on

---

[17]   The phrase is from a report from the governor of Bombay to the viceroy, see Lumley to Linlithgow, Confidential Report No.110, 24/27-8-1942, London, British Library, India Office and Records, L/P&J/5/163, f.160.

10 August in Bombay in the confrontations and six the following day, though thereafter the toll was in injuries rather than in deaths. Concurrent with the direct action of street-corner groups, those Gandhian Congress members not yet in jail attempted to maintain peaceful nonviolent protest but their demonstrations were also forcibly stopped. After a fortnight, the applications of force imposed a modicum of order on Bombay, but it was never complete, and resistance continued through into 1944 (Masselos 1998).

The story of Quit India is complex, but its interest here is that it illustrates how protest in the 'Indian' quarters emerged in street-level localities through residents joining together. Such unity was not novel but drew on existing locality organization, formal and informal, and on how individuals had become accustomed to behave conjointly in their localities. Localities already had coherence, authority structures, and even distinctive organization, particularly apparent at festival time. Important in this regard was the Hindu Ganapati festival and the ten-day period of mourning that was Mohurrum for Muslims (Masselos 1977, 1982). Both events had similar trajectories: the installation of revered or symbolic objects, a programme of activities for the ten-days' duration of the installation and, finally, the taking of the objects to the sea for immersion. For Hindus, it was clay statues of Ganesh, elaborately painted and decorated, that were taken to the sea; for Muslims it was equally elaborate and impressive model reproductions of the tombs of Husain and Hassan, nephews of the Prophet.

Localities of streets and associated lanes and byways were basic units with their own social integrity, their own structures of formal and informal authority, and with established customary modes of behaviour. They were modules whose existence as entities had been demonstrated over the years in street-level action, most prominently so in the communal riots that shook Bombay from the second half of the nineteenth century. The localities were the sites for such outbreaks. At such times they became bristling fortified enclaves, protecting their own space against the forays and attacks of rival *mohollas* and *wadis*. Much of any riot was about testing the strength of boundaries and locality perimeters or, put differently, about attempting to invade and take over an opponent's space. Much of it was also about attacking individuals from the other, the opposed, space. Thus, while specific issues may have started the hostilities, territorial imperatives play a large part in explaining the shape of riots in urban Bombay. Nevertheless, despite relatively frequent riots in the city over the years, the division and hostility between localities were not necessarily permanent. According to occasion and need, previously rival *mohollas* and *wadis* could come together in joint street actions; and it was then former rivals became allies. The locality module was constant, not the issues that powered its engines into action.

British control over the localities varied, and from the late nineteenth century the government put considerable effort into accessing and controlling them. It stationed police in the areas; used informers, secret police, and undercover agents; and worked through locality leaders who were active in local-level politics, mediated in religious disputes and the like. Quit India brought the issue of who controlled the space of the locality to the fore and by the strength and spread of the opposition confronted the government in the various localities of the city. In doing so, it challenged the very capability of the government to govern. The government deployed its usual armoury of tactics to establish control such as those blunt instruments of force they were to operate to telling effect in Shivaji Park in 1942. They were also slightly more subtle when they imposed curfews on affected areas and levied collective fines on troublesome localities. They were eventually able to quell disorder and show that the writ of the raj was present, but it was always tenuous in the 'Indian' quarters.

*The nation and its spatial past*

When independence did finally come all raj space became Indian (and Pakistani). The contestation with a foreign power was over and the celebrations during the week of independence were euphoric, at least in those cities and regions not immediately affected by the rising tide of anarchy. Elsewhere, as in Calcutta where Gandhi fasted on the day of independence and businesses were closed in fear, the mood was of deep gloom. But Bombay had celebrations that lasted a week with the whole city magnificently illuminated. Lights bedecked buildings and outlined government buildings, a spectacle that everybody had to see. Enthusiasm was so intense that through the night people drove around the city in cars, on the backs of trucks, and in victorias (horses and carriage) to take in the sights. To handle the crush of traffic much of the city was converted into a one-way grid. People were jubilant and sang and danced in the streets. Apart from members of extremist Hindu organizations, virtually everywhere and literally almost everybody celebrated in Bombay in those nights, regardless of whether they had participated in the various nationalist agitations or even whether they had opposed or disapproved of them.

At the critical moment on the midnight hour of 15 August when the national flag was finally raised ceremoniously over a free India, the crowds went wild. They milled about and pushed past the guards around official buildings. At the Secretariat they were unstoppable as they literally took over the government space and turned the bastion of British power in Bombay Presidency into Indian space.[18] Through the night till dawn people surged

18   *Times of India*, 15-8-1947, p. 1.

through the buildings, but it was not long thereafter before a new power structure asserted itself. Within a day entry into government buildings was stopped except for official purposes even though the buildings were now under Indian authority and control. The old template of raj power had become a template of Indian governmental power.

Similarly, the successor government replicated raj attitudes to the control of public space, albeit with modification. Flag raisings and singing of national songs were now acceptable and no longer carried the challenge they had presented in the days of the raj. Needed now for nation building they were to play key roles in ceremonials and national days. As for meetings and marches, political parties not in government and with their own policies and political interests still needed to use them so as to promote their own causes. Here the Congress government was less sympathetic: it permitted meetings and demonstrations, but since it had administrative responsibility to maintain public order it could justify banning meetings. There was a major confrontation early in the postindependence period that showed it could impose controls as stringently as the government it had replaced. Thus when a left-wing activist student group proposed to meet in a public park in the mill areas of the city, the government banned it on the grounds it might enflame communal relations in the city, though in the area concerned there was no communal tension and the issues involved had nothing to do with religious issues. The students tried to hold their meeting regardless, pushing their way through police cordons into the park and were met with the same force used against Congress in the Shivaji Park meeting, including *lathi* charges and tear gas.[19] As had happened before independence, so too afterwards, political battles for expressing viewpoints would take the form of contestations over meeting places, over the space in which to express viewpoints and programmes.

The message delivered by the confrontation is clear. The successor Congress government could not and did not alter the basic relationship between the state and the people. Congress control of public space was in practice much like that of the preceding imperium. What was different was that control was now vested in an Indian national, as distinct from an alien external, force. Generally, it might be expected of the new government that it would be more sympathetic to issues that concerned its population and more sympathetic also to the use of those techniques of agitation, the panoply of all that was involved in offering nonviolent civil resistance, those techniques it had invented and had been the first to deploy. Over time, two key but contradictory considerations were to constrain its handling of street-level protests. The first derived from the fact that after independence Congress had become a political party. It was no longer the nationalist movement that had operated

---

[19] *Times of India*, 1-1-1948, pp. 1, 7.

through struggle and tried to bring everybody into the struggle. Its objective now was to govern and stay in power, something that required it to score points over rival parties and contenders to its *gadi* (throne) and to control those who challenged its popular base. Its interest was to ensure it continue ascendant as a political party. On the other hand, as the government and the one imbued with implementing all the ideals and dreams of the nationalist struggle, including the maintenance of freedom and the ensuring of personal dignity, its role and logic went beyond merely preserving preeminence and power – perhaps the prime considerations that had driven its foreign prede-cessor as ruler.

Congress was thus in an ambivalent position as it assumed the mantle of governance: it sought to make real the enlightened ideals of the freedom struggle while it also needed to assert its power as the government. In assert-ing its position, in making difficult choices it found itself largely repeating the familiar patterns of raj controls. In practice, the people who were impos-ing and implementing them, civil servants, officials, and police, were much the same people as had been responsible for implementing earlier controls. Only the politicians in government were different. Thus, neither the agents of control nor the idea of public space altered in any structural sense after independence, even if they were no longer of the raj. What did change was a heightened sympathy with the means of *satyagraha*, though that did not prevent the government from stopping its public practice whenever it chose to do so.

Similarly, the nature of what had been the raj, that is the British, parts of the city, was not dramatically affected by the changeover of political rulers. As the British left, the racially exclusive clubs opened themselves to Indians. Indians replaced European managers in foreign-owned business enterprises and moved into company accommodation in elite areas. Generally what hap-pened was that one dominant and wealthy social group replaced another. Social exclusivity continued though the earlier criteria of race, or connection to raj power no longer applied. Much the same areas still attracted the power-ful: the locales no longer had a raj flavour, but they continued to be centres of privilege.

Likewise, there was little structural alteration in the 'Indian' parts of the city or in its customary sense of space. The *wadis* and *mohollas* continued to maintain their coherence as locality units and were not affected by decoloni-zation despite changes in population concentrations following the arrival or departure of refugees. Though Muslims went to Pakistan from Bombay, the entity of the *mohollas* remained intact and continued to be predominantly Muslim in character, as likewise did the *wadis* in relation to Hindu concen-trations of residents and businesses. Communal rioting did break out in Bombay late in 1947 as news and rumours spread details of the carnage in the northwest and as refugees brought their stories to the city. The rioting was not, however, citywide but occurred at the boundaries between specific Hindu and Muslim localities and in this sense followed the pattern of rioting that had developed over the preceding century. There were similar inter-locality confrontations, similar attacks on neighbouring and rival localities, and similar defence of territory. The police handled the situation by applying the usual armoury of measures – they controlled the formation of crowds, increased the police presence, ordered curfews on troublesome localities, imposed collective fines, and worked through local leaders. There were even large peace processions that made their way through the localities, proces-sions that apart from the usual political worthies and local notables now included Bollywood film stars.

If the local space of Bombay was largely unaffected by decolonization, what of Delhi? Old Delhi retained its character, though the composition of specific parts changed as Hindu refugees took over the houses of Muslim families who had fled to Pakistan and thus altered the predominant char-acter of some quarters. At this time Old Delhi became a staging ground for displaced people, victims of the carnage, so that for a year or so it looked like an enormous camp until people were absorbed into the city or left it. In large open spaces like the grounds of monuments such as the Purana Qila (the Old Fort) were big camps of Muslims waiting to go to Pakistan. Hindu refugees were more visible and in greater numbers in Delhi than in Bombay. Even New Delhi became affected. The outer ring of Connaught Circle, the key shopping and business centre for New Delhi, saw an influx of refugees who set up kiosks and food stalls and gave the area a character it had not had before. British space was being Indianized through the migrant presence just as at an elite level; New Delhi became Indianized as Indian politicians took over the sites of power and Indian bureaucrats replaced British officials and moved into the grand buildings and housing created for the raj and gave it a different flavour. The British face of New Delhi and its attribution as British space thus changed after independence. It was still the location of elite power structures and hierarchies, but they were Indian, not British.

In the days after independence the message of Indian agency and freedom was popularly demonstrated in the extraordinary enthusiasm of the crowds at the formal events and celebrations. They were there early on 15 August in thousands to cheer as the members of the new Indian Cabinet went to the Durbar Hall in the Viceroy's House to be sworn in before the chief justice, and they were there in hundreds of thousands in the early evening at Prince's Park for the salutation of the new national flag. The crowd, estimated at between 250,000 to 600,000, was so immense that a planned march of the armed ser-vices was abandoned and the flag-raising hurriedly completed, though with the fortuitous appearance of a rainbow at the end, after which India's first governor general, Lord Mountbatten, tried to leave with the nation's prime minister, Jawaharlal Nehru, perched on the front of the carriage. As it pushed slowly through the throng, people from the crowd surged forward cheering and trying to shake hands with the governor general and his wife. [20] Spatial barriers were being broken down in all sorts of ways.

Nehru brought Old Delhi back into the picture with an address at the Red Fort on the morning of 16 August, the second day of independence. He used the location as a symbol of the continuity of Indian governance and as a means of pointing out that the period of British rule was short in terms of the history of the nation. He legitimated the new government by bringing it into the context of a place full of memories and associations, some those of the 1857 Mutiny and some of the recent imprisonment in the Red Fort of freedom fighters. Just as the raj had tried to absorb the aura of the Mughal Empire through appropriating durbars, so Nehru and his government located themselves under a similar umbrella of association. Each year after 1947 it became customary for the prime minister to deliver an address from the ramparts of the Red Fort in the early morning of 15 August as the major set piece in commemorating Independence Day (Masselos 1990).

The other major national day likewise played on spatial symbolism – not that evoked by Old Delhi, but that inherent in the British imperial geography of New Delhi. The occasion was the celebration of India's becoming a Republic on 26 January in 1950 (Masselos 1996). In that year there had been a march in Irwin Stadium in the afternoon, but the following year it was decided to take the celebration into the streets, five miles of them, starting at the top of Rajpath (Kingsway) at the President's Palace, down along the avenue, past India Gate, and on into the twin cities. The parade over the years became progressively grander: the army, navy, and air force marched; there were displays of weaponry; cadets and school children joined in; and there were floats illustrating every part of the Republic, which was presented as a vibrant and diverse entity, not a truncated territory. The parades celebrated Indian national achievements and the Indian nation. The quality of the spectacle in part derived from the grand avenue where the parade started, an avenue designed for grand imperial statements. But after 1947 the statements were about the Indian nation, not the British empire.

In contrast, Pakistan did not have a custom-built imperial capital at the time of independence nor did it have within its territories major Mughal monuments around which to build new national imagery. Instead the transfer ceremonies were held in Karachi, a raj colonial port city, commercial centre, and provincial capital of Sind. On 13 August 1947, Mountbatten flew

[20]   *Times of India*, 17-8-1947, pp.1, 7. See also Mountbatten's 'Description of events on 15-8-1947 (Written on the following day)', reprinted in Hodson 1969:390-3; Hough 1983; Ziegler 1985:425.

in from Delhi as the last viceroy of India in order to be present the next day as Pakistan came into being and Jinnah was sworn in as the first governor general of Pakistan. The crowds in Karachi were as tumultuous and as exultant as they were to be in Delhi the next day; they cheered Mountbatten enthusiastically and hailed Jinnah triumphantly as the great leader, the creator of Pakistan. His speeches around this time reflected the ethos of the new nation, that of its basis in the idea of two nations on the subcontinent, the Hindu and the Muslim, and the achievement for Muslims of a national territory, a space of their own, a homeland. But the new Muslim homeland was not to exclude the minorities who remained in Pakistan; he promised their rights would be secure.[21] A couple of days earlier he had pointed out that 'we are all citizens and equal citizens of one State'.[22] The overall idea of Pakistan that was being conveyed was of course that which had driven the demand for Pakistan, a homeland for Muslims, even though it should encompass others who were not. The actual space of Pakistan, with its two wings on either side of India, was less important in the new nation than the idea that it was the homeland for subcontinental Muslims. Jinnah died the year following the winning of Pakistan and the impressive mausoleum built for his body became a national monument, a commemoration of his achievement as the founder of the nation. Karachi remained the capital until it was replaced in the 1960s by a new custom-built planned city, Islamabad, to the northwest of (West) Pakistan, which became the focus of national identity and of the symbolic nation. The national imagery that Pakistan had thus forged differed significantly from that which India created for itself on the basis of its being a successor nation – of the British, of the Mughals, and of all of India's pasts and the places associated with them.

*Conclusion*

Decolonized space thus became Indian (or alternately Pakistani), a point that the national symbolism inherent in the new and evolving national ceremonials unequivocally asserted. But national values were not only imposed on the new nation-space – that space also provided legitimation and reinforcement for the new nation through the accretions of its history and their pervasive continuance into the present. What was largely rejected was the European and alien past; it was still too close to be absorbed. The nation itself had to be rethought once the process of achieving independence had been completed, given the way in which the freedom struggle's ideas of what would be the

---

[21]   Broadcast speech, 15-8-1947, cited in Saiyid 1962:446.
[22]   Speech to Pakistan Constituent Assembly, 11-8-1947, cited in Wolpert 1985:337.

national territory had not been fully met. The ceremonials in Delhi and, on a smaller scale, the parallel ones in each province and territory, aided in the spatial adjustments required. Viewed not in terms of ideas and values attaching to space but to the structural relations involved in public space, access to it and control of it, the government maintained its rights of control just as had the British. The maps of power and function still continued to operate in people's minds, though the British character that such templates once presupposed was replaced by Indian determinants. As for accustomed space, once new populations of refugees and migrants had been absorbed, the basic patterns of urban configurations remained much as before, even if some of the specifics had changed. There was now a different raj, but raj there was.

## *References*

Butalia, Urvashi
1998        *The other side of silence; Voices from the partition of India*. New Delhi: Viking.
Cohn, Bernard S.
1983        'Representing authority in Victorian India', in: Eric Hobsbawm and Terence Ranger (eds), *The invention of tradition*, pp. 165-209. Cambridge: Cambridge University Press.
Frykenberg, R.E. (ed.)
1986        *Delhi through the ages; Essays in urban history, culture and society*. Delhi: Oxford University Press.
Gupta, Narayani
1981        *Delhi between two empires, 1803-1931; Society, government and urban growth*. Delhi: Oxford University Press.
Hasan, Khalid
1987        'Introduction', in: Saadat Hasan Manto, *Kingdom's end and other stories*, Translated from the Urdu by Khalid Hasan, pp. 5-7. London/New York: Verso.
Hodson, H.V.
1969        *The great divide; Britain – India – Pakistan*. London: Hutchinson.
Hough, Richard
1983        *Edwina; Countess Mountbatten of Burma*. London: Weidenfeld and Nicolson.
Hutchins, F.G.
1971        *Spontaneous revolution; The Quit India Movement*. Delhi: Manohar Book Service.
Low, D.A. and Howard Brasted (eds)
1998        *Freedom, trauma, continuities; Northern India and independence*. New Delhi, Thousand Oaks, London: Sage.

Manto, Saadat Hasan
1987　　　　*Kingdom's end and other stories*. Translated from the Urdu by Khalid
　　　　　　Hasan. London/New York: Verso.
Masselos, Jim
1977　　　　'Power in the Bombay "Moholla", 1904-15; An initial exploration into
　　　　　　the world of the Indian-urban Muslim', *South Asia* 6:75-95.
1982　　　　'Change and custom in the format of the Bombay Mohurrum during
　　　　　　the 19th and 20th centuries', *South Asia* New Series 5-2:47-67.
1987　　　　'Audiences, actors and Congress dramas; Crowd events in Bombay city
　　　　　　in 1930', in: Jim Masselos (ed.), *Struggling and ruling; The Indian National
　　　　　　Congress 1885-1985*. Delhi: Sterling. [Asian Studies Association of
　　　　　　Australia South Asian Publications Series 2.]
1990　　　　'"The magic touch of being free"; The rituals of independence on
　　　　　　August 15', in: Jim Masselos (ed.), *India; Creating a modern nation*, pp.
　　　　　　37-53. New Delhi: Sterling.
1991　　　　'Appropriating urban space; Social constructs of Bombay in the time of
　　　　　　the Raj', *South Asia* 14:33-63. [Special issue 'Aspects of "the public" in
　　　　　　colonial South Asia'.]
1996　　　　'India's Republic Day; The other 26 January', *South India* 19:183-204.
　　　　　　[Special issue 'Asia and Europe: Commerce, colonialism and cultures;
　　　　　　Essays in honour of Sinnappah Arasaratnam'.]
1998　　　　'Bombay, August 1942; Re-readings in a nationalist text', in: Biswamoy
　　　　　　Pati (ed.), *Turbulent times; India 1940-1944*, pp. 67-107. Mumbai: Popular
　　　　　　Prakashan.
2002　　　　'Time and nation', in: Sujata Patel, Jasodhara Bagchi and Krishna Raj
　　　　　　(eds), *Thinking social science in India; Essays in honour of Alice Thorner*, pp.
　　　　　　342-54. New Delhi/Thousand Oaks/London: Sage.
Masselos, Jim and Narayani Gupta
2000　　　　*Beato's Delhi, 1857, 1997*. Delhi: Ravi Dayal.
Nehru, Jawaharlal
1946　　　　*The discovery of India*. Calcutta: Signet Press.
Norman, Dorothy
1965　　　　*Nehru; The first sixty years*. Vol. 2. London: Bodley Head.
Pandey, Gyanendra
1988　　　　'Congress and the nation, 1917-1947', in: Richard Sisson and Stanley
　　　　　　Wolpert (eds), *Congress and Indian nationalism; The pre-independence
　　　　　　phase*, pp. 121-33. Berkeley, CA: University of California Press.
2001　　　　*Remembering Partition; Violence, nationalism and history in India*.
　　　　　　Cambridge: Cambridge University Press.
Philips, C.H. and M.D. Wainwright (eds)
1962　　　　*The Partition of India; Policies and perspectives 1935-1947*. London: Oxford
　　　　　　University Press.
Prasad, Rajendra (ed.)
[1929]　　　*Young India, 1927-1929*. Madras: Swatanthara Press.
Sahai, Govind
1947　　　　*'42 Rebellion; An authentic review of the great upheaval of 1942*. Delhi:
　　　　　　Rajkamal Publications.

Saiyid, M.H.
1962        *Mohammad Ali Jinnah; A political study.* Lahore: Sh. Muhammad Ashraf.
Talbot, Ian
1996        *Freedom's cry; The popular dimension in the Pakistan movement and partition experience in North-West India.* Karachi: Oxford University Press.
Wolpert, Stanley
1985        *Jinnah of Pakistan.* Delhi: Oxford University Press.
Ziegler, P.
1985        *Mountbatten; The official biography.* Glasgow: Fontana and Collins.

FREEK COLOMBIJN

# Solid as a rock, or a handful of dust? The security of land tenure in Indonesian cities from 1930-1960

*Land tenure and regime change*

Land tenure systems are culturally specific or social conventions (Deiniger 2003:xxii).[1] In precolonial societies land tenure was usually embedded in a network of social relationships. A transfer of rights, if possible at all, was determined by rights and obligations towards kin, fellow villagers, and rulers. Land had both a practical and a symbolic value. The symbolic value of land could be expressed in different ways, for example, in myths regarding the origin of its occupants and reinforcement of such myths by the presence of ancestral burial places. Territorial conflicts thus enhanced the symbolic value of the land. As Michael Saltman (2002:3) rightly argues, 'identity achieves its strongest expression within the political context of conflicting rights over land and territory'.

Both colonization and decolonization had a profound impact on land tenure systems. When Europe colonized other parts of the world, Western companies and settlers needed land and pushed indigenous residents to marginal areas. Land became a key commodity in the colonial economy of these hitherto noncapitalist societies and thereby acquired an exchange value. This new system of land control thus had a great impact on precolonial society and often met with stiff opposition (Bernstein 2000:263; Berry 2003:641; Deiniger 2003:xviii). Because of the interests involved, rules pertaining to land are by nature always political; they promote the interests of either those who have some form of control over land, or those who do not. A regime change is usually followed by a change of state regulations pertaining to landownership. This new set of regulations tends to favour the new power holders or a group they are trying to protect.

If we look at the Philippines, we see an example of the kind of impact that changes to the landownership system can have. Washington established the

[1]  I am very grateful to Martine Barwegen for her assistance with data collection. I would like to thank the editors, the members of the Kring van Leidse Urbanisten, the Kotagroep, and my colleagues from the 'Indonesia across orders' research group, all of whom have made helpful comments about drafts of this chapter. I would also like to thank Mischa Hoyinck and Robert Chesal for editing my English.

Philippines Commonwealth in 1935 as a first step towards full independence within twelve years. The most important Philippine politicians were part of the landed elite and were of a Catholic, Spanish-Creole background. These politicians defined the emerging Philippine nation along ethnic lines. Non-Christian, indigenous people living in the uplands were excluded from the Philippine nationalist project. The maximum landholdings of indigenous non-Christians and the Muslim Moros (who were considered a separate category) were legally reduced from 25 to 10 acres, while Christians were allowed holdings of no more than 40 acres. Land grants issued by sultans or chiefs without consent from the former Spanish and American colonial governments were declared void. The landed elite profited from the political changes by introducing new legislation that allowed them to reinforce their hold over land. Private titles were granted to capitalists who bought large tracts of land from which indigenous people were then barred. This long process, culminating in Commonwealth Act 141 of 1936, created rampant landlordism in the Philippines (Church 2003:132-3; Molenkamp 2003:33-9).

Another example of how land changed hands after a political sea change is the apartheid regime of South Africa (1948-1991). The Groups Area Act (issued in 1950) prescribed that each racial category (Black, Coloured, White, Asian) be restricted to its own residential and commercial districts. This was to be achieved through controls on the purchase of land and buildings. District 6 was one of the most vibrant, ethnically-mixed areas of Cape Town until it was declared a Whites-only area in 1966. About 60,000 people were forcibly moved out of District 6 under the Groups Area Act; their houses were bulldozed. Simon's Town is another notorious case of forced resettlement in Cape Town. In 1994, Restitution of Land Rights Act 22 gave people who had been dispossessed of their land under racial legislation the right to claim restitution. The Land Claims Court mediated in the restoration of land to the original owner or lawful descendants, or, when this was impossible, awarded compensation in money or an alternative plot of land. The first cases of thousands of claims were handled by the Land Claims Court in May 1998.[2]

The South African example supports the hypothesis that a supplanting of political regimes is often followed by a change in land tenure rules. These are particularly clear illustrations of the ethnic (racial) undertones of discriminatory legislation and of how quickly a political change can be followed by new rules.

---

[2]   Royston 2002; Land Claims Court of South Africa (www.server.law.wits.ac.za/lcc/), District Six Beneficiary & Redevelopment Trust (www.d6bentrust.org.za), District Six Museum (www. districtsix.co.za) and *Sunday Times* of 17-5-1998 (www.suntimes.co.za/05/017/) (accessed on 4-12-2003). Even at the height of apartheid, though, control of the very strict separation of Black and non-Black land ownership broke down in the face of unplanned urbanization (Coquéry-Vidrovitch this volume; Royston 2002:166).

In colonial Indonesia we see two cases of how drastically land rules are changed following a political watershed. Immediately after the British assumed control of Java in 1811, the Lieutenant Governor, Thomas Stamford Raffles, nationalized every last acre of privately owned land and imposed a land rent. Later, when state policy for the archipelago was once again determined in The Hague, the ascendant Liberals in Dutch parliament pushed through the Agrarian Law of 1870, creating opportunities for big capitalist interests. This law not only favoured Western enterprises, it also protected indigenous landowners against land-hungry foreigners.

The focus of this article is a third regime change in Indonesia, namely the postwar decolonization and the accompanying agrarian reforms. The Dutch ruled Indonesia until they were defeated by Japanese forces in 1942. Indonesian leaders proclaimed independence in 1945, two days after the Japanese surrender that marked the end of the Pacific War. The Dutch did not recognize independence at first. Between 1945 and 1949 they resumed colonial administration in the largest towns and all of the outer islands, while the Indonesian Republic ruled most of rural Java and Sumatra. When the Dutch finally transferred sovereignty in 1949, they insisted on the creation of an Indonesian federation. However, this lasted less than a year, and in 1950 Indonesia became a unitary state.

*Security of tenure*

As can be expected, Indonesian independence had an impact on land tenure systems, or 'regimes of rights to land' (Slaats and Portier 1990/1991:56) as well. The young state experimented with socialist economic ideas, and Article 33 of the 1945 Constitution explicitly stated that land should serve the interest of the people (rather than big companies). This policy was elaborated in the Basic Agrarian Law (Undang-Undang 5 tentang Pokok Agraria) of 1960. The law had two main objectives: to abolish the colonial legacy of racially-inspired distinctions between European and indigenous land tenure, and to strengthen legal certainty. Legal certainty and security of tenure overlap but are not exactly the same; security of tenure may include illegal occupation secured by political protection and legal certainty may become insecure when power holders ignore the rule of law. Here I will study how Indonesian independence made an impact on security of tenure; I will concentrate on ownership because other rights (renting, pawning, and other) are usually derived from ownership.

In general, the security of landownership is far from self-evident. People cannot physically possess land in the same way they hold movable property (clothes, food, vehicles, and jewellery). In the case of land, one may have a right to use a plot, and this right is vested in the title. Outsiders, however, can claim ownership too, even when they do not (yet) physically occupy the land. The owner of a plot only feels the property is secure when he or she believes others will acknowledge the title, and all the more so when titles are not written down in deeds. In cities, a feeling of security is created when there is a system of landownership that determines unequivocally who controls a given plot of land. This feeling in turn encourages investment. Insecurity, on the other hand, makes landowners and the state hesitant to invest; it thwarts provision of shelter, undermines long-term planning, and hinders the provision of basic services (Durand-Lasserve and Royston 2002:7-8; Deiniger 2003:xix, xxv; Nwaka 1996:126). The UN Centre for Human Settlements (Habitat) concludes that 'Access to land and security of tenure are strategic prerequisites for the provision of adequate shelter for all' (quoted by Durand-Lasserve and Royston 2002:2).

From an agrarian perspective, insecurity of land tenure increased during decolonization. People could lose their rightful claim to a plot of land through outside manipulation of the individual title or by changes in landownership regulations in general (Berry 2003:640; Goldberg and Chinloy 1984:37-8, 222-3). In the chaos of revolution, manipulation of individual titles always becomes easier and the rules of tenure change, as they did in Indonesia's Basic Agrarian Law 5/1960. In the West, and therefore also in Western-dominated social sciences, security is considered desirable while insecurity is best avoided. However, one person's insecurity can be another's opportunity for change. Decolonization might also be regarded as a process of emerging opportunities. Rusty structures are discarded by force, and the resulting insecurity leads to creativity. In terms of land tenure, decolonization created many new opportunities for squatting, which overrides all formal claims. By focusing on agrarian reform and the new opportunities it creates, decolonization can be viewed in a nonteleological way and considered an open-ended process (Cooper, this volume).

Principles of tenure were laid down in Indonesia's 1945 Constitution, and the formulation of a new agrarian law began in 1948, before the war of independence was over. However, the key legislation, the Basic Agrarian Law, was not proclaimed until 1960 (Gautama and Hornick 1972:91). While new regimes tend to create new land tenure systems, it took Indonesia 15 years to do so. This is a puzzling fact, though to an extent the lapse of time is easy to understand. Drafting a new agrarian law with potentially far-reaching consequences was an extremely complicated affair and a major accomplishment at a time when the young state was facing so many other urgent tasks.

The slow pace of agrarian reform can be attributed partly to local variations in land tenure rules. A major policy aim at the time was to overcome the tension between nation building and local diversity, though this was not specifically addressed in the Basic Agrarian Law. Local diversity had been at odds with the idea of national unity for as long as the archipelago had been regarded as a whole. The sheer size and cultural variation were enough to hamper national cohesion. The archipelago spans five thousand kilometres, about the distance from Ireland to the Ural Mountains, while its people speak some three hundred different languages. The tension between national unity and local diversity was also manifest in urban land tenure systems, which varied from city to city and complicated any state law. Agrarian rules were, in the words of the Dutch head of Medan's Municipal Agrarian Office, of 'a bewildering diversity' (Jansen 1930:145). The reason why it took 15 years for Indonesia to promulgate the new Basic Agrarian Law may lie partly in the fact that local tenure arrangements were quickly adapted to independence. Perhaps the need for a new national law was not so urgent because the necessary agrarian changes were already taking place locally. If this is true then nation building, in the sense of increased unity, was not achieved in agrarian terms.

The aim of this chapter is to shed light on two aspects of decolonization: the enhanced insecurity of property and the attempt at nation building by overcoming local diversity. So far, agrarian studies in Indonesia have either focused on national laws and overlooked local deviations or focussed on one local situation and missed the wider pattern. I will try to give an overall view of local variation. Below, I will first analyse the national reforms intended by the Basic Agrarian Law of 1960. Subsequently, I will deal with the entire spectrum of tenure systems and their various, but changing, degrees of security.

## Agrarian changes at the national level

In colonial times, landownership rules basically distinguished between European law (*Europees recht*) and indigenous law (*inlands recht*). Late-colonial agrarian policy was based on the 1870 Agrarian Law, which entitled the government to offer land in long lease (*erfpacht*) to Western companies. However, the state could only lease land when it had the right to dispose of it. The Agrarian Law was therefore accompanied by the so-called Domain Declaration (*Staatsblad* 1870 no. 118), which declared that all land of which ownership (*eigendom*) could not be proven in accordance with European law was considered state domain. Land held under indigenous law was formally state domain as well, but in practice the state respected land titles regulated by indigenous law. People holding land with indigenous rights (mainly indigenous smallholders) were forbidden to sell land to nonindigenous persons. This was meant to prevent the emergence of a landless class (Commissie voor het grondbezit 1934a; Gautama and Hornick 1972:75-81; Logemann 1936:7-8). The most important categories of land were, therefore, state domain; smallholdings with indigenous rights (only *de jure* property of the state); state domain given to companies in long lease (only in rural areas); and land that had acquired a European title of full private ownership.

The European land title was almost exclusively found in cities and towns. Colonial jurists realized that if the prohibition of land sales from indigenous to nonindigenous people was applied in urban areas, development there would be severely hampered. To solve this problem, the state had the right to distribute new plots with property rights based on European law, but only in cities and towns. The state could also grant the right to construct buildings on state land (*recht van opstal*), but this did not have much impact because full property was clearly the preferred title. Urban land with a European title was relatively expensive. Owners had to pay the administrative costs of surveying their land parcel and transferring its title at the cadastre upon acquisition. They also had to pay an annual land tax (*verponding*). Such costs and effort were only warranted if the land had certain specific purposes. One advantage of a European title was that it offered the highest degree of security, and this was considered necessary if the owner intended to carry out major and expensive construction work in brick or cement. The precise measurement of a land parcel with a European title was also necessary in shopping areas, where shops were built in an unbroken line up to the exact boundary of the plot.[3] Security depended not only on precise measurement and registration, but also on the type of law which applied. A European title was based on the elaborate and written Civil Code, whereas indigenous rights were based on the customary law (*adat*), which was at best partially codified. When it came to credit, banks would only approve a mortgage on land with a European title (Logemann 1936:8-11).

The legal distinction between a European and indigenous title was absolute, but the difference in levels of security was gradual. Land with an indigenous title was also registered, not by a cadastre but by the neighbourhood administration. The neighbourhoods, or kampongs, were formerly rural settlements that remained autonomous administrative units when they were swallowed up by the expanding towns. The kampongs had land registers based on the collection of land rent in the early nineteenth century. The tax form was the only written proof of ownership. The register itself consisted of a map (scale 1:5,000) indicating the location and dimensions of the plots. The plots had been measured by a *plontang*, a bamboo stick, often warped, with a length of one *roede* (3.76 m). Shortly before World War II this was replaced by a 5-metre *plontang*, which was more consistent with the metric system.

---

[3] Registration at the cadastre required the greatest possible precision. It took up a full 16 sections of the law just to describe how the name of the owner should be recorded (Kadastrale Dienst in Nederlandsch-Indië 1938:36-43).

Hedges, trees, and ditches served as boundary markers. Changes in ownership were reported to the neighbourhood head and secretary, who were summoned as witnesses by the law court (*landraad*) whenever an ownership dispute arose.

During the Japanese interregnum (1942-1945) no thought was given to land tenure systems, but, as we shall see, squatting was often condoned, and this represented a *de facto* change of tenure. After the proclamation of independence in 1945, the Indonesian government declared that all old (colonial) laws that did not conflict with the Constitution would remain valid until a new regulation came into force. In the case of the colonial landownership rules, that took until 1960.

The Basic Agrarian Law of 1960 was aimed at redistributing agricultural land from the wealthy to the landless peasants, and at eliminating the colonialist dualism between indigenous and European titles. To this effect all existing titles were converted to a uniform system consisting of eleven rights to land. Of these eleven rights, *hak milik* gave the tenure holder the widest competence right. It meant freehold: full ownership of a plot that could be freely sold, bequeathed, or otherwise transferred. Ownership could only be enjoyed by Indonesian citizens, either individually or collectively, and a number of specified legal bodies. Plots with a formerly European and indigenous title of ownership were automatically converted to the new right of *hak milik*; both colonial types of ownership were thus unified under one term in the 1960 law. However, foreign owners of a European title – in practice mostly Chinese residents – had their freehold reduced to land in long lease because only Indonesian citizens were permitted to own land (Gautama and Harsono 1972:21-4, 31; Gautama and Hornick 1972:82, 86, 90-105; Leaf 1992:109-14).

The distinction in the East Indies between indigenous and European tenure systems was not unique in the colonial world. In their East and West African colonies, the English and French also distinguished between traditional indigenous communal ownership and colonial individual ownership. In contrast to colonial Indonesia, their discourse included the term 'traditional' rather than 'indigenous' to denote the opposite of European; this term explicitly places the two land-rights regimes in an evolutionary framework in which the European system is deemed the more modern, superior one. Both traditional and colonial law were products of the colonial situation. The so-called traditional rules were invented or reinterpreted by colonial regimes, creating a racialized system of property rights. The colonizers profited from this dichotomy because it laid the foundations for the expropriation of land on which their plantation economy rested. The indigenous chiefs also profited from this system because they controlled communal land. During decolonization, the communal tenure systems in these English and French African colonies did not disappear. They proliferated. A convincing claim to land not only rests on a persuasive narrative revealing who first arrived on a territory; it also depends on effective social networks and political power (Berry 2003:642-5, 649; Chanock 1992:280-90; Lentz 2005; Reyntjens 1992:123-5).

## *Unregistered, legally held land*

In post-1960 Indonesia, there was a gap between the law and actual practice. Judges often overruled decisions based on local customary law by applying national rules even though this was contrary to the spirit of the Basic Agrarian Law of 1960. Landowners also subverted at least one aim of the Basic Agrarian Law, namely to have all property registered (Colombijn 1994:179). Many owners preferred the informality of unregistered plots.

Until 1960, parcels of land not registered at the cadastre were considered 'plots with an indigenous title'; the word 'indigenous' refers here to the tenure system and not to the owner, who could be of a nonindigenous background as well. After the proclamation of the Basic Agrarian Law, such plots were referred to as 'not yet' registered; the implied temporality could in practice be continued indefinitely. Given the shortage of skilled staff and funds, land registration was a daunting task. Many landowners consciously did not apply for a cadastral deed because of the cumbersome procedure and high costs. The formerly European plots remained 'islands in the middle of the sea of adat land' (Gautama and Harsono 1972:31; see also Slaats and Portier 1990/1991:59). The Basic Agrarian Law therefore introduced a new dualism between plots already registered under the new system (formerly European plots for the most part) and those that had 'not yet' been brought into the system (Leaf 1992:88, 114, 127-36, 145). In some cases there was written proof of ownership of these unregistered plots, such as property tax payments or a deed of purchase drawn up by the owner (Leaf 1992:100-1).

Tenure based on such written proof of ownership was not as secure as a title deed from the cadastre. In colonial times, conflicts about these relatively weak types of proof did occur once in a while, but their number increased significantly during the Japanese occupation and the subsequent decolonization. One example is the case of a plot in Padang, West Sumatra. It was owned by a Eurasian man named Vermeer and his indigenous wife. During the Japanese occupation, the man died in a Japanese detention camp, while his wife fled to Jakarta. After independence, their son Alex Vermeer stayed with his mother in Jakarta. Two daughters migrated to the Netherlands. During the Japanese occupation and through the late 1940s and 1950s, Vermeer's maid looked after the land and paid land tax to the administration. She allowed 16 families to build a house on the land and collected rent from them. In 1958, a certain Rahman saw an opportunity for land speculation. He came up with a forged letter from the Netherlands, stating that the two sisters of Alex Vermeer had died childless in Europe – making Alex the sole heir – and persuaded Alex Vermeer to sell the plot to him. Rahman parcelled the plot and forced the 16 families to purchase their respective lots. The conflict then escalated, became entangled in the political turmoil of the late 1950s and 1960s, and dragged on until the 1980s (Colombijn 1994:138-42). If it had not been for the uncertainty caused by decolonization, Rahman could never have launched this scheme.

The legal pluralism was in itself a source of insecurity; often it was not the exact location or ownership of an individual plot that was at stake, but the question of which tenure system applied. The Basic Agrarian Law of 1960 declared that *adat* law (customary law) remained valid as long as it did not contradict other articles of the Basic Agrarian Law (Gautama and Hornick 1972:93). Cornelis van Vollenhoven, a Dutch law professor and expert on *adat* law, had identified – some people say 'invented' (Burns 2004:225) – 19 areas in the archipelago, each with its own version of *adat* law (Vollenhoven 1981:44). *Adat* law applied mainly in rural areas, but was also valid in towns with a clear ethnic majority that belonged to one of the 19 recognized *adat* law areas. Most of the larger cities, however, had ethnically mixed populations, so that no specific *adat* law system could be applied. In these cities, indigenous rights were called 'hereditary individual property rights' (*erfelijk individueel bezits-recht*), which resembled the rules of European property (Jansen 1930:148).

It was not self-evident that the colonizers would recognize indigenous tenure systems in Indonesian towns. To give a counter-example, the legal construction of communal land in Africa was based on a rural situation and not suited to urban land. The convention that communal land is inalienable because it belongs as much to the ancestors as the kin yet unborn (Sonius 1962:23) was impractical in towns. Migrants in towns did not always live with their kin. Moreover, illegal land markets had been developing since the nineteenth century in response to pressure on land. Residents often circum-vented the official system by applying simpler, informal rules (Chanock 1992:288-91; Lentz 2005; Nwaka 1996:125). On the whole, the situation in African towns was less conducive to indigenous tenure systems than in Indonesia, where the existence of indigenous, individually-owned titles was more widely accepted.

Indonesia's 'legal pluralism' grew more complex after 1960 (Hooker 1975:6, 251). Contrary to its aims, the Basic Agrarian Law of 1960 increased land tenure insecurity. Partly as a 'postcolonial reaction' and a denunciation of colonial law (Burns 2004:250), the Basic Agrarian Law gave precedence to *adat* law over the Civil Code. Its preamble, in a reference to the national char-acter of the agrarian law, stated that it should be based on *adat*. In this context *adat* was an empty phrase because the preamble did not specify which of the 19 *adat* law areas or other local law systems was meant (Harsono 1994:141-

2, 154-71). Moreover, most of the *adat* regulations were unwritten, so the bar, which had more faith in written statutory law, was frequently at a loss as to which rule to apply (Gautama and Harsono 1972:24-9). Gautama and Hornick (1972:106) concluded in the 1970s that at that time there was 'probably more legal uncertainty about agrarian law and rights in land than there was before enactment of the basic law'.

An added source of potential uncertainty was communal landownership. In such cases, a given community enjoyed full ownership, but the individual members of the group of landowners did not. A good example can be found in the town of Padang, where the Minangkabau constitute the ethnic majority.[4] According to the Minangkabau, *adat* land is communal property of the female members of matrilineal (sub)lineages. Although some legal experts have claimed that it was not permitted to sell lineage land, it did happen in practice; sales dating back as far as 1828 have been recorded. A transfer of title was possible when all sublineage members agreed, and it is precisely here that problems arose because membership was not always clearly defined. Every sale, division, donation or inheritance of a plot could be contested by any sublineage member who felt short-changed. Land disputes were often brought to court and as long as a plot was *sub judice* a real estate developer could neither sell it nor build on it. The Minangkabau's *adat* rules of ownership led to a high incidence of land disputes and hence insecurity, which greatly hampered urban development. In order to avoid such inconvenient disputes, many people preferred to deal with plots with European titles (Colombijn 1994:182-202).

The following case reconstructed from various files at the Padang court of justice demonstrates the complexities of legal pluralism that were exacerbated – but not caused – by independence. In 1919 a man from lineage A donated part of his land to his two daughters, who, according to Minangkabau *adat*, belonged to lineage B (their mother's lineage). The donation fell under Islamic law as *hibah* – meaning a gift and contradicted Minangkabau *adat*; according to *adat* the man should have kept the land in lineage A because the land was property of his sisters and nieces. After the man died, his lineage members contested the legality of the gift to his daughters of lineage B. In 1921, 1936, 1938, and 1940, lineage A sued lineage B, but in all these lawsuits the judge upheld the gift to the daughters of lineage B, acknowledging the correct application of Islamic law. In 1962, when each 'clan' was headed by a member of a younger generation, lineage B brought lineage A to court, claiming that it not only owned the land donated to the two daughters in 1919, but all lineage land in the possession of lineage A (none of this other land had been litigated

---

[4]    Another Indonesian example of communal urban land is the *kalakeran* land in the town of Manado (Nas 1985).

in the earlier lawsuits). Lineage B claimed that the land occupied by lineage A had been its own ancestral land, but that the members of lineage B had fled from the Dutch army during the war of independence; when they returned they had found the land occupied by lineage A (Colombijn 1994:199-202). It is telling that lineage B filed this case in 1962 after the new Basic Agrarian Law provided extra support for cases based on *adat* law, and not immediately after the war of independence. The land was still contested in the 1990s.

## Aristocratic land

The communal land in Padang is one example of an idiosyncratic situation more complex than envisaged by the new national law of 1960. Two other cities with a unique agrarian situation were Yogyakarta and Medan. Local aristocrats claimed a considerable share of urban land in these two cities. The distinction between indigenous and nonindigenous 'races' (Asian and European respectively) was further problematized because only Asians were considered subjects of the local rulers. Access to land was mediated via the local aristocratic family, but it was only open to the ruler's subjects, who received preferential treatment.

The sultanate of Yogyakarta (on the island of Java) was a semi-autonomous state that issued its own laws. The sultan claimed ownership of the land but gave kin and servants apanages, some of which were in town. People could obtain a plot of urban land on condition they built a yard and provided services to the sultan or apanage holder. On 1 January 1925, the sultan reclaimed the urban apanages. All legal users of land – subjects of the sultan – received an indigenous title deed. The four kampongs that surrounded the royal palace (*kraton*) held a special position in the sense that the property was not freely alienable; a transfer of the title required royal approval. Yogyakarta also knew European titles, which were issued to nonindigenous residents until 1918, when the sultanate promulgated its own Domain Declaration. From then on, nonindigenous residents could only acquire a new plot by renting it from indigenous owners or by securing building rights (*recht van opstal*, not ownership) from the sultan.[5] Nothing changed in Yogyakarta during the Japanese reign in terms of landownership rules. After the proclamation of Indonesian independence, the Sultan of Yogyakarta decided to support the Republic, thereby retaining, if not enhancing, his prestige and authority.

---

[5]  Schwencke 1932; Bousquet, Nota betreffende den rechtstoestand van den grond ter hoofdplaats Djokjakarta, Djokjakarta, April 1918, Royal Institute for the Tropics, Amsterdam; E.M. Stork, Overgang van Inlandsche grondrechten in het gewest Jogjakarta, 10-8-1936, Royal Institute for the Tropics, Amsterdam.

Following independence and pending a national agrarian law, Yogyakarta issued local regulations called Peraturan Daerah Istimewa Yogyakarta 1954/2. Coming six years before the Basic Agrarian Law of 1960, this swiftly introduced local legislation may have increased confidence in the tenure system during the chaotic postindependence period. Even under the new regulations, however, ownership of individual plots could be insecure. In the 1950s many Dutch nationals sold their building rights and fled Indonesia, but often such hurried transfers were not recorded at the cadastre (Dinas Agraria D.I.Y. 1974). Apparently it was not only the Dutch sellers but also the buyers of these rights who lacked confidence that their ownership would be respected.

Although the Sultan of Deli in Medan (North Sumatra) had lacked the wide administrative powers and prestige of his counterpart in Yogyakarta, he had nominally claimed a considerable part of the town as his ancestral domain. A current resident of royal descent told me that in the late colonial period the sultan gave away parts of his domain in Medan to people who needed small plots. The sultan issued deeds, so-called sultan's grants, as proof of his permission. It seems that, in practice, many people were allowed to live on the sultan's land as long as they acknowledged his sovereign rights. No substantial payment was required to obtain a sultan's grant. As the sultan only gave grants to his subjects, neither Chinese, European, nor Indian residents could acquire land from him (Jansen 1925:101). Even Tjong A Fie, a well-known property owner in colonial Medan who allegedly owned half of the housing stock in the 1920s, did not own land in town.[6]

The sultan did not keep a central registry of all his grants, but many prudent grant holders carefully saved their deeds. As the sultan's grants were registered less meticulously than deeds at the cadastre, they were more likely to become the focal point of conflicts. Nevertheless, a sultan's grant was regarded as such firm proof of ownership that it was even considered collateral for a mortgage. Creditors provided capital in return for the right to the first share in a forced auction of a sultan's grant. This practice continued for years, albeit at a relatively high interest rate because a sultan's grant was considered slightly less secure collateral than a European title deed (Jansen 1925:103).

Eventually, the practice of using sultan's deeds as collateral proved to be less secure than hitherto assumed. In 1923, the trading company NV Handelmaatschappij Djoe Sen Tjong went bankrupt. As was customary, two creditors wanted to auction the grant they had received as collateral (in the presence of a notary).[7] However, the state claimed first right to the

---

6    Dirk Buiskool and Tuanku Luckman Sinar, oral communication.
7    In this case it was a Deli Maatschappij grant, issued on the sultan's authority.

auction's yield because Djoe Sen Tjong still had a very large tax debt. In its final ruling the Supreme Court decided in 1927 in favour of the tax collector. Suddenly, creditors lost confidence in their collateral. As a result of the ruling, creditors wanted the sultan's grants they had accepted as collateral converted into European titles, but owners of sultan's grants remained reluctant to do so because of the costs. In the hope of ending the insecurity, the Handelsvereeniging Medan (Trade Association of Medan) urged the government to convert all grants into European titles free of charge. However the government did not heed the call.[8]

The validity of the sultan's grants was based in part on the sultan's prestige. He had been held in high esteem during the Dutch colonial period and had remained in place during the Japanese occupation of Indonesia. As a descendant recalled, the sultan used to hang a portrait of Hirohito on the wall behind him whenever he received Japanese officers. As the officers bowed to their emperor, they were unwittingly also paying homage to the sultan as well. However, after independence was proclaimed a social revolution swept this part of Sumatra. Most royal families were discredited as colonial puppets; many aristocrats were murdered. When Dutch forces recaptured the city of Medan, they partially restored the sultan's authority. His role was most important when Medan was made capital of the State of East Sumatra (Negara Sumatera Timur), one of the constituents of the new Federal State of Indonesia, a short-lived Dutch creation (1949-1950). After East Sumatra's subsequent dissolution, all that remained of the sultan's land was nationalized.

The aristocracy's loss of power in the Sumatran social revolution weakened the sultan's status and may have eroded the value of his grants. Many migrants arrived from other parts of Sumatra in the postwar years. They had little respect for the sultan and settled on the sultan's land without his formal consent. The sultan no longer had the power to prevent this. The best he could hope for was that the newcomers would acknowledge his status as landowner and pay some land rent. The plots of land that were occupied in this way were subdivided over time.[9] In a sample of cases filed in the court of justice of Medan after 1945, there appears to be a disproportionate number of cases about land held with a sultan's grant. This suggests that titles with a sultan's grant were especially lacking in credibility after decolonization. This may be connected to the general decline of the sultan's status.

One example of how the sultan's status changed after independence was a lawsuit filed by the sultan's family against the National Land Agency

[8]    Jansen 1925:107-111; Verslag Handelsvereeniging Medan 1930 1931:5-8; Verslag Handelsvereeniging Medan 1931 1932:5. A swiftly issued temporary law declared the sultan's grants valid collateral from 1927 until 1933, but after 1933 a sultan's grant was no longer considered valid collateral by a court of law (Verslag Handelsvereeniging Medan 1938 1939:8).
[9]    Tuanku Luckman Sinar, personal communication.

(Badan Pertanahan Nasional). In the late nineteenth century the Sultan of Deli leased out a plot of land for 75 years. When the term of lease expired in 1954, the plot was not returned to the sultan's heirs but to the district authorities, who issued a new lease and a building permit to a private third party. The sultan's descendants claimed full ownership of the plot and filed a complaint at the administrative court. Three experts of land law summoned by the judges were divided; this left the judges groping in the dark. The court of first instance and court of appeal rejected the claim by the sultan's heirs. The supreme court at first granted the claim in cassation, but, finally, in 1996, quashed its own judgement in revision (Bedner 2001:162).[10]

In short, the aristocracy's claim that it had the right to issue titles was a secure basis for land tenure. However, it was only secure to the extent that the aristocratic ruler was locally acknowledged and respected. In Yogyakarta, where the sultan remained in power throughout the decolonization process, the aristocratic basis of titles did not cause any problems, while in Medan, where the sultan lost prestige and influence, decolonization eroded the validity of the sultan's grants and the security of tenure.

*Registered land owned by individuals*

The most secure property was land with an individual title acknowledged by statutory law. In colonial times, the most formal type of ownership, or freehold, had a European title. Colonial European land was encumbered with rights defined in the Civil Code of the East Indies, which was kept as consistent as possible with the Civil Code in the Netherlands. An ordinance of 1834 (*Staatsblad* 1834 no. 27) required that land with a full title be registered at the cadastre; local cadastral registers could date back further (Colombijn 1994:178; Gautama and Hornick 1972:7, 82). After promulgation of the 1960 Basic Agrarian Law the most secure title was registered as full ownership (*hak milik*).

Title deeds of full ownership gave the highest security of tenure in colonial times, but some deeds did not survive the years of war and revolution. A common problem stemming from the Japanese occupation was that people had lost their title deeds and needed an authenticated copy after the war.[11]

---

[10]   There were several juridical irregularities in this case. Adriaan Bedner notes that it was not about bad governance but disputed ownership and that, therefore, the plaintiffs should have gone to a civil, not administrative, court. The supreme court revised its decision on the basis of a re-evaluation of evidence. According to Bedner (2001:162), this is 'very strange', for Supreme Court revisions are generally only allowed when new facts are discovered.

[11]   See, for example, the request of the NV Administratiekantoor Kamerlingh Onnes, Pengadilan Negeri Medan, Pdt. 139/1950 and 140/1950, or several specimens (1948) at the Koninklijk Insti-

Lists of lost deeds were regularly published in the local newspaper, presumably in an effort to retrace the deeds. It was not only individual landowners who lost them; sometimes the cadastre itself lost an entire archive of deeds. The archives of the cadastre in Semarang, Pekalongan, Ambon, and Tanjung Pinang were either largely or entirely destroyed. The cadastral archive of Padang had been moved to the interior of Sumatra during World War II. There it remained during the Indonesian Revolution, in a place beyond the control of the Dutch-dominated city administration.[12]

Another problem was that for some time the cadastre did not operate properly. In 1945 the normal transfer of titles at the cadastre was temporarily suspended (*Staatsblad* 1945 no. 139); this measure was revoked in early 1947, but due to a lack of trained staff it would take some time before the cadastre was fully functional.[13] In 1941 the cadastre employed 297 staff; in April 1947 the number was down to 159 (although the number of high-ranking staff had hardly changed, declining from 46 to 45) (*Jaarboekje* 1941:40-57; *Jaarboekje* 1947:4-10). Employing new inexperienced civil servants endangered the uniformity of procedures (a vital concern for a reliable cadastre).[14] In short, the decolonization process put even the titles considered most secure, those based on European law, at risk.

## Government land

The central colonial government already owned state domain in most towns when autonomous municipal governments were established, one after another, in the first quarter of the twentieth century. The new municipal administrations enviously eyed the state domain within their borders, but the central government would not donate its land to them for free. Therefore local governments could acquire land only by becoming a player on the land market and many urban administrations did so with relish. These major players created public development corporations (*grondbedrijven*) as part of their urban development strategy. These corporations acted as land banks, owning land that was needed for future urban development. They also prepared sites for construction; levelling them, laying paths, constructing roads,

---

tuut voor Taal-, Land- en Volkenkunde, Leiden (hereafter KITLV), Manuscript H 1156[2].

[12] Rondschrijven Secretaris van Staat voor Binnenlandse Zaken, H. van der Wal, 14-9-1948, no. A.Z.26/1/50, Arsip Nasional Republik Indonesia, Jakarta (hereafter ANRI), Archives Algemene Secretarie (AS) 609.

[13] Rondschrijven Hoofdkantoor van het Kadaster 440/47, 18-3-1947, KITLV, Manuscript H 1156[2].

[14] Kennisgeving Hoofdkantoor van het Kadaster 3823/49, 21-10-1949, KITLV, Manuscript H 1156[1].

and digging drainage canals. They bought strips of land that were deemed necessary for future infrastructural works or state buildings. They also purchased plots in order to build up a stock of land; the aim was to swap this for specific privately-owned plots that the administration might need later. Some development corporations bought large tracts of rural land bordering the cities and towns for future urban development. The last aim of development corporations was to combat speculation; the municipality eased rising market prices when it put enough land up for sale at low prices (Devas 1983; Gemeente Bandoeng, Dienst van het Grondbedrijf 1931:17; Jansen 1930:149). Transactions of municipal land eventually took up such a large share of total land sales that the administration was often setting, rather than following, the market price. In the town of Bandung, for example, land speculation indeed disappeared in the areas where the development corporation operated, but remained common where the corporation was inactive (Verslag 21e jaarvergadering 1933:16).

However, there were also times when the public development corporations themselves (or municipalities) could be accused of speculation (Jansen 1930:157). Some development corporations neither sold nor rented out their plots, just leaving them to waste instead (Verslag Planologische Dag 1939:30). When they neither built on the land nor withheld it from the market, they could be considered land speculators. A notorious case is Bandung. The public development corporation there invested large amounts of capital in land that yielded no return, plunging the municipal administration into a financial crisis. In the municipal council of Bandung, in 1923, nationalist politician G.S.S.J. Ratulangie made a telling remark: 'Pinter sekali pembesar2 gemeente' ('The urban authorities are very clever'; Otto 1991:209). He was referring to the cynical observations of indigenous people who had sold land to the development corporation and seen the profits reaped by the administration.

The distinction between sound urban planning and speculation was bound to be a fine line. Bandung administrators were seduced to overinvest by proposals to relocate the central capital from Batavia (Jakarta) to their own city. In a prospectus, the municipality of Bandung advertized plots where housing could be built for the bureaucratic elite (Gemeente Bandoeng, Dienst van het Grondbedrijf 1931). The municipality would probably have turned a profit if the plans had materialized (Nas 1990:106). Around the same time, a similar thing happened in Padang when the urban administrators erroneously assumed that their town would be made capital of the new province of Sumatra (*Sumatra Bode* 9-5-1930, 20-1-1932, 29-4-1932).

Colonial civil servants could not agree whether development corporations should pay their own way. Jac P. Thijsse, member of the technical staff of Bandung municipality, remarked dryly that a development corporation need not be profitable because urban development costs money (Verslag Planologische Dag 1939:27). Yet, at the same time, he advised that land be bought as early as possible at rural prices (Verslag Planologische Dag 1939:24-28). Gerard Jansen (1930:155), head of agrarian affairs in Medan, thought a development corporation should be run according to social principles rather than the profit principle.

The regime changes – from Dutch to Japanese and from Japanese to Indonesian – probably also had an impact on the management of government land. However, evidence for this is scarce. It is possible that after independence municipalities used more government land for communal purposes, but rent-seeking behaviour is equally plausible. The one thing we do know is that during regime changes local administrations became more tolerant of homeless squatters. By the time administrators' attitudes changed, their grip on municipal land had seriously weakened – as we will soon see.

*Long lease to large companies and private estates (particuliere landerijen)*

Two other forms of land tenure controlled by large corporations – long lease and private estates with seigniorial rights (*particuliere landerijen*) – are rather well documented. These corporations were usually in Dutch or Chinese hands, and their interests were fairly well protected by the colonial state. Here, too, we may assume that the shifting balance of power after independence had an impact on these tenure systems.

Long lease is a tenure right derived from property rights. Leased land controlled by the large companies is an important separate category because of the concentration of land in the possession of a single owner. The central Sumatran town of Pekanbaru, for instance, was developed on land between the oil companies' concessions. Medan provides material for a more extensive analysis. The Deli Maatschappij (Deli Company), the most powerful tobacco company in North Sumatra, controlled large tracts of land in the Medan area. In town, the company also controlled land granted by the sultan. The company used some of this land for housing its employees, but also allowed others to use it. The rights of these others were laid down in a so-called Deli Maatschappij grant.

Not surprisingly, the Deli Maatschappij had a big say in municipal affairs. In 1930, for instance, the company asked the local government to adjust the road plan in a new suburb (Polonia) and to swap a strip of land. The administration cooperated. The Deli Maatschappij had often come to the municipality's aid in the past, and the administration knew it would need the company's cooperation in the future as well. The administration stated that its compliant attitude towards the company should not be seen as a precedent for other, ordinary claimants who might want to change a road plan.[15]

Once the Deli Maatschappij lost the protection of the Dutch colonial government, its land became the target of squatters. Nevertheless, the company continued its operations. In 1958, a state-run company, Perseroan Terbatas Perkebunan Negara II, nationalized the possessions of the Deli Maatschappij, including plots of urban land. Soon PTPN II began to cash in on this boon, quietly selling the land off in small parcels to members of powerful political parties.[16]

The other form of land tenure controlled by large corporations was private estates with seigniorial rights. These were established in the seventeenth and eighteenth centuries when the Dutch and English East India Companies granted and sold large tracts of land with the concomitant seigniorial rights to retired officials and well-to-do Chinese. The Dutch and Chinese owners established estates to which labourers were tied, either as slaves or kampong residents with limited freedom of movement. The land was cultivated either by descendants of the slaves or by newcomers until well into the twentieth century. The estates, called *landerijen*, were found near the major port towns of Java: Batavia (including large areas in the mountainous hinterland of West Java), Semarang and Surabaya, and also near the town of Makassar on the island of Sulawesi. Colonial planners of the nineteenth and twentieth century deemed such large estates at the urban fringe ideal for building because extensive tracts could be developed as a whole. However, owners were forbidden to sell their estates for development because peasants usually held the right to cultivate the land (*oesaharechten*). The peasants who tilled the soil, in turn, were not allowed to build a house on the plot without consent of the owner of the estate (Jansen 1930:152-4; Logemann 1936:20). Therefore, it was difficult to make the estates available for urban development (Dick 2002:114-7).

In 1910, the central government started purchasing these estates, not only for the benefit of urban development but also because seigniorial rights had been considered obsolete since the nineteenth century. Every purchase required lengthy negotiations, all the more so because the administration had the reputation of paying the full market price. At one point the office that dealt with the purchases, the Particuliere Landerijen Kantoor, employed eight civil servants and seventy other staff. Between 1912 and 1931, more than 1,1 million acres were repurchased on Java, but this costly policy was abandoned during the Depression years in the early 1930s.[17] In 1935 the state founded a

---

[15]  *Gemeenteblad gemeente Medan* 2 no. 42 (1930).
[16]  Tuanku Luckman Sinar, personal communication.
[17]  Kort verslag vergadering Voorlopige Federale Regering 16-2-1949, ANRI, AS 610. See also: Gautama and Harsono 1972:5-7; Leaf 1992:102, 104.

semi-public company that purchased another 200,000 acres using money borrowed at a commercial rate.[18]

The Dutch colonial government started buying land again during the four post-Pacific War years when it controlled most of the cities. In 1949 a commission composed of representatives of the government and 43 large estates near Jakarta negotiated a standard agreement of purchase by the state. Most estates were limited liability companies run by Chinese directors. The state thus acquired another 1,1 million acres. However, the commission was unable to strike a deal with the owners of estates near Semarang and Surabaya. All the latter estates were smaller, in dispersed locations, and had a variety of seigniorial rights, requiring negotiations to be conducted on an individual basis.[19]

In 1958 the Republic of Indonesia enacted a new law regulating the liquidation of private estates; the law declared the remaining estates to be state land. Financial compensation was set unilaterally by the state. The 1960 Basic Agrarian Law shut the door to the last estates by setting the maximum size of a landholding (Dick 2002:120; Gautama and Harsono 1972:5-6; Leaf 1992:104, 120).

Not all estates were liquidated in this formal way. According to Michael Leaf, in a somewhat ambiguous passage, the Japanese had abolished all *landerijen* and given the land to the tillers. After independence, he wrote, the Indonesian government returned the land rights to the original owners as a temporary measure. During the late 1940s and 1950s many of the claims on the estates' land 'passed from foreign hands into the control of wealthy [...] Indonesians, [...] military officers or other well-connected individuals' (Leaf 1992:103). It may be presumed that these new owners sooner or later managed to have their claim formalized in the shape of a cadastral deed.

Among those who did not have their new property registered were people who occupied a part of an estate but were less well-off. These included people who acquired land under the Japanese land-to-the-tiller policy or during the turmoil of the revolution. Much of this was kampong land. Today these plots are most easily manipulated by the Jakarta municipal government in its attempt to plan the city (Leaf 1992:106-7).

---

[18] Letter Secretaris van Staat voor Binnenlandse Zaken, 9-7-1948, no. A.Z. 12/2/47, ANRI, AS 610.

[19] Ontwerp-besluit 8-4-1949, ANRI, AS 610; Letter H. van der Wal, Secretaris van Staat voor Binnenlandse Zaken aan Hoge Vertegenwoordiger van de Kroon, 19-12-1949, no. A.Z. 12/5/12, ANRI, AS 610; Letter C.M. Dieudonné, waarnemend voorzitter Aankoopcommissie, aan Hoge Vertegenwoordiger van de Kroon, 20-12-1949, no. APP/251/16922, ANRI, AS 610.

*Squatters' land*

Squatting is occupying a plot of land to which one has no legal right (Durand-Lasserve and Royston 2002:4-5). During Dutch colonial rule, landless people had little opportunity to squat, but there might also have been less of a need for squatting because urban populations were smaller. In the late colonial period, state control over the urban population gradually tightened; squatting was prohibited while street vending and begging were restricted. Once Dutch and Japanese colonial powers were broken, after 1945, the kampong dwellers reclaimed the town as their own. At the same time a huge number of migrants were looking for living space in the towns. Public land was the most obvious choice; squatters took up residence on the banks of canals and rivers, in graveyards, along railway tracks, and in fire access lanes. The Indonesian Communist Party encouraged occupation of private estates in anticipation of land redistribution in the 1950s (Abeyasekere 1989:197; Dick 2002:118-9).

During the Indonesian revolution, when Jakarta was in Dutch hands, Republican leaders even encouraged people to squat on European-owned land with unequivocal titles, in defiance of colonial rule (Abeyasekere 1989:197). This Republican policy muddled the rights to land, of course. For some time in the 1950s nothing was done about the squatters because the topic was too sensitive and there was no capital to invest in the squatted land anyway. The insecurity of property felt by the owners of occupied land was the window of opportunity for squatters. In the words of Susan Abeyasekere (1989:197), '[M]ost Jakartans must have found this a period of great freedom'.

In the mid 1950s the Jakarta government stepped up efforts to remove squatters from land needed for urban development projects. At the same time, the administration tried to be fair; it offered land for resettlement whenever possible and attempted to negotiate fair compensation for removal. These negotiations were expensive and time-consuming. In 1953, for example, a major thoroughfare connecting the centre of Jakarta with the new satellite town Kebayoran Baru was still uncompleted seven years after it was planned because five hundred houses still had to be demolished (Abeyasekere 1989:197).

From 1956 onward, the policy became firmer. Even then, however, the municipal council wanted squatters who had settled between 1950 and 1955 to be offered assistance in the form of money and land. Buildings erected illegally after January 1955 had to be torn down. The stricter policy was supported by the proclamation of martial law in 1957 and a military regulation prohibiting the occupation of land without consent of the owner.[20] It then

---

[20]  Regulation of the Army Chief of Staff No. Prt/Peperpu/011/1958 of 14-4-1958.

became much easier to move people in the interest of development projects (Abeyasekere 1989:198; Gautama and Harsono 1972:13). Nevertheless, communist organizations provided some protection to squatters in the early 1960s. This ended when the Indonesian Communist Party was outlawed in 1965. By the mid 1960s, eviction had become so easy that squatters felt deeply insecure. In 1966, after both civilian and military officials as well as private individuals began to evict people for their own benefit, Jakarta's governor issued a decree warning local government officials not to assist in evictions without consent of the governor (Gautama and Harsono 1972:14). The timing of this move in 1966 suggests that eviction had become a focal point in the struggle between communist organizations on the one hand, and landowners and military on the other.

In Medan, squatting went through a similar cycle of tolerance and repression. Large parts of tobacco plantations near Medan had been occupied by squatters after 1942. The Japanese authorities had allowed, or urged, people to cultivate food crops on the plantations. After independence, the plantations released part of their land for squatting smallholders, but these plots were also used by dock workers, clerks, and petty traders employed in Medan and others who commuted to the city. Immediately after independence, the state urged the labourers to be steadfast in their conflict with the plantations, but by the mid 1950s it viewed the occupants as common squatters who should be forcibly removed. In practice, it seemed impossible to evict the squatters, but martial law gave the military the green light to take firm action against the squatters. Later, the squatters' plots were gradually absorbed into the expanding city.[21]

There were different perceptions of the legal status of squatting. Formal land proprietors, the state, and the squatters each had their point of view. Nicole Niessen (1999:269) remarks that 'the uninterrupted possession, sometimes for more than one generation, of abandoned or vacant land is a traditional means of founding *adat* rights to the land'. This type of land acquisition was only acknowledged in areas with an established *adat* tradition, in other words in rural areas. In urban areas, squatting was deemed unlawful. Being in many cases from a rural background, the squatters may have thought differently and considered their occupancy perfectly rightful. This point of view was backed by *adat* rules about developing new land and reinforced by the squatters' regular payment of land and building tax. The taxpayers may have erroneously believed that the receipts of their tax payments had a status equal to a title deed (Niessen 1999:269-70).

---

[21]    Pelzer 1978:123, 1982:101-6, 147-150; Sinar 2000; Slaats and Portier 1990/1991:58.

*Conclusion*

I have used land tenure as a lens through which to gain insight into Indonesian decolonization. Security of tenure is very important to people. During decolonization, the legal certainty of tenure is questioned. During any regime change, and this certainly applies to the decolonization of Indonesia, security of tenure is endangered in two ways: entire tenure systems change and the legal certainty of individual titles is undermined.

New rulers sometimes change land tenure systems to suit their own interests or the interests of those they protect. In colonial times, the two main categories of landownership were known by ethnic or 'racial' labels: indigenous and European ownership. The European tenure rules were characterized by a high degree of formality and tenure security. Such security made this kind of tenure attractive to upper and middle-class people with long-term investment plans. The Basic Agrarian Law of 1960 ended the use of the terms 'indigenous' and 'European' plots, but continued the distinction between plots with a formal, secure tenure and those with an informal and less secure status. In that respect little changed. Rural landownership in postcolonial Indonesia was complicated by local variations in tenure systems that went back to colonial times. All these idiosyncratic tenure systems were mixed with practices that had become common throughout the archipelago – such as registered and unregistered individually-held land – to form unique, local land rights regimes. These local systems of land tenure responded more quickly to decolonization than to national law. There are many examples of such rapid, local adjustments to the new balance of power after independence. These include the purchase and subsequent abolition and partition of the large private estates with seigniorial rights (*particuliere landerijen*), and the weakening of aristocratic claims such as the sultan's grants in Medan.

The legal certainty of individual plots was often imperilled because the usual legal protection broke down. The conventional wisdom that land 'has always been one of the safest forms of investment in politically unstable situations' (Evers 1984:483) did not apply to the Indonesian revolution. The main victims of land invasions must have been the Eurasian and Chinese populations, who, unlike most of the white European elite, resided permanently in Indonesia. The Japanese occupation and the change of regime in 1945 briefly heightened the insecurity of tenure. Some owners were put in internment camps or were forced to flee their property when the course of the war turned against them. Later they found that others had occupied their land. Another vulnerable group was Western companies that had lost the protection of the colonial administration; their lands in long lease became a prime target for squatters. The risk of illegal occupation was increased when the Japanese occupation ended and the revolution began because the registration of title deeds at the cadastre was temporarily suspended. When peace had been more or less restored a score of lawsuits were filed. These lawsuits show that owners had to fight hard to regain control of their land, and that their success was limited.

While property owners feared the insecurity of tenure, for others it represented an opportunity. In Indonesia, the legal uncertainty of individual former owners made it possible to squat. Although squatting did not lead to legal certainty, it did seem to be an accepted form of tenure for a while. This lasted as long as the squatters had powerful allies and protectors in the Japanese administration, the Republican government, and the Indonesian communist party.

To sum up, the decolonization of tenure systems in Indonesia culminated in the Basic Agrarian Law of 1960, which aimed to increase tenure certainty and abolish the distinction between European and indigenous titles. With regard to these goals, the law was hardly successful. The European-indigenous dichotomy was merely replaced by a distinction between registered and 'not yet registered' titles, implying a similar difference of formalization and (in)security of tenure. At the height of the decolonization process, security of tenure was deeply undermined, albeit temporarily. This was a loss for some categories of owners and an opportunity for landless squatters. The Basic Agrarian Law also failed to achieve its other implicit goal, namely to overcome local diversity and promote national unity as part of the great nation-building effort.

Indonesia's agrarian issues were not unique. Similar situations arose in Africa. Nevertheless, colonial Indonesia appears to be different in several respects: the formal acceptance of indigenous, individual titles, the smaller difference between indigenous and European titles, and the possibly greater local diversity with an accompanying adjustment of tenure systems to local needs. It is for these reasons that the decolonization of tenure systems in Indonesia was generally characterized by continuity, despite the temporary insecurity of titles.

*References*

Abeyasekere, Susan
1989            *Jakarta; A history.* Revised edition. Singapore: Oxford University Press.
                [First edition 1987.]
Bedner, Adriaan
2001            *Administrative courts in Indonesia; A socio-legal study.* The Hague: Kluwer
                International Law. [The London-Leiden Series on Law, Administration
                and Development 6.]

Bernstein, Henry
2000            'Colonialism, capitalism, development', in: Tim Allen and Alan
                Thomas (eds), *Poverty and development into the 21st century*, pp. 241-70.
                Oxford: Oxford University Press.
Berry, Sara
2003            'Debating the land question in Africa', *Comparative Studies in Society
                and History* 44:638-68.
Burns, Peter
2004            *The Leiden legacy; Concepts of law in Indonesia*. Leiden: KITLV Press.
                [Verhandelingen 191.]
Chanock, Martin
1992            'The law market; The legal encounter in British East and Central
                Africa', in: W.J. Mommsen and J.A. de Moor (eds), *European expansion
                and law; The encounter of European and indigenous law in 19th and 20-th
                century Africa and Asia*, pp. 279-305. Oxford/New York: Berg.
Church, Peter (ed.)
2003            *A history of South East Asia*. Singapore: John Wiley. [Revised edition.]
Colombijn, Freek
1994            *Patches of Padang; The history of an Indonesian town in the twentieth century
                and the use of urban space*. Leiden: Research School CNWS. [CNWS
                Publications 19.]
Commissie voor het grondbezit
1934a           *Summier overzicht van de beginselen en hoofdzaken der agrarische wetgeving
                en van de voor Europeanen in Nederlandsch-Indië verkrijgbare rechten op
                grond*. [Batavia]: Commissie voor het Grondbezit van Indo-Europeanen.
1934b           *Verslag van de Commissie voor het Grondbezit van Indo-Europeanen,
                3 Volumes*. [Batavia]: Commissie voor het Grondbezit van Indo-
                Europeanen.
Deiniger, Klaus W.
2003            *Land policies for growth and poverty reduction*. Washington: World Bank,
                Oxford: Oxford University Press.
De Soto, Hernando
2000            *The mystery of capital; Why capitalism triumphs in the West and fails
                everywhere else*. New York: Basic Books.
Devas, Nick
1983            'Financing urban land development for low income housing; An
                analysis with particular reference to Jakarta', *Third World Planning
                Review* 5-3:209-25.
Dick, Howard
2002            'Urban development and land rights; A comparison of New Order and
                colonial Surabaya', in: Peter J.M. Nas (ed.), *The Indonesian town revisited*,
                pp. 113-29. Münster: Lit Verlag, Singapore: Institute of Southeast Asian
                Studies.
Dinas Agraria D.I.Y. [Daerah Istimewa Yogyakarta]
1974            *Sejarah hukum agraria di Daerah Istimewa Yogyakarta*. [Yogyakarta: Dinas
                Agraria Pemerintah Daerah D.I.Y.]

Durand-Lasserve, Alain and Lauren Royston
2002        'International trends and country contexts; From tenure regularization
            to tenure security', in: Alain Durand-Lasserve and Lauren Royston
            (eds), *Holding their ground; Secure land tenure for the urban poor in
            developing countries*, pp. 1-34. London: Earthscan.
Evers, Hans-Dieter
1984        'Urban landownership, ethnicity, and class in Southeast Asian cities',
            *International Journal of Urban and Regional Research* 8:481-96.
Gautama, Sudargo and Budi Harsono
1972        *Agrarian law*. Bandung: Lembaga Penelitian Hukum dan Kriminologi,
            Universitas Padjadjaran.
Gautama, Sudargo and Robert N. Hornick
1972        *An introduction to Indonesian law; Unity in diversity*, Jakarta: Alumni Print.
Gemeente Bandoeng, Dienst van het Grondbedrijf.
1931        *Prospectus voor de uitgifte van gronden*. Bandoeng: Vorkink.
Goldberg, Michael and Peter Chinloy
1984        *Urban land economics*. New York: Wiley.
Harsono, Boedi
1994        *Hukum agraria Indonesia; Sejarah pembentukan Undang-Undang Pokok
            Agraria, isi dan pelaksanaannya*. Cetakan 5. [Jakarta]: Djambatan. [First
            edition 1962.]
Hooker, M.B.
1975        *Legal pluralism; An introduction to colonial and neo-colonial laws*. Oxford:
            Clarendon Press.
*Jaarboekje*
1941        *Jaarboekje voor de ambtenaren van het kadaster in Nederlandsch-Indië tevens
            overzicht van de voornaamste wettelijke bepalingen, welke betrekking hebben
            op het kadaster*. Batavia: Olt.
1947        *Jaarboekje van het kadaster in Nederlandsch-Indië*. [Batavia]: Vereeniging
            van Landmeters van het Kadaster in Nederlandsch-Indië.
Jansen, Gerard
1925        *Grantrechten in Deli*. Amsterdam: Oostkust van Sumatra-Instituut.
            [Mededeeling 12.]
1930        'De decentralisatie en de grond', in: W.F.M. Kerchman (ed.), *25 Jaren
            decentralisatie in Nederlandsch-Indië 1905-1930*. Semarang: Vereeniging
            voor Lokale Belangen.
Kadastrale Dienst in Nederlandsch-Indië
1938        *Instructie voor de kadastrale perceelsregistratie (Registratie-Instructie,
            Volume 1. Voorschriften en bepalingen*. Bandoeng: Strafgevangenis
            'Soekamiskin'.
Leaf, Michael
1992        *Land regulation and housing development in Jakarta, Indonesia; From the
            'big village' to the 'modern city'*. PhD thesis, University of California,
            Berkeley.

Lentz, Carola
2005        'First-comers and late-comers; The role of narratives in land claims',
            in: Sandra Evers, Marja Spierenburg and Harry Wels (eds), *Competing*
            *jurisdictions; Settling land claims in Africa and Madagascar*, pp. 157-80.
            Leiden and Boston: Brill Academic Publishers. [Afrika-Studiecentrum
            Series 6.]
Lissa Nessel, R.C.A.F.J. van
1940        *De mogelijkheid van een gemeentelijk inlandsch 'kadaster'; Prae-advies*
            *uitgebracht voor het 30e Decentralisatie-Congres te Bandoeng, op 2, 3 en 4*
            *mei 1940.* Bandoeng: Stichting 'Technisch Tijdschrift'.
Logemann, J.H.A.
1936        *Stedelijk agrarisch recht en stadsvorming.* [Bandoeng]: Stichting Technisch
            Tijdschrift. [Technische Mededeeling Vereeniging voor Locale
            Belangen 8.]
Molenkamp, Iben
2003        'Whose nation? Social and ideological divisions versus national unity
            in the Philippines, 1930-1945'. MA thesis, Leiden University.
Nas, Peter J.M.
1985        'Miniatuur van Manado', *Orion: Oriënterend Tijdschrift Nederland/*
            *Indonesië* 2-3:20-1, 56-7.
1990        *De stad in de Derde Wereld; Een inleiding tot de urbane antropologie en*
            *sociologie.* Muiderberg: Coutinho.
Niessen, Nicole
1999        *Municipal government in Indonesia; Policy, law and practice of*
            *decentralization and urban spatial planning.* Leiden: Research School
            CNWS. [CNWS Publications 77.]
Nwaka, Geoffrey I
1996        'Planning sustainable cities in Africa', *Canadian Journal of Urban*
            *Research* 5:219-36.
Otto, J.M.
1991        'Een Minahasser in Bandoeng; Indonesische oppositie in de koloniale
            gemeente', in: Harry A. Poeze and Pim Schoorl (eds), *Excursies in*
            *Celebes; Een bundel bijdragen bij het afscheid van J. Noorduyn als directeur-*
            *secretaris van het Koninklijk Instituut voor Taal-, Land- en Volkenkunde*, pp.
            185-215. Leiden: KITLV Uitgeverij. [Verhandelingen 147.]
Pelzer, Karl J.
1978        *Planter and peasant; Colonial policy and the agrarian struggle in East Sumatra*
            *1863-1947.* 's-Gravenhage: Nijhoff. [KITLV, Verhandelingen 84.]
1982        *Planters against peasants; The agrarian struggle in East Sumatra 1947-1958.*
            's-Gravenhage: Nijhoff. [KITLV, Verhandelingen 97.]
Reyntjens, Filip
1992        'The development of the dual legal system in former Belgian Central
            Africa (Zaire-Rwanda-Burundi)', in: W.J. Mommsen and J.A. de
            Moor (eds), *European expansion and law; The encounter of European*
            *and indigenous law in 19th and 20th-century Africa and Asia*, pp. 111-27.
            Oxford/New York: Berg.

Royston, Lauren
2002        'Security of urban tenure in South Africa; Overview of policy and practice', in: Alain Durand-Lasserve and Lauren Royston (eds), *Holding their ground; Secure land tenure for the urban poor in developing countries*, pp. 165-81. London: Earthscan.

Saltman, Michael
2002        'Introduction', in: Michael Saltman (ed.), *Land and territoriality*, pp. 1-8. Oxford/New York: Berg.

Schwencke, G.
1932        *Het Vorstenlandsche grondhuurreglement in de practijk en het grondenrecht in Jogjakarta.* Djokja: Buning.

Sinar, Tengku Luckman
[2000]      *Konflik Vertikal; Persoalan tanah adat ulayat di Kabupaten Deli-Serdang & Langkat.* [Medan]: n.n.

Slaats, Herman and Karen Portier
1990/1991   'Urban land ownership relations and the role of traditional law concepts among the Karo Batak in Medan, Indonesia', *Netherlands Review of Development Studies* 3:49-62.

Sonius, H.W.J.
1962        *Inleiding tot begrippen van gewoonte-grondenrecht in Afrika en enige vergelijkingen met Indonesisch recht.* Leiden: Universitaire Pers.

Stork, E.M.
1936        *Overgang van Inlandsche grondrechten in het gewest Jogjakarta.* Amsterdam: Royal Institute for the Tropics.

Stuers, H.J.J.L. de
1849        *De vestiging en uitbreiding der Nederlanders ter Westkust van Sumatra.* Vol. 1. Amsterdam: Van Kampen.

*Verslag van de 21e jaarvergadering*
1933        *Verslag van de Een en twintigste jaarvergadering van de Vereeniging voor Locale Belangen en van het Drie en twintigste Decentralisatiecongres [...].* [Semarang]: Vereeniging voor Locale Belangen. [Mededeeling Locale Belangen 98.]

*Verslag Handelsvereeniging Medan*
1931-1939   *Verslag van De Handelsvereeniging te Medan over het jaar [1930-1938],* Medan: Varekamp.

*Verslag Planologische Dag*
1939        *Verslag Planologische Dag Bandoeng, 1 en 2 juli 1939,* [Bandoeng:] Planologische Studiegroep van de Vereeniging voor Locale Belangen. [Technische Mededeeling Vereeniging voor Locale Belangen 16.]

Vollenhoven, C. van
1981        In: J.F. Holleman (ed.). *Van Vollenhoven on Indonesian adat law; Selections from Het adatrecht van Nederlandsch-Indië.* 2 vols. (Volume I, 1918; Volume II, 1931). The Hague: Nijhoff. [KITLV, Translation Series 20.]

BILL FREUND

# The African city
# Decolonization and after

This chapter is a response to a particular question: what happened to the colonial city in Africa following decolonization? What was the colonial city? If one can generalize from the African continent as a whole, colonialism was an historic phase that tended to occur between the late nineteenth century and somewhat past the middle of the twentieth, thus well under a century, and very often only the duration of one old person's lifetime. There is a large body of social science literature to inform us that colonial urbanization was a very significantly expanding phenomenon of note. All colonial cities were not alike, and there have in fact been some noteworthy attempts to create an appropriate typology to make sense of these distinctions. I am not going to explore such a typology here.[1] Instead, for the purposes of this chapter, I prefer to focus on what I shall term the 'classic colonial city'.

The classic colonial city created from scratch was subjected to the intense gaze of modern planning ideas from which it really was inseparable.[2] Typically,

---

[1]   One of the most frequently cited and useful attempts can be found in O'Connor 1983. A distinction has to be made between existing cities in which elements of continuity from precolonial social forms were strong or even dominant – Salé in Morocco (Brown 1976), Ilesha in Nigeria (Peel 1983), and Accra in Ghana (Parker 2000) to name cities that have been studied in important English language monographs, and the more numerous cases where cities were formed *de novo*. This latter case was especially true in the southern half of the African continent. One might make a further distinction between cities that were largely passed by colonial developments such as Ilesha or Salé and those cases such as Accra, Kano in Nigeria, or Rabat in Morocco where the 'native' city was encapsulated in a more dynamic new colonial city. A further complication exists where cities such as Freetown, Sierra Leone, or St. Louis de Sénégal were 'old' but essentially colonial creations, redolent of pre-twentieth century commercial ways. In all of these examples, inevitably the modernist thrust was either significantly muted or perhaps nonexistent entirely. For a more thorough discussion of African cities and their history, which uses the material in this paper, see Freund 2007.
[2]   By modern, I mean a striving towards the rational and functional in planning and in architecture. Modernist cities would inevitably concentrate on the typical industrial production and transport methods of the time and tended towards a sense of urban centralization, showing scant respect for past technique and tradition, but it is not at all true that all modernism is or was reactionary or exclusive in the way described for colonial Africa. There were inclusive variants suitable for societies with little differentiation between rich and poor where the market played little role and where the centrality of an industrial working class was pivotal, for instance in the Soviet Union and the Communist world.

colonial subjects were permitted to reside only on sufferance to the extent that they fulfilled an essential economic purpose. To take one of the most famous figures of early-twentieth century modernism, an instance can be made of Le Corbusier's (in)famous unfulfilled plan of a giant overhead causeway linking the harbour to the new parts of Algiers, literally passing over and isolating the ancient Casbah (Çelik 1997). In southern Africa, the Rhodes-Livingstone Institute's school of anthropologists became famous for pleading simply for the recognition of black labour migrants as potentially permanent urbanites, but it cannot be said that they wrote much about the concomitant need to replan spatially the new cities of the Northern Rhodesian Copperbelt (Epstein 1958; Mitchell 1987). The planned part of the city related to the settlement of Europeans, to the crucial structures of the administration, and to the over-whelmingly extractive economy in general.

Even in the colonial heyday, this colonial impulse met very significant con-tradictions. These contradictions, exemplified in Frederick Cooper's edited book on the *Struggle for the city* (1983), became more apparent with the rela-tively prosperous times for colonial economies in the late 1930s and the years of World War II when urban populations expanded without the essentials for making urban life bearable. A rapidly growing African population began to fill and expand urban space, but the planning structures of colonialism left them out or treated them as an afterthought. Only through various forms of struggle, which quickly resonated with the emergence of nationalism, could a way be forced open to alter, or at least bypass, these structures. The question of how to accommodate a crucially important working class came to the fore.

## Decolonization: Modernity and nationalism conjoined

The following discussion means to question the binary divide between the colonial and the postcolonial. Instead I suggest that there were important his-toric continuities between the late colonial period, when colonial authorities in their pursuit of what we call development, tried to accommodate popular forces while pursuing and extending colonial urbanism and the early decades of nationalist rule. In other words, there is important continuity between the period 1945-1960 and 1960-1980 that form a long transitional period. During this period, the concept of development changed relatively little.

In Africa, the collapse of colonialism needs to be dated somewhat later and to be taken through a somewhat longer time period than in most of Southeast Asia. The *annus mirabilis* of African independence was 1960 when French West and Equatorial Africa, Togo, Cameroon, and the Malagasy Republic all became independent as did Nigeria and the Belgian Congo. By this time, the countries of North Africa, except Algeria, together with the Sudan and Ghana, had also become independent. However, the end of Portuguese colonialism only dates from 1975 and there continued to be an armed struggle over the future of Rhodesia and South-West Africa later than that. It is perhaps appropriate to date the end of a very long era of conflict with the creation of a democratic, nonracial dispensation in South Africa as recently as 1994.

If this last event ends what John Saul likes to term a 'thirty year's war' for southern Africa where a settler identity enters powerfully into the equation, the early decolonizations did not often occur in an atmosphere of massive disruption through an epochal event such as World War II, as was the case in Southeast Asia. African decolonization rather took into account the events in South Asia, the Middle East and elsewhere, but in most African countries it was much more of a peaceful process inaugurated by the colonial powers. There was a political conscientization, an indigenous radicalization of importance, which certainly raised the price of continuing with the status quo for the colonizer, but independence had much to do with the realization that local interlocutors would be required in any event to play a growing political role and also, very crucially, that the colonial impetus to transform and modernize old societies along capitalist lines would be hazardous, expensive, and best done under the auspices of such interlocutors. The older forms of colonial exploitation, after boom-like conditions in many commercial fields following the Second World War began to be exhausted, showed little potential for profitable extension and not up to deeper transformative tasks.[3]

Movements speaking to the growing African population so poorly catered for found strong impulses in the cities. Trade unions, organizing workers in critical transport and communications sectors especially, were often based in towns; they agitated against the harsh working and living conditions that the rapidly growing and strategically important membership experienced. The spirit of the Mau Mau rebellion – triggered by the British policies of pushing Gĩkũyũ from their farmlands in Kenya in the 1950s – was so strongly implanted in the poor quarters of Nairobi that the British regime determined to expel the entire Gĩkũyũ-speaking part of the city's population early in the Emergency (Furedi 1973; Anderson 2005). Tens of thousands were driven away to be replaced by Kenyans from other 'uninfected' parts of the country. At the same time, cities could become the place where European anxieties were violently vented. Douala, the port city of Cameroon, was the site of violent anti-African riots immediately after World War II on the part of settlers, as was Luanda in Portuguese Angola in 1960 (Joseph 1974; Cahen 1989).

---

[3]  For decolonization, see Cooper 1996; Freund 1998; for a standard source, see Gifford and Louis 1982.

Algeria was notorious for the violence and hostility to democratic concessions on the part of its colons.

However, if we try to capture the typical situation under late colonialism, it was one where the state attempted to reconcile a modernist approach
to urban development and planning with increasing openings towards the
incorporation of the rapidly expanding African populations. This involved
substantial plans for housing construction and the expansion of urban planning bureaucracies and mechanisms to the extent that resources existed.
Independence did not really alter this situation very much. Particularly again
in the best-endowed countries, the modernist impulse was sustained and
indeed most typical aspects of colonial planning continued in terms of legislation and even implementation, as happened, for instance, in the heyday of
Houphouët-Boigny's Ivory Coast and in oil-boom rich Nigeria and Gabon.

Throughout colonial Africa, a major twentieth-century characteristic of
town life had been racial segregation. Modified in significant ways in North
and even West Africa, it was still transparently dominant as a feature further
east and south. In South Africa, this system was developed on a remarkable
scale with exceptions ruthlessly eliminated. European quarters were isolated
from the native city with 'cordons sanitaires' (sanitary corridors) of parks,
boulevards and natural features, and large-scale population removals made
key central districts white. The planning regulations regarding the two kinds
of urban structures were startlingly different – and these were typically
refined to deal with other minorities and populations that did not fit the
binary divide between African and European.

Deracialization of the urban space under the aegis of the colonizing power
was usually instituted before the grant of independence, thus setting the scene
for the possibility of structural continuities that no longer were governed by
a racial code. A new elite could move into what had been the white side of
town without breaking down the barriers between the city and the 'location'
(the black labourers' neighbourhood). This new elite erected monuments to
itself in the form of prestige projects such as sports stadia and luxury hotels,
which played a far more important role in many African capitals than they
did in Europe or America. Within the precincts of such hotels, the elite could
apparently enjoy the amenities of its international counterparts. However, it
should also be mentioned that, especially in the many new regimes that had
a populist basis, substantial social infrastructure such as universities and high
schools, hospitals, and clinics were created that not only spoke to the prestige
of modern living but offered real services to the urban population. The stadia
were not only for sport; they were the scene of party rallies and celebrations
aimed at recognizing national integration.

At the same time, countering this impulse was the reality of unplanned
growth from below. The concentration of social infrastructure in the cities,

the suitability of the cities as sites of individual reinvention for rural men and women, the many spin-offs that were involved in greatly increasing state expenditure and, to some extent, import substitution industrialization, also attracted unprecedented numbers of migrants to the cities of Africa. This growth, which had started in colonial times, accelerated after 1960 and everywhere spun out of the control of the forces at the disposal of the state for controlling the cities. Thus the planning of urban space increasingly became inoperative as forces from below started to remould African cities. In this chapter I will argue that in the early independence phase there was a balance – of course marked by a lot of conflict – between such disruptive forces from below and the continued elan of the state, which continued to enjoy some capacity to pursue projects that glorified the new regimes and provided patrimonial support for a wide range of economic activities. During this period, it became clearer too that new urban cultures were emerging in Africa.[4]

By 1980, however, the picture was beginning to be far more negative. Urban growth was increasingly fuelled by rural economic collapse and warfare; the postcolonial urban economies were, in general, in decay, often even in chaos, and a new urban literature began to write about dysfunctional cities and parasitical urbanism. It can be argued that for better and for worse the 'neocolonial' era marked by substantial continuities was tending to come to an end in Africa and cities, seen by some as diseased and crisis-ridden and – to a far lesser extent, it must be said – by others as the site of new cultural and economic creativity, were entering a new stage. As the cities changed further, making too great a distinction between old cities with a long sense of continuity and new cities emerging from the blood and sweat of colonialism began to be less meaningful. At this point, 'conventional' modern planning ceased to have meaning in most of the continent. However, in those numerous African countries where a more stable form of accumulation continued to develop, we can see a bourgeoisie, even if primarily a service middle class, stake out its claim for survival and space in this new context.

*Early portents: Algeria and the Congo*

One might usefully first consider those cases where a historic break was more dramatic and decolonization most dramatically intrusive. An obvious place to explore here is Algeria. With independence, the cities suddenly lost a huge share, often a majority, of their population at a stroke, as 'Europeans',

---

[4]    For an excellent exposition, see Dorier-Apprill 1998. That the Francophone tradition is really much stronger in this regard owes much to the classic sociology of Balandier 1957 and Meillassoux 1968, stretching into colonial times.

Jews, and those Muslim Algerians who felt too implicated in the colonial project departed quickly and dramatically. Depopulation was a very temporary phenomenon in fact; in a short time the availability of built urban space and the new opportunities created by transformed Algeria attracted massive immigration from the countryside. Thus the settled population of the Algiers Casbah in good part shifted towards what had been the European parts of town with their far superior infrastructure and amenities while they were replaced in the Casbah with poor rural migrants happy to have a very cheap and central place to live. In Algerian cities, the symbols of Frenchness – statuary, churches, nomenclature – were quickly and systematically replaced in terms of a new Arab iconography to a remarkable extent.[5]

Thanks to the oil discoveries in the Sahara, this was a postcolonial state with means. A nationalist-minded state that controlled much of the economy and saw a socialist road as essential attracted large numbers of students and employees, potential and actual, to the cities but especially to the capital Algiers whose growth became noticeably disproportional to that of other cities. This was to be a typical phenomenon in postcolonial Africa: where cities had previously reflected colonial extractive economic needs with mining and port-based centres often quite large, now the role of the patron-state became more important. In Algiers, this state also created and promoted import substitution factories in expanded industrial districts. This was accompanied by a massive construction programme aimed at housing Arab families in large council estates on the European model. As the recent earthquake revealed, some of these estates have proven unsustainable to local environmental conditions in extreme circumstances. By contrast, the high quality residential and commercial neighbourhoods (or for example, the beaches) established under French rule were now of little interest and usually became very degraded in maintenance and urban quality. Far more people migrated to Algiers than could be accommodated, and the result was the growth of squatter settlements on the city periphery. In the heyday of radical Algeria, these were seen as an unhealthy growth that needed to be uprooted. Such settlements were actually torn down and their inhabitants expelled in the 1960s, although, of course, they tended to be reconstructed elsewhere quickly enough. Thus up through the 1970s Algerian cities continued to be governed by a modernist outlook albeit one with some very different prerogatives than what had prevailed under French rule. These patterns typified the days of Ben Bella and Boumediene. By 1980 they were coming unstuck as the state proved less and less able to sustain modernization projects and the difficulties imposed by

[5]    This is captured in the concluding pages of Prochaska 1990. After military coups put paid to conservative regimes, a parallel evolution can certainly be discerned in Libya and in Nasserite Egypt.

the failure to accommodate what we now call 'informal' activity mounted. In Algiers and presumably elsewhere in Algeria, the result has been a relaxation, if not often collapse, of modernism, and a growing tolerance of laissez-faire activities, not just on the part of impoverished squatters but also a middle class beginning to search for a more privatized and property-orientated way of life in the city.[6]

The other model that emerges from a dysfunctional transition to independence is observable in what had been the Belgian Congo. Without rehearsing the unfolding of events there from 1960, one can first point to a quick and poorly planned push to independence by the Belgian regime, which seems to have anticipated very little change at the socioeconomic level[7] and successful continued dominance through divide-and-rule tactics. Instead, mutiny and rebellion quickly began to tear the country apart and destroyed the tissue of neocolonialism as conceived in Brussels. Later massive areas of the Congo went into revolt in the hopes of a more genuine 'second independence', while ineffectual and weak governments ruled in Léopoldville, renamed Kinshasa. Eventually Mobutu succeeded in consolidating a new system of sorts. In this chaotic series of events, many aspects of the highly-articulated extractive economy virtually disappeared together with basic social services and most of the fairly large Belgian population. However, Katanga copper, together with growing diamond mining, sustained a famously corrupt state. Much wealth was funnelled through Kinshasa in consequence.

The consequences for urban demography were very dramatic. Kinshasa itself, both as a source of what wealth there was and as a place of refuge, grew spectacularly and dramatically. With a population of 400,000 at the time of independence, much of the growth took place in the following several years; today Kinshasa has an estimated population of five million and upwards. By contrast, many of the country's important provincial cities such as Elizabethville a.k.a. Lubumbashi, the main centre for copper mining, and Stanleyville a.k.a. Kisangani, the great river port in the centre of the country as a whole, have grown only very slowly and have far below one million populations.[8] The only real exceptions are those places that have profited from continued mineral extraction or have successfully harboured refugees from rural dislocations and conflict.

At the same time, while Mobutu presided over the construction of the predictable sports stadium and a few other durable prestige projects we could

---

6   For postcolonial Algiers, see Hadjiedj, Chaline and Dubois-Maury 2003.

7   One is reminded in the recent film 'Lumumba' of the infamous equation laid out on the blackboard by Belgian General E. Janssens, 'After independence = Before independence', to a not very pleased class of newly promoted Congolese soldiers, who began to mutiny within hours (Young 1965:316).

8   For an account of the degradation of urban life in Kisangani, see Omasombo Tshonda 2002.

call modernist, the remarkable thing about the built environment of Kinshasa itself has been its attenuation. The old colonial core remains and continues to house government buildings and those commercial activities that cement the Democratic Republic of the Congo's ties with the West, especially the loan-givers and mineral dealers; otherwise one has a massive expanse of compounds stretching into the Congolese interior, primarily to the more populous south, the annexes. For the majority of urban Congolese, this is the real Kinshasa and life goes on with little reference to the old centre: on se débrouille. People acquire land through negotiations or survive as tenants through the presence of patrons with more or less legal right to property. Of course, the urban infrastructure is badly lacking. Nonetheless a hinterland has developed where food for this conurbation is grown, mainly in Kongo-speaking territory to the south. The Kinois are famous for their talent at survival and their joie de vivre. Kinshasa is the critical home of Congolese popular music, the admired visual art with its haunting symbols of this society, of the Kinois dialect, of the radio-trottoir as a form of communication. A whole urban culture has emerged and with it multiple forms of mutual aid and association, often linked to new forms of Christian worship, but virtually lacking in the classic economic and social advantages of city life, of classic citizenship. It has been possible for modern scholarship to comprehend Kinshasa, the postcolonial city, in terms both of urban decay and catastrophe – Jean-Luc Piermay, for instance, sees this dysfunctional city as one that could dramatically attenuate – or in terms of some kind of genuine affirmation of African recovery and identity in urban life – as witness the recent *Under Siege* collection.[9]

## Postmodern elements take over: African cities after 1980

By about 1980, it was possible to discern many of the same tendencies elsewhere. Quite a number of African cities (Mogadishu, Freetown, Monrovia, Khartoum) have become swamped by refugees from warfare in various regions, for instance.[10] These include cases where the colonial and postcolonial infrastructure – sewage, electricity, and so on – have fallen into ruin or been swamped by crisis. Growth has been overwhelmingly fast at the same time, and much of the population could be found in camps and unserviced shelters.

However, even where disaster has never struck, few countries have been able to maintain modernist forms of development with systematic construc-

---

[9]    Piermay 1997. For more celebratory approaches, see Nlandu 2002 and especially De Boeck 2002.
[10]   Freetown is the subject of Abdullah 2002.

tion of new housing or effective planning. In more prosperous situations, centre cities have decayed while the middle class looks after its own needs in a securer suburban environment. The divide between the formal plans and governance of the city and the actual way that people survive and cope with urban life has widened into a yawning gap.

Modernist plans are no longer internationally fashionable. Growing African indebtedness after 1980 brought about the adoption of so-called structural adjustment policies that can be associated with a neoliberal economic outlook. As in nineteenth century liberalism, the state became the target of attack from international agencies and associated social scientists. The role of the state in the economy was denounced as authoritarian and wasteful; what was required was the freeing of market forces, whatever the consequences. In this context, planning traditions were discredited and discarded, lumped together with 'urban bias' that stacked the dice against productive rural cultivators and burdened African economies unnecessarily. This has had a major impact on the way African cities have been described in the last twenty years. Modernist disasters became cradles of innovation as we have already begun to note for Kinshasa.

Sub-Saharan Africa's largest city by far is Lagos. It is Nigeria's main port but no longer capital. If the national capital has moved to Abuja[11], it has not slowed down the development of Lagos, which now extends beyond the state that bears its name functionally and which is overwhelmingly dominated economically by the informal sector. For those 'Afro-pessimists' who see the decayed African city as a symbol of African failure, Lagos is almost as omnipresent an image as Kinshasa. In fact, it is a rather different tale. Lagos's growth has not been driven by catastrophe; Nigeria's tumultuous history so far has not force-fed its big cities with vast numbers of refugees. Lagos contains a large middle class and a certain number of very wealthy people as well as established functioning institutions, and it remains a significant industrial centre and port. It is true, however, that in vast parts of metropolitan Lagos most people see little of the old historic centre. Living on the mainland, they rarely have a need to explore or exploit Lagos or other islands that belong to the city. This is thus a city that has been reconfigured from colonial times.

There are certainly many signs of acute dysfunctionality in Lagos. Its highways, which brought relief to the transport sector in the 1970s, are poorly maintained and clogged. There are endless traffic hold-ups, petrol shortages, electricity outages and vast, visible dumps of rubbish near human habitation. Lagos has massive squatter settlements and brutal crime: its 'area boys'

---

[11]   It has to be said that Abuja is very much an exercise in continued modern development focused on the state and made possible by Nigeria's oil revenues. It 'works' in Western terms far better than Nigerian cities established before or during colonial times.

shake down sections of the city very effectively. Lagosians have died in large numbers from terrifying explosions and fires in recent years, not to speak of 'intra-ethnic' violence. Nonetheless, the *Under Siege* collection contains more plausible positive statements about Lagos than Kinshasa. On the one hand, there is Rem Koolhaas's photo-essay that tries to give meaning to a new architectonic, to the idea that traffic jams and rubbish heaps can and are made functional in a city where the formal sector is so deficient in absorbing job seekers and, further, that this functionality contains a logic that forms the basis for a new African city, operating according to a different logic than the old colonial city. On the other, Babatunde Ahonsi tries to convince us that community-based organizations are slowly upgrading and civilizing communities within Lagos and turning them into liveable and sustainable neighbourhoods: 'The CDAs [community development associations] successfully paved streets, constructed security gates, routinely cleaned and cleared their surroundings (including dealing with the aftermath of flooding), maintained public water pipes and taps, and devised vigilante security arrangements for dealing with the problem of armed robbery'.[12]

Here it might be useful to turn to what I would identify as one of the dominant themes in studies of the postcolonial city in Africa, the development paradigm that seeks to identify accumulation from below, to fasten on Western-based NGOs as sources of organization and service on the one hand, and African-based NGOs and CBOs as sources of legitimate governance that need to share power with the formal municipal authorities or even to usurp them on the other hand. The contrast between state and community or 'civil society' marks many studies from Andrew Hake's pathbreaking 'self-help city' study that re-interpreted the character of contemporary Nairobi.[13] There is often a cultural dimension to such contrasts with the genuine African city, compared to the artificial European or colonial city. Where once progress was measured by how much an African town reproduced the amenities of a European counterpart, now it is authenticity, liberation from the colonial chrysalis, that can be celebrated. In addition, there may be a gender dimension: the autonomous forces of urban development allow women, usually at a great disadvantage in obtaining wage employment, to support and empower themselves as they transcend established boundaries of gender activity.[14]

I should like to point as well here to two other tendencies that appear systematically. The decline of the state sometimes can be empowering for racial

---

[12]   Ahonsi 2002:148. In the same volume, Koolhaas is quite remarkable. For solid accounts that are perhaps less imaginative see Aina, Etta and Obi 1994; Peil 1991.
[13]   Hake 1977; Stren and White 1989. Note that Hake's work coincides with the ILO mission to Kenya that famously discovered the development potential of the newly dubbed 'informal sector'.
[14]   Tripp 1997. For an influential account that sees the city in some senses liberating for African women, see White 1990.

or ethnic minorities who became outsiders – if they had not been before – after the coming of independence. However, in the urban consciousness there now exists increasingly the sense that the amount of wealth available in the city is finite and limited. It gives rise to what South Africans call xenophobia, a conflict between groups, sometimes only identifiable through urban social evolution, that can have very serious consequences for the functioning of the city.[15] This tendency casts a long shadow particularly over cities that have thrived through their cosmopolitan character. This is thus a localized mercantilist reaction – wealth is a zero-sum game – to international neoliberal hegemony.

This is how I would interpret changes that have overcome Abidjan, the largest West African city after Lagos.[16] Abidjan was established by the French administration of the Ivory Coast in French West Africa in 1920.[17] At that point, its population consisted only of those inhabiting a couple dozen Ebrié and other villages around a network of islands and peninsulas on a lagoon. The French goal was to establish the ideal site for a railway terminus that would evacuate useful tropical commercial products and could be connected easily to a seaport. They wanted to find a relatively healthy site that they meant to develop as a territorial capital. Abidjan became the capital of the Ivory Coast only in 1934, and in 1950 a cut through the island of Petit Bassam brought deep-water ships directly through to the lagoon, confirming Abidjan's location as the dynamic plug-point of colonial development not merely in the Ivory Coast but in French West Africa more generally. Under self-government and then independence, it was the purpose of the long-lived Houphouët-Boigny administration to make Abidjan a splendid gateway to the prosperity of this unusually successful territory. The air-conditioned modern towers of the urban core, the Plateau (Abidjan des tours), rose over shops that made available the full array of French consumerism to what was by West African standards a large affluent population. For a casual visitor, a striking feature of Abidjan lay in the presence of numerous French people and the apparent replication of a provincial French city. The wealthy districts seemed to be a West African echo of the settler cities of East and South Africa.

Many observers would ascribe a very large part of the success of the city, and of the Ivory Coast, to its tolerance and its capacity to engage the energies of large numbers of outsiders. Not only were there many French residents, there was an even larger number of Lebanese who played a role in most aspects of the economy. The agricultural export economy was dependent on the migration of northern Ivorians into the lightly-peopled south

---

[15] For the city as a cauldron in the creation of new ethnic identity, see Bernault 2000.

[16] There is a very substantial and rich literature on Abidjan. Important titles include Antoine, Dubresson and Manou-Savina 1987; Yapi Diahou 2001; Cohen 1984; Dubresson 1997.

[17] For an earlier attempt on my part to compare Abidjan and Durban, see Freund 2001.

but also hundreds of thousands from the savannah countries, particularly Burkina Faso (Upper Volta), once joined as a colonial territory to the Ivory Coast, and Mali. There were also many migrants from other neighbouring countries such as Dahomey (Bénin), Togo, Liberia, and Ghana. Immigrants often were able to own land and to find their way into the professions and civil service as well as the informal commercial sector where Ivorians were able to exert dominance in general in government work and in the formal working class. Up to a third of the population can be defined as being of 'foreign origin'.[18]

Establishing the correct balance between different parts of the hetero- geneous Ivory Coast, between the natives and the outsiders, was certainly the focal point of the system created by Félix Houphouët-Boigny, compared at an early stage to a big city political machine playing to a myriad of ethnic communities in the USA by the political scientist Aristide Zolberg (1964). On the one hand, the final supremacy of the Ivorians who deserved the finest fruits of the harvest was to be sustained. But foreigners were to be welcomed and had their place in the pecking order, although there were outbreaks of violence against foreigners at different points in time. Indeed, the Ivory Coast government was critical in causing the break-up of the French West African federation in order to retain the rewards of regional success within the territory. Zolberg already wrote in 1964 of xenophobia as an Ivorian characteristic. But problems were inevitably resolved in terms of firming up a political and social order that promoted the Ivorian miracle socially and politically, elegantly defined in terms of the African hospitality of the Ivorian people. The state fostered ethnic identity, ruled the countryside through networks of ethnically defined chiefs, and then established an expert and flexible balance offering something to everyone, which usually worked.

This was the synthesis that revealed much continuity between the late colonial and early independence decades. Urban wealth was dependent on the growing productive earnings of its hinterland. Unfortunately, the Ivorian miracle did not endure past 1980. From 1980 to 1995, GNP per capita fell by approximately one-third. Despite various initiatives, the Ivorian economy failed to branch out and diversify very effectively. Indeed, in the 1990s it tended to focus more narrowly around cocoa. The neoliberal world order promotes exports but not generally peasant crop production that can be pro- duced in a wide range of countries; prices fell, and the indebtedness of the state mounted enormously. From 1990, Houphouët-Boigny, who had always bought out and incorporated political opposition, was forced to accept a

---

[18]   Pierre Janne in *Le Monde Diplomatique* (Octobre 2000). Offical figures are considerably lower, only 26% and declining in the last census (Kipre 2002:106). This is a useful guide to the first phases of the current Ivorian political crisis.

multiparty system that threatened his political machine's smooth running. When he died in 1993, he was succeeded by a far less smooth or effective political operator, Henri Konan Bédié. Bédié was the promoter of what was called *ivoirité* – a philosophy that exalted those who could prove that they and their parents were indigenous Ivorians. This opened a Pandora's box. On the one hand, it took off as a popular slogan for Ivorians who could identify with it in their frustration at a stagnant or declining economy and blame it on outsiders or foreigners. On the other, it was seen with mounting anger as a ploy by northern and western Ivorians on the part of the cocoa belt forest dwellers to retain state power to themselves. In 1990, foreigners lost all residual rights to vote in the Ivory Coast, while since 1999 they have lost the ability to own land and have been obliged to formalize their status as non-Ivorians by accepting a system of relatively costly identity cards. Accusations about faking cards preceded this step. The minister who introduced the cards, Alassane Ouattara, was a northerner himself, and his rivalry with other leaders was regionalized and turned into religious and ethnic competition. A key state-commissioned report by the Conseil Économique et Social asserted that the number of those of foreign origin in the Ivory Coast, although no longer increasing, surpassed by far the limit that one could find 'tolerable'. Konan Bédié's opponents demanded democracy, but they too wanted a sharper distinction between Ivorians and foreigners.

As this impulse advanced, Abidjan was plunged into prolonged waves of political crisis marked by considerable violence that ripped off layers of its cosmopolitan character. Violent youths have been the bearers of the chauvinist politics that is taking on unprecedented strengths. Tensions, curfews, and political murders have taken place in an environment where popular nightclubs feature singers who bemoan the illegitimate influence of foreigners. In the nightclub of Joël Tichi, former captain of the national soccer squad, Ivorians danced to 'Libérez', by which they meant: liberate us from the foreigners (*Hindustan Times*, 25-4-2003). One of the Ivory Coast's best-known comedians, a resident of Adjamé known to support Ouattara, was murdered, sparking violence in Adjamé amongst his supporters.[19] Gangs set torch to informal settlements, and tens of thousands of their inhabitants made their way back to Liberia, Burkina Faso, and so on. Burkinabé, arriving back in Burkina Faso, described themselves as 'harassed, beaten and … arrested' in large numbers, and as 'treated like cocoa bags'.[20] Students burnt down the Burkinabé embassy in January 2003.

Abidjan is too large and too complex a city to say that globalization has finished it off; its capabilities remain large compared to almost any other

[19]   Voice of America online 3-2-2003.
[20]   http://afrol.com (accessed 25-01-2003).

West African city. But there is no question that this classic city of import substitution, of the strong state, of peasant export crops, of the neocolonial bargain of 1960, is reeling from the impact of a turn inwards. This turn inwards must be related to the decline and present limited prospects of the previous economic system that created the Ivorian miracle. And initiatives at reconstruction on the basis of more modest forms of growth were really aimed at hardening class lines and creating a new and potentially less humane kind of urbanism in Abidjan where they have come on line; they are about identifying and privileging the minority still able to feed the circulation of money in a substantial way (Bredeloup 2002). Nor is there the sign of a new moral order creating a new rainbow on the horizon. Abidjan is not dying, but it is altering in the new environment in important ways. The neocolonial is becoming postcolonial.

This is effectively the second point I wish to make: the decline of modernist planning has led to the opening of opportunities accruing to the rich and privileged by the collapse of conventional state planning controls. In the ensuing mayhem, the rich are often well able to care for themselves and to strike out on development paths that divide some African cities more dramatically and ferociously along class lines than in colonial times. A noticeable feature of all the North African cities today also has been uncontrolled building on the periphery by the favoured and fortunate (Chabbi 1988).

This leads us to the question of whether South Africa, the wealthiest country in Africa, fits the pattern or represents a successful attempt to counter the tendencies we have examined. Perhaps a caveat is needed to bring in a South African case study. It is incorrect to describe South Africa after 1910 as a colony or as colonial, although some elements of British hegemony remained constitutionally present for some while; it was an independent country from that time. However, the African majority continued to be administered along lines typical of African colonies. The urban population was considered transient and only of doubtful legitimate status, and much of the rural population ruled through chiefs and an adaptation of precolonial rule convenient to the hegemonic white powers in society. In consequence, many of the trends that characterize the colonial African city and the consequences of the end of colonialism can be applied to the South African city under segregation and apartheid. In southern Africa, the modernist paradigm has not died. It continues to powerfully motivate well-resourced urban regimes, notably in Durban, as well as the government ideology in South Africa, and in fact is still significant in Namibia, Botswana, Zimbabwe, and elsewhere. In the important case of South Africa, the postmodern paradigm is probably at least only partially applicable to date.

## Durban: A postmodern urban centre in South Africa?

Since 1994, urban problems have been the challenge faced by a new government determined to destroy the traces of apartheid. We shall consider here the example of Durban, South Africa's third largest city – approximately the size of Abidjan – linked to the heart of the national economy through the presence of the continent's busiest port.[21] From 1996, a new administration presided over more than forty previously extant, racially defined municipal structures merged into a metropolitan council with sub-metropolitan bodies. This was restructured again from 2001 into a Unicity given the isiZulu name of Ethekweni on a considerably more centralized basis that draws in a substantial rural periphery. Obviously, the new structure is committed to equity in services, employment, and so on as part of the 'new South Africa'. Moreover while the globalization model predicts a growing dominance of ethnic and racial identity as other issues are predetermined by the needs of capital, the ruling African National Congress is committed to forging a new national identity, even while privileging the 'previously disadvantaged', as they are termed, and with a strong bias towards centralized government dominating governance. In a comparative research project, it was estimated that city revenues in Durban were perhaps twenty to thirty times as great as in Abidjan. Thus, a particular form of the modernist paradigm carries on.

Numerous commentators have in recent years emphasized an ideology of 'modernity' as promoting a South African city where residential and business areas were distinctly separate, where the newer suburbs extended themselves on garden city lines, highways allowed the middle class to move through the city very rapidly, and where the shabby, the indeterminate, and the irredeemably poor tended to be entirely left out of the city plans. Transport was governed by commuter rail lines and buses aimed at ferrying workers back and forth to work from relatively distant townships. The growing dominance of big firms and multinationals dovetailed with this process. However, the South African dimension to this meant that the class aspect was subordinated to racial politics. Particularly following the Group Areas Act of 1950, Durban was being reconstructed on precisely this basis. Security concerns were flagrantly emphasized in this segregatory planning phase that partitioned the residential part of the city between white, Indian, Coloured, and African areas while making sure that in every sense the whites retained power over the core.[22] The South African version of modernism gathered strength after

---

[21] For Durban over the past twenty years, see Freund and Padayachee 2002. Vital earlier references are Kuper, Watts and Davies 1958; Maylam and Edwards 1996.

[22] For the South African city under apartheid, there is a large monographic literature. However, see Smith 1992, and the special issue of the *Journal of Southern African Studies* 23-1 (1996) on urban studies and urban change in southern Africa.

mid-century, especially in the years of economic recovery following the withdrawal from the Commonwealth and the establishment of the republic in l960. The following decade witnessed more rapid growth in Durban than average for the country.

Well before the end of apartheid, the material conditions allowing for this pattern began to become less favourable. This created particular challenges for the new era that dawned from the late 1970s as this segregated structure began to manifest growing cracks in the wall. The city had carried out the construction of large family orientated housing estates for African and Indian people, but these estates were poorly serviced with basic amenities, especially the African ones. Servicing required money and after 1980 employment ceased to expand in the city, particularly for the working class, creating increasing tensions and politicizing struggles over rent and over payments for electricity and other basic services. There were few licit economic activities in the African townships, although market and even production activities gradually emerged despite the planning laws in some Indian areas. The centre of Durban witnessed the arrival of growing numbers of street traders while private taxis greatly increased the possibilities of movement for those who did not own cars. The bad fit between the 'modern' structuration of the 1960s and the actual needs of a city thronged with poor people looking for means of survival on their doorstep became apparent.

A detailed look at two sections of the city exemplifies how the city has evolved since 1994. On the one hand, we see the tendency towards fragmentation and privileging of an elite that fits into the patterns we have already noted and, on the other, there is also the effort to create a progressive modern city in line with the ideals of the struggle against apartheid.

One visible index of the new Durban is the very rapid growth of the northern areas of Umhlanga Rocks/Umhlanga Ridge. In the postwar decades, this section of the city essentially consisted of sugar cane fields while a small settlement around a lighthouse and hotel attracted white tourists seeking an unspoilt seaside environment. From the 1970s, this settlement built up rapidly with flats and time-share units as the well-to-do in Johannesburg searched for an outlet to a warm place by the sea away from the traditional Durban beachfront, too easily reached by public transport and beginning to fade as leisure tastes changed. However, just inland the sugar fields remained, in good part due to the tax regime that discouraged conversion from agriculture. One large company, Tongaat-Hulett, itself linked to the finance-mining giant Anglo-American, owned them in large part.

However, starting with shifts towards economic liberalization, powerful forces began to make new plans in the late 1980s. Tongaat-Hulett hired some of the best minds in the city to think about future spatial planning and has been a major force in the growing environment of public-private partnership planning in Durban. Consequently, Tongaat-Hulett organized the sale of large amounts of cane land to create the foundation for what has been classically termed in the USA by Joel Garreau an 'edge city' (1991). On the ridge overlooking the sea and leisure orientated built environment, one now finds hundreds of houses of the newly rich (no longer racially defined, of course), the largest shopping complex 'in the southern hemisphere' modelled on activity-based US shopping malls, and a growing array of corporate service offices and headquarters. These now extend directly above the beach suburb of Umhlanga Rocks. Meanwhile, further north, gloriously or hideously unplanned new beach suburbs on the so-called Dolphin Coast, much like Umhlanga Rocks, are expanding very rapidly to cater to the wealthy retired and the need of the well-heeled to recuperate from the pressures of life in Johannesburg or Pretoria. Mount Edgecombe sugar estate has been largely turned into a golf course and adjoining network of affluent gated suburbia. Farther inland is land designated for the less affluent and the site of what will be towards the end of the first decade of the twenty-first century a new international airport partly aimed at the tourist market. By contrast, the central business district of Durban, although still a centre of government and harbour-related business and still a thriving shopping district for the working poor and lower middle class, is now largely bereft of boutiques, entertainment facilities, and up-market office premises.

In more than one sense, Umhlanga symbolizes the typical features more generally associated with the globalized city: sharp division between a cut-off and protected rich and a growingly unwanted and irregularly supported poor, an obsession with security and the hunger of capital for exploitation of new land for constructing houses and commercial property. The architectural models used are eclectic and international with little or no attempt to adapt South African indigenous building forms. Like most international examples, the gentrification option is, however, also present in the form of upgrading the wealthiest parts of inner suburbia of Durban. Stereotypically it is often assumed that Africa, the entire continent, is simply cut out of these trends and banished to some outer hell by globalization. In reality, the example of Durban, just as in Abidjan, shows that these new divisions also form within Africa itself.

A short account of Cato Manor development gives an interesting contrast to Umhlanga. Cato Manor is a large tract of hilly, relatively unstable land beyond the Berea Ridge but very close to and directly inland from the central business district of Durban. It was sub-divided in large part and sold to Indian smallholders who were the dominant element when it was incorporated into Durban in 1931 at a key stage in the segregatory modernization project. During World War II, already notorious as a locale for illicit activity, especially the brewing and sale of alcohol to Africans, Cato Manor attracted some tens of thousands of poor African arrivals from the countryside to whom Indians rented land or shacks. In 1949 it was the scene of the infamous Cato Manor African-Indian 'race riots' that were partly instigated by ambitious African would-be entrepreneurs. In the 1950s it became associated with pockets of militant antigovernment organization and violent conflict between women beer brewers and the police. It was a zone that urban authorities could not control and were anxious to shut down.

Before the Group Areas Act, Durban de facto had been largely segregated by race. Now the state was determined to put segregation into force more thoroughly. Cato Manor was almost entirely uprooted and its Indian and African inhabitants forced to move into townships elsewhere in the early 1960s. However, there was no commercial interest in developing the area for white suburbia, and in effect a huge area left undeveloped near the centre of the city languished for decades.

In the late apartheid era, the state had proclaimed the Cato Manor area suitable for Indian housing, and some Indian families had returned through purchasing new little bungalows from the middle 1980s. Indian claims for Cato Manor were strong; the compensation money doled out in the past was minimal and the sense of dispossession a burning part of the legacy of apartheid. And yet, in 1992 impatient Africans living nearby in crowded circumstances were so upset at the new Indian arrivals that they invaded the last lot of this housing, seizing these properties for their own. Moreover, during the transition era, a considerable number of Africans, perhaps up to 20,000, felt emboldened to build shacks in parts of Cato Manor. Many were refugees from violence in the politically contested countryside, and here again there was some sense of wanting justice about the past. But equally pressing were the activities of shacklords and gangs that were dominated by so-called veterans of the liberation struggle who preyed upon the illegal shack dwellers.

Given this fraught context, in 1992 the city was prepared to authorize the creation of the Cato Manor Development Agency to administer and further the development of the area. This agency was staffed with committed ex-activists associated with alternative housing NGOs and foreign sympathizers; while there was a board of control with local representation, political circumstances allowed these bureaucrats to operate free of political pressures, democratic and otherwise, to a large extent. They were able to devote the first years of CMDA activity to knife-edge political negotiation at which they proved very skilful, gradually stabilizing conditions. They also proved very effective at attracting outside funding to what was billed a model project, particularly from the European Union, that was desperate to find funding outlets of a high quality in Africa.

This situation controverts neoliberal policy making in important ways: a strong central state eager to make centre-left interventions, a set of enlightened bureaucrats willing to dispense with overly much stakeholder intervention, although acting with a certain structural autonomy, and large-scale state intervention financially. The results have been correspondingly positive in important ways. Housing has proceeded and has included some interesting experiments involving more quality and potential for community construction than is typical. Sites have generally been allocated as fairly as possible without patronage taken into account, thus creating citizens rather than patrimonial clients. The foundation for far more building has been laid. Indian ex-residents, uninterested in the end in returning to mixed neighbourhoods, have accepted compensation on a large scale for their previous losses. The smaller shack settlements have been destroyed and replaced by permanent housing. In the biggest site where perhaps 15,000 people live, some upgrading has taken place, the shacklords' power has been broken, and there have at least been no further successful attempts at illegal settlement. A striking feature of the settled areas of Cato Manor has been the early provision of health facilities, schools, and community halls. Some green space has been left in many areas. A major road has been driven through the area opening it up to easy access to the city, and commercial and industrial properties have begun to develop. A small number of African contractors (approximately 100) have been used locally, although, as is so typical of South Africa, construction remains overwhelmingly performed by public or corporate contractors with capacity 'at scale'.

The limitations of Cato Manor success need, however, to be spelled out equally. The residents suffer just as much from AIDS and unemployment as elsewhere in the city. The special features of the CMDA from early in 2003 will be a thing of the past; the city has adjudged crisis conditions to be over and will start to administer Cato Manor like anywhere else. Patronage in the form of elected councillors and their activities will no doubt return, diluting the CMDA thrust on turning residents into pure citizens free of dubious forms of mediation.

Some of the housing in Cato Manor is pathetically tiny and basic and unsurprisingly gets sold illegally for less than the official value of the house (houses are supposed not to be legally sold for a fixed but considerable period of time). Given how rarely inhabitants are in steady employment, the private sector has effectively refused to get involved for the most part in Cato Manor. South Africa has a dearth of small businessmen living on the margins and prepared to take big risks to fill this gap. There are beginning to be problems with nonpayment of bills; an experimental densely settled rental area is refusing to pay rent. Why should they, after all, if houses have been made available to others for nothing? These issues highlight the basic contradictions in government policy in general. On the one hand, an urgent and intense desire exists to 'make up for' apartheid by making available some funds for housing and infrastructure, but there is no capacity to intervene massively to create jobs and no desire to try to channel private funds forcibly in directions business does not seek. A thriving private sector has been adjudged to be the bedrock of any national future and, in the globalized environment, this dramatically limits structured interventions. And, finally, Cato Manor is only very marginally 'nonracial'; it is a black community, in part due to the choice to create almost no middle-class housing, although the income mix is greater than in many other South African state housing schemes. At best, Cato Manor is now another urban township with all the problems experienced by the others, no worse but not dramatically better either. In conclusion, this major site for inspecting the new South Africa conveniently located almost a stone's throw from the city centre reveals in and of itself some of the realities of the globalized city.[23]

## Conclusion

This paper has looked at how decolonization transformed African cities. In contrast with other parts of the world, decolonization in Africa took place over several decades and in many cases can be seen as a gradual process involving many kinds of continuities. It is argued that modernist planning and state policy, while altered after independence, contained much the same in the way of ideas about development allowing for considerable continuity so long as the economy, often categorized as neocolonial, held up.

Modernity came to Africa in one fairly standard form through colonial domination. Where possible, the postcolonial state tried to shift that modernity in statist and deracialized directions and become a yet more powerful patron of the very rapid growth of primate cities. However, the circumstances of postindependence development intensified pressures that made continued state intervention difficult or impossible and led to the collapse of the late colonial planning formulae. The patronage of the state has coupled with the declining purchase of peasant life of the mass of African people to lead to an explosive growth that has far surpassed the capacity of the formal economy to accommodate migrants with jobs and has led to the emergence and indeed seeming dominance of the 'self-help' city. The possibilities of modernity led by the state now look far more limited given the triumph of neoliberalism and the crisis of the African state. Through its attack on 'urban bias', neoliberalism has slowed urban migration, and today most African cities grow very largely through natural means rather than in-migration. The future of the self-help city is seen less negatively than in the past and indeed promoted by neoliberal enemies of the African state in almost glowing terms. The potential of

---

[23] For one of many attempts to generalize about global trends and urbanization, see Marcuse and Van Kempen 2002.

'civil society' in the form of nongovernmental organization and community development organizations to create basic services for the majority is much discussed although it is not clear that important integrative urban functions can really be developed in this way.

At the same time, modernist visions remain on the books and continue to have real potency in South Africa and some other countries. In terms of postcolonial cities, it can be said that even within Africa there is no simple formula for understanding the evolution of cities. If in some cases, xenophobic zero-sum ethnic politics, as in Abidjan, have become more and more oppressive, in others, neoliberal constraints on ethnic groups more than able to look after themselves in the marketplace have been reduced, and indeed the bourgeoisie has been able to carve out space for itself as dramatically or more dramatically than before, as in Durban. If 'urban bias' has come under the spotlight, the 'rural bias' of colonial times that tended towards seeing African urbanization as unnatural as well as undesirable is not dead. There is as well a current view of the African city, in the wake of the decline of the modern project in many places, as an iconic dystopia.[24] This latter literature is not entirely to be dismissed because it highlights formidable problems that are barriers in giving urban Africans a better life. Yet this chapter also in a qualified way points to at least this validity in analyses influenced more or less unconsciously by neoliberalism: they highlight examples that show variety, continued choice, and vitality in African urbanity, the key source of the contemporary art and music of Africa so much admired internationally. The African city will continue to develop and expand; it will continue to exhibit human virtues, and it will more and more be the place where African futures are decided as the colonial era drifts further back into the past.

*References*

Abdullah, Ibrahim
2002            'Space, culture and agency in contemporary Freetown; The making and remaking of a postcolonial city', in: Okwui Enwezor, Carlos Basualdo, Ute Meta Bauer, Susanne Ghez, Sarat Maharaj, Mark Nash and Octavio Zaya (eds), *Under siege; Four African cities, Freetown, Johannesburg, Kinshasa, Lagos*, pp. 201-14. Ostfildern-Ruit: Hatje Cantz.
Ahonsi, Babatunde A.
2002            'Popular shaping of metropolitan forms and processes in Nigeria; Glimpses and interpretations from an informed Lagosian', in: Okwui

---

[24]   For a powerful recent example very sympathetic to the plight of Africans in a deteriorating economy with reference to the Zambian Copperbelt, see Ferguson 1999.

Enwezor, Carlos Basualdo, Ute Meta Bauer, Susanne Ghez, Sarat Maharaj, Mark Nash and Octavio Zaya (eds), *Under siege; Four African cities, Freetown, Johannesburg, Kinshasa, Lagos,* pp. 129-53. Ostfildern-Ruit: Hatje Cantz.

Aina, Tade Akin, Florence Ebam Etta and Cyril I. Obi
1994        'The search for sustainable urban development in Metropolitan Lagos', *Third World Planning Review* 16:201-19.

Anderson, David
2005        *Histories of the hanged; Britain's dirty war in Kenya and the end of empire.* New York: Norton.

Antoine, Ph., A. Dubresson and A. Manou-Savina
1987        *Abidjan; 'Côté cours'.* Paris: ORSTOM/Karthala.

Balandier , Georges
1957        *Sociologie des Brazzavilles noires.* Paris: Presses de la Fondation Nationale de Sciences Politiques.

Bernault, Florence
2000        'The political shaping of sacred locality in Brazzaville', in: David Anderson and Richard Rathbone (eds), *Africa's urban past,* pp. 283-302. Oxford: James Currey.

Boeck, Filip de
2002        'Tales of the invisible city and the "Second World"', in: Okwui Enwezor, Carlos Basualdo, Ute Meta Bauer, Susanne Ghez, Sarat Maharaj, Mark Nash and Octavio Zaya (eds), *Under siege; Four African cities, Freetown, Johannesburg, Kinshasa, Lagos,* pp. 243-86. Ostfildern-Ruit: Hatje Cantz.

Bredeloup, Sylvie
2002        'Abidjan, un dispositif marchand en mutation', in: A. Bouillon, B. Freund, D. Hindson and B. Lootvoet (eds), *Governance, urban dynamics and economic development; A comparative analysis of the metropolitan areas of Durban, Abidjan and Marseilles,* pp. 255-83. Durban: Plumbline Publishing.

Brown, Kenneth L.
1976        *People of Salé; Tradition and change in a Moroccan city, 1830-1930.* Cambridge, MA: Harvard University Press. [Harvard Studies in Urban History.]

Cahen, Michel (ed.)
1989        *'Vilas' et cidades; Bourgs en villes en Afrique Lusophone.* Paris: L'Harmattan.

Çelik, Zeynep
1997        *Urban forms and colonial confrontations; Algiers under French rule.* Berkeley, CA: University of California Press.

Chabbi, M.
1988        'The pirate developer; A new form of developer in Tunis', *International Journal of Urban and Regional Research,* 12-1(March):8-21.

Cohen, Michael
1984        'Urban policy and development strategy', in: I. William Zartman and Christopher Delgado (eds), *The political economy of the Ivory Coast.* New York: Praeger.

Cooper, Frederick (ed.)
1983        *Struggle for the city; Migrant labour, capital and the state in Africa*. Beverly
            Hills/London: Sage.
Cooper, Frederick
1996        *Decolonization and African society; The labor question in French and British
            Africa*. Cambridge: Cambridge University Press. [African Studies
            Series 89.]
Dorier-Apprill, Elisabeth, Abel Kouvouama and Christophe Apprill
1998        *Vivre à Brazzaville; Modernité et crise du quotidien*. Paris: Karthala.
Dubresson, Alain
1997        'Abidjan; From the public making of a modern city to management
            of a metropolis', in: Carole Rakodi (ed.), *The urban challenge in Africa;
            Growth and management of its large cities*, pp. 252-91. Tokyo: United
            Nations University Press.
Enwezor, Okwui, Carlos Basualdo, Ute Meta Bauer, Susanne Ghez, Sarat Maharaj,
            Mark Nash and Octavio Zaya (eds)
2002        *Under siege; Four African cities, Freetown, Johannesburg, Kinshasa, Lagos*.
            Ostfildern-Ruit: Hatje Cantz.
Epstein, A.L.
1958        *Politics in an urban African community*. Manchester: Manchester
            University Press. [Rhodes-Livingstone Institute.]
Ferguson, James
1999        *Expectations of modernity; Myths and meanings of urban life on the Zambian
            Copperbelt*. Berkeley, CA: University of California Press. [Perspectives
            on Southern Africa 57.]
Freund, Bill
1998        *Making of contemporary Africa; The development of African society since
            1800*. Second edition. Basingstoke: Palgrave, Boulder, CO: Rienner.
            [First edition 1984.]
2001        'Contrasts in urban segregation; A tale of two African cities; Durban
            and Abidjan', *Journal of Southern African Studies* 27:527-46.
2007        *The African city; A history*, Cambridge: Cambridge University Press.
            [New Approaches to African History 4.]
Freund, Bill and Vishnu Padayachee (eds)
2002        *(D)urban vortex; South African city in transition*. Pietermaritzburg:
            University of Natal Press.
Freund, Bill, Brij Maharaj and Maurice Makhathini
2004        'Development in Cato Manor, Durban; Political interpretations',
            in: Peter Robinson, Jeff MacCarthy and Clive Forster (eds), *Urban
            reconstruction in the developing world; Learning through an international
            best practice*. London: Heinemann.
Furedi, Frank
1973        'The African crowd in Nairobi; Popular movements and elite politics',
            *Journal of African History* 14-2:275-90.
Garreau, Joel
1991        *Edge city; Life on the new frontier*. New York: Random House.

Gifford, Prosser and William Roger Louis (eds)
1982          *The transfer of power in Africa; Decolonization 1940-1960.* Second print.
              New Haven, CT: Yale University Press.
Hadjiedj, Ali, Claude Chaline and Jocelyne Dubois-Maury (eds)
2003          *Alger, les nouveaux défis de l'urbanisation.* Paris: L'Harmattan.
Hake, Andrew
1977          *African metropolis; Nairobi's self-help city.* London: Sussex University
              Press.
Joseph, Richard
1974          'Settlers, strikers and sans-travail; The Douala riots of September 1945',
              *Journal of African History* 15:669-87.
Kipre, Pierre
2002          'Les discours politiques de décembre 1999 à l'élection présidentielle
              d'octobre 2000; Thèmes, enjeux et confrontations', in : Marc le Pape
              et Claudine Vidal (eds), *Côte d'Ivoire; L'année terrible*, pp. 81-121. Paris:
              Karthala.
Koolhaas, R.
2002          'Fragments of a lecture on Lagos', in: Okwui Enwezor, Carlos Basualdo,
              Ute Meta Bauer, Susanne Ghez, Sarat Maharaj, Mark Nash and Octavio
              Zaya (eds), *Under siege; Four African cities, Freetown, Johannesburg,
              Kinshasa, Lagos*, pp. 175-85. Ostfildern-Ruit: Hatje Cantz.
Kuper, Leo, Hilstan Watts and Ronald Davies
1958          *Durban; A study in racial ecology.* London: Cape.
Marcuse, Peter and Ronald van Kempen (eds)
2002          *Globalising cities; A new spatial order?* London: Blackwell.
Maylam, Paul and Iain Edwards (eds)
1996          *The people's city; African life in twentieth century Durban.* Pietermaritzburg:
              University of Natal Press.
Meillassoux, Claude
1968          *Urbanization of an African community; Voluntary associations in Bamako.*
              Seattle: University of Washington Press. [Monograph 45.]
Mitchell, J. Clyde
1987          *Cities, society and social perception; A Central African perspective.* Oxford:
              Clarendon Press.
Nlandu, Thierry
2002          'Kinshasa; Beyond chaos', in: Okwui Enwezor, Carlos Basualdo, Ute
              Meta Bauer, Susanne Ghez, Sarat Maharaj, Mark Nash and Octavio
              Zaya (eds), *Under siege; Four African cities, Freetown, Johannesburg,
              Kinshasa, Lagos*, pp.185-200. Ostfildern-Ruit: Hatje Cantz.
O'Connor, Anthony
1983          *The African city.* London: Hutchinson. [Hutchinson University Library
              for Africa.]
Omasombo Tshonda, Jean
2002          'Kisangani and the curve of destiny', in: Okwui Enwezor, Carlos
              Basualdo, Ute Meta Bauer, Susanne Ghez, Sarat Maharaj, Mark Nash
              and Octavio Zaya (eds), *Under siege; Four African cities, Freetown,
              Johannesburg, Kinshasa, Lagos*, pp. 401-16. Ostfildern-Ruit: Hatje Cantz.

Parker, John
2000        *Making the town; Ga state and society in early colonial Accra.* Portsmouth: Heinemann, Oxford: Currey. [Social History of Africa.]
Peel, J.D.Y.
1983        *Ijeshas and Nigerians; the incorporation of a Yoruba Kingdom 1890s-1970s.* Cambridge: Cambridge University Press. [African Studies Series 39.]
Peil, Margaret
1991        *Lagos: The city is the people.* London: Belhaven.
Piermay, Jean-Luc
1997        'Kinshasa; A reprieved mega-city?' in: Carole Rakodi (ed.), *The urban challenge in Africa; Growth and management of its large cities,* pp. 223-51. Tokyo: United Nations University Press.
Prochaska, David
1990        *Making Algeria French; Colonialism in Bône, 1870-1920.* Cambridge: Cambridge University Press, Paris : Éditions de la Maison des Sciences de l'Homme.
Rakodi, Carole (ed.)
1997        *The urban challenge in Africa; Growth and management of its large cities.* Tokyo: United Nations University Press.
Smith, David M. (ed.)
1992        *The apartheid city and beyond; urbanization and social change in South Africa.* London/New York: Routledge, Johannesburg: Witwatersrand University Press.
Stren, Richard E. and Rodney R. White (eds)
1989        *African cities in crisis; Managing rapid urban growth.* Boulder, CO: Westview Press. [African Modernization and Development Series.]
Tripp, Aili Mari
1997        *Changing the rules; The politics of liberalization and the urban informal economy in Tanzania.* Berkeley, CA: University of California Press.
White, Luise
1990        *The comforts of home; Prostitution in colonial Nairobi.* Chicago: University of Chicago Press.
Yapi Diahou, Alphonse
2001        *Baraques et pouvoirs dans l'agglomération abidjanaise.* Paris: L'Harmattan.
Young, Crawford
1965        *Politics in the Congo; Decolonization and independence.* Princeton, NJ: Princeton University Press.
Zolberg, Aristide R.
1964        *One-party government in the Ivory Coast.* Princeton, NJ: Princeton University Press.

CATHÉRINE COQUÉRY-VIDROVITCH

# Racial and social zoning in African cities from colonization to postindependence

This chapter addresses an issue that has barely been studied in a comparative perspective, that of urban residential segregation – the policies and practices of urban residential zoning during colonialism, and their continuation after independence.[1] The question is whether and how decolonization and the change of power affected urban policies of residential zoning. Of course, the situation differed for every city. Colonial residential segregation was instituted in many ways, sometimes imposed by the government (as in East and South Africa), at other times indirect (in the case of both anglophone and franco-phone West Africa). Moreover, segregation went much further than simple residential segregation: it could involve the separation not only of housing but of practically every substantial element of daily life: public spaces, laws, schools, livelihood, and culture. Colonial life was often organized along lines of inclusion or exclusion of specific groups, and residential zoning was only part of this general pattern of segregation. Yet, the built environment was an essential and conspicuous expression of the compartmentalizing spirit of colonialism. As Anthony King (1984:99) noted, 'How people think governs how people build. And how people build [...] also affects how people think.'

The manifestations of residential zoning in colonial times were very diverse. Self-evidently, in many ways colonial urban policies have left an imprint on the postcolonial developments of the African city. However, formal residential zoning did not have such a strong impact in either period. In this chapter, I argue that the residential laws and rules played a relatively minor role during both colonial and postcolonial times. The colonial period can be divided in two phases: first, up to the 1930s, when urban planning was given little attention and residential policies barely existed; second, between the early 1930s and the 1960s, when residential policies and plan-ning began to be more seriously planned. This colonial town planning con-tinued without great changes in the early decades of independence.

---

[1]  A first draft of this argumentation was tried at the conference 'African urban spaces; history and culture' in Austin, Texas, March 2003. The author and editors thank Elsbeth Locher-Scholten for her expert help in editing this chapter.

The change of power at independence did not bring an enormous shift in the structure of the African city. Indeed, independence created a pattern that before had only existed in West Africa: segregation as a political ideology became unlawful everywhere. As a consequence of the transfer of sovereignty, a sudden mobility was put in motion: an African bourgeoisie rushed to occupy the former white settlers' districts, while people at the bottom of society moved to downtown districts to extend their 'informal' trade activities to the quarters where they had been forbidden in the past. Nevertheless, the change of power little affected residential habits; at most, racial zoning was substituted by social zoning. Therefore, just prior to or after the transfer of sovereignty, it even appears that decolonization strengthened rather than weakened previous trends. In Johannesburg racial (and social) zoning increased rather than decreased; Soweto, the southwestern township of Johannesburg, became larger than ever before. So did Pikine in Senegal, which came into existence in the late 1950s as a result of the forced removal of urban shantytowns to the fringes of the city. Residential evolution after independence was more or less similar everywhere (post-apartheid South Africa included). Since then, urban growth has been so intensive, partly due to globalization, that the development of sprawling African megacities of later years differs little from urban growth elsewhere in the world.

This article does not deal with the desegregation of the middle classes at independence, which in a sense is self-explanatory: the national bourgeoisie benefited from the new political situation. Independence made many African political expatriates return to their countries in tropical Africa and occupied the houses and quarters of the former colonizers. In settlement colonies, former settlers emigrated in sufficiently large numbers to leave behind comfortable and luxurious villas and buildings in the residential quarters that until then had been reserved for whites. In the case of Maputo, for instance, about one million settlers departed at Mozambique's independence, leaving behind their empty houses.

More interesting is the situation of the common people. How and in what rhythm did they take over former colonial cities? In what way and how did the state intervene to attempt to regulate their migration process and housing problems? What were government visions at the time? Although detailed case studies for the postcolonial period are scarce, existing studies conclude in general that social zoning replaced racial zoning soon after independence. Except for South Africa, white settlers remained a minority, and class differentiations did not have racial consequences. For instance, Lebanese traders in West Africa, or Indian traders in East Africa, as well as 'coloured' people in South Africa, had during colonial times (and under apartheid) been used as go-betweens between the 'natives' and the whites. They were accustomed to trade and therefore to live side by side with people of other backgrounds. This did not change in the postcolonial period.

But social zoning there was. As a rule, the state did not pay attention to 'tribal' localities in towns. New migrants often settled in parts of town where they had relatives or acquaintances from the same background. The rapid acceleration of urban migration even favoured a higher mixed urban population than before. Usually migration knew at least two stages: the first arrival was more or less improvised, when newcomers would be forced to settle in far-away shantytowns. Only after awhile the household would seize the opportunity to improve housing and to settle in a better place, or at least closer to work.

*Colonial cities; mixed populations and sanitation syndrome*

It is a misunderstanding to think that under colonial rule residential segregation was legally enforced from the beginning. The authoritarian colonial regime did not prevent the cohabitation and even melting of different groups in the cities. Thus, Cape Town in South Africa was for a long time a mixed city, and apartheid had to destroy entire quarters of it – as it also did in Johannesburg – to apply its principles (Davenport and Saunders 2000:272-3, 396-7). There were a few exceptions. Fort-Lamy in Chad or Pointe-Noire in Congo were cities created by colonization with city plans that imposed residential segregation from the beginning, *de facto* if not *de jure*. South Africa, South Rhodesia, and Kenya were the only countries where residential segregation was legalized early on. But at first this segregation primarily concerned rural areas, where the British colonizer confiscated land rights from the autochthonous inhabitants to the profit of white planters. Thus, the South African Land Act of 1913 did not give Africans the right to own land anywhere except in the 'reserves'. However, this as yet did not concern the black population that lived in the cities, where settlement was subject to few rules. Although entire quarters of the cities would soon be reserved for them, some blacks would keep their property rights even if their property was located in white areas. Generally, it was income level that was most decisive in the selection of a place of residence: settlers had the means to buy their tranquillity. They established themselves, as a general rule, in areas far from the harbour and industrial zones, but close to the principal services and the most sought-after region: at the seaside or on the heights that were considered most sanitary and enjoyed a good view.

Before apartheid, the city of Cape Town was as mixed as Lomé in Togo, and for similar reasons: the history of the city was that of a harbour that had been founded before colonization (Lomé) or during early colonialism (Cape Town) (Marguerat 1994:71-95). Only after 1950 their paths went in different directions, when Lomé, having become the capital of an independent state, continued to be mixed – it is today probably still the most residentially mixed African city – while apartheid created an authoritarian and late white order in Cape Town. In Dakar, measures of exclusion were also taken in the name of order and seemliness: thus, a police rule forbade the use of donkey carts, a mode of transportation commonly used by the autochthonous people on the Plateau, the centre of business and colonial government. This measure effectively denied access to these places to 'natives' of the popular classes because they were unable to get there, as has been immortalized in the film *Borom Sharet* by Ousmane Sembène as late as the 1950s.

Urban zoning was rarely officially galvanized by law. However, from the beginning of colonial urbanization, colonial governments have displayed a so-called 'sanitation syndrome'. It authorized colonial officers and later colonial planners to differentiate between two parts of the city: the 'healthy' white one, the only 'true city' part in their opinion, and the 'native' one. The latter was often known under the denigratory term of 'villages', although they were true urban districts, but built and maintained in an autochthonous manner. Residential zoning under the justification of this 'sanitation syndrome' was attempted almost as early in Dakar – where the expulsion of the inhabitants of the Plateau and their relocation to the Medina occurred in 1914 after the plague epidemic – as in South Africa, where it remained restricted to mining compounds.[2] Ironically, one of the first African city quarters to be exclusively reserved to white settlers was not built in South Africa, but in Freetown (Sierra Leone). Hill Station was supposed to keep the British protected from malaria on the provision that African families were excluded from the area. For just before the twentieth century, British doctors had asserted that malaria was carried and spread by African babies; hence, their mothers had to live elsewhere. In this case, residential segregation was officially gendered. Only in 1902 would the role of the anopheles mosquito in spreading malaria be recognized. Nevertheless, the sanitation syndrome lasted long: it was claimed to be necessary to isolate African households suspected of ignoring elementary rules of hygiene. In 1914, Kenyan settlers obtained the *Public Health Ordinance* that constructed the notion of 'inherently unhygienic races' to demonstrate the racial 'inferiority' of non-Europeans (Murunga 2003). Here, as well as elsewhere, the 'sanitation' argument remained in use when the first urban planning proposals were adopted before and after World War II.

---

[2]  On the hygienic and segregationist transformation, see: Call 1986 (on Western Africa) and Curtin 1985 (on Accra); Cohen 1983; Goerg 1996; Swanson 1977; Frenkel and Western 1988; Gale 1979, 1980 (on Lagos); Betts 1969, 1971; Mbokolo 1982; Ngalamulume 2004; Western 1981:35-6.

*Origins of colonial urban land legislation*

Colonial policies for the rural and urban areas differed. As a rule, African people were considered to be 'naturally' rural people and 'strangers to the city', as the majority of them lived in the countryside (Plotnicov 1967). Hence, rural land laws came in many forms, and regulations might differ from one colony to another. The major differences existed between British and French West Africa (and Uganda) on the one hand, and the rest of Africa on the other. In the western African colonies, the entire land was supposed to be reserved for the production of cash crops by African 'natives'. In British West Africa, British settlers were not allowed to enjoy rural land rights, while in the French part French settlers – if not completely absent – were very few. In the other parts of the continent, British settlers were favoured with fertile lands (such as the Highlands in Kenya), and 'natives' were supposed to live only in 'reserves'. This was legalized by an extensive corpus of land laws that might vary from one colony to the other.

Until around World War II, matters were quite different in the cities. Urban laws, when they existed, aimed at controlling people's migrations. Few thoughts were spent on permanent urban housing for Africans as they were considered only as nonpermanent migrant workers. Laws were few and mainly aimed to control 'vagrancy', that is, of people not supposed to be in town. This was especially the case in Southern Africa and Kenya, where the coming and going of migrant workers were regulated by compulsory passes.

Women held a special position. Even in South Africa women's passes were not made compulsory before the 1950s. Only in Belgian Congo a special control of migrant women was organized by law. In most cities, like Elizabethville (now Lubumbashi, originally a mining compound) a special tax and an ID was imposed for all adult women between 16 and 50 years old, theoretically living alone as 'independent' women because they were supposed to be 'free women', which meant they were prostitutes. They were not expelled from the city because the community needed their tax money. Fifty-five percent of Elizabethville's urban revenues depended on it, and probably as much in Stanleyville (Kisangani), where one third of the adult women during World War II were registered as 'free women'. The municipal authorities were divided between the desire to keep these reportedly dangerous independent women from entering the city and the satisfaction of exploiting them, since they were vitally necessary both for the work they did and for the percentage of city revenues they brought in (Coquéry-Vidrovitch 1997:91-2). Hence, nearly everywhere women might freely migrate to the cities, and very little or nothing was done to regulate their housing (apartheid excepted).

Colonizers thought of colonial cities as white cities. The reality was of course different. African cities, except Cape Town for a while in the nineteenth century, were always inhabited by a large majority of African urbanites. Yet, colonizing regimes did not recognize them as such. Parts of the city occupied by these African residents were not 'true' cities, or 'European-like' cities. Therefore, these residents were left to manage their own affairs with their supposed 'customary' habits. Probably, the most striking example is Nairobi because from its beginning in 1900 it was a mere creation of the colonizers. The initial growth of Nairobi was strongly influenced by city building in British India: in fact, all the engineers and the labour force originated from India.[3] White settlers were strongly encouraged to settle in Nairobi: in 1933, and again in 1947, 51 percent of all Europeans in Kenya lived in this city. At that time, in theory at least, no places were authorized to Africans in Nairobi. Nevertheless, Africans always outnumbered the white settler population, their numbers hovering between 60 or 70 percent of the entire population of the city until independence in 1963, when it increased to 80 percent. In fact, in 1919 permission was granted to create 'native areas' in town, and in 1928 the Municipal Native Affairs officer for Nairobi was installed to 'accept responsibility for native affairs within its boundaries', whereby formerly the presence of Africans in Nairobi was acknowledged for the first time (Campbell 2005:143). From the onset the African population grew rapidly. The first official census taken in 1948 counted 64,397 Africans, 43,749 Asians, and 10,830 Europeans (Hake 1977). As was mentioned before, the colonial government considered Africans, in particular young men, as short-term wage-earners and temporary residents. Hence, the segregated 'native locations' to the East of the railway and downstream from the industrial discharge were designed in the cheapest possible way. The municipal authorities' attitude toward African housing was well-expressed in 1930:

> It seems only right that it should be understood that the town is a non-native area in which there is no place for the redundant native who neither works nor serves his or her people. (Van Zwanenberg and King 1975:268.)

Between 1932 and 1947, the Nairobi City Council spent only one to two percent of its revenue on services for Africans.

In Northern Nigeria, the colonial state had all the urban land recognized as crown land and thus in principle disposed freely of the urban land market. But it used this right only if it needed land for the 'modern' part of the city. Colonial authorities could not proceed similarly in South Nigeria, where the entanglement of customary rules of lineage made it necessary to compensate the autochthonous people who were recognized as eminent owners of the

---

[3]   Preston 1938, quoted in Campbell 2005. This innovative work contains several precise historical views on colonial Nairobi.

land. It was only in 1978, well after independence, that the Land Use Act planned to uniform these laws. Until now, the local people have not respected this law at all. It is no exception that the same owner sells his land rights to constructors several times, creating complicated situations that generate quarrels, law suits, and violence (Oruwaro 2003). These kinds of affairs popped up as early as colonial city construction started.

The situation was similarly complex in the cities of Francophone Africa where, officially, the colonial authorities only recognized private property. It did not recognize customary property rights, except in certain cases. The Lebous of Dakar offer an example; they pugnaciously made themselves known as the first occupants and, therefore, the legitimate owners of the land. Legally, since the land decree of 1904 in French West Africa, the state was the eminent owner of lands and it classified them as 'vacant and without master' each time that an act of registration of private ownership had not been filed.[4] However, this registration was unknown to the majority of the rural autochthonous population, who were largely illiterate and uninformed. The French state thus had the opportunity to disown whomever they wanted without taking into account the rights of local usage. Contrary to the colonies of settlement, the French administration made little use of this privilege in the countryside. Yet, in the cities it did as it wished, although the authorities often tried to negotiate. As in southern Nigeria, African customary chiefs were persuaded to cede their rights after compensation. French officials even had a special vocabulary to solve these urban land quarrels between 'customary' landlords and the state or urban authority. In the case of an urban extension that needed to expel 'illegal' (not controlled) urban inhabitants, the question was, and still is, how to *'purger la coutume'*, which means how to make the 'traditional' owner, who usually had created his own business with his tenants, agree to give up his land. The usual method was (and still is) to recognize, in exchange, part of the land as his private, regularly registered property. The method was often used for urban extensions but became, of course, less effective in downtown quarters. Thus, each time an official edifice had to be built, or if the land was conceded to a private entrepreneur, 'removal' (*déguerpissement*) became the rule for city-dwelling autochthonous people who did not have a title to their property. The quarter was razed and the inhabitants were summoned to reestablish their quarters elsewhere. Similarly, in Cape Town each time a city expansion was planned, Africans were expelled.

In this way, partly organized by the officials themselves, vast shantytowns arose, such as Crossroads in Cape Town or Pikine in Dakar (Senegal), both in the colonial and in the postcolonial period. While political conditions between these cities were strikingly different, the same scheme originally

[4]    Decrees of 23-10-1904 (organization of property) and of 24-7-1906 (system of landownership).

was followed in both places. In the late 1950s, Pikine, a dozen kilometers from downtown Dakar, had spontaneously grown as a shantytown for the new arrivals who came to the city in increasing numbers (Vernières 1977). It was enormously boosted by the official decision to destroy Colobane in Dakar. The latter was a very large shantytown north of the centre, stretching for several kilometres from the highway to the airport, and was not destroyed until 1970, as the independent government pursued the same politics of removal from quarters judged to be unhealthy or illegal. In 1975 in Cape Town, people were instructed by officials to leave their squatter camp (known as Brown's Farm) to come to a 'transit camp' for African families, which was to become Crossroads near Cape Town (Cole 1987:chapter 1). Similar policies were applied all over the continent, from Abidjan to Nairobi. They were limited, however, by the lack of housing for African labourers. The *leitmotif* was everywhere the same: to receive only those hands necessary for colonial development in the city. Urban lodging for families was not provided at all, and the workers themselves were considered rural residents that were only temporary town dwellers (Collins 1969:1-32; Coquéry-Vidrovitch 1988:47-68). They were, therefore, left to themselves, building slums or shantytowns as close as possible to their places of work, such as the port, offices, and commercial centres, therefore near economic activity centres led by white people.

*Blueprints of urbanism; the emergence of colonial town planning*

Once colonial urban planning took off, authorities started to provide low-cost housing for Africans at a distance from white districts. This policy accelerated when the political mood in the colonies started to change, which would eventually lead to decolonization. In Dakar (Senegal), an Office pour habitations économiques (OHE) was created as early as 1926, but the first buildings were built only in 1941-1942 under the Vichy regime, the Cité des Capverdiens. Some houses were constructed in the Medina too. In Nairobi (Kenya), as early as 1917 residential segregation was supposed to be realized. All natives had to move to a special location, Pumwani. But reality followed at a snail's pace: only in 1923 were three slums destroyed: Kaburini, Marikini, and Mombasa. In 1930, Pumwani still remained a project, except for a few hostels for bachelors. Only in the 1930s the old shantytown of Pangani, created at the beginning of the railway construction and inhabited by 3,100 residents, was destroyed, while Pumwani was only completed in 1938. It sheltered 4,000 Africans, while probably 31,000 lived in Nairobi (Kimani 1972; Van Zwanenberg 1972). Africans were forced to relocate into government-planned residential quarters, which collectively came to be known as 'the location' – the centre of African settlement in colonial Nairobi. As most of them were shantytowns, unsanitary shacks and other unregulated settlements were often demolished, offsetting any efforts by the City Council to build sufficient, officially authorized permanent African settlements. By 1940, the pattern of racial residential segregation was firmly entrenched in Nairobi. Low-density European housing was located on the highest grounds, away from the damp areas, and north of the central business area. The majority of the Asian inhabitants lived in areas across the Nairobi River in the bazaar and commercial zone. African housing was concentrated in Nairobi's Eastlands where, at the independence in 1963, an estimated fifty percent of Nairobi's total population, and seventy percent of the African population of Nairobi was living.[5]

While Nairobi is an early example of a colonial city created from scratch, Lusaka, the new capital of Northern Rhodesia, was the first example of a fully planned city in Africa. Decisions in that direction were taken in 1929; the British architect and urban planner S.D. Ashley presented his project two years later. He chose the location and designed the city following the garden-city model as it was elaborated by Ebenezer Howard at the beginning of the century (Howard 1898). Then, in 1933, P.J. Bowling proposed a plan for a city that would house 20,000 Europeans. A kind of a perfect zoning was conceptualized, organizing three main areas, an industrial area, a business area, and a trading area, in order to spare both transportation costs and energy (Williams 1986). Nothing was planned or provided for Africans, except a 'location', *Old Kampala*, far away from the city. It was badly drained and far too small, as it was able to shelter at most 3,000 inhabitants. Except for a marketplace, everything was left to the natives' will and ability (Coquéry-Vidrovitch 1996:110-5). Only in the next generation of plans after World War II (of 1952, 1958 and 1962) were arrangements made to open parts of the city to Africans and provide housing. The 1962 plan reckoned for 125,000 inhabitants, among whom were only 22,000 Europeans. At the same time most master plans were elaborated for French Africa, notably Dakar and Abidjan (Côte d'Ivoire). In fact, it was the period when urban planning developed in Africa, as it did in Europe, and embraced the idea that cheap housing had to be provided for African urban workers and their families.

Legal residential segregation intensified after the World War II. Colonial governments, of whatever kind (South Africa included), made necessary decisions to house their African population of urban workers – it was these decisions that made legal residential segregation possible.

In terms of city planning, South Africa was a good half-century ahead. It had, therefore, a certain attraction for European tropical-zone urban planners, who had much influence on planning in other parts of the continent. Notably,

---

5   This quarter is especially studied by Campbell 2005:chapter 3.

it was a prestigious South African team of an architect, an engineer, and a sociologist that originated the 1945-1946 general plan of Nairobi (Comhaire 1971). In their work, they explained the following:

> The Nairobi populace is a multiracial one. [...] It is a fascinating task to investigate whether different planning principles should apply to each of these various peoples and their specific cultures. And indeed if on examination there emerge such striking differences in the management of these activities which are the subject of town planning, the Plan will have to particularize for each community. The more there are divergent and complex interests, the more will the municipal area be broken down in separate specialized zones. [...] Race rather than family status, class, religion, generation, is the social determinant which fixes and circumscribes the life of the individual. (White, Silberman and Anderson 1948:3, 21.)

Around this time, expert meetings were held, at which problems of housing construction in tropical Africa were discussed. Thus, in 1952 an international conference on housing was held in Pretoria (South Africa), where many representatives from other colonies were present. For instance, an engineer of Public Works of France Overseas, Crouzat, represented France. Three years later, France organized its own congress in Paris, this time on indigenous housing (Dulucq and Goerg 1989:14-5). There is no doubt that South African specialists, considered the best experts, attended the meetings.

France witnessed the official appearance of colonial urban politics after 1943. It was stimulated by the fallback on African soil of several large European companies during World War II. A Committee of Colonial Urbanism was instituted in 1945; it was followed by laws that provided financing for city works and equipment and stimulated urban development in the colonies. Finally, in 1946, an order from the minister of France Overseas enumerated the cities and regions that had to provide, before 1948, works classified as serving the general interest.[6]

---

[6]    Law of 15-6-1943 on colonial urbanism; Ordinance of 28-6-1945 (no 45-1423) relating to urbanism in the colonies; Committee on urbanism in the colonies created by the decree of 28-6-1945; Law of urban legislation overseas of 30-4-1946. The Decree of 18-6-1946 (n° 46149) specifies the modalities of the urban projects overseas. The Order of the Minister of France Overseas of 8-8-1946 designated the target zones: apart from the Cap Vert peninsula (Dakar, Rufisque, and Thiès), were included: Saint-Louis, Kaolack (Sénégal), Bamako, Ségou, Gao in Sudan (Mali), Niamey (Niger), Conakry, Kindia, Kankan, Labé, Dalaba (Guinea), Abidjan, Sassandra, Bouake and Man (Côte d'Ivoire), Bobo-Dioulassou and Ouagadougou (Haute Volta), and Porto-Novo and Cotonou (Dahomey). The Decree of 18-6-1946 (no 46149) specified the modalities of application. Finally, list of registered urbanists in AOF by an order of 20-5-1947, followed 25-6-1947 by an ordinance recognizing the profession of architect in AOF, by virtue of the institution of the order in AOF (law of 31-12-1940). With respect to the Federal Habitat Service followed the Habitat Service

Colonial urban planning was born in these immediate postwar years. Of course, rough drafts of city plans had previously existed, particularly for the establishment of the colonial capitals, such as Nairobi in Kenya or Conakry in Guinée at the beginning of the twentieth century. But with the exception of South Africa, and of Lusaka in the 1930s, developments in those cities did hardly conform to the will of the public authority.

Under the aegis of the new urban planning, 'modern' cheap housing was provided for wage-earners. In spite of the dreams of white colonizers, these wage-earners were only a small minority among urban Africans. Most of the urbanites were people (in particular women and an increasing number of jobless youth) who remained invisible in official documents and statistics. Their jobs as well as their houses were part of the so-called 'informal' sector, that is the majority of social and economic life of urban Africa. 'Informality', or activities not controlled by law, increased with the urban boom that took off slowly after the mid 1930s and accelerated from the 1950s onward, at the very moment when population growth was at its highest and decolonization started to take hold of public opinion.

## Decolonization: Change or continuity?

In most countries, planning and managing urban development changed little after decolonization, even in countries where former racial rules were abolished. Governments were preoccupied with national political and economic issues; policies pursued by the new elites had both to favour national integration and to improve relations with the world economy. Usually, these elites paid little attention to issues of urban administration. They had to intensify housing construction for the middle classes and to decrease – if not to solve – the shantytown pressure as much as possible. Where centralized institutions existed, as in Francophone Africa, these were maintained. Where urban local government had been established according to the British model, it was kept more or less intact too. New urban laws were necessary only when previously the legal apparatus had been insufficiently developed (Simon 1992; Stren and White 1989).

In most places, urban trends tended to accelerate rather than reverse. Any preexisting legally imposed residential segregation disappeared. But this did not spark off a sudden mobility or reshuffle. The greatest dynamic was to be seen in townships and shantytowns, which tended to receive more and more inhabitants and expanded at a high pace. Within 20 years, Pikine near Dakar

---

instituted in 1926, it was created by an order of the general government on 10-3-1951. Inventory of the Archives of Senegal, volume 4P, Urbanism, introduction, Dakar, 2000.

jumped from half a million to probably more than two, and Soweto more and more became a huge satellite dormitory town for Johannesburg wage-earners of all kinds.

Ironically, in South Africa the apartheid regime had begun in the early 1950s with a tremendous building programme aiming at housing urban black workers out of reach of the other races. The trend of destruction and reconstruction during the first twenty years of the regime was impressive until the officials discovered that housing the urban black population might favour urban migration. Hence, in the 1980s they stopped housing programmes for black workers in townships, which usually were located at the periphery of the big cities. However, most of the government's efforts had not gone into urban housing but to relegate the black population to their 'homelands' (Bantustans); deportations to these regions were tremendously important in the late 1970s. But the results were the opposite of the nationalist whites' wishes. Urban migrations did not decrease. Certainly, the effects of the so-called Group Areas pattern, which aimed to settle races apart, had in general been realized. But new waves of people, consisting mainly of blacks and coloured landless people who had been expelled from their overcrowded homelands, tried to reach the cities and find a place there, disturbing the apartheid rules. Informal residencies mushroomed, either in backyard shacks in formal townships or in squatter communities usually far away from easy commuting distance to the urban labour markets. In the 1980s, this massive growth of informal settlement proved the failure of state policies set up to solve the housing problem, especially after the escalation of violence from 1976 onwards. The last brutal destruction of new squatter communities occurred around Crossroads in 1986. By that date the private and industrial sector became involved in the issue. Grey areas in town made it possible for large corporations to organize housing for their relatively skilled workers. These projects were meant for lower-middle-class people and were situated closer to their workplaces than the remote shantytowns. Meanwhile, the idea grew among the administrative boards that labour should be free to move within developing regions, which implied that the pass system had to be reduced or abolished. Of course, this was fully realized only after the end of apartheid in 1990. Community organizations now planned and organized land 'invasions', taking over land adjacent to the townships. This policy was exactly opposite to the one that had resulted, a few years earlier, in expelling most of the inhabitants of the satellite communities around Crossroads.

When freedom of movement was reestablished after the fall of apartheid, urban migration accelerated. In spite of a real effort, the government found itself incapable of solving the double heritage of the apartheid regime: a considerable lag in urban construction for the black population that had been stopped nearly completely for almost twenty years, and the new migration waves triggered by the regrouping of families that had been split by apartheid between the city and the 'Homelands' (Tomlinson 1990). People were allowed to move freely; the city centre was now no longer forbidden ground and shantytowns too expanded more than authorities could control.

A similar overcrowding of the city occurred in Salisbury/Harare (Rhodesia/Zimbabwe), long before the eviction of the white power in 1980. An extensive urban manufacturing sector had developed by the 1970s, assisted by Southern Rhodesia's isolation during the Second World War and the markets provided by Northern Rhodesia and Nyasaland during the Federation (Rakodi 1995:18). The influx of refugees that fled the fights during the liberation and civil war swelled the ranks of squatters occupying land in and around the city. As in South Africa, the rescinding of the restrictions on the movement, residence, and property ownership of black people triggered new urban migration, when wives and families joined the urban workers, changing the gender composition of the urban population. Even more than Johannesburg downtown, Harare downtown now is the dominion of African urbanites.

As in South Africa, township development was the result of segregation policies. Segregation on the basis of race had been introduced as early as 1894. Since the 1960s, urban areas were managed by Town Management Boards by and for the benefit of the European population. When the boundaries of Harare were extended, the Urban Councils Act (1973) was promulgated. Closely modelled on the British local government system, the Act gave urban local authorities a wide range of powers. Because the black inhabitants were considered nonpermanent city dwellers, they had no voting rights. As in Nairobi, Lusaka and Johannesburg, African housing areas were spatially separated from the (European) city, but were administered by the city council and organized into townships. The initial proposal to establish a township to the south of Salisbury (Seki) was made in 1951. Construction started in 1954, and in 1974 a second town was added adjacent to the former one (Rakodi 1995:53-5). Basic infrastructure and housing construction was rapid: 20,000 units were completed by 1979. In the 1980s, facilities gradually improved, but provisions did not keep pace with population growth: although the population had reached at least 274,000 in 1992, only 5,000 local industrial jobs were available.

A similar evolution occurred in Tanzania (former Tanganyika), although the political regime was different. Dar es Salaam was not a newly created colonial city, but already existed in precolonial times. The place had been chosen by sultan Sayyid Majid of Zanzibar in the late 1860s, and about 5,000 Africans already lived there when the Germans chose to make it their capital city of German East Africa. Only in 1912 did the Germans begin to divide the town into three segregated building zones to avoid racial intermingling; the

British completed this scheme after 1918, locating the African zone west of the commercial centre (Iliffe 1979:385). Avoiding the terms 'African', 'Asian', and 'European' housing, residential quarters were described as high-, medium-, and low-density residential areas. The physical layout reflected social distances. Europeans lived in attractive suburbs, in large houses with spacious gardens. Streets were well-maintained and illuminated by streetlamps. Houses had water supplies, electricity and sewage connections. Golf courses and other recreational facilities were offered. In colonial times, these districts were called *Uzunguni*, a Swahili word meaning 'European area'. Next to it was the *Uhundini* area, where people of Asian origin lived and had their shops and trading businesses. Most of the houses here were built on medium-density housing plots. Africans were left to reside in areas of high population density, often unplanned settlements without tap water, street lights, or a modern sewage system. Residential segregation went hand in hand with segregation in the provision of social services and schools (Lugalla 1995:14).

In the course of time, social segregation even hardened; it became more and more unusual for Africans to live outside these areas. In 1952, the municipality was 'busy cleaning the town by demolishing the older African houses in order that multi-storeyed houses may be built reaching to the skies, without considering the suffering caused to Africans compelled to move because they are powerless'.[7] As the city of Dar es Salaam continued to grow, settlements for Africans were located at considerable distance from the city centre. Lack of housing led to the emergence of shanty settlements and also forced the colonial government to start providing housing.

Since the late 1940s, Dar es Salaam, a major port with modern port facilities, doubled its population every ten years. The national government after independence in 1961 proved as unable to stop the trend as the colonial government had been. To the contrary, as immediately after independence the state abolished all colonial laws and regulations intended to restrain the flows of Africans migrants to urban areas.

Apart from the continuing influx of migrants into the city, things changed very little until 1968, when the government of independent Tanzania decided to prepare a new master plan. However, the only major change was that the state seized control of the land. All land was declared national property. As all freehold land was converted to government leasehold, previous owners were obliged to pay land rent. But the urban zoning system itself was not changed.

---

[7]    *Zuhra*, 15-2-1952, quoted in Iliffe 1979:387. Exactly the same statement might be made about Dakar. On the Plateau just a few plots were (and still are, but in a quickly diminishing number) left for Lebous' shacks (invisible from the streets because hidden behind their walls). Here, the municipality and the private sector were prevented from buying the plot, due to the complexity of Lebous' land customary rights: it has proven nearly impossible to decide who is supposed to be the official landlord.

The former policy of the colonial government that divided residential urban land into low-, medium- and high-density areas remained in force, even if residential segregation by race was abolished. Spontaneous self-segregation followed the lines of previous enforced legal residential segregation. In the period between independence and the Arusha declaration of 1967, by which President Julius Nyerere proclaimed his human socialism, most of the former colonial policies were perpetuated, resulting into a similar unequal regional distribution of resources, hence of housing and unemployment problems. The post-Arusha period brought few improvements for Dar es Salaam. Urban development focused on decentralizing urban growth through the dispersion of industrial investments in so-called 'growth pole centres'. Another policy was to reduce rural-urban migration by laws and regulations aiming at repatriating jobless or wandering people to their rural home areas.

It reminded the onlooker of the urban politics in the preceding era: the removals, now on behalf of the independent governments. These removals also occurred in Johannesburg after Nelson Mandela's rise to power. For example, a shantytown, the densely populated township of Alexandra, was situated near the highway leading to the airport. Family members wishing to join squatters there organized themselves in order to occupy some neighbouring 'vacant' land (the Far East Bank of Alexandra), between the highway and a high-tension line. This land was part of a larger area where the municipal authorities envisaged a large social housing project for 80,000 inhabitants. In May 1996, the Far East Bank was cleared by bulldozers. Some land had been provided for the squatters to rebuild their shacks, but at great distance from their former dwellings and their job locations in the Alexandra sector.[8]

These urban policies were nothing exceptional; neither were they strictly reserved to Southern Africa or Tanzania. They were routinely used by municipal and national authorities in a number of capitals that were more or less invaded by an ever-expanding migrant population, such as Dakar, Abidjan, and Nairobi. The construction of a new city quarter resulted almost automatically in the concomitant deportation of a mass of poor people who had to find housing elsewhere. Most often they found a place farther away from the city centre, in a new makeshift habitat that would be razed to the ground several years later. One big difference between the cities of Africa and those in Western countries is that, while the latter seem to have attained a certain demographic equilibrium, or even regression, the former continue to expand. This is not so much the result of rural migrations but of a high natural demographic growth: more than three-quarters of city dwellers are less than 25 years old.

---

[8]    *The Star*, 7-5-1996; *The Citizen*, 8-5-1996; *The Saturday Star*, 11-5-1996.

*Urban globalization?*

The contention here is not that all colonial urban systems were alike. But from a bird's eye perspective, the major problems of African cities do not appear to be very dissimilar from each other today. Whatever the colonial heritage, of legal segregation or not, of having been colonized by either British or French, or whether situated in the north or the south of the continent, the situation of cities is analogous: everywhere its centres are congested as a result of the explosion of urban population growth. Housing and mass transportation are falling far behind, a backlog which seems extremely difficult to solve. If we add to this the ever-growing number of cars resulting in an increasing congestion of traffic and parking space, it is clear that the economic centres of the cities become more difficult to reach for the less fortunate of the country. The urban poor try to do as they always did: to slip into a habitat that is hyperdense but as close as possible to their work. An ironic consequence is that previous trends that were introduced or encouraged by colonial powers, far from disappearing tend to be strengthened. Where racial segregation had been legally enforced, it did not disappear by changing the law. Segregation laws or habits were abolished, but cultural trends were maintained and were even strengthened. Today, Kibera is just one of Nairobi's 199 slums, in which more than 1.6 million people live, representing at least 50 percent of the total population of the city. Around 60 percent of Nairobi's population lives on only 8.7 percent of the land. The persistence of slums is connected to the history of colonial policies and its uneven allocation of resources, reinforced by legal or informal residential segregation, when most of the urban land surface was reserved for the European quarters and the Africans received little to none. Moreover, rapid urban population growth continues to outstrip attempts to organize and plan cities.

The cases of Johannesburg and Nairobi, among others, show the burdens of the colonial heritage; residential segregation has a tendency to increase rather than to disappear. Not only did the former townships remain the main focus of urban migration, but the 'invasion' of downtown by the poor has accelerated a reaction that American cities got to know not so long ago: the mushrooming of gated suburbs. In Dakar they expand all along the Cap Vert peninsula 'Grande Corniche'; in Johannesburg they occupy the northern part of the city, where a rich bourgeoisie migrated to safer districts. After independence, the three Nairobis – European, Asian and African – merged into one, but resegregated 'in the process of exchanging social for economic characteristics'.[9] This is not new, and even began earlier than is usually supposed. Resegregation was already foreseen by Nairobi city planners in 1948:

---

[9]    UNDP (United Nations Development Program) report, 2004, quoted by Campbell 2005:148-9.

Even the formulation of the problem as a racial one is slowly becoming inoperative as class differentiation takes place in every social group. As soon as there are rich and poor, intellectual and lowbrow, professionally trained and unskilled, as recognizable types in every race, with interracial organizations, each pressing for bigger slices of the cake, multiracial society is normalized. (White, Silberman and Anderson 1948:10.)

As always, the bourgeoisie has tried to distance itself from these dirty and noisy areas where informal activities, especially those related to commerce, have become denser and denser. The very rich have moved to well-to-do neighbourhoods with good access from large highway arteries; the least well-off go still farther away and are submitted to longer and more problematic daily commuting. Only the very poor accept the risk of downtown life because it becomes the kingdom of informality and they cannot hope for more.

Thus, in most African metropoles, a typical residential partitioning has evolved. Dakar or Abidjan today does not differ much from Johannesburg or Nairobi. The large cities of Africa tend to become the 'gated cities' of Johannesburg and Los Angeles. Only the Francophone cities of medium size and several less-developed capitals such as the city of Lomé (Togo) have kept a less strictly zoned layout (Beall, Crankshaw and Parnell 2002). Elsewhere, social zoning is the rule. The poor live the daily dangers and discomfort of the gangs of taxi drivers and bad buses. Markets, long the points of contact between different classes, do not have this function anymore, as the higher and middle classes embrace the Western supermarkets and shopping habits. The idea is growing among the middle classes everywhere that any market seller or informal worker is a bandit. In Nairobi, under colonial rule, every African was considered dangerous. The same phenomenon exists today. The target is no longer colour but refugee status.

Like most cities of the South, African cities are mainly populated by poor people who owe their livelihood to the informal sector and who are not housed as they should be – an everyday reality that should be studied as such and not as a deviation from the modernist, colonial path.

*References*

Beall, Jo, Owen Crankshaw and Susan Parnell
2002      *Uniting a divided city; Governance and social exclusion in Johannesburg.*
          London: Earthscan.
Betts, Raymond F.
1969      'The problem of the Medina in the urban planning of Dakar, Senegal',
          *African Urban Notes* 4-3:5-15.

1971          'The establishment of the Medina in Dakar, Senegal, 1914', *Africa*
              41- 2:143-52.
Call, John W.
1986          'Anglo-Indian medical theory and the origin of segregation in West
              Africa', *American Historical Review* 91-2:307-35.
Campbell, Elizabeth
2005          *UNHCR and contemporary protection challenges; The case of urban refugees
              in Nairobi.* PhD thesis, Binghamton University, New York.
Cohen, William
1983          'Malaria and French imperialism', *Journal of African History* 24-1:23-36.
Cole, Josette
1987          *Crossroads; The politics of reform and repression 1976-1986.* Johannesburg:
              Ravan Press.
Collins, John
1969          'Lusaka; The myth of the garden-city', *Zambian Urban Studies* 2:1-32.
Comhaire, Jean L.
1971          'Lubumbashi et Nairobi; Étude comparée de leur évolution', *Revue
              française d'études politiques africaines* 61:54-72.
Coquéry-Vidrovitch, Cathérine
1988          'Villes coloniales et histoire des Africains', *Vingtième siècle. Revue
              d'histoire* 20:47-68.
1996          'À propos de la cité-jardin dans les colonies; L'Afrique noire', in :
              Cathérine Coquéry-Vidrovitch and Odile Goerg (eds), *La ville européenne
              outre mers; Un modèle conquérant?*, pp. 105-126. Paris: L'Harmattan.
1997          *African women; A modern history.* Translated by Beth Gillian Raps.
              Boulder, CO: Westview Press. [Social Change in Global Perspective.]
              [Originally published as *Les Africaines: Histoire des femmes d'Afrique
              noire du XIX au XX siècle.* Paris : Éditions Desjonquères, 1994.]
Curtin, Philip. D.
1985          'Medical knowledge and urban planning in tropical Africa', *American
              Historical Review* 90-3:594-613.
Davenport, Rodney and Christopher Saunders
2000          *Southern Africa; A modern history.* Foreword by Desmond Tutu. Fifth
              edition. Basingstoke: Macmillan, New York: St. Martin's Press. [First
              edition 1977.]
Dulucq, Sophie and Odile Goerg
1989          *Les investissements publics dans les villes africaines (1935-1985); Habitat et
              transports.* Paris: L'Harmattan. [Villes et Entreprises.]
Frenkel, Stephen and John Western
1988          'Pretext or prophylaxis? Racial segregation and malarial mosquitos
              in a British colony: Sierra Leone', *Annals of the Association of American
              Geographers* 78-2:211-28.
Gale, Thomas S.
1979          'The history of British colonial neglect of traditional African cities',
              *African Urban Studies* 5:11-24.
1980          'Segregation in British West Africa', *Cahier d'études africaines* 80, XX-4:
              495-507.

Goerg, Odile
1996       *Pouvoir colonial, municipalités et espaces urbains; Conakry et Freetown, des années 1880 à 1914*. Paris: L'Harmattan. Two vols. [Racines du Present.]

Hake, Andrew
1977       *African metropolis; Nairobi's self-help city*. London: Sussex University Press.

Howard, Ebenezer
1898       *To-morrow; A peaceful path to real reform*. [reprinted as: *Garden cities of to-morrow*. London: Swan Sonnenschein, 1902.]

Iliffe, John
1979       *A modern history of Tanganyika*. Cambridge: Cambridge University Press. [African Studies Series 25.]

Kimani, S.M.
1972       'The structure of land ownership in Nairobi', *Canadian Journal of African Studies* 6-3:379-402.

King, Anthony D.
1984       'Colonial architecture re-visited; Some issues for further debate', in: Kenneth Ballhatchet and David Taylor (eds), *Changing South Asia; City and culture*. London: Centre of South Asian Studies, University of London; Hong Kong: Asian Research Service.

Lugalla, Joe
1995       *Crisis, urbanization, and urban poverty in Tanzania; A study of urban poverty and survival politics*. New York/London: University Press of America.

Marguerat, Yves
1994       'La naissance d'une capitale africaine: Lomé', *Revue française d'histoire d'outre-mer* 81 (302):71-95.

Mbokolo, Elikia
1982       'Peste et société urbaine à Dakar; l'épidémie de 1914', *Cahiers d›études africaines* 22-1/2:13-46.

Murunga, Godwin R.
2003       '"Inherently unhygienic races"; Race and hygiene in the making of colonial Nairobi, 1896-1914'. Paper, Conference on 'African urban spaces; history and culture', Austin, Texas, March.

Ngalamulume, Kalala
2004       'Keeping the city totally clean; Yellow fever and the politics of prevention in colonial Saint Louis du Senegal 1850-1914', *Journal of African History* 45-2:183-200.

Oruwaro, Yomi
2003       'The emerging formal and informal urban land markets in southern Nigeria; A case study of Port Harcourt'. Paper, Conference on 'African urban spaces; history and culture', Austin, Texas, March.

Plotnicov, Leonard
1967       *Strangers to the city; Urban man in Jos, Nigeria*. Pittsburg: University of Pittsburgh Press. [Pitt Paperback 22.]

Preston, R.O.
1938       *Oriental Nairobi (Kenya Colony); A record of some of the leading contributors to its development*. Nairobi: Colonial Printing Works.

Rakodi, Carole
1995        *Harare, inheriting a settler-colonial city; Change or continuity?* Chichester:
            Wiley. [World Cities Series.]
Simon, D.
1992        *Cities, capital and development; African cities and the world economy.*
            London: Belhaven, New York: Halsted Press.
Stren, Richard E. and Rodney R. White (eds)
1989        *African cities in crisis; Managing rapid urban growth.* Boulder, CO:
            Westview. [African Modernization and Development Series.]
Swanson, W. Maynard
1977        'The sanitation syndrome; Bubonic plague and urban native policy in
            the Cape Colony 1900-1909', *Journal of African History* 18-3:387-410.
Tomlinson, Richard
1990        *Urbanization in post-apartheid South Africa.* London: Unwin Hyman.
Vernières, Marc
1977        *Dakar et son double; Volontarisme d'Etat et spontanéité populaire dans
            l'urbanisation du tiers-monde. Le cas de Dagoudane-Pikine.* Paris:
            Bibliothèque nationale pour le Comité des travaux historiques et
            scientifiques.
Western, John
1981        *Outcast Cape Town.* Minneapolis: University of Minnesota Press.
White, L.W.T., L. Silberman and P.R. Anderson
1948        *Nairobi; Master plan for a colonial capital, 1948.* London: His Majesty's
            Stationery Office.
Williams, Geoffrey J.
1986        *Lusaka and its environs; A geographical study of a planned city in tropical
            Africa.* Lusaka: Zambia Geographical Association.
Zwanenberg, R.M.A. van
1972        'History and theory of urban poverty in Nairobi; The problem of slum
            development', *Journal of Eastern Africa Research and Development* 2:165-
            203.
Zwanenberg, R.M.A van and Anne King
1975        *An economic history of Kenya and Uganda, 1800-1970.* London: Macmillan.

# Contributors

Greg Bankoff is Professor of Modern History at the University of Hull, specializing in historical disaster studies and environmental history in an Asian and a global context. He is the author of *Cultures of disaster; Society and natural hazard in the Philippines* (London and New York 2003). His most recent book is (co-edited with Uwe Lübken and Jordan Sand) *Flammable cities; Urban conflagration and the making of the modern world* (Madison 2012).

Raymond F. Betts (1925-2007) was Professor of History at the University of Kentucky. He wrote numerous books on French and European colonialism, among which *Uncertain dimensions; Western overseas empires in the twentieth century* (Minneapolis 1985) and *France and decolonization, 1900-1960* (London 1991). His latest books are *Decolonization* (London and New York 1998/2004) and *A history of popular culture; More of everything, faster and brighter* (New York and London 2004).

Els Bogaerts taught Indonesian languages and culture at Leiden University. From 2002-2007 she was coordinator of the research programme 'Indonesia across orders; The reorganization of Indonesian society 1930-1960' at the Netherlands Institute for War Documentation in Amsterdam. Her current research is about the representation of Javanese culture on Indonesian television.

Anne Booth is Professor of Economics at the School of Oriental and African Studies and specializes in the economy of Indonesia and Southeast Asia in the twentieth century. She authored *Indonesian economic development in the nineteenth and twentieth centuries; A history of missed opportunities* (London 1998), *Colonial legacies; Economic and social development in East and Southeast Asia* (Honolulu 2007) and *The economic performance of the ASEAN economies from the mid-1990s* (London 2009).

Freek Colombijn is associate professor in anthropology at the Vrije Universiteit, Amsterdam, specializing in Indonesian urban and environmental studies. His most recent book is *Under construction; The politics of urban space and housing during the decolonization of Indonesia, 1930-1960* (Leiden 2010). He is editor of the *Bijdragen tot de Taal-, Land- en Volkenkunde* of KITLV.

Frederick Cooper is Professor of History at New York University. He is the author of a number of books on slavery and labour in (post)colonial Africa and of *Colonialism in question; Theory, knowledge, history* (Berkeley: 2005) and (with Jane Burbank) of *Empires in world history; Power and the politics of difference* (Princeton 2010).

Cathérine Coquéry-Vidrovitch is professor emeritus at Université Paris VII-Denis-Diderot. Over the decades she has published numerous books on Africans, such as *L'Afrique noire; De 1800 à nos jours* (first editon Paris 1972), *Histoire des villes d'Afrique noire; De origines à la décolonisation* (Paris 1993), *Les Africaines; Histoire des femmes d'Afrique noire du XIXe au XXe siècle* (Paris 1994), and *Enjeux politiques de l'histoire colonial* (Marseille 2009). Her most recent book is *Petite histoire de l'Afrique; L'Afrique au sud du Sahara, de la préhistoire à nos jours* (Paris 2010).

Bill Freund is emeritus professor, University of KwaZulu Natal, Durban South Africa and has written extensively on urban history and development issues of Durban, South Africa and Africa. Among his books are *The making of contemporary Africa; The development of African society since* 1800 (Boulder 1998), The *African city; A history* (Cambridge 2007) and, most recently (with Harald Witt), *Development dilemmas in post-Apartheid South Africa* (Durban 2010).

Karl Hack was associate professor at Nanyang Technological University in Singapore and is currently at Open University, where he produced and chairs the History Department course on Empires. His research interests include decolonization, violence and 'empire from below'. Among his latest books are *Defence and decolonisation in Southeast Asia* (Richmond 2001), (edited with Tobias Rettig), *Colonial armies in Southeast Asia* (London 2006) and (with Kevin Blackburn), *War, memory and the making of modern Malaysia and Singapore* (Singapore 2012).

Jim Masselos is honorary reader in history at the University of Sydney. He is the author of a large number of books on India and Mumbai, among which are the oft-reprinted *Indian nationalism; A history* (fifth edition 2010), *The city in action; Bombay struggles for power* (Oxford 2007). His latest book (ed.) is *The great empires of Asia* (London 2010).

Remco Raben teaches global, Asian and colonial history at the University of Utrecht. His latest book (co-edited with Sita van Bemmelen) is *Antara daerah dan negara Indonesia tahun 1950-an; Pembongkaran narasi besar integrasi bangsa* (Jakarta 2011).

Willem Wolters is emeritus professor economic anthropology at Radboud University Nijmegen. He has published on land tenure, agricultural marketing and credit, in particular in Indonesia and the Philippines. His current research concerns monetary systems in Southeast Asia.

# Index